Socialism, Politics, and Equality

Socialism, Politics, and Equality

Hierarchy and Change in Eastern Europe and the USSR

WALTER D. CONNOR

New York COLUMBIA UNIVERSITY PRESS *1979*

Printed in the United States of America

Columbia University Press
New York Guildford, Surrey

Library of Congress Cataloging in Publication Data
Connor, Walter D
Socialism, politics, and equality.

Includes bibliographical references and index.
1. Social classes—Europe, Eastern. 2. Social classes—Russia. 3. Social mobility—Europe, Eastern. 4. Social mobility—Russia. I. Title.
HN380.Z9S638 301.44'0947 78-14780
ISBN 0-231-04318-X

To Eileen

Contents

Preface

THIS, as the title indicates, is a book about three things. *Socialism*, not as theory or ideal, but in the shape of the concrete political-economic systems of the Soviet Union and Eastern Europe, has provided the broad context, the reality at the level of society or nation-state upon which the study is based. *Politics*, albeit of a different sort than that of Western democracies, has shaped this socialism, both in the early stages of its construction and in the current phase of relative maturity, and continues to do so. *Equality*, in the spheres of power, prestige, material possessions, and the opportunity to strive for all of these, has been both the beneficiary and the victim of the political processes of socialism which were set in motion in the USSR in 1917 and in the Eastern European states after World War II. The populations of these countries have also been beneficiaries and victims of those processes, and it is with both processes and outcomes that this book is concerned.

The business of researching, writing, and editing has spanned a good deal of time, and several locations. I have incurred along the way a number of personal and institutional debts that it is a pleasure to acknowledge. The American Council of Learned Societies' Committee on Soviet Studies awarded the author a grant in 1973, and in conjunction with the Committee on East European Studies, another grant in 1975–76 which together allowed three unhindered semesters for work on the project. The Ford Foundation, through a grant to the University of Michigan's Center for Russian and East European Studies on "Studies of Industrialization, Mobilization, and Mass Attitude Change in East European Countries," provided funding for research assistance, summer support, and for a visit to researchers in Poland, Hungary, Bulgaria and Yugoslavia in 1974. The International Research and Exchanges Board receives my gratitude for nominating me to the exchange of senior scholars with the USSR in 1973, although unforeseen complications prevented the visit at Moscow State University which was the object of the application.

Debts to colleagues are many, and my thanks go to Zvi Gitelman,

William Zimmerman, Morris Bornstein and Roman Szporluk at Michigan's Center for Russian and East European Studies, and to Robert Cole, Martin Whyte, Gayl Ness and Werner Landecker of the Department of Sociology there, as well as to Michael Flynn, Elwood Beck, and Irving Louis Horowitz. David Powell and Mark Field of the Russian Research Center, Harvard University, also deserve thanks for their interest and encouragement over the years, as do more recently my colleagues at the Foreign Service Institute.

Research assistance at Michigan, for which I will remain long grateful, was provided by Christine Sadowski, Judy Clodfelter, Marta Johnson, Vera Berceanu, and A. C. Tanner. Kathleen Vargo, Debbie Polzin, Margaret Grillot and Mary Nensewitz typed the first draft at Michigan, Leslie Butterfield the final draft in Washington in 1977. John Moore and Karen Mitchell of Columbia University Press have my thanks for their support and patience on this project, as on an earlier book.

Finally, my wife Eileen deserves more thanks by far than the dedication of this book can provide; but to her, and to Christine and Elizabeth who may one day read it, much gratitude.

The views expressed in this book, of course, are my own, not those of the government or of any government agency.

Prologue

THIS BOOK deals with patterns of social stratification and mobility in the Soviet Union and the socialist states of Eastern Europe. It is thus a work about equality and inequality in societies whose births were attended by the *promise* of greater equality among men than had existed in the previous history of those societies—or indeed anywhere else on the globe.

This is not the first book to focus on the performance of the socialist (or "state-socialist," communist, "bureaucratic-collectivist," as one prefers) societies in delivering on their promise. I am indebted to numerous authors who have gone before, evidenced by my citing them and, at times, challenging some of their views. But it does attempt to deliver a more comprehensive and systematic consideration of the socialist experience, in a broader comparative context, than earlier authors have provided.

Such an effort requires attention to a wide range of topics, from the beliefs, values, and attitudes about equality and subordination that characterized the presocialist societies and their peoples, to the social and economic impact of continuing postrevolutionary processes of economic development, to some of the minutiae of everyday life in the area stretching from the Oder-Neisse boundary to the Pacific coast of the USSR. Some of the content will be familiar to some readers, some of it rather exotic.

This is not, however, a book intended solely for specialists—either those concerned with stratification and mobility in general, or students of socialist politics and society. Like many other authors of what seem "specialized" works, I hope (perhaps, like many others, vainly) to reach a somewhat larger audience. The widely discussed controversies over the distribution of economic rewards, the broadening or narrowing of income gaps, the acceptability of compensatory and preferential treatment for historically deprived minorities, employment goals or quotas in the United States (and in Western Europe as well) testify to the existence of that audience.

These are civic concerns, on which public choices are being made; they are thus also concerns of that audience of general readers most likely to attend to the current controversies. I do not suggest that this book, exploring the Soviet and Eastern European experience, will provide them with readily applicable lessons for their own very different environments. But, in broadening the factual framework at a reader's disposal, it may help; it may render the various issues more complex than they seem at present, but this is not a bad thing.

OBJECTIVES

The purposes of this work are both descriptive and analytic. A primary aim is to describe as fully as possible socialist patterns of stratification and social mobility—which requires a good deal of data. These include indicators of educational and income differentials, rates of intergenerational occupational inheritance and mobility, and other quantitative indices familiar to specialists. But also included are qualitative data of diverse sorts—journalistic, ethnographic, even belletristic materials that give some feeling for the human realities lying behind what might otherwise be a rather barren, if concise, recital of statistics.

I seek to analyze—but not only by applying quantitative measures and techniques to data. More use is made of such implements here than in previous Western works on socialist stratification, but their total is modest by contemporary standards of sociology and political science. A broader kind of analysis, using qualitative and quantitative data to explain *why* certain patterns occur, is the goal.

Thus I am concerned not only with how unequal income distributions are, but with how interaction of official wage policies, personal decisions, patterns of family composition and employment produce particular per capita income figures in occupational strata. My concern is not only with the fact of increased access to higher education, and the shortfall from equal access, but also with the operation of those mechanisms by which some "opening" has been accomplished, and of those which underlie the persistence of inequalities. I contrast not only national rates of occupational mobility, but also the factors that seem to shape these differences. The final product—a portrait of the statics and dynamics of inequality under socialism—is sometimes quantitative, sometimes qualitative; sometimes diachronic, sometimes synchronic.

It will scarcely satisfy everyone. The Soviet/Eastern European specialist may wish for more detail on some topics unfamiliar to him than he will find. The sociologist to whom socialist countries are not a matter of special interest may want more of the kind of analysis he expects in a subfield grown increasingly quantitative over the years. General readers may find too much jargon, though the aim has been to stick to ordinary language as much as possible. The author can only hope that all take from the book enough to satisfy some of the concerns that brought them to it in the first place.

COMPARATIVE ASPECTS

This work is also comparative in intent, the comparison being between the socialist countries and those of the industrial West. There are many rationales for such a choice. Socialism of the Soviet type has been *in fact* a program of modernization and industrialization. Its announced objectives have included the "overtaking" of the industrial Western countries in productivity, welfare, equality, and the like. With the West thus adopted as a yardstick of performance *by* socialist regimes, comparison of the "two world systems" on various stratification and mobility indicators is scarcely "forced," for all the historical differences that divide the two areas. One might have set a comparison with the Third World, to which communist regimes hold out their own experience as a relevant model, but two reasons militate against such a comparison. First, the problems of traditionalism and underdevelopment in the Third World are of quite different magnitude than those that were faced by the new socialist regimes, and much more acute. Second, the Third World cannot provide a broad enough range of even roughly comparable data for our purposes.

Hence, I compare "East" and "West"—but since this book is primarily about socialism, the West, whose experience is better known and more elaborately studied, does not receive equal space. While the following chapters do not proceed according to a mechanical comparative plan, where data permit and where the nature of certain issues demands it, I present the socialist experience against a

Western background. Finally, the concluding chapter expands on comparative themes in an attempt to tie threads of similarity and diversity together.

Comparisons within the socialist camp are another focus. The broader East-West comparison highlights differences and similarities in the performance of systems of different types; the narrower seeks to isolate the common and the particular among the socialist states. Few would claim that the Eastern European states are "miniatures" of the USSR, but they are all too frequently still treated thus. No Eastern European state, in its presocialist history, mirrors the Russian imperial experience. Nor do the Balkan states share many common experiences with Poland, Hungary, and Czechoslovakia. Historical differences condition diversity among the socialist states today, but they are not its only source. The Soviet model has been received to quite varying degrees in the Eastern European states, and this too underlies a contemporary diversity less familiar on the whole than are East-West differences.

This is not, on the other hand, a "comparative" study of the sort that is based on highly aggregated quantitative indicators, frequently derived directly from national handbooks, for large numbers of nations about none of which authors necessarily claim any expertise. Such studies, increasingly common, represent an on the whole welcome reaction to the noncomparative thrust of American sociology, which has included American writings about "society," "modern society," "industrial society," or whatever based almost solely on contemporary *American* society. Such comparative work has also set itself against "area studies," taken to mean research on a single foreign country or set of countries, with the implication that such work is too often descriptive, lacking in analytic content, and peripheral to the central concerns of the disciplines—generally sociology and political science—with which its practitioners are identified.

No doubt there is something to react against. But it seems far from certain that such comparative multinational studies are a panacea. Sophisticated and impressive as many such studies are in the manipulation of data, they frequently seem almost devoid of content. The quantitative indices are the closest one gets to the societies involved, and in the process of testing hypotheses against these data (all in the form of equally "concrete" numbers, though their quality may range from reliable to quasi-imaginary), the societies themselves are lost sight of. Men do not live "in society," they live in *particular* societies; it is these whose impact they feel in their lives. To say this is not to deny the possibilities of comparison, or to overemphasize the unique, but to state fact. A major problem of the large-scale comparative multinational study, then, seems to be that techniques of quantitative manipulation have outrun our ability to understand, in a more general but no less important sense, the diversities and similarities within large samples of nations. We may learn a good deal, but we miss a good deal too, in such studies.

Moreover, the sorts of aggregate indicators necessary for such work are frequently not forthcoming from the socialist states at all. A recent and on the whole impressive effort at explaining social inequality and its variations among nations, based on a 60-nation sample including states as diverse as Sweden and Ceylon, Luxembourg and Mauritius, includes none of the socialist states—a real lack, as its author realizes,[1] and one that is especially troubling given the socialist challenge to the inequality of the industrial West. Even if one lacks my own reservations about this sort of comparative study, one can only deplore the fact it must ignore the socialist countries and their experience.

A final reason for our sort of comparative approach is a desire to emphasize some useful aspects of an area-studies perspective. The opposition, noted above, of the "discipline" to area studies—especially, it seems, those concerned with communist systems—has gone on for some time. "Discipline" practitioners have often tended to see area specialists as peripheral exotics, and indeed *mea culpas* have been forthcoming from the area specialists as they have accepted some of the criticism, and called for greater integration of disciplinary perspectives and concepts into area studies. Much of this may be to the good, but one might also be concerned here about a possible deemphasis of disciplinary shortcomings. Much of the conceptual development in sociology and political science has been parochial, reflecting the experience of modern liberal-democratic societies, and especially the concerns of Americans who make up the majority of the practitioners of these disciplines. Trends toward ever more sophisticated analytic techniques that outrun the quality and availability of data, toward emphasizing "analysis" to the denigration of description, toward generality and away from specificity, all may seem progressive. In reality they have, as often as not, narrowed our concerns and our understanding. Here, I shall try to tread a middle course, hoping to serve adequately the legitimate ends of both disciplinary and area inquiries.

SOURCES OF DATA

Apologies for a paucity of data are, by now, a standard component of the introductions to Western books on communist societies. The apologies, it seems to me, come from the wrong source, and I intend to offer none here. The foreign specialist is scarcely to blame for the shape and quantity of data over whose collection and availability he has no control. His socialist colleagues often have little more control over the sorts of data they may collect, and even less over their eventual publication. The situation differs among the countries, for reasons of disciplinary development and politics. Yugoslavia, Poland, and Hungary provide better conditions and more room for scholarly maneuver than do the other states. Romania and Bulgaria boast less of sociological tradition than does Poland, and in those countries sociological research suffers the combined pains of adolescence and political uncertainty. For varying reasons, neither the German Democratic Republic nor Albania has yet produced sufficient data for their experience to be included in this book. The USSR, which boasts some social researchers of great sophistication, remains notable for the small proportion of research completed that ever sees publication. The situation in Czechoslovakia after "normalization" has been little short of disaster (we are fortunate here that much of our Czech data dates from shortly before the Prague Spring of 1968).*

*This somewhat dismal picture, of course, must be seen in context. Generally, data availability has improved over the last fifteen years for all the countries mentioned: without such improvement, the present book could not have been written. But as readers familiar with discussions of some of the issues dealt with here in Western countries will find, we are scarcely yet at the point where a flood of high-quality data confronts the researcher.

But data there are, and this work is based on several sorts. Most standard are the quantitative data on incomes, education, etc. generally available in one form or another in national statistical yearbooks, although often varying maddeningly in exact definition and categorization from year to year. The reader can also anticipate standard national mobility data, in varying complexity, for all the countries of interest here save the USSR. The survey techniques, nature of the samples, and other research conditions vary, but generally no more than have the conditions under which mobility data have been collected in the past thirty years by researchers in the West.

I make use as well of newspapers and general periodicals from the socialist countries. Such sources, while hardly "scientific," are important for the light they cast on everyday life, on mass concerns with equality and equity, and on official policy and its variations. That the material is often didactic or tendentious does not reduce its value as an index of certain themes and concerns.

From time to time, I also take advantage of what Russian and Eastern European *belles lettres,* both pre- and postrevolutionary, yield by way of insight into the problems of equality and inequality. These sources are often pithy, to the point, and state, better than the social scientist who might paraphrase them, some typical aspects of the ways individuals and groups experience the stratification systems in which they live. Literary sources also provide, relatively effectively, some of the general background of societies with which many readers will be unfamiliar. A Western reader addressing himself to a book on stratification in his own society comes to it with a great deal of background, gained painlessly from childhood on, at a low level of intellection but effective nonetheless. He is in a different situation with respect to alien societies, and here the author must help as best he can. It is no easy matter to convey the background, indeterminate but valuable, one derives from language, from walking the streets of Moscow, Warsaw, Budapest, etc., from simply talking and *listening* to people without writing a travelogue. This is not a travelogue—hence I have, mindful of the unavoidable selectivity involved, let literary sources make some observations and impressions I find accurate but could scarcely convey so well.

ORGANIZATION

The chapters that follow vary in length and focus. While they follow one another according to a logic evident to the author, the reader might be helped by some guidance as to that logic.

Chapters 1 to 3 are devoted to prefatory material of different sorts. The first deals with "Equality as an Issue": the controversies that have engaged those who see equality as *sine qua non* for a just society in combat with those who defend certain inequalities as inevitable and tolerable components of a social order; the forms these controversies take in the contemporary West and in the socialist world as well; and the crucial problem of equality and individual liberty. These discussions should sensitize readers to problems that will again be addressed in the concluding chapter. "Tradition, Deference and Egalitarianism," the second chapter, provides a historical dimension, examining the prerevolutionary socioeconomic structures of Russia and the Eastern European states, the values and attitudes about equality and hierarchy that characterized them, with a brevity no doubt shocking to historians but adequate, I hope, to the purposes of this book. Chapter 3, "Old Hierarchy and New," completes the preliminaries and moves toward the major preoccupations of the book as a whole. It deals with the displacement of the old stratification structures by the new regimes, and the social strata that have persisted into or developed under socialism, arriving at a rough model of the new hierarchy. Finally, it provides space for discussions of the relevance of power and prestige in socialist stratification, thus clarifying, better than if consideration of these dimensions had been postponed, the meaning of occupational mobility under socialism.

Chapters 4 and 5 both deal with mobility: the former with a general survey of mobility (in presocialist, early postrevolutionary, and maturing socialist society), and questions of how much and what sort of mobility (structural versus "circulation" mobility), and how different the patterns are from those in a broad range of Western states. The latter examines the human context of contemporary mobility—the distribution of aspirations and resources, and the relevance of social origin to one's propensities to strive, and to succeed or fail.

Chapter 6, "The Stratification of Incomes," explores the income dimension that completes the stratifying triad of power, prestige, and "property." Chapter 7 focuses on families, or households, the basic unit of stratification systems, examining status persistence and change through marriage patterns and stratum-related differences in the material contexts of family life (housing and consumption patterns) as well as life-style and leisure activities.

Chapter 8 concludes the book, returning to a comparative frame to counterpose the socialist experience to two experiences of the West—that of the United States, once a "new nation" born of a break from Europe, and that of Western Europe itself—on the rationale that, however different the states of the parliamentary West and the socialist revolutionary East, they are both European, and thus elements of continuity and similarity should be sought as well. This chapter also provides a summary of the characteristics of social stratification under socialism, and the opportunity to readdress the general problems of equality and freedom raised in chapter 1.

As will become evident to readers as they proceed, this book does not attempt to treat *all* forms and dimensions of inequality in the socialist states. The focus is on groups rather than individuals, and foremost on groups as formed by similarities in occupation. Thus, though each is recognized and noted at the appropriate points, the book does not concentrate its main focus on inequalities of *place* (the different rewards gathered from similar work depending on one's location in large cities versus small towns, the differing availability of life's amenities depending on region in unevenly developed countries), or of *sex* (although some major elements of economic stratification explicable in terms of discrimination toward, and/or assumptions about, women in their work roles are explored). Socialist societies, as others, are mosaics of such inequalities, intertwined yet separable. All are important, all likely to be interesting: here the choice among them has led to a book that gives its main attention to the dimensions generally indicated by the terms *class* and *stratum*.

Chapter One

Equality as an Issue

> The angel gave orders to Cain that for his whole life he should work not only for his own children but also for the descendants of Abel, whom he permitted to live on earth, doing nothing but faring well. So from Abel come the kings and the lords, but from Cain the serfs working for the benefit of the masters . . . What good did Cain do? He created serfdom; now the poor must work for the rich men.
>
> —Polish legend

> At the beginning of the world God created a certain number of men and women and gave to them the flocks that were necessary for their subsistence. Afterwards he created some others, to whom he gave nothing. When they demanded their share, God said to them, "Serve the others, and they will give you what you need." This was the origin of master and servant—in other words of nobles and common people.
>
> —American Indian legend

OBSERVING THROUGH the ages the inequalities in their access to scarce goods, material and spiritual, men have sought the roots, the origins, the rationale of inequality. Fable has sometimes given answers, as the passages above show; other modes of inquiry have provided them as well. The quest has not been a purely intellectual or historical exercise, for inequality has been, and is today more than ever, a source of controversy. Differing values, differing perceptions of justice and social order have led some men to denounce inequality as evil, others to defend it as natural, inevitable, and beneficial to the life of man in society.

Enduring as the controversy between partisans of equality and their opponents has been, its terms have changed over the centuries. In premodern societies, where concrete economic and political conditions were extremely inegalitarian by later standards, the partisans of equality were few but vocal nonetheless. Hebrew prophets denounced the rich, their extravagance and predation on the poor in ancient Israel; some Greek philosophers rejected the "natural" and immutable division of men into free and slave. Christian thinkers divided as well. John of Salisbury could view society as a divinely designed organism, like the human body, wherein the common people, the "feet," were subordinate to higher components, all benefiting from this subordination as did the "head" from its superordination. The English "levelers," not much later, could view the division of society into gentleman and commoner as a perversion of divine design, a departure from the time "when Adam delved and Eve span" and no gentleman was to be found.

Defenders and attackers of inequality had recourse to much the same rationales—human nature, divine decree—to support their positions: generalized rationales, quite resistant to disproof. With the onset of the modern era, the age of revolutions, the picture changed somewhat. Theology gave way to philosophy, old feudal-localistic structures of social organization gave way to the increasing power of the centralized state. Men in the mass became more accessible to central governments and their purposes, and *philosophes* argued in new terms about the relationship of man to society. *Liberté* and *égalité* were raised on the banners of the French revolution.

The revolution brought a new agenda, to some men's delight, and others' fear. "Equality" had won the day—but not entirely. What, precisely, did it mean, and what should it mean? Legal and civic entitlements that made each man, fundamentally, the equal of any other? Or something beyond, some more radical break with the past inequalities of men's general condition? No less important, to some, was the question of liberty in the context of the new acceptance of equality. What did liberty mean, how was it to be guaranteed, if equality, a goal that might restrict men's autonomy, was to be pursued? Some saw no conflict; others, like Tocqueville, saw this dilemma as the central one of the modern age, yet unresolved; conservatives like Edmund Burke saw a clear trend against liberty and autonomy in the assault on old, often inegalitarian social institutions. Men continued to debate, as they had in the past.

They continue today, and not only in the advanced states of the West, where the Enlightenment was born and whose capitalism has moved far from the *laissez-faire* of the past. In the socialist states—the USSR and its Eastern European followers—their birth with the promise of equality has not, over the years, guaranteed the acceptance of equality as a goal by all, nor has it stifled controversy over what equality means.

The modern debate, East and West, is in fact not simply about equality versus inequality, but about the *kind* of equality that is right, desirable, and attainable—and herein the present diverges greatly from the past. "Egalitarians" still press the claim that "justice" abhors inequality, increasingly defining inequality very broadly indeed as the differences in men's conditions or in outcomes. On the other side of the controversy are those whose definitions of justice require not equal results, but equality of opportunity—equality before the law, equality in certain basic resources at the start of a competition whose unequal results, once reached, are to be tolerated. This position obviously defends some inequality in terms of what we may call here the "performance principle."

This principle, no less than that of justice as equality of result, represents a radical break with the past. It is a notion of *merit*—antithetical to claims that divine will, immemorial tradition, or noble birth gives a particular kind of person entitlement to certain rewards. It dictates reward according to what one does and how well one does it, accepting and operating on the position that some modes of activity are more beneficial to society and therefore more deserving of reward than others. It thus asserts the differing entitlements of different persons on the basis of roles they perform. In this, it may even resemble the beliefs that declared the Brahman's entitlement greater than the Shudra's, the lord's greater than the villein's.

But the resemblance is apparent more than real. The performance principle diverges markedly from older legitimations of inequality. First, to be *born* a Brahman or a knight was sufficient to collect on one's "entitlement," whether one performed the attached role well or badly. The performance principle demands, and judges, activity, effort, and success or failure. Second, older ideologies of inequality saw these as fixed at birth, by and large—they made no consistent place for effort to improve one's position. The performance principle, though it defends a certain measure of inequality, endorses, as we noted above, equality of opportunity as a way to ensure that the best qualified, of whatever origin, can all strive to attain the most important, and hence best rewarded, positions. Chances for social mobility are to be equalized; outcomes are not. To the older ideologies, such distinctions, and the notion of equality of opportunity, were alien and irrelevant.

Equality neither of result nor of opportunity is to be found totally realized in any society, of course. We write here of principles, of ideals. Yet these are no less real, no less important in modern industrial societies, capitalist and socialist, than the factual deviations from them.

THE EQUALITY DEBATE: WEST

The terms of the contemporary debate are thus set. Equality of condition remains the goal of egalitarians. Those who oppose them no longer have recourse to traditionalistic legitimations of inequality, but rather rely on the performance principle—something quite close to "functionalist" sociological[1] interpretations of the sources of inequality—and endorse equality of opportunity. The interesting thing is that in both the West and the communist states of the East, the debate takes place, *mutatis mutandis,* in much the same terms.

It is not surprising that the debate over equality has probably been sharpest in the United States (of the Western countries) in recent years. America's historical experience as "the first new nation," consciously breaking with monarchic and feudal European tradition, supported the development of a new ethos, whose existence (as well as its imperfect observance) was evident to European observers such as Tocqueville, Martineau, and others. This ethos combined two values—in Lipset's terms, equality and achievement[2]—each authentically and sharply in contrast to traditional Europe, yet creating a tension between them difficult to reconcile. For those who would argue that an historical reconciliation was achieved, the formula was one in which "equality" came to mean civic and moral equality, the notions that all men are "created equal" and that they shall thus be treated as equal "before the law," whatever their differences of wealth, learning, etc. The achievement aspect of the ethos found its reflection in the acceptance of unequal outcomes from a competition to take place within a rough context of "equality of opportunity"—the Horatio Alger stories were a characteristic expression of this, and a quite American product. Such reconciliations cannot be totally successful, of course, as Lipset makes clear: "Achievement is a function of equality of opportunity," he writes. "That this emphasis on achievement must lead to new inequalities of status and to the use of corrupt means to secure and maintain high position is the ever recreated and renewed American dilemma."[3]

A recent response to this dilemma is that of the "new egalitarianism"—the moral position that *only* equality of result is just. This position is reflected in philosophical form in Rawls's *A Theory of Justice*[4] and in two sociological works—Herbert Gans's essayistic *More Equality*[5] and the controversial work of Christopher Jencks and his collaborators, *Inequality: A Reassessment of the Effects of Family and Schooling in America.*[6] Gans, confronting the traditional view, asserts that "America has not had an egalitarian tradition," and that equality of opportunity is a *libertarian* rather than egalitarian principle.[7] For him, the only "truly egalitarian principle is equality of results," and though he is aware of the utopian nature of some of his arguments, he does not shrink from noting that its achievement may require unequal treatment for the initially advantaged and disadvantaged, "so that they eventually wind up equal in resources or rights."[8] It does Gans no injustice, then, to say that his position clearly opposes the ideal of equality of opportunity, insofar as the latter would produce an inequality of result.

Most influential among recent American works has been that of Jencks et al. *Inequality*, after an attempt to trace the familial and educational roots of economic success and failure through a large body of data, concludes that success depends mainly on "luck" and a job-related "competence" having less to do with technique than with the imponderables of personality. The findings are not undisputed, but our major concern here is with the policy implications the authors draw.

Equalizing luck or personality is inconceivable, but reducing or abolishing their different results is not. In Jencks's view, this means that social mobility and the quest for equality of opportunity through equal access to schooling, etc. are irrelevant to his objective.

> Increasing social mobility is a policy for reducing inequality between groups (the initially advantaged and the initially disadvantaged) without reducing inequality between individuals. It assumes

> that the economic, social, and psychological distance between occupations is fixed, and tries to tinker with the factors determining success and failure. We can see no great virtue in such a policy. We do not want to randomize inequality; we want to reduce it. Merely ensuring that every group is proportionately represented in high-status occupations would not achieve this, even if we knew how to do it.[9]

For the authors of *Inequality,* then, the whole general notion of "achievement" is false, because they do not find enough evidence to convince them that achievement in the sense of a general, "entitling" property exists. Their emphasis is on the "random" nature of economic outcomes, the instances in which persons of similar family background and similar educational levels wind up diverging in income virtually as widely as the total population in all its diversity of background and schooling. With achievement gone, justice seems to suggest that we manipulate the system, even in quite radical ways, "to reduce the rewards of competitive success and the costs of failure."[10]

Like other egalitarians, Jencks et al. concentrate first on equalization of the most quantifiable reward—money. That resistance to its equalization exists, they are well aware: "Americans have a strong feeling that once they have 'earned' a sum of money, it is theirs to do with as they please. They view taxes as a necessary evil. . . ."[11] How, then, to proceed? By equalizing pretax wages:

> Equalizing the distribution of initial wages takes money from those with unusual luck or skill before they have formed a precise idea of what they really "deserve." Likewise, it allocates extra money to those with bad luck or little skill before others have decided they are not "worth" it.[12]

In the words they choose to set in quotes, the authors emphasize their denial of performance or achievement as things giving sanction to any given amount of inequality. *No one* has, by and large, "earned" or become entitled to more than another, whatever his education, his "replaceability," or the "critical" nature of his job.

This position is, of course, more radical than the one that has characterized the defenders of "equality of opportunity" in the American context. Thus, it has its opponents, no less articulate.

Those who feel that rewards are indeed earned, that achievement is real, and that equality of result itself would signify injustice and imply ominous levels of governmental intervention in life, beyond those acceptable in the pursuit of equality of opportunity, have in recent years come to be called by some the "neoconservatives." Lipset, Nathan Glazer, Daniel P. Moynihan, Daniel Bell, Robert Nisbet, Irving Kristol, and others are often so characterized. Whatever the accuracy of the label, it can be said that they wish to "conserve" certain values and institutions that they see seriously threatened by the pursuit of equality of result. Equality before the law, equality of opportunity, they do not question—but the *sole* idealization of equality they view as a threat. In Nisbet's words, the ideal of equality, once it becomes uppermost, can become "insatiable" in its demands, resembling "some of the religious ideals or passions which offer, just by virtue of the impossibility of ever giving them adequate representation in the actual world, almost unlimited potentialities for continuous onslaught against institutions."[13] Their concerns are with equality, but go beyond it, as we shall see in the last section of this chapter.

This is, of course, scarcely the whole of the equality debate in the West. Among partisans of equality of opportunity, there is disagreement over policies and their implementation, over the desirable degrees and modes of intervention in education and the labor market to secure a competition fairer in nature, allowing for the acceptability of unequal outcomes. These debates, indeed, come closer to the realities of social policy; their outcomes are more likely to have direct effects on people's lives than the more general debates over opportunity versus results. But it is in the latter sort of confrontation that the most fundamental issues are truly joined.

THE EQUALITY DEBATE: EAST

The differences between West and East are many—different histories, vastly different contemporary political systems that have an impact on how explicitly social and economic issues can be verbalized, different ideological languages in which those issues are couched. Yet for all this, an "equality debate" is going on in the socialist states, and the issues around which it focuses are much the same, even though the names and points of argument may be less familiar to readers than those we have already examined.

First, it must be understood that the success of socialist revolutions has set up a tension between equality and achievement not unlike the tension Lipset sees as characteristic of the United States. Equality has been part of socialism's long-term "promise." Achievement, on the other hand, is a value implied and immediately promoted by socialism in the concrete historical circumstances in which it came to power. Marxian socialism, with its emphasis on man's capacity to transform his existence, applied achievement values to tasks of economic development in previously traditional, underdeveloped societies whose religious heritage (predominantly Roman Catholic and Eastern Orthodox, with an admixture of Islam) and political histories (Ottoman domination in the Balkans, rule by landowning aristocracies in Poland, Hungary, and the eastern portions of what would become Czechoslovakia) militated against development. Marxism brought a secular equivalent of the Protestant Ethic to these societies to mobilize both societal and individual energies—the latter through expanded educational opportunities, the recruitment of peasants from the overpopulated countryside to the new industrial complexes, and the combined political-educational "merit" system of promotion and placement. "Achievement" has coexisted tensely with "equality." However much ideologists have stressed social orientations and nonmaterial means of stimulating effort, socialism in fact has emphasized *individual* striving, individual effort to qualify for and achieve better jobs and enjoy the large rewards that go with them. This tension between equality and achievement has generated a debate between two lines of socialist thought, which we call here "ideological egalitarianism" and "pragmatic reformism."

Ideological egalitarianism expresses a discontent with the persistent results of adherence to the socialist principle of reward "according to work" (in force until whatever time communism replaces it with reward "according to need"): discontent with income stratification, discontent with the continued cultural differences that see overuse of higher education by children of nonmanuals and its underutilization by those of workers and peasants—discontent, essentially, with the performance principle as it operates under socialism.

Of such persuasion are some of the Yugoslav philosophers and sociologists grouped around the journal *Praxis*, and intellectuals both "established" and dissident in other Eastern European states. One of the most concise and pointed in her comments is the Budapest sociologist Susan Ferge, who argues for "the reduction of differences of social origin and of *social consequences*, that stem from the actual character of the social structure, where socially significant differences are interrelated, forming a hierarchical system."[14] While Ferge cautions against trying to eliminate "all differences," and says that society "should not aim at rigid conformity or 'egalitarianism,'"[15] it seems clear that more equality of results in Hungary is her goal. Like Jencks and Gans, Ferge is not impressed by opportunity per se, or even by high rates of intergenerational mobility. Individual vertical mobility may be instrumental "not in changing but in conserving the structure."[16] That a peasant or worker child may succeed in becoming a professional, an academician, a responsible official is not bad; but the gap between the economic and cultural worlds of elite and mass that makes such a transition noteworthy (though more common today than in presocialist Hungary) is objectionable. The strata must be drawn closer together by governmental action to abolish the "dirty" jobs, to uplift the lower strata until the distance is not so great, and "collective mobility" becomes a natural and unremarkable phenomenon.

More subtle and less readily classifiable as an ideological egalitarian, but all the more interesting in his sophisticated Marxism, is the Yugoslav Svetozar Stojanovic. In his view, "distribution according to the products of labor [work]" is not simply a convenient principle on the "road to communism," but is ethically and humanistically an advance over capitalist distributive principles ("ownership, hierarchy, power and inherited and acquired privilege").[17] In a complex society where the results of individuals' labor are dependent one upon another, the principle harmonizes interests: "it is in each person's interest that everyone, rather than simply himself, do more and better work." [18] Stojanovic sees distribution according to need *not* as reachable in the communist future but as utopian, since needs are infinite and can never be completely satisfied. Even if all needs could be satisfied, reward according to need alone would result in injustice, for Marx "overlooked differences of capability resulting from *personal effort.*"[19] Two persons, equally endowed in their basic capabilities, may invest more or less effort in developing those capabilities. Borrowing from Aristotle, Stojanovic suggests that rewarding all according to their (presumably equal) needs would be unjust, in "treating unequals equally."

> With two equally capable people the principle of distribution according to need would actually favor the person who had invested less effort in developing his capabilities. Even worse, since this principle would favor the person who works less, as both would receive according to their needs, inequality and injustice would only be intensified. . . .[20]

Stojanovic does not reduce effort to something predetermined by an individual's genes or upbringing and thus something for which the individual can claim no credit, no entitlement to differential reward. But he is far from invoking the performance principle as the sole guide in "socialist distribution."

This, in his view, is not simply a matter of the products-of-labor principle, but of the principle plus modifications in its operation. Stojanovic argues for two types of modification: first, the equalization of chances to select, prepare for, and find employment corresponding to one's capabilities—an equal-opportunity package that seems to cut deeper than "equality of opportunity" as understood in contemporary Yugoslavia. Second, arguing that a society "cannot be socialist unless elements of communism are already developing within it," he calls for the introduction and broadening *now* of distribution of certain "goods" (schooling, medical care, social insurance, cultural goods) on a need basis. To the degree that this is possible in the here-and-now, it is not "utopian" but a justified egalitarian corrective to the performance principle.[21]

On these grounds, Stojanovic attacks those Yugoslavs he calls "anarcho-liberals," whom he sees as unlimited partisans of the "market," since they "*identify* distribution according to the products of labor with distribution according to successes on the market."[22] While willing to accept the market as the principal standard for judging productivity, he also sees in it elements of monopoly, chance, and luck that open a gap between success and labor invested—a gap socialism should narrow as much as possible. The market might indeed provide incentives; Yugoslavia might thereby become a "society of abundance," but not a *communist* society. Hence the market must, at points, be curbed for egalitarian reasons. Finally, he reads the anarcho-liberals out of socialism, noting that they, in criticizing the inadequacy of economic differentiation in Yugoslavia, use as their standard the scales of developed captialist countries: "the very nature of their standard reveals the true color of their communism!"[23] Stojanovic may be right. Socialist values stretch only so far before they become something else. "Capitalism" has produced socialists; why should socialism not produce some "capitalists," or at least persons whose "socialism" is no more intense than that of Western European social democrats? His attempt at a synthesis of principles reflects, inter alia, the problems of reconciling ideals with reality, of translating a reading of Marx into a viable social policy.

What then of the other side, the critics of the egalitarianism socialist states have produced? These we call "pragmatic reformers" for two reasons. First, their arguments have been couched in pragmatic terms: higher yields in productivity have been advanced as justifications for greater income differentiation, greater wage-salary inequality between professionals and rank-and-file workers, between industrious and "lazy" workers, etc. Second, such proposals have come in the context of general economic reform programs, advocated and adopted at various times (generally or piecemeal) in most socialist countries, with support most vocally from economists but also from a broader spectrum of intellectuals and professionals.

"Pragmatic reformism" arises from an aspect of the equality-achievement tension that the United States and the socialist states do not share. Extremely high levels of productivity and of affluence have characterized the United States, moderating that tension. Even those whose relative share of the total was small have enjoyed a standard of living higher in absolute terms than their European working-class counterparts. But the countries where socialism triumphed were on the whole neither rich nor productive. To those who pressed the claims of equal distribution, there were those who replied that equality meant little when there was so little to distribute. The promise of socialism would be, they argued, better served by a (temporary?) expansion of inequality in pursuit of greater productivity, an increase in the stock of goods and services sufficient so that egalitarian distribution, when readopted, would lead to comfortable circumstances rather than austerity.

Yugoslavia, at least until quite recently, has gone the way of pragmatic reformism—and with it swallowed the pill, bitter to some, of contrast between new affluence for the qualified, energetic, and lucky, and markedly less for others; of unemployment handled by the export of *Gastarbeiter*. In Hungary, the New Economic Mechanism, operating with much the same logic but with the trimming necessitated by Soviet tutelage, has also brought dislocations as it has modified the economic status of various groups. But perhaps the most explicit presentation of the pragmatic reformist critique of egalitarianism was that of the Czech economic reformers of the 1960s, whose long dissatisfaction with the performance of the economy in that most egalitarian of socialist states grew into major and articulate participation in the events leading to the Prague Spring of 1968.

Ota Sik, the renowned economist, pointed to the "increasingly damaging leveling of wages, which in turn had a harmful effect on progress in science and technology"[24]—an effect economists saw reflected, inter alia, in the diastrous "negative growth" achieved by the Czech economy in the early 1960s. His sentiments were echoed by the sociologist Pavel Machonin, who found the degree of wage differentiation "absolutely insufficient from the viewpoint of the postulates of a mature socialist society and especially from the viewpoint of the immediate needs of further development of science, technology and culture."[25]

On the agenda was a de-leveling that would increase the often small distance between the wages of university-trained personnel and workers who had not gone beyond primary school; a situation which, at its extremes, suggested that some "educated" professionals, given their later start, might *never* overtake in lifetime earnings a rank-and-file worker in heavy industry. That this would be difficult to accomplish was clear in the words of another economist:

> Implementation of the anti-equalization program and the carrying out of a more clear-cut differentiation of wages . . . require consider-

able work in the areas of political education and organization, since they depend above all on personal relations and on a purposeful tightening of discipline—of both wages and workers.[26]

The Czech working class, as the economists (probably rightly) saw it, was reasonably happy with economic policies that, if they could not guarantee a worker much, did guarantee that others would not do much better. Galling to the economists was their conviction that such working-class attitudes, anti-incentive and antiperformance, prevented the development of a more productive and abundant economy; that they grew from an underestimation of the value of skill, technology, "science," and the dependence of the mass on those who could make advances in these areas. As Frank Parkin notes, the Czech reform economists were, in their advocacy, close to the "functional" justification that "inequality of reward is a necessary feature of any complex society, since it is a key mechanism for ensuring that talent is utilized in the most effective way."[27] Indeed, the reformers were pressing the performance principle, with uncharacteristic directness, in a sensitive political and economic situation.

The reformist aims of 1968 amounted to a complex package, of course. Economic de-leveling was combined with a program for political liberalization whose unpalatability to the USSR brought the tanks of August. For the workers grown used to egalitarianism, the economic program probably detracted from their support of the political package—and, as Parkin observes, there were probably elements of self-interest involved on the reformers' side, since the vociferous supporters of reform were the "white-collar specialists who seemed most likely to gain from the erosion of egalitarianism."[28]

For all the qualifying complications of different national policies and different economic situations—which will become clearer as we go on—the division between "ideological egalitarians" and "pragmatic reformers" seems clear. For the first, like Jencks, Gans, and others in the United States, the most impressive fact is persistent inequality—a phenomenon defined as a moral problem, not to be assuaged by general affluence. Egalitarians are distrustful of arguments that present a logic of unequal endowments, effort, or energy as justification for unequal results, and find the promotion of equality of opportunity per se irrelevant to the results they desire.

On the other hand, those we have called "pragmatic reformers," without generally endorsing a free-for-all operation of the performance principle, do accept the logic of Polish sociologist Wlodzimierz Wesolowski's words that "the scale of skills seems to be greater than the scale of income" in socialism, underrewarding those of extraordinary skill and training while overrewarding those at the other end of the spectrum.[29] For them, as for American opponents of the new egalitarians, education, effort, scarcity of skills *are* "entitling" and deserve extra reward. Ignoring this is seen to lead not only to injustice but to inefficiency, which hampers the whole economy and thus the welfare of all.

In the East as in the West, however, the equality debate also encompasses issues less general, more closely related to concrete governmental policy. Thus, controversy over the structuring of educational opportunity, quite independent of the issue of final results, is a continuing phenomenon. In states ideologically committed to a class-conscious policy, it is not surprising that the focus of concern is largely the social profile of higher education—the relative shares of white-collar, worker, and peasant children in university-level study and how accurately these reflect the distribution of groups in the broader population. Thus, in the USSR, diverging conceptions of justice fuel a debate over strictly "meritocratic" versus egalitarian principles of admission to higher education, over the logic of admissions-examination performance as sole criterion as opposed to policies which would recognize, in something of an "affirmative action" sense, the cultural disadvantages under which worker and peasant children compete for admission with children of the intelligentsia.[30]

In Poland, with the greater frankness characteristic of discussions in that country, Wesolowski likewise outlines the conflict of interests inherent in the intelligentsia's espousal of purely "merit" principles for admission, as opposed to the worker-peasant interest in a social "preference" principle wherein the presumably culturally disadvantaged receive extra "points" toward university entrance. The conflict is real—for to the degree one group's principle is adopted over another's, the supply of places in higher education for the losing group decreases.[31]

The debate remains, perhaps permanently, unresolved in East and West. The issues of value and perceptions of reality tied to it make its treatment important in any attempt to grapple with the realities of stratification in the socialist states. That socialist governments, with a monopoly of power, have chosen to pursue a middle course—retaining the promise of greater equality in the future, and claiming that much of it has already been achieved, while citing the socialist performance principle as a contemporary guide to reward—has not really moderated the debate. The tension between achievement and equality persists, and the affluent future that might moderate it remains quite distant.

LIBERTY, EQUALITY, AND INDUSTRIAL SOCIETY

We live, now more than ever, in an age of equality. Demands for a more equal sharing of resources and benefits arise in international politics, and take on ever greater urgency in the calls from Third World nations for a reallocation of wealth from industrialized countries, for a new economic order to alter the current scene of a (relatively) rich "North" and (relatively) poor "South." *Within* nations, certainly within the industrialized nations, politicians and leaders of whatever conviction *must* pay tribute to equality. (It becomes increasingly difficult to appreciate the fact that, in the not so distant past, even parliamentary democracies at times defended principles and operations in elitist terms.) The manifestoes of the "new egalitarianism" do not sound so strange or so radical as they once might have. And even those who counter these demands with the position that equality of opportunity is as ambitious a goal as democratic societies should pursue argue that its attainment will produce somewhat greater equality of result.

The pursuit of equality of result brings up the broader question of liberty. Equalization of status, economic or otherwise, requires intervention by the state, and intervention, of its nature, restricts individual liberty. Of course, individual autonomy is restricted in all societies in the pursuit of civil order; in modern democracies, *legal* equality is itself the outcome of restrictions on some earlier, exclusive autonomies. In modern industrial societies, at least, it is generally further restricted to ensure that persons do not fall below a certain minimum standard of material welfare. But the more radical the demands for equality, the more they focus on equality of condition, the more intervention will be required, and the greater the concern of those who fear such intervention, who accord liberty a place equal to or higher than equality in their scheme of values. Nisbet, commenting on Rawls's principle that inequalities that give some persons large advantages are only justified insofar as they redound to the benefit of the least advantaged, observes that the "mind boggles at the thought of the political apparatus necessary to give expression to and to enforce such a principle."[32]

Crucial issues are joined here. Gans, Jencks, Rawls, and their partisans, do not denigrate liberty, but they do stress equality. None seem to be open *partisans* of state omnicompetence. But their concerns about increased intervention seem dwarfed by perceptions that existent inequalities are the product of the exercise of private power not morally superior to public or state power and by their overriding concern with equality of results as moral imperative for a just society.[33] Gans is, in some senses, quite correct in identifying equality of opportunity as a libertarian rather than egalitarian principle—the critical point is that, for many if not for him, libertarian principles are no less compelling than egalitarian ones.

Thus, the "neoconservatives" are inclined to assess the issues quite differently: to concern themselves with the costs, foreseeable and unforeseeable, to liberty that arise from attempts to intervene in favor of equality, to emphasize the possibilities of an outcome wherein "more equality" is achieved at the cost of lessened freedom. This is no new concern—in the American context, it goes back to questions Tocqueville raised—but we may say that those who are labeled neoconservatives show *more* concern with it today than do the egalitarians. Despite the homage that the egalitarians pay to freedom, the neoconservatives question the effectiveness of that commitment when they see so little appreciation of the consequences of the growth of state power that an equality program would require. *Which* value is paramount? People may differ on the practical reconcilability of the two, but egalitarians and neoconservatives are clearly on opposite sides. When Gans, rejecting the notion that equality of income and power would produce "sameness," argues that each person would be free to do with these as he saw fit, well and good. But, since he goes on to anticipate that some would use their money to make more money (rather than purchase consumption goods) and warns that society would have to "find ways of discouraging"[34] such developments, one can anticipate Nisbet's observation that such egalitarian measures would be "destructive of political freedom."[35] To the conservatives, the calls for equality of result manifest something that goes beyond equality—a rejection of the notion that "imperfect" societies can be legitimate, a rejection of "the bourgeois notion of the common good" and its everyday concerns, by intellectuals who despise the bourgeois ethos of the United States and Western Europe as unheroic, deficient, and unworthy.[36]

The debate in the West goes, then, well beyond narrow concerns with equality. In the socialist states, separated from the West by a great political divide, the debate is more circumspect—for these issues cannot be discussed so openly there. For all the evident imperfections of democracy in Western societies, individual liberties, press freedom, an open electoral politics, and the rule of law obtain as they do not in the socialist world—even allowing for wide variations among socialist countries. But, if the issues of equality versus liberty are not openly aired, they are still relevant to our inquiry into the structure of inequality under socialism. The relations of equality and freedom in the socialist states raise a number of questions that we note now and will return to in the final chapter.

Their form is peculiar to the historical experience of Russia and Eastern Europe—one that distinguished it from the West before as well as after the socialist revolutions. Autocracy persisted in Tsarist Russia. Imperial domination of Eastern Europe before World War I gave way to unstable regimes of an authoritarian-fascist character in most of the successor states, manifesting the weakness of traditions of civil liberty and democratic process. Socialism brought yet tighter and more effective political control, as well as mobilization in the economy. One must ask whether whatever has been accomplished in achieving greater equality under Soviet and Eastern European socialism—in comparison to the presocialist period in these states and in comparison to realistic possibilities—has been reached at too high a cost in liberties for the individual and for groups; cost that might have been lower had equality not been so pursued. This is a complex question. The sorry record of the presocialist regimes must be taken into account in judging the degree of freedom lost, as must the relevance of freedom versus greater equality to the mass of the population. But also to be placed on the balance scales are the protections against death, exile, and imprisonment that democratic institutions afford even those people whose concern with freedom takes second place to the proverbial full stomach. Socialist citizens have clearly lacked such protection, and have suffered dearly from the lack. Their sufferings must be balanced against whatever benefits of greater equality they may enjoy. We need not decide these or related questions at this early point, nor need we yet dispose of the objection that liberty versus equality is a false issue, freedom on an empty stomach an illusion. Here, we need only observe that the large and enduring machinery of the party-state socialist regimes, demonstrably capable of mobilizing and guiding human energies toward impressive social transformations—among them possibly a greater degree of equality—are by the same token capable of other things. Machinery that can do things for people can do things to them. If this machinery was necessary to achieve a certain level of equality, the question for egalitarians will be, Has the achievement been sufficient to discount or outweigh the costs in realistic prospects of "liberty" postponed or denied? For neoconservatives or libertarians, it might be posed thus: Are any conceivable achievements in equality and welfare attributable to the socialist regimes sufficient to balance both the threats, and already registered costs, to individual freedom such regimes pose? Both will require an answer.

Chapter Two

Tradition, Deference, and Egalitarianism

[Among the Poles] . . . the contrast between the lower classes and the noblesse is very striking, the latter being physically and in character refined to an almost excessive pitch of elegance.

—Baedeker's *Russia* (1914).

. . . Bulgaria is a land of peasant farmers, without a nobility, where by the standards of other countries there are neither rich nor poor.

—K. J. Jirecek, *Travels in Bulgaria* (1888).

OF NECESSITY, this chapter presents a simplified and brutally condensed treatment of diverse historical realities. The history of presocialist Eastern Europe, even that segment of social history most directly relevant to this book, fills many pages and fuels enduring controversies among scholars—and much remains yet unwritten. What we offer here is a modest amount of discription, data, and interpretation, with the purpose of conveying elements of unity and diversity in roughly the century before the coming of centralized socialism on the Soviet model, against a background of the imperial Russian society whose transformation in the wake of war and revolution gave rise to that model.

"Eastern Europe," as even a casual acquaintance with the area shows, is not a convenient unit of analysis—indeed for many purposes it is no unit at all. Nor is it clear that such internally diverse states as Czechoslovakia and Yugoslavia (to say nothing of the USSR) are themselves always appropriate units of analysis. But for the most part, we must take the national boundaries as they come, and in the case of imperial Russia and the USSR that succeeded it, restrict ourselves largely to the European, predominantly ethnically Russian areas, whence came the force for domestic and foreign transformations.

This chapter focuses on the two most relevant aspects of historical diversity. First, the actual levels of economic development and the social structures of the presocialist states, which varied considerably, claim our attention. Second, we address diversities of belief, attitude, and rationalization concerning systems of stratification—the structures of dominance and subordination, advantage and disadvantage. To view the relations of urban "elite" to peasant "mass" as similar throughout the area would be a gross oversimplification. To see the sources of elite legitimacy as the same would be an error. The relative weights of "egalitarianism" and "legitimate subordination," as national characteristics recognized by outside observers and citizens alike, varied in historically conditioned ways. This was a critical source of some of the differences a homogeneous program of socialist transformation would face in the period after World War II. Here we are concerned not only with stratification and inequality, mobility and inheritance of status, per se, but with beliefs about them, their justification and appropriateness. Such matters are not easily captured in statistics, but they are nonetheless important for an understanding of issues and realities in the socialist world today.

ECONOMIC DEVELOPMENT: A PATTERN OF DIVERSITY

The states of interwar Eastern Europe—newborn in the wake of World War I or emerging at that time with the 1914 borders altered, manifested different patterns (essentially three) of economic development and labor force composition. These patterns themselves were as much a product of over a century of pre-1914 history as they were results of postwar drawing of boundaries. The data in table 2.1, simple though the categorizations are, serve to make the essential point. Czechoslovakia, on the whole, was not an "underdeveloped" country; Poland and Hungary, with the balance of the labor force in agriculture, were underdeveloped, but had regional cores of industrial development. The Balkan states—Yugoslavia, Romania, and Bulgaria—were thoroughly peasant societies, reflecting the effects of the long Ottoman domination of the Balkans.

Table 2.1.
Working Population, by Sector of Economy, "Before Socialism"

	Czechoslovakia (1934)	*Hungary (1930)*	*Poland*[b] *(1931)*	*Romania (1930)*	*Bulgaria (1935)*	*Yugoslavia (1936)*
Industry[a]	38.3	24.1	19.4	7.7	8.0	9.9
Agriculture	25.6[c]	53.0	60.6	76.9	80.0	76.3
Trade	9.2	5.9	6.1	3.3	2.4	4.2
Other	26.9	17.0	13.9	12.1	9.6	9.3
Total	100.0	100.0	100.0	100.0	100.0	99.7

[a]Includes mining and construction [b]Includes dependent non-earners
[c]Probable underestimate; see figures for 1950 in table 2.2, below.

SOURCE: adapted from Nicholas Spulber, *The Economics of Communist Eastern Europe* (New York: MIT–Wiley, 1957), p. 5 (Czechoslovakia); F. S. Pisky, "The People," in Ernst C. Helmreich, ed., *Hungary* (New York: Praeger, 1957), p. 71 (Hungary); *Concise Statistical Year-Book of Poland 1938* (Warsaw, 1938), p. 30 (Poland); Stephen Fischer-Galati, ed., *Romania* (New York: Praeger, 1957), p. 57 (Romania); F. S. Pisky, "The People," in L. A. D. Dellin, ed. *Bulgaria* (New York: Praeger, 1957), p. 80 (Bulgaria); Spulber, *Economics*, p. 5 (Yugoslavia).

Czechoslovakia throughout its history has been Eastern Europe's deviant case. Its exceptionalism was a product of political and cultural history, and of the borders of the Czechoslovak Republic created by the victors of World War I. The western parts of the country—the "Czech lands" of Bohemia and Moravia—contained the main industrial centers of the old Austro-Hungarian Empire, and hence large numbers of skilled industrial workers, "hereditary proletarians" who felt at home in the urban factory environment in a way rare elsewhere in Eastern Europe. Education levels and living standards in the Czech lands, among the Czechs as well as the Austro-Germans, were not notably inferior to the standards of neighboring Western European countries.

The Czech lands had benefited, relatively, from their long administration by Vienna. If Hapsburg dominance was unwelcome in 1914, and had been since the Czech nobility lost the Battle of the White Mountain in 1620 to the Hapsburg forces, it was nonetheless far better for economic, educational, and cultural reasons to reside in an Austrian-administered part of the Dual Monarchy than to be ruled from Budapest.

But interwar Czechoslovakia, much like contemporary Italy, was a country with a "South"—or, more accurately here, an East. Slovakia, joined to the Czech lands in the new state, was the classic Eastern Europe. Peasant-agricultural in profile, Slovakia, with little industry, showed the effects of hundreds of years of Hungarian domination in its large estates owned by Magyar nobles, its agricultural overpopulation (a small problem, if one at all, in the Czech lands), its low indices of literacy and other marks of modernity. Land reform after 1918 redistributed the lands to the Slovak peasantry, but differences in developmental levels persisted. In 1937, almost twenty years after the birth of the Republic, Slovakia, with 24.6 percent of the population, produced only 7.3 percent of the total national industrial output, receiving 15 percent of the total national income. With 35.6 percent of the national acreage, Slovakia's contribution to the total agricultural output was 22.9 percent and only 17.4 percent of the output for market.[1] Forestry (which had employed large numbers of Slovak peasants before 1914) and some industrial capacity in iron and textiles suffered in the Republic from the rupture of governmental and trade relations with Budapest, since it was originally toward the Hungarian market that these were oriented.[2]

The Slovak problem was a large one for interwar Czechoslovakia, exacerbated by the Czech civil servants and officials who largely ran the area—though in truth the absence of a Slovak intelligentsia of any size made such tutelage unavoidable. But as a whole, the Czechoslovak Republic was a "developed" country by the standards of the time. Czechoslovak society was balanced—relatively prosperous Czech middle farmers and smallholders balanced the depressed Slovak smallholders and landless laborers, while in the secondary and tertiary sectors a numerous urban working class and an essentially "bourgeois" ruling class with a mix of commercial, manufacturing, intelligentsia, and government officialdom distinguished the nation from the rest of Eastern Europe. It can scarcely be accidental that this relatively modern population mix was accompanied by a rather effective democratic government in the interwar years. For the purpose of this study, presocialist Czechoslovakia possessed a modern social structure, whose stratification patterns were by no means exotic in the context of Western Europe.

In contrast to Czechoslovakia's modernity, the weight of tradition lay heavily upon Poland and Hungary, both in economic development and, as we shall see, in the complex of attitudes and values concerning equality and status. Despite some differences, it may be said that both these states remained in the interwar years, as they had been in the century before, countries of landlord and peasant, dominated by national elites who, for reasons of history and culture, remained traditionalist in orientation and, maintaining a deeply entrenched anticommercial attitude, never came adequately to grips with the economic problems their nations faced.

Poland was restored to the map of Europe, from which it had disappeared in 1795, out of pieces of the Prussian, Austro-Hungarian, and Russian empires that had been its partitioners. Hungary at the end of the war was a truncated state, shorn of its imperial holdings but not of irredentist aspirations. Both interwar states inherited traditional elites and underlying social structures, which were to endure until World War II.

In Poland, the development of cities and an urban commercial class had been arrested in the sixteenth century by the landowning aristocracy, the *szlachta,* a class jealous of its own considerable authority in a land where kingships were elective and where, although economic differences between the large landowning "magnates" and the remainder of the aristocracy were large, a sort of "one noble, one vote" formal democracy prevailed within the group. Two centuries of relative stagnation followed, until events in the eighteenth century began a process of social mobility crucial for the formation of the interwar Polish ruling class. Agricultural crises and the political consequences of partition led to a loss of land and power for much of the aristocracy. Downwardly mobile, but clinging to their aristocratic values and economic attitudes, they created a new urban class, an intelligentsia of the free professions, the arts, and to some degree the government service. Commerce and industry, such as they were, were largely left to foreign (German and Jewish) entrepreneurs and merchants. In spirit, this urban stratum remained part of the gentry, more closely allied in attitude and self-conception to the landed magnates who survived than to the new urban classes that grew slowly during the nineteenth century. During the partition period gentry and intelligentsia had united to claim a role as preservers of the national identity. This claim they successfully pressed later, to become the core of the greatly expanded native ruling administrative class with the restoration of Poland after Versailles.

The interwar social structure, then, had much of the prewar in it.[3] Large landowners (those with over 50 hectares), less than 1 percent of the nation, owned 27 percent of the land. (There had been some agrarian reform, but the conservative policies from the mid-1920s on stabilized the situation.) The richer bourgeoisie, the urban financial and industrial elite, made up about 2 percent of the population. Often without social pedigree, this small stratum and its interests were, along with landowners and theirs, dominant in the economic policy of the interwar Polish state. The urban intelligentsia, about 6 percent of the population, was almost evenly divided between those whose education fitted them for professional, managerial, and academic posts and those who, in the manner of lower functionaries elsewhere, pushed paper and lorded it over those who worked with their hands. This group gave the tone to much of the Polish urban style. A petit bourgeoisie of small producers, purveyors of services, craftsmen, etc. made up an additional 11 percent.

The remainder of Poland was submerged in the world of manual labor. Roughly 20 percent of the nation made up a working class, much of it wage labor in small workshops, domestic service, etc. A small core of skilled workers in areas of older industrial development in Silesia, Lodz, and later the Warsaw region was more than balanced by a predominantly semiskilled and unskilled labor force whose grip on urban jobs, always precarious, was made more so by the Depression. Peasants, about 52 percent of the population, ranged from the minority of large to medium proprietors (50 to 5 hectares) to the almost two-thirds who, possessed of less than 5 hectares and hampered by low educational levels, inefficient farming methods, and high birthrates, had to seek additional sources of income as laborers on large estates. Finally, the rural landless—the lowest layer of society—amounted to about 9 percent of the population.

Much the same picture applies to interwar Hungary as to Poland. While national political histories differed, a large segment of the traditional Magyar landowning aristocracy had also become residentially urbanized, losing its lands in nineteenth-century agricultural crises and moving, again, not into commerce but into the professions and civil service. They formed, in Seton-Watson's words, "a middle class, which occupied the social position of a bourgeoisie, but retained the mentality of an aristocracy."[4] The landed aristocracy that survived (for while the Potockis and Radziwills still were large landholders in Poland, so were the Fesketics and Esterhazys in Hungary) dominated an agrarian sector in which dwarf landholders, with under 5 hectares, made up a vast majority of all landholders, while 48.3 percent of the land was in holdings of more than 100 hectares. These holdings, which made up less than 1 percent of all holdings, were in the hands of the magnates. The under-5-hectare smallholders, however, were themselves exceeded or at least equaled in number by landless agricultural laborers and estate servants.[5]

For the landless laborers and estate servants, their life at the bottom of society was harsh indeed. The populist writer Gyula Illyes, in his 1936 book *People of the Puszta,* drew the memorable picture of large estates where one could see fat farm animals but no fat laborers, where laborers' children cried and kicked at the locked lids of breadboxes, while the parents, knowing well how food had to be hoarded against greater hunger later, turned deaf ears toward them.[6]

As in Poland, the nonagricultural working class made up only a modest share of the total employed nationwide; and even this was a product of relatively modest growth from a very small base. According to one source, the industrial population grew, between 1870 and 1910, by 127 percent.[7] In the latter year, data from a different source indicate that 21.8 percent of the population was in industry.[8] The war—in which Hungary, unlike Poland, took part as an existing power—spurred the growth of industry. But just as industry in Poland was concentrated in a few restricted areas, so in Hungary industry was largely limited to Budapest and its environs.

What has been said thus far should not be taken to mean that in interwar Poland and Hungary, a "landlord anti-industrial" stratum exclusively dominated governmental policy. In both countries, the ruling class included some commercial and industrial interests, drawn (since 1918) moderately but increasingly from the aristocracy as well as from successful bourgeois entrepreneurs. With time, indeed, the interests of the latter became dominant in state economic policy.[9] But dependence on foreign capital and the general disaster of the Depression made for difficult times, slowing potentially rapid transitions to modern economies. The ruling classes, agrarian and industrial, were conservative, wary of the costs of rapid social and economic change yet seeking the benefits of economic modernity; and they were unsure of the direction their increasingly "statist" economies should take. Official figures show moderate patterns of change in the decade between war's end and the onset of depression. In Poland in 1921, 15.4 percent of the population depended on industry; in 1931, the figure was 19.4 percent, while the proportion dependent on agriculture dropped from 63.8 percent to 61.0.[10] In 1920 in Hungary, 19.1 percent of earners were in industry, 58.2 in agriculture; a decade later in 1930 the comparable figures were 23.2 and 53.0.[11] The Depression, of course, presented a considerable setback to the economies of both nations, the impact of which was felt well into the late 1930s. With an increasingly pro-German political orientation and German economic penetration, the Hungarian industrial sector resumed growth around 1937,[12] and continued to grow through most of World War II. Poland did not do so well; and in any case, normal life ceased to exist in Poland in September 1939.

The old political orders perished in Poland and Hungary in the destruction of World War II. But as table 2.2 shows, in 1950 both countries, in the beginning of the socialist phase, possessed social structures that in their balance of agriculture to industry much resembled the interwar period. Their relative position among the countries that would become socialist had not changed. Well behind Czechoslovakia's level of development, these countries of the "second tier" were still, it might be said, frozen in transition toward modernity, but well ahead of the peasant societies of the Balkans.

To a Polish or Hungarian observer of the interwar years, the Balkan states—Bulgaria, Romania, and Yugoslavia—would have looked underdeveloped by his own domestic yardstick. And indeed they were, for here Asia had come to Europe, and stayed for centuries, in the form of the Ottoman Empire. By the fifteenth century, the lands that were later to be reassembled as Romania and Bulgaria and most of the territory of the future Yugoslav state had fallen under the Ottomans. There most of this land would remain until the latter part

Table 2.2.
Working Population, by Sector of Economy, 1950

	Czecho-slovakia	*Hungary*	*Poland*	*Romania*	*Bulgaria*[a]	*Yugo-slavia*[b]
Industry	30.1	19.4	20.6	12.0	11.5	16.7[c]
Construction	6.3	3.1	5.0	2.2	3.4	—
Agriculture	38.7	52.0	54.5	74.3	73.2	68.3
Trade	7.0	5.3	5.3	2.5	2.9	1.7
Transport and communications	5.2	4.0	4.5	2.2	2.5	2.1
Other	12.7	16.2	10.1	6.8	6.5	11.3
Total	100.0	100.0	100.0	100.0	100.0	100.1

[a]1952 [b]1953 [c]Includes construction

SOURCE: adapted from *Statisticka rocenka CSSR 1966*, p. 112; *Hungarian Statistical Yearbook 1973*, pp. 6–7; *Rocznik statystyczny 1974*, pp. 109–10; *Anuarul statistic al Republicii Socialiste Romania 1974*, p. 61; *Statisticheski godishnik na NR Bulgariia 1973*, p. 82; *Statisticki godisnjak Jugoslavije 1971*, p. 76.

of the nineteenth century, the European extension of an empire that sought little except tax revenues and territorial domination.[13]

In 1859, with Ottoman power fading under the pressure of European imperial competition, a Romanian state was reborn from the union of the two principalities of Moldavia and Wallachia. The year 1878 saw, among the consequences of a Balkan war, the emergence of Bulgaria as a state entity. Yugoslavia's roots extended further into the past. A revolt against the abuses of Ottoman administration in Serbia in 1804 began a series of conflicts, revolts, and suppressions culminating in 1815 in the establishment of Serbia as an autonomous state. Effective Ottoman power in Bosnia and Herzegovina was displaced in 1878 by Hapsburg administration. Of the remaining regions that were to make up Yugoslavia, Montenegro remained inaccessible, backward, and independent, Macedonia continued under Turkish rule until 1913, and Croatia and Slovenia remained under the Hapsburgs until the collapse of the old empire in 1918.

At the lower extreme of the developmental continuum, the new Bulgaria and Yugoslavia shared, nonetheless, an important characteristic with the more modern Czechoslovakia—the virtually complete absence of a historically entrenched native landowning nobility. Ottoman and Hapsburg rule had long since wiped out this stratum. Kings there might be in the interwar period, but not nobility. (The relative newness of "dynasties" in the area is evident. Bulgaria and Romania imported their monarchs. Indicative too are the early years of the Serbian state—the 1804 revolt was led by George Petrovic, who, assuming the title Karageorge, "Black George," gave his name to the ruling house of Karageorgevic. The second, 1815 revolt, led by his rival Milos Obrenovic, succeeded and established the house that would contend for national power until the beginning of the twentieth century. Both Petrovic and Obrenovic sat on the throne of Serbia; both were, at the time of their revolts, pig breeders and merchants—prosperous, but far from nobility as the Europe of 1800 understood the term.) Bulgaria emerged into independence a state as authentically peasant as Serbia. Romania, on the other hand, followed a more complicated path. Turkish administration had not been extended to the Principalities in quite the same way as to the rest of the Balkans, leaving some native landowning nobles, as well as the Phanariot Greeks, in possession of large estates. By the 1820s, the native nobles had largely displaced the Phanariot servants of the Turks. With independence, they became the new ruling gentry, dominating a nation of peasants who, freed from serfdom in 1859, remained land-poor as the implementation of an 1864 agrarian reform law proceeded at a glacial pace. Romania was closer in many senses to the Polish and Hungarian pattern than to that of Serbia and Bulgaria, remaining so until the onset of World War I. Its territorial acquisitions at Hungarian expense left it much larger at war's end, and facilitated what two distinguished economic historians have called a "rather radical land reform," redistributing land from both old and newly acquired estates, and generated a peasant economy that made interwar Romania rather similar to the rest of the Balkans.[14]

This peasant character was thus largely a product of political and military history—a history that had precluded economic development and dispensed with native aristocracies. But it was also to some degree designed—especially in Serbia, and later much of Yugoslavia, which came to bear the stamp of Serbia's dominance.[15] In 1836, Milos Obrenovic promulgated the first "protected minimum homestead" decree, forbidding foreclosure on a minimal plot with a small number of animals even for a peasant deep in debt. A revised, stronger decree, aimed at advancing the principle that "the land belongs to him who works it," appeared in 1873. The principle of peasant ownership, however, did not "usher the peasants into the millenium of freedom, progress, or plenty"; with feudal lords and aristocrats gone, the peasant faced, in the nineteenth and twentieth centuries, "the state bureaucracy, the trader and the usurer."[16] This was equally true of Bulgaria and Romania. Not surprisingly, the peasant, despite his numbers and secure ownership, came off second best against the new competition, as he had against the old.

The life of peasants in the Balkans was far from idyllic. Whatever the psychological consolations of ownership, their diet, clothing, and living standards were little, if at all, better than those of the rural populations of unreformed Poland and Hungary.[17] Even had the peasants' conscious horizons expanded, there was little to do but remain on the land. The late nineteenth century and the interwar years saw little industrial development, and what there was relied largely on foreign skilled labor, foreign markets, and foreign capital. "The greater portion of domestic capital," Tomasevich reports, "was used for ventures in trading and in usury, and after 1918 in urban real estate, rather than in industry."[18] As both tables 2.1 and 2.2 indicate, the share of the industrial working class remained low in Balkan societies during the whole period—not surprisingly, given their backward status in 1918 and the political and economic problems of the interwar years. The smallness of landholdings, the overpopulation and underemployment in rural areas, and the low living standards amounted to "push" factors that, hypothetically at least, made the rural population a reserve for industry. The absence of concerted efforts at industrial development, however, resulted in a lack of the equally critical "pull" factor.

The interwar Balkan states were, as even peasant states must be, possessed of elites. But the elites differed from the modern bourgeoisie of Czechoslovakia, and even more from the aristocracies of Hungary and Poland. They lacked the former's modern admixture of industrialists and productive entrepreneurs and the latter's historical "legitimacy." We will return to this later in the chapter, but for now it seems adequate to characterize the upper classes as composed largely of the free professions, professional politicians, the civil service (whose size grew, naturally, with independence but for various reasons continued to grow beyond the needs of countries so poorly developed), and those who profited from commerce and trading. While the predominant cast of the Balkan societies was noncommercial, and the money economy came only gradually to the majority of cultivators in the countryside, the new elites of Yugoslavia, Romania, and Bulgaria did not share the disdain for commerce which marked the gentry-intelligentsia elites of Poland and Hungary.

Such, in rough outline, were the presocialist Eastern European states, their populations, and their economies. Divergent histories and locations had conditioned their development (or stagnation) in the nineteenth century, and in the wake of World War I Eastern Europe, with the exception of Czechoslovakia, was an underdeveloped area: along with Russia, in fact, probably the first area in the world to think of itself as such and to be recognized as such by others. The two decades between the wars brought changes aplenty in politics and some changes in the economies; but as the data in table 2.2 show, in the first years of socialism, before the economic policies of the new governments had worked their effects, those changes had been far from massive.

EGALITARIANISM AND SUBORDINATION IN EASTERN EUROPE

While inequality was ubiquitous in Eastern Europe, before and after World War I, it was not of the same sort from country to country. It looked different, it "felt" different, its base lay in diverse rationalizations or in a lack of them. Depending on the country, it was either more or less apparent, blatant, evident to the outside observer. One may find the lines from Baedeker and the words of the Czech traveler Jirecek that begin this chapter quaint, florid, or simply wrong (for surely there *were* some rich, even in the Bulgaria of the 1880s)—but they express something important about these societies, and, what is more, they reflect perceptions with which many natives at the time would have agreed.

Poland and Hungary, one might say, were countries of a "great tradition," somewhat in Redfield's sense,[19] a tradition that legitimated the subordination of the masses—peasant masses, on the whole—to an aristocracy/nobility that conceived of itself as *the* nation. The claims of the aristocracy rested on their heredity, on "breeding," manners, knightly conceptions of honor, on a tradition that was military-agrarian, antiurban, and anticommercial. If the term is not too vague (and it is difficult to use specific terms here), the "model" aristocrat was an arrogant, heroic individualist, little concerned with counting costs, in a monetary sense or otherwise: this had its consequences.

Something of this can be seen in the comments (1840) of an Englishwoman and traveler in Hungary:

> The besetting sin of the Magyar is vanity. He is proud of his nation, of his liberty, of his antiquity, and above all, of his privileges. In short, he admits no superior, scarcely an equal, when he has high blood, a long pedigree, and an apparent rent-roll. I say apparent, for perhaps Europe cannot present collectively so pauperized a nobility as that of Hungary, when their circumstances and positions are thoroughly understood. From the gorgeous and princely Esterhazy, with his debt of two millions sterling, to the minor Magnate who rattles over the pavement of Pesth behind his four illgroomed horses, there are not twenty nobles in the country who are not *de facto* bankrupts.[20]

In the same vein, a domestic observer, the Hungarian national poet Sandor Petofi, described the nobleman in a verse of 1845:[21]

Serf, repair that road! Your horse
Has to carry me, of course.
Walking's not for me—and why?
A Magyar nobleman am I!

Shall I then a scholar be?
Scholars live in poverty.
I can't write or read, or try,
A Magyar nobleman am I!

....

Tax I do not pay, that's fine!
Few the lands that I call mine,
But debts enough to reach the sky:
A Magyar nobleman am I!

The virtues and vices of aristocrats were proper to them, and them alone—not to be emulated by the lower orders except at the risk of ridicule for attempts to rise above their station. The muteness, isolation, and illiteracy of the peasant mass meant that these "noble" traditions were the preemptive traditions of the nation. No other stratum could elaborate a tradition, or behavior models appropriate to itself, that could compete effectively with them.

Despite the agrarian, antiurban aspects of the tradition, the nineteenth century, as noted above, saw a large portion of both the Polish and Hungarian aristocracies leaving the land for the cities. With them went their tradition, determining the character of life in Warsaw and Budapest as the gentry moved into the free professions and governmental service while avoiding commerce and manufacturing.

Linguistic usage was elaborate and stratified, well beyond the *tu* and *vous* of French, and the similar use of singular and plural "you" in other West European languages to denote age and/or status. The Polish *pan* and *pani* (Sir, Madam) might be used as terms of address among gentlefolk but not among peasants or workers, and certainly not by a superior addressing a subordinate or by an urbanite to a farmer. Some of the strangness of any such behavior emerges in a passage from the Polish emigré novelist W. S. Kuniczak's *The Thousand Hour Day.* Pawel, an aristocratic officer, finds himself, in the first disorganized days of World War II, in a peasant cottage, eating the food provided by the peasant wife, and deviates from the customary mode of address.

—Thank you, madam, Pawel said. She laughed, embarrassed, covering her mouth. Her teeth were yellow and her breath was bad and she had a great scarlet face like an angry moon and arms like a man. Her hands had the texture and the color of a crust of bread.

—Madam! Me? She was, of course, a peasant, and such words as *pani* or madam or lady had never been addressed to her. She worked hard and her life was difficult.

She would not know about ducks and apricot stuffing. She would not know about the Brandy of Napoleon. Oh but, he thought, you could see she liked it: This was the first time, perhaps, that anyone had called her anything but mother. Therefore he smiled as though this was, indeed, a Warsaw drawing room, and spoke to her as if she were that kind of hostess. She in turn, made her voice gruff: —It is simple. It is only bread and cheese. But (and her voice was suddenly soft and shy and girllike) if the Sir Officer will eat it will be an honor.[22]

While Pawel could condescend, the housewife would never have considered responding other than by calling him *pan oficer.*

Such a society is an unlikely place to look for open elites, for aristocracies of talent. Success in activities such as commerce or manufacture, which, however honest or useful, were "beneath" aristocratic values, may have generated status aspirations, but these were frequently frustrated. Money, certainly, conferred power—but it could not buy everything, when "everything" included social acceptance. This is the central theme of the nineteenth-century Polish novel *Lalka (The Doll)* by Boleslaw Prus. The hero, Stas Wokulski, a self-made, rich Warsaw merchant (and a more sympathetic character, on balance, than Moliere's *bourgeois gentilhomme*), confronts aristocratic prejudices as he seeks to win his distant love, Isabella Lecka, daughter of a socially impeccable but impecunious aristocrat. On a business trip to Paris Wokulski compares the city, where the openness of society to talent and enterprise impresses him, to Poland.

"Am I to go back there? What for? Here at least I have a nation living by all the talents with which man is endowed. There, on the other hand, labor stands in the pillory, and depravity triumphs! He who makes a fortune is called a miser, a skinflint, a parvenu; he who wastes money is called generous, disinterested, open-handed. . . . There, simplicity is eccentric, economy is shameful, artistry symbolized by shabby elbows. There, in seeking to acquire the denomination of a man, one must either have a title derived from money, or a talent for squeezing into drawing rooms. Am I to go back there?"[23]

From the other side of the gulf between noble and *parvenu,* Thomas Lecki, Wokulski's intended father-in-law, plays the "revolutionary" in the drawing room society by breaking with tradition and mixing with his social inferiors (all of whom possess more money than he).

. . . Thomas had broken with society and joined the merchant's club as a sign of his revolutionary sympathies. He used to play whist there with persons he had formerly despised, such as tanners, brushmakers and distillers, telling all and sundry that the aristocracy had no right to wall themselves up in exclusive society, but should lead the way for the enlightened bourgeois and, through them, for the whole nation.[24]

It would never have occurred to Thomas Lecki that, whatever the instability of his finances (and theirs), any stratum but his own aristocracy should "lead the way."

This, however, is only a partial picture, leaving out an important phase in the transition of gentry to intelligentsia in Poland, and the basis of the distinction between the Polish and Hungarian upper classes from the late nineteenth century through the interwar period. The economic and political processes that drove so much of the gentry of partitioned Poland to the cities created, despite the continuing "parasitism" of this stratum, an elite that did achieve a measure of genuine acceptance as leaders. Historically conscious of themselves as successors to the gentry who had guarded Poland's independence, the intelligentsia found themselves the keepers of the flame of national identity, culture, and language when Poland ceased to exist as a political unit. Alexander Gella observes in a perceptive essay:

Because there was no Polish state in the nineteenth century and because the Polish propertied classes were divorced from the political apparatus, the intelligentsia preserved most of its moral independence. Hence it felt itself to be a charismatic stratum, and was recognized by the other classes as the leading force in the nation.[25]

With all its undoubted imperfections, the intelligentsia, before and after 1918, claimed and received allegiance from the Polish masses, acting on behalf of the nation first as fighters for and then as guardians of national independence. Independence was something of which peasants and workers as well as aristocrats could partake.

A large literature addresses the problems, genesis, and fate of the presocialist Polish intelligentsia;[26] perhaps the most interesting indicator of a different situation in Hungary is the lack of such a literature. This is not surprising, since Hungarian conditions were different. The flow to the cities of the gentry had much more directly economic causes. Moreover, by 1867 (when Poland had been off the map of Europe for some seventy years) Hungary had achieved something like parity with Austria within the Empire, and the nobility, civil servants, and urban professional classes went about the common business of dominating, exploiting, and Magyarizing the parts of the Empire subject to Budapest's administration. Thus they could not claim to be acting on behalf of the masses. National independence was a card the Hungarian, unlike the Polish intelligentsia, could not play. The Hungarian masses, like the Polish, may have been in awe of the leaders and their historical claims to dominance; but it is likely that the Hungarian awe had less gratitude in it, less feeling that rural landowners, and the urban officials who came from and owed allegiance to the gentry, were linked with common folk in common concerns.

In both nations, the interwar period saw a multiplication of government functions and other changes that, however moderate and gradual, led to a swelling of especially the lower ranks of the bureaucrat-functionary stratum—the "lower white-collar" stratum, as we might call it today. The attractiveness of association with the *cachet* of the urban upper classes evoked a strong tendency for these routine functionaries, clerks, and the like to identify with and claim membership in the Polish intelligentsia, the Hungarian ruling class. Insofar as this signified an attempt on their part to distinguish themselves from all who worked with their hands, it was by and large successful. Hard evidence is lacking, but the observations of various scholars tend to support this picture. Of interwar Poland, Wesolowski observes that "the intelligentsia stratum was sharply distinguished from the rest of the population. . . . All mental workers, including lower officials, secretaries, bookkeepers, had higher social prestige and status than workers—even highly skilled specialists in their trade."[27]

Similarly, Zygmunt Bauman stresses the gulf between those who worked with their hands and those who did not, the

> lofty scorn for hard work deeply ingrained in the traditional gentry culture. The contempt for hard work, especially manual, was something like the first commandment in the decalogue of the dominating culture. Making one's living at this kind of work was sufficient to exclude one from well-bred society. The other side of the medal of the same cultural system was the extremely high prestige ascribed to all kinds of "clean" jobs, "cleanliness" being a value in itself, independent of any estimate of the social utility, rationality, and appropriateness of the job and its role in increasing wealth.[28]

In Hungary, much the same gulf yawned between the classes, expressed often in the deference of peasants toward the few from among their number who achieved an education, and the reciprocal contempt of the latter for those from whom they had sprung. As the writer Illyes observed, recalling his own confronting, as an adult and man of accomplishment, the estate-servant background from which he had come, it was "then I realised how difficult a thing is equality and how far one is tamed by one's social status."[29]

This signifies that the ranks of the white-collar workers, as the size of the category grew, did not remain closed to all except those born into them. While social mobility scarcely achieved a revolutionary pace in either society, the extension of modern educational institutions to large segments of Polish and Hungarian society in the interwar period allowed some to climb to "clean hands." Inclusion in the Polish "intelligentsia" generally required not a university education but rather that of the classical high school, and some whose parents lacked education managed to complete the course.[30] Those who completed training that was less demanding but still provided access to minor bureaucratic-clerical positions also could cross the manual-nonmanual line and achieve some social recognition—if not from their superiors, at least from those whose ranks they had left.

Similar processes—the "pull" of increasing numbers of jobs in administration, the "push" of somewhat greater educational opportunities—allowed many Hungarians in the interwar years to rise to positions that represented, both materially and culturally, real advances over their artisan, worker, or peasant origin. Relatively crude but illuminating Hungarian census data of 1930 (see chapter 4) show quite moderate movement of peasant and worker sons into nonmanual occupations. Most remained where they had been born. But those who moved up formed a fairly large share of the petty officialdom—a fact less evident than it would have been in a society where a rise from humble origins was something to pride oneself on.

Such were the elements of status in the consciousness of elite and mass Poles and Hungarians in the presocialist period. The picture is overgeneralized, of course. Among the urban working classes, affected by socialist ideology, some dents in this facade had appeared.[31] But all generalizations are dubious, and the picture presented here seems more accurate than any alternative.

The meaning of the dominant "great tradition" that gave Poland and Hungary landlord-peasant characteristics, that suffused their urban upper classes with rural gentry values, however, only becomes clear in the light of the contrasting situation of the Balkans. Lacking an upper class with historical claims to guardianship of national identity, the Balkan states were countries of a "little tradition."[32] History there was, but a remote one—the Siberian kingdom of Tsar Dushan which fell to the Turks before 1400, the Bulgarian empire of Simeon, also long vanished. No human links, no remnants of ancient historical families, connected the states of the nineteenth century with their distant past.

The Ottoman domination removed much of the diversity in the predominantly Christian population of the Balkans.[33] Taking little or no account of ethnic "nationality," the Turks favored those who converted to Islam, treating the rest essentially as outcasts. Religion remained the crucial means of differentiation. With the Christian nobility and landowners displaced by Turks and Slavic converts to Islam, the indigenous populations were reduced to the common status of peasants. Despite generally heavy taxes, chance, enterprise, and the quality of land differed, so that there emerged over the centuries poorer and richer peasants (and from the latter the leaders of revolts, such as Petrovic and Obrenovic). But the critical point is that self-identification as peasant was apparently accepted by rich and poor alike—no magnate class emerged.

For a long time, the Balkan city and urban life remained alien to the broader national life—more alien than Budapest and Warsaw, set though they were in predominantly peasant countries, were in their own contexts. Vuk Karadzic, the Serbian writer, folklorist, and ethnographer of the earlier nineteenth century, wrote that there were "no members of the Serbian nation but peasants. The small number of Serbs who live in towns as traders . . . and craftsmen . . . are called townsmen. They wear Turkish costumes and live according to the Turkish way of life. . . . They are not called Serbs by the people and indeed are despised by them. The Serbs, as peasants, live only from land and livestock."[34] Its alien quality limited the impact of the city on national life well into the late nineteenth century. An anonymous foreign traveler confirms some of what Karadzic wrote:

> In most European countries wealth, intelligence, prestige and power are unequally distributed between town and country, with the towns receiving the lion's share. . . .
>
> In little Serbia the position is quite different: here it is the country, not the town, which predominates. The capital has not more than 20,000 inhabitants, who are less militant and, in the opinion of the peasants, less patriotic than the inhabitants of the countryside.[35]

Thus, the city in the nineteenth century was alien not because of a great tradition of landowning aristocracy that looked down upon urban life and pursuits, but because of a widely diffused "little tradition" that viewed it as irrelevant, not really a part of national life. In Poland and Hungary, an aristocratic tradition would percolate down to shape values in the interwar period; in the Balkans, the peasant tradition, the only real tradition, would move into the cities as they developed, giving the politics, society, and economy of the Balkan capitals their particular flavor. The absence of a great tradition as model for behavior, deportment, and deference—a model the ambitious and prosperous might adopt—was probably as important as the presence of the little tradition (which could not easily be transplanted to urban life, except perhaps in the profusion of "peasant parties" in Balkan interwar politics and the constant exaltation of peasants as the "soul" of the nation). The competition for mobility, for status, rewards, and respect in the interwar period had little in the way of traditional upper-class norms to regulate it in the Balkans.

Who was to judge, by what standards, when a person had "arrived"? The fluidity of social life in the early years after World War I has been captured nicely in Ivo Andric's fiction, here in passages dealing with life of the time in Belgrade—Serbia's old capital, now the capital of a new Yugoslav state: "The new community which was being forged of Belgrade residents and a swelling number of newcomers . . . did not as yet have any of the basic attributes of a real society; it had no common traditions or a common outlook on life. . . ."[36] Belgrade, as the new capital, was expanding rapidly in population, new elements mixing with and threatening to engulf the small, provincial society of the city: "Here were many young people from all parts of a state that was still in the process of formation, who looked forward to the next day and expected great things of the changed circumstances, and also a number of older people who looked for a means of adjustment and for salvation in this very flood, hiding the fears and the loathing which it inspired in them."[37] In such situations, different from those in Poland (where an elite knew what it wished to restore) and Hungary (where an elite tried to cling to what was left in a "rump" state), there were few rules to follow, few channels that led unerringly to status:

> At midday or toward evening, between Slavia Square and Kalemegdan, you might unexpectedly meet some childhood friend and, thanks to that accidental meeting, find yourself the very next day in some fine position of sudden wealth, without anyone's demanding to know in detail who or what kind of person you were. And by the same token, you might spend many futile weeks knocking at the doors of various authorities, with a briefcase full of the best references and most emphatic credentials, and never get your rights recognized. There was something of the lusty chaos of the golden land of Eldorado in the life and appearance of this capital of a large new state, which so far had no clear frontiers, no internal order, not even a final name.[38]

Playing an important role in the capital of a new Yugoslavia while achieving economic success was, of course, attractive—no less so was life in Sofia and Bucharest for Bulgarians and Romanians. For all the peasant quality of these countries and the alien quality of their urban life, many from the countryside looked with ambition and longing to the cities and a break with the poverty, monotony, and toil of agriculture. However, economic development, as we have seen, was quite slow in the interwar Balkans. Where, then, did the ambitious young aspire to go? What sorts of occupation offered opportunity and conferred status?

In the answer to this question, we find a parallel between the Balkans on the one hand and Poland and Hungary on the other. For, with a rather limited number of commercial and entrepreneurial opportunities (and a culture that, while it did not wholly look askance at such pursuits, did not particularly favor them either), it was again the civil service and the free professions which drew them. Security, "official" status, clean hands were attractive, even if salaries were often low.

There was historical precedent for this—perhaps a legacy of a view of civil service posts as sinecures, derived from witnessing Turkish administration; perhaps simply a conviction, ever-present to some degree among those with imagination, that leaving the land was *possible*. Though we may allow for exaggeration, the comment of an English traveler of the early 1870s that "Roumania is, *par excellence,* the land of officialism, and, small country that it is, possesses more civil servants than either France or Prussia"[39] is instructive, when we reflect on the situation that created such an impression. (Similarly, it is interesting that a Yugoslav sociologist, writing in 1966 about the interwar period, characterized his land as "one of the rare countries in which officials outnumbered workers.")[40]

A bloated civil service with more than a whiff of corruption, weak industrial, commercial, and financial development (with these sectors largely in the hands of foreign capital)—the interwar Balkans, in this system and in the channels of achievement within it, resembled more than a little the new nations of Asia and Africa which emerged in the colonial decline after World War II. Of the university students of the period (many of whom in the Balkans did come from peasant households,[41] despite later claims of the socialist governments) Seton-Watson writes:

> Only a comparatively small proportion were inspired by a love of learning or a desire to train their intellects for the service of their countries. Their idea of such service was rather that they had an automatic right to a place in the State administration after spending a given number of years at the university. A university diploma was considered a claim on the State for the rest of life.[42]

What sort of civil service was thus produced out of the successful winners of degrees? We quote Seton-Watson again, not only for the quality of the picture conveyed but also because more recent travelers in the Balkan socialist states will not find it entirely outdated:

> The Balkan official regards himself as immeasurably superior to the peasants among whom he lives and from whose ranks he has sprung. To be an official is the fondest dream of every able young

son of a peasant. The Balkan official does not like to work. He considers himself so fine a fellow that the State and the public should be proud to support him for life, and should not ask him to make efforts that will tax his intellect or character. A visitor to a Balkan Ministry or Police Headquarters in the middle of the morning will find the rooms filled with good-natured fellows comfortably enjoying a cup of Turkish coffee and a chat with their friends. The papers lie on their desks. Outside stand, sit and squat patient queues of peasants awaiting their various permits and receipts. Foreigners and citizens with 'protekcija' obtain swift and polite attention, but the people can afford to wait. They have waited many hundreds of years already for justice, and a few more hours will not make much difference. Time counts little in the Balkans.[43]

Such were some of the characteristics of the Balkan societies prior to socialism. Even less developed than Poland and Hungary, lacking a "great tradition," they remained societies where an evident rupture, for all the "peasant" rhetoric, existed between the rural mass, the barely existing urban industrial stratum, and the urban elite and semielite. The social strata, large and small, lacked consensus on their respective places in society. Few stable rules of conduct, rooted in any upper-class culture, existed. Such a culture itself was lacking, except for the borrowing of Western styles in clothing, leisure, and so forth by those who could afford them. By any *economic* measure that contrasts the rewards of the elite with those of the mass, the Balkans were inegalitarian. But the Balkan elites, however jealous of their positions, could scarcely fall back on national traditions legitimating their exclusive claim on privilege, nor elevate inegalitarian *values* to a level that would deny the legitimacy of mobility aspirations. Balkan society had much of the unfamiliar about it, from a Western European perspective, but it was also far removed from the Polish-Hungarian pattern.

Czechoslovakia appears here once again as a deviant case. Developmentally advanced at the start, the Czech lands assumed the dominant position in the new state, which lacked either Slovak or Czech native aristocracy. A nationally balanced economic structure, in which commerce and industrial entrepreneurship were not beneath the dignity of the upper classes or of those who aspired to join them, supported, and was supported by, values and attitudes with few specifically Eastern European elements (except for some values of the Slovak peasantry). For those who sought them, the channels of social mobility and the models of success to be striven for were more diverse in a Prague than in a Warsaw or Budapest. Even the Czech peasantry, relatively prosperous and less burdened with overpopulation and underemployment, was a part of the nation—as one scholar has it, "participating more deeply than usual in a national culture above the folklore level."[44] Czechoslovakia's "great tradition" was a recent one, civic rather than aristocratic—the republic of Masaryk and Benes was its child. Only its central European location, the problem of the underdeveloped Slovak lands, and the political fate that brought it socialism in 1948 account for its falling within the purview of this book.

IMPERIAL RUSSIA: THE ESTATE SOCIETY

None of the three Eastern European patterns thus far outlined adequately encompasses the social structure and value system of the imperial Russian society of the mid-nineteenth to the early twentieth century. Similarities there were, of course—inequalities as extreme, or more so, than in Hungary and the Polish lands,* economic backwardness and a population as heavily agrarian as in the Balkans. But dissimilarities even more striking make Tsarist Russia in its twilight years a separate case—relevant not for its nineteenth-century impact on the structure and ideologies of inequality in Eastern Europe, but for the fact that the transformation it underwent in the 1917 revolution's aftermath set what would emerge, in the wake of World War II, as the agenda for social change in the Eastern Europe to which Soviet hegemony now extended.

Russian history—political, economic, institutional—had diverged from that of the remainder of Europe in the thirteenth century, with the coming of the Mongol domination—the "Tartar yoke." Two centuries of this burden were sufficient to ensure, even after Russian princes and nobles reasserted control over the Russian lands and expanded their reach to the Pacific, that Russia's course would not bend back to parallel Europe's again. Nineteenth-century

*It should be remembered, of course, that a large portion of the Poland that emerged as a restored nation from Versailles in 1918 was, in the "Congress Kingdom," part of the Russian empire in the period of immediate concern.

Russia, then, presented a peculiar picture: a society combining elements of stagnation and change, pushing by the end of the century toward a peculiar and uncomfortable modernity with which neither elite nor mass could make its peace.

Elite, mass, class—all such words take on exceptional meanings in this Russian context. Russia was a peasant society throughout the nineteenth century, by virtue of a legacy of backwardness, but one with its own specific elements. Serfdom, gradually abolished in Western Europe in previous centuries, and indeed on the decline in Eastern Europe, only was concretized and codified in the Russian lands in a decree of 1649. A growing debt-bondage to landowners combined with the state's need to assure a stable, accessible peasantry for tax exactions (and landowner's desires for a cheap and stable labor force) to produce a system of bondage that would remain in effect until 1861. Only nobles were accorded the right to own serfs, in exchange for their service to the autocracy. Peter the Great further defined and expanded the service duties of the nobility, and tightened the squeeze on serfs and remaining free peasants through a poll tax, introduced in 1718. Thus, the nobility's exclusive domination over the serfs had a quid pro quo—their service to the Tsar-autocrat, on terms to be determined by him. The lack of an independent nobility would have far-reaching effects as other social strata emerged. Despite the rescinding, in 1762, of compulsory state service for the nobility, it maintained its exclusive domination of serf labor and developed along a different course than that of the nobility and gentry classes in the West.[45]

Characteristic of Russian peculiarity was the legal division of the population into "estates" defined by their privileges and liabilities.[46] Some of the names of estates are deceptively easy to fit into a hierarchy (hereditary nobility, serfs—after 1861, peasants); others defy such classification ("honored citizens," merchants, townsmen, cossacks). Indeed, though hierarchy was implied in the estate system, and though imperial Russia was a hierarchical society, it would be a great mistake to think of the estates as "classes" in any generally accepted sense. They were *categories,* often cross-cut by economic and occupational characteristics, with little internal cohesion. However hereditary it might become in practice, membership in one or another estate was ultimately at the will of the Tsar. The estates, though they possessed corporate organizations at the local level, never developed fully into aggregators or articulators of particular interests, nor effective "reference groups" for their members. In Western Europe, struggles among the feudal nobility, monarchs, and emergent commercial-enterpreneurial middle classes had imparted group unities that Russian history, basically a chronicle of ever-centralizing autocracy, withheld. As one scholar put it, "the Russian estates, unlike those of Western Europe, were not so much the accommodative outcome of a struggle between a powerful autocrat and a powerful nobility (and later, a powerful bourgeousie) as they were, both in law and in accepted tradition, the tsar's instrument for preserving his own power."[47]

Power without legal limit, the "omnicompetence" of the Tsar, was reflected at the top of the estate system, in the nobility: for all the popular images of the vast gulf between noble and knave, the Russian nobility could not even control its own composition. Divided into a "hereditary" and a "personal" nobility, it was a permeable category. "Hereditary" noble families retained their status, but both hereditary and personal nobility were achievable through state service. Reaching a certain position on the fourteen-step "Table of Ranks" of civilian or military service resulted in personal ennoblement—noninheritable—while higher rungs made the achiever *and* his descendants noble. Not all nobles, then, were landowners (many who had been left their land after the emancipation of the serfs) and the conditions of obligatory or the later attractions of voluntary state service combined to make of the nobility a "bureaucratic service class," wherein even landowners "never fully lost sight of their initial indebtedness to the state," and were unlikely to assert claims against that state.[48]

Between the nobility and the peasant mass were intermediate estates: "honored citizens" *(pochetnye grazhdane),* the nonnoble issue of personal nobles, or persons who had distinguished themselves moderately in state service or other activities; the "merchant" estate, divided into three "guilds," according to their ability to pay admission fees and their accumulated capital; artisans, organized into corporations; and finally the category of *meshchanstvo*—sometimes loosely rendered "townsmen"—a loose aggregate of petty traders, artisans, and others of the urban "lower class" who did not belong in a "higher" estate.

Thus was the society of imperial Russia divided.* Legal status as a member of one estate or another determined, for a long time, one's privileges and liabilities. One was subject to the poll tax or not, liable to or free from corporal punishment, free from or subject to military draft, by virtue of one's official status.

Such a system seems archaic, and indeed it was—increasingly so as the nineteenth century wore on; as the emancipated peasantry began to differentiate itself into a majority of land-poor cultivators scarcely less dependent on state and landlord than they had been as serfs, and a minority of middling and prosperous farmers; as industrial development, fostered from the 1880s on, rapidly increased the size of these categories not covered in the concept of "estate." Thus, the imperial census results of 1897, while they tell us something of the official structure of privilege, leave many questions unanswered. The composition of the population by estate, in millions, was as follows:[49]

hereditary nobility	1.22 million
personal nobility and nonnoble officials	.63
clergy	.34
honored citizens	.34
merchants	.28
"townsmen" (including artisans)	13.38
peasants	96.90
cossacks	2.93

Where were the rich, where the poor? Where are the industrial workers here, however small their number? Where is the middle class, the bourgeoisie? One can answer, roughly, *throughout* these figures, since the official classification, especially with respect to the urban population concentrated in the intermediate estates, "bore little relation to economic realities."[50] Nobles might or might be forced to engage in nonnoble pursuits, merchants might grow rich beyond some nobles' dreams of avarice, peasant sons move to the small but growing industrial settlements in Moscow, St. Petersburg, or other cities, and leave no reflection in these figures, since "there

*Cossacks, as noted above, formed a separate estate, as did the clergy (though some of its members were simultaneously nobles), while some of the population, because of special regulations, fell outside the system completely (Finns, Jews, some of the peoples of the Asiatic part of the Empire).

was less rigidity in occupational mobility than in the formal transfer from one class [estate] to another."[51]

If peasants were poor, and the urban *meshchanstvo* as well, the nobility as a whole was far from rich. Some great landowning magnates weathered emancipation well, but much of the nobility, despite compensation arrangements favoring the ex-landlords and serf owners as against the new "free" peasantry, found its place, predictably, in service to the state at modest pay—and much of the rural nobility had never been rich in any case. (As County Lieven, a Minister of Education in the earlier nineteenth century, put it, "the boundary of the noble estate is so far extended beyond sight that at one end it touches the foot of the throne and at the other it is almost lost in the peasantry.")[52] Some nobles maintained their fortunes through ownership of factories; some of the merchant class, risen from the *meshchanstvo* and even from the peasantry, became wealthy—but not many. The poor in Russia, as elsewhere, vastly outnumbered the rich, and despite a certain fluidity in the estate structure and in occupations, there was little room at the top.

Even so overwhelmingly peasant an empire needed industrial workers, of course—and there were some in small but increasing numbers throughout the last century of Tsarism. Factory labor had existed from Peter the Great's time, and indeed before it, in mines, armament production, and metal work—but that labor force had little in common with a "working class" as the term is generally understood. Serfs worked in factories as they did in the field: "state peasants" in state-owned factories, nobles' serfs in the enterprises they owned, and state peasants also in those enterprises owned by merchants, where they were attached to the factory rather than to its owner.[53] Free labor, however, worked better, and various provisions for the liberation of serf workers produced a situation in which, on the eve of emancipation in 1860, serfs formed only about one-third of the total industrial labor force (itself amounting only to a tiny 800,000).[54] Emancipation, however, did less to urbanize the workers than might be expected. The newly freed peasants, organized into the system of the rural commune (*obshchina, mir*), needed the commune's approval before leaving to seek factory work. They retained the right to participate in the periodic redistribution of the communal land (emancipation had not made them independent smallholders) and the burden of liability for their share of the communal taxes. Some gradually made the city their home, but harsh factory conditions and insecure employment meant that much of the labor force, even as it grew rapidly under the industrialization programs of Alexander III in the 1890s, retained its rural linkages and character. It also retained its membership in the peasant estate—about 10 million of those recorded as peasants in the 1897 census figures (see above) were, in fact, engaged in industrial work, perhaps 3.5 million on a permanent basis.[55] These, plus some in the *meshchanstvo* category, made up the "working class" at century's end. In all, about 90 percent of all urban workers—some second- or third-generation industrial laborers—carried a peasant passport.[56] These workers were an economic reality. Their retention of legal peasant status reflected both the regime's uneasiness with the new category and their own divided consciousness, which "delayed their transformation into a modern industrial labor class,"[57] their emergence as a political reality.

Nor were the normal elements of a bourgeoisie—merchants, bureaucrats, the intelligentsia, and those in the free professions—ever to coalesce into one in imperial Russia. With emancipation, the nobility increasingly moved into state service as a primary source of income—but as was true of Poland and Hungary, then and later, their "ethos was that of a military landowning class, not of a civilian middle class, such as had grown up in the West since the Reformation."[58] The merchants, despite some changes in outlook as they dealt more with foreign counterparts, remained for the most part quintessentially Russian in attitude—seeking not freedom in which to exercise their talents, but state protection and preference. Even in the spurt of industrialization in the last decade of the nineteenth century, the merchants and capitalists of late Tsarism played roles essentially subordinate to that of the state as actor and promoter of development.[59] With an intelligentsia generally barred from responsible political participation, oppositional in its attitudes toward the autocracy, and distant from the merchants and bureaucrats, no bourgeoisie in the Western sense was possible.

Russia in the late nineteenth century was a land of unstable balance. An archaic estate system and economic backwardness, manifested in a huge peasant population living near subsistence levels and generally employing only the crudest of technologies, represented the "traditional" elements, as did the general acceptance of massive inequality. Yet from the very top—from the autocracy itself—counterforces were being set in motion.

The ripeness of the Empire for reform was demonstrated to many by Russia's catastrophic participation in the Crimean War. In a sense, from this may be traced both the emancipation of 1861 and the reforms in law and local government in the reign of Alexander II. Though an emancipation that left peasants land poor, heavily in debt, and tied to their rural communes, and court and administrative reforms that were too often subverted at local levels, may be regarded by history as too little, too late, they *were* real in their impact. One cannot speak of the establishment of true "citizenship" or of legal equality in this time, but some estate privileges and liabilities were modified. By 1863, townsmen, while still subject to corporal punishment, could have it imposed on them only by the courts; and in 1874, the military service obligation was extended to all estates.[60] Slowly, changes were being wrought in the old structure of inequality.

Alexander III (1881–1894), conservative autocrat though he was, presided over the beginnings of a profound change—the industrialization alluded to several times above. Together with his minister Sergei Witte, he pursued a program of industrial development that, continued into the reign of Nicholas II, yielded a high rate of growth throughout the last twenty-five years of the regime. The struggle against backwardness created new opportunities for the technical portion of the intelligentsia to involve themselves in professional work,[61] spurred the growth of an urban proletariant, and lay behind attempts under Stolypin to disengage excess peasant labor from the commune, legally and economically, to make it available for more effective cultivation. However heavy the autocratic overlay, Russia was in a period of profound economic change that impinged on the old order of stratification.

Increasing urbanization drew the disparate worlds of city and countryside closer, though the gap remained wide. An urban population of about 7 million in 1861 grew to double the size by 1900 and to more than 20 million by 1914 as new hands were added to the industrial workforce. High birthrates, especially in rural areas, moderated the impact—urbanites amounted to about 11 percent of the population in 1861, and 14.6 in 1914.[62]

All these forces manifested change, and implied adjustments in the hierarchical organization of society, yet change and adjustments came hard to the last two Tsars. The "modernization" of the late years was, after all, defensive in intent, as had been Peter the Great's innovations two centuries past. Aimed at converting imperial resources into effective power on the international scene and at stabilizing the autocracy, it was a process undertaken for the preservation of traditional, rather than modern, ends. Thus, for all the social mobility generated by economic change, all the new fluidity, the regime was far from ready to relax its hold on society.

Ascent through the estate system and the proper role of education were two areas where concern with restricting mobility in the interests of social and political stability found focus. Recognizing the desire of the merchant and other middle strata for more social recognition, yet setting itself absolutely against granting them entrance to the nobility, a decree in 1832 attempted to resolve the problem by creating the category of "honorary citizenship," to be awarded for state service short of the ninth rank, or merit in other fields. If it was hereditary rather than personal, this status guaranteed to the possibly indolent or untalented offspring of achieving fathers that they would not fall back into the *meshchanstvo,* and exempted them from military service, the poll tax, and corporal punishment.[63] Access to noble status was tightened in 1845 by raising the notches in the Table of Ranks at which personal or hereditary ennoblement could be reached[64]—but still, noble status was "achievable," not completely a function of birth.

Education had been a desideratum since Peter the Great had begun to stress it as a necessity for the elite who would manage his empire. Yet Russia wavered between seeing it as an investment, to encourage the free rise of talent from whatever stratum, and as training for the elite service to be given only to those who were preselected for the elite on other criteria. An 1827 recommendation, while asserting that Russia's few universities should remain open to those of all free estates, concluded that generally the type of education made available to individuals should "fit the social status and future destination of pupils, and should not encourage excessive efforts to rise above their station."[65] In 1845, Nicholas I's minister of education, Uvarov, raised the fees for the classical gymnasium in an attempt to reduce the numbers of nonnoble students therein, with the same end of discouraging excessive aspirations.[66]

All this, in the "prereform" period of the first half of the nineteenth century, is not so surprising. But social conservatism continued to play a role in maintaining the "natural order" well into the period when the economy's need for trained personnel was growing. Thus, the famous words of a Ministry of Education decree in 1887:

> Gymnasiums and progymnasiums are freed from receiving the children of coachmen, servants, cooks, laundresses, small tradesmen, and the like, whose children, with exceptions, perhaps of those who are gifted with extraordinary capacities, ought by no means to be transferred from the sphere to which they belong and thus brought, as many years' experience has shown, to slight their parents, to feel dissatisfied with their lot, and to conceive an aversion to the existing inequality of fortune which is in the nature of things unavoidable.[67]

Even in such a state, decrees cannot completely determine reality. In the late nineteenth and early twentieth centuries, *more* persons than ever before entered Russia's universities, and the social mix of their student bodies grew more diverse. But despite a growing need for the educated of whatever origin, and despite a growing supply of such, imperial policy often seemed to come down on the side of "station," immobility, subordination, and deference. Social arrangements and structures changed more slowly than did the aspirations and attitudes of many peasants who were "mobile" into the urban working classes, and of many of middling station who sought careers of greater prospects. Political structures appropriate in some ways for the fostering and sponsoring of economic development were less appropriately organized to cope with the social outcomes of that development.

Imperial Russia in its twilight years, then, diverged as significantly from as it resembled the societies of Eastern Europe. In some ways like Polish and Hungarian society, it boasted a nobility as arrogant as they—but the Russian nobility had, in a sense, less *raison d'être*. Russia's independence not being threatened, the role of the Polish gentry-intelligentsia as defender of national identity was closed to it. Nor was it faced with the task the Hungarian nobility shouldered of achieving co-equality within the Hapsburg empire (albeit only on their own behalf, with little or no thought for peasant Magyars). Most critically, however, the persistence of the Russian autocracy and its dominance over a compliant nobility deprived the latter (as well as other strata) of the opportunity to develop political responsibility as articulators of broader interests, or even of their own narrower ones. Some nobles might be more arrogant, some less; some kind to their serfs, some bestial; some "enlightened," some obscurantist—but as a whole, the noble estate provided little dynamism or leadership, and its *legitimacy* as a privileged class was on the decline.

Like the Balkan societies, Russia was demographically an overwhelmingly peasant nation. Yet unlike them, it never fully institutionalized the notion that "the land belongs to him who works it," nor did its history remove the "old nobility" from the peasant's back. A peasant society, it never became, even rhetorically, a peasant *state*, nor did it develop peasant politics. Quiescent for the most part and prepolitical, the peasantry occasionally manifested resentment in revolts of a local nature, anomic violence, etc. But the stories of the Stenka Razins and Pugachevs remain the chronicles of bandit leaders who failed—very different from the peasant Obrenovics and Petrovics who eventually won their battles with the Turkish occupiers.

Russia came no closer to developing a "modern" middle class than did the rest of Eastern Europe. Most nobles continued to look down on trade and commerce, and civil servants, if they were not noble already, sought the entrance into the nobility a bureaucratic career might provide. In the independent professionals, in the "responsible" intelligentsia that participated in the work of the *zemstvos* (local government councils), in some forward-looking entrepreneurs, the roots of a middle class existed—but they were poor, weak, as was the soil in which they might have taken root. A lack of opportunity to participate in politics in any real sense, a lack of *social* authority that could have worked a change in the hierarchical-bureaucratic ethos of Russia, and their small numbers and late development when the demands on the system were growing—all these made impossible any new stabilization of Russian society on a bourgeois basis.

In summary, Russian society in the hundred years before it became the Soviet Union was backward (though developing) and inegalitarian (though fluid in some respects). Its inegalitarianism was ancient, but in the realms of property and power came to diverge from the lines of the estate hierarchy. Nobles might exist in rural poverty, urban merchants and even townsmen of no pedigree or culture might grow rich. Power, as an ultimate characteristic of estates, was not a great differentiator—at critical junctures, nobles and rich merchants might possess no more, against the autocracy, than did the peasant mass. Their privileges were, in the final analysis, conditional and revocable, however seldom they actually were revoked.

The fluidity of Russian society (moderate, to be sure—we do not mean to suggest that this was, on the whole, a society of "mass mobility" in any modern sense) did not contradict its other characteristics. Though the absence of data makes such observation speculative, one can guess that movement into the nobility in Russia was easier than in Poland and Hungary, and indeed that movement into the urban working class from the peasantry, and mobility among the various strata and sectors of the intermediate urban categories, may have been easier in the late Empire than in the Balkans, or in Budapest or Warsaw. This fluidity, partially the product of economic development, was otherwise, however, no manifestation of a high degree of autonomy in society, but rather a product of the continuing dominance of the autocracy over society as a whole. In the area of class, stratum, or group autonomy, Russia had probably come a shorter distance on the road toward modernity than any of the other countries which would later join it in socialism. This made for strata which were *not* "classes" in the sense of politically participant groupings[68] but were untutored in political responsibility. The peculiar system of stratification thus created would allow the Bolsheviks to preserve centralized dominance of the society and influence the new patterns of stratification that would emerge under Lenin and Stalin.

AFTERTHOUGHT

Is all this history necessary to a work whose main focus is contemporary? Clearly, the author would answer yes. Had we a great deal of the sort of quantitative data we lack, we would find ourselves later attempting to "explain the variance" in stratification and mobility patterns among the socialist states. One variable worthy of close examination would be the structures of stratification predating socialism in each country—not only their concrete elements (occupational distributions, degrees of economic inequality, etc.) but also beliefs, attitudes, acceptance or rejection of the prevailing order by various groups. To be sure, we shall not arrive at neat conclusions, wherein a certain percentage of the variance can be assigned to historical differences. But at the less quantitative, less rigorous level of analysis available to us, the impact of history is important. It is likely that many differences in stratification among the contemporary socialist states will require some historical analysis, some attention to elements of continuity, in their explanation. The fact that they are all, in a sense, postrevolutionary societies tends to direct the attention to change, to radical transformation. But, like all societies, these too are in some degree captives of their pasts. Here, we may anticipate somewhat arguments which follow.

In the USSR, even after sixty years of socialism, certain basic elements of stratification seem to some analysts reminiscent of Tsarism. Differentials in income, perquisites, and prestige are evident now as then, but they are the conditional rewards of the regime for services rendered rather than the possessions of certain categories of people, of different autonomous *classes* with their own private resources. In a sense Soviet society is "classless" in the same manner as Tsarist society.[69]

Here, many would argue, the main thread of continuity is the omnicompetence of the state, its refusal to tolerate the coalescence of categories into classes under Tsarist and later under totalitarian dictatorship (and perhaps even today, under a fairly stabilized "collective leadership"). The degree to which privileges still depend on bureaucratically regulated access, on papers of different sorts rather than on money and the market, cannot fail to impress even those to whom the changes wrought in the Soviet period are more significant than the continuities.

If continuity is an element sometimes of stability, to the newer Eastern European regimes continuity of old patterns and attitudes may seem more of a threat. It is, in fact, striking to note the occasional evidence of real political concern with the aristocracy of what propagandists would call a vanished and vanquished era. In April 1973, the Warsaw weekly *Polityka* published a two-part article, "The Coronet under the Hat," by the writer Malgorzata Szejnert; the subject was the families of the old aristocracy and their current role and place in People's Poland. A chatty, sympathetic treatment of the Potockis, Radziwills, Czartoryskis, and so on, it was scarcely analytic or politically explosive, basically asserting that the present-day members of the great families "differ from other citizens of the Polish People's Republic only in the fact that their children encounter their own names in the history books." For all of this, the article swiftly provoked from several other newspapers sharp ideological attacks, citing "the disregard of the class approach . . . all the more startling because the part of the article appeared in the May Day issue of the weekly," and similar responses.[70] In a sense, surely, this was a tempest in a teapot. The old families have retained their identity, but they constitute no real political force, either in Poland or in the emigration. Yet, as the authors no doubt remembered, with the *coming* of People's Poland, many people with peasant-sounding surnames changed them under new laws for others with a more aristocratic sound.[71] A sort of semantic upward mobility? Evidence of the persistence of the old order, a widespread acceptance of some of its social premises in the face of the new order? Whatever the answers, it is only at great risk that we *assume* the effects of revolution, and ignore the continuities, at whatever level, that shape forms of inequality under socialism and enter into the debate over it.

CHAPTER THREE

Old Hierarchy and New

> You are horrified at our intending to do away with private property. But in your existing society private property is already done away with for nine tenths of the population; its existence for the few is solely due to its non-existence in the hands of those nine tenths. You reproach us, therefore, with intending to do away with a form of property the necessary condition for whose existence is the non-existence of any property for the immense majority of society.
>
> In one word, you reproach us with intending to do away with your property. Precisely so; that is just what we intend.
>
> —Marx and Engels, 1848.

> Socialism has solved a great social problem—it has abolished the exploiting classes and the causes engendering the exploitation of man by man. There are now two friendly classes in the U.S.S.R.—the working class and the peasantry. . . .
>
> A new intelligentsia, coming from the people and devoted to socialism, has emerged. The one-time antithesis between town and countryside, between labor by hand and by brain, has been abolished. The common vital interests of the workers, peasants and intellectuals have furnished a basis for the indestructible socio-political and ideological unity of the Soviet people.
>
> —Program of the CPSU, 1961

> Q.: What is the difference between capitalism and socialism?
>
> A.: Under capitalism, man exploits man—under socialism, it's the other way around.
>
> —Soviet joke.

THIS CHAPTER is transitional, exploring several topics that link the last chapter's treatment of socialist "prehistory" with our major foci—mobility and stratification patterns in the near-past and present.

The first and second sections address the collisions of the new socialist regimes with the "old orders," the old hierarchies of power, property, and prestige, and the conflict between commitments to revolutionary "inversions" of the old order and the construction of new, industrially based social and economic regimes. The third section examines alternative models of the stratification structure that emerged and settles on one that will be utilized through the remainder of the book. The fourth and fifth sections, respectively, address the prestige and power components of stratification. These, less readily quantifiable than income or property (chapter 6), are for various reasons critical to an understanding of the significance of social mobility, and thus we deal with them at this fairly early point in the book.

THE OLD ORDER: EMBATTLED AND VANQUISHED

In the wake of wars a generation apart, the social orders of imperial Russia and the Eastern European states retreated before the attacks of new regimes. In Russia, where the Bolsheviks had no previous pattern to follow, the assault may be divided into two phases. The first, primarily political-military in character, extended from 1917 to 1928. Civil war and "Red Terror" ended in Bolshevik political supremacy and were combined with state control of the "commanding heights" of the economy. However, some representatives of the past—small artisans, traders, and the peasants, now owners of their own plots—were left with a private sector to work in during the period of the New Economic Policy (1921–1928). The second phase, the great leap into industrialization and collectivization, "the plan era," and the rise of Stalinism followed, leaving a radically altered Soviet society as the 1930s ended and Europe went again to war. This series of experiences, history's first example of "socialist construction," became the model that would be exported.

The socialist revolution involved a politicized, often violent assault on the old distribution of power, property, and prestige. Power was most important, and the "new men" rapidly seized it. In Russia, the collapse of a government overstrained by a war it lacked the resources to fight left the field open for the Bolshevik coup of November 1917. The Civil War, which followed a series of urban Bolshevik takeovers, led within a few years to a new nationwide political order, with the old elites vanquished by death, emigration, or dissolution into the new society.

Twenty years later, World War II began the process that destroyed the traditional Eastern Europe. Communist partisans in Yugoslavia and Albania successfully fought German and Italian occupiers and domestic opponents, carrying off political revolutions that were indigenous as Russia's had been. Elsewhere, in nations whose old power structures had been compromised or destroyed by Nazi Germany, revolution was imported by means of Soviet power. Hungary, Romania, and Bulgaria (in a qualified way) had been German allies: the fates of their ruling classes were sealed. Czechoslovakia, sundered after Munich into the Bohemian-Moravian Protectorate and the puppet state of Slovakia, ranked among the "victors." It moved toward a mixed economy with heavy socialist components in the 1945–1948 period, spurred by a large Communist parliamentary bloc, and maintained a multiparty system until it underwent full incorporation into the Soviet sphere in 1948. Poland, another "victor," emerged with redrawn boundaries that moved it toward the West and for the first time an ethnically homogenous population. In the extremes of devastation and exhaustion, Poland came rapidly within the Soviet orbit as noncommunist politicians were pushed aside to make way for a communist government, in which "Muscovite" leaders gradually assumed dominance over "home communists" who had spent the war years underground in their country. In each state, new elites emerged. All, whatever their routes to power, were "interventionist," committed to political and economic mobilization. They would hold power more tightly, and use it with greater purpose over a larger number of objectives, than the old elites had ever envisioned.

Both concomitant and result of the new hierarchy of power was the new structure of property. The large landowners, and large and middling (and, eventually, most of the petty) capitalists were taxed and confiscated out of business. Accumulations of wealth fell to confiscation, currency "reforms," and "voluntary" contributions. The intensity and pace of the attack varied, but generally the early to mid-1950s in Eastern Europe saw (as had the end of the first Soviet Five Year Plan in the early 1930s) the end of private property in the means of production as a major factor in national life. For a time, private artisans and small traders would survive in some states, but only as tolerated appendages, without resources to protect their own interests vis à vis the state. The nation became, by and large, the legal proprietor of the nonagricultural means of production.

Just as the "exploiters" were thrust down, the bottom of society, the peasantry, was for a time elevated. Land reform in Poland and Hungary (and in Slovakia) generally eliminated the rural landless, as Lenin's decree had in the Russia of 1917–1918. Thus new peasant proprietors were created in the non-Balkan states. Yet, however appealing the program of "land for the landless," however responsive to desires, the phenomenon of independent peasant within a socialist economy represented ambiguity. What, after all, *was* the peasant? An owner, a *private* owner of means of production—and therefore a capitalist? Yes, in a sense. But a *poor* man for the most part, a victim of market forces and moneylenders like the urban proletarian? Yes again. Still, however much he remained one of those have-nots for whom the revolution was carried out, the peasant represented, in his productive capacity, latent power that might be used against a revolutionary regime that sought to use his output, to force "savings" from the agrarian sector for industrial development. The ambiguity had to be resolved.

In the USSR, resolution came with the collectivization drive of the late 1920s and early 1930s, a chaotic and bloody change that produced a "collectivized" peasantry. Co-owners of farmland merged from individual holdings, "proprietors" of property legally midway between private and state (and therefore regarded as inferior to the latter), the *kolkhozniki* were in fact as much the state's workers and the soil as much the state's property as urban workers, the factories, and mills. By the mid-1930s, the Soviet peasants, formerly "rich," poor, and middle alike, were locked into an economic-organizational system that guaranteed the state's ability to extract the "surplus," and a peasant living standard so low that they lived, as they would throughout the Stalin era, close to the margin of existence.

Collective agriculture thus became an element in the Soviet model, one that evoked different outcomes when attempts were made to apply it in Eastern Europe. Neither new communist elites nor their Moscow supporters, concerned though they were with rendering the peasantry powerless and their product accessible, desired a reprise of the disastrous Soviet experience, and the watchword, for a time, was gradualism. Gradualism, however, was not voluntarism. With two exceptions, the Eastern European peasantry had moved, by the late 1950s to early 1960s and at much lower cost in human life, into the framework of collective farming. In Yugoslavia, the Titoist concern with proving the socialist essence of the state after the 1948 break with Moscow led to an aggressive and forceful collectivization campaign that was abandoned rapidly as Tito came to seek domestic support in the early 1950s, leaving the maverick socialist state with private agriculture to the present. In Poland, the gradualist approach to collectivization had not gone very far when the events of the 1956 "Polish October" restored Gomulka to power and produced an indefinite "deferral" of collectivization. Most of the ambiguity, then, has been resolved. The remnants of rural private property and proprietorship are of a sort that the Polish and Yugoslav regimes have learned to tolerate in the interests of tranquility and productivity.

Property in productive resources, its *legal* ownership, has then ceased to be an important factor in hierarchy under socialism. It is in conjunction with power—the power to effectively utilize and control the nation's wealth—that property is significant. Such control is lodged in the political elite. The main economic dimension of inequality in socialist states involves *income* and job-related perquisites—significant in the context of socialist life, but different in fundamental ways from the economic hierarchies of capitalist countries which still are heavily influenced by private property and the advantages accruing to those who possess it in significant amounts.

The old hierarchy of prestige formed a third target of the new rulers. The superiority of nonmanual work to manual, of salary-earner to wage-worker, of gentry to commoner were assaulted. Marxian economics provided some of the thrust—if manual work, the production of "material values," was the only really productive work, to what should it be inferior in honor? Similarly, the Marxist critique of "exploitation" provided a moral rationale for turning out the old capitalists and landowners in dishonor (along with the nonowning but affiliated professionals and employees who rendered them services and had sided with them against the proletariat). The new order had no use for them. To these rationales were added the basic forces of envy of the old ruling classes by the new rulers of rank-and-file origin and guilt over past advantage felt by many communist intellectuals, who sought to purge it by actively participating in the destruction of the moral and social authority of the strata from which they had defected. The revolutions brought new themes in poster art—the stern-visaged, horny-handed proletarian as the "new man," the repository of a new prestige; new slogans—"I am a miner (or steelworker, or bricklayer): Who is more?"; and new priorities. In times of rationing, workers were to receive more than white-collar functionaries. Worker and peasant children, for whom the universities had allegedly been unattainable under the old regimes, would now receive special preference, and children of the old bourgeosie would be barred from them. Ideology, and allocation policies immediately after the revolution, promised a new situation where better wages and more power for the workers would be paralleled by a greater prestige than they had hitherto known.

Delivering on the promises has been a different matter. Scarce goods by definition, power, income, and prestige are not so easily reallocated—especially the latter two—in societies whose resources are not abundant. Old evaluative criteria have changed in some measure, but also show persistence. The agenda of revolution, after all, was not solely upheaval and inversion, but encompassed developmental objectives as well. In their pursuit, the leaders of the new regimes found that prudence dictated allocations of power, income, and prestige that differed from egalitarian ideals and were distant as well from the promise that those "who had been nothing, would be all."

LEVELING AND DIFFERENTIATION

Egalitarian policies and rhetoric in the first socialist state, the USSR, survived Lenin (who had once declared that a Party functionary's pay should not exceed that of a skilled worker) by less than ten years, their abandonment being signaled by Stalin's denunciation of *uravnilovka,* "equality-mongering," in 1931. The widening of gaps between strata and the new inequality that resulted arose in response to two perceived needs. First, talent and skill—scientific, technical, and managerial—were in short supply. Though coercion would play a role in their mobilization, in itself it was not sufficient to guarantee adequate servicing of a rapidly industrializing economy, nor could it alone motivate people to train for the required specialties. Though scarcely a theorist of stratification, Stalin was an advocate of the performance principle, an "applied" functionalist to the core. Managers, engineers, and other scarce technical personnel came to enjoy wage and bonus levels many times higher than those of workers. Within the working class, the differentials between skilled and unskilled were wide. At the bottom, the peasants, who were a "surplus" group, toiled on between scarcity and starvation, this poverty a "push" factor that combined with the pull of higher industrial wages to aid the great movement from field to factory in the 1930s. To these income differentials were added preferential access to housing, elaborately stratified networks of special stores and outlets to serve the favored with foods and durables unavailable to the masses, and other subsidies.

Equally important was the need Stalin felt to bind the Party and state bureaucracies, the industrial managers, favored artists, and other regime servitors to the center of power, to alienate them from the mass. Stalin sought to demonstrate that advantage was to be gained not by "serving the people," or satisfying their spontaneous wants, but by serving the *leader*. The high incomes and special sources of supply, the reserved apartment buildings and special resorts all served this purpose, as did various symbolic recognitions of inequality and subordination that went back to Tsarist times. The numerous "commisariats" once more became "ministries." The old military rank system, with appropriate uniform decorations and a traditional system of military etiquette, was restored. Uniforms and epaulettes also came into the Foreign Ministry and other civilian hierarchies. All emphasized rank, status, the gap between top and bottom. Formal education's prestige was enhanced, and the tough-talking, diamond-in-the-rough factory manager promoted from the factory floor came to be seen as a negative and objectionable stereotype rather than a model.[1] With the institution of fees for advanced secondary education, the access road to the university was closed to those whose parents could not afford it. The Stalinist elite, however insecure as individuals in their status (as the Great Purge of 1937–1938 proved, and as they were indeed meant to be), formed a distinctly elevated stratum, whose children could expect to benefit in many ways from their parents' "accomplishments." The quotation marks are justified—it was not simply an elite of talent and skill that was so rewarded, but also the operators of the "means of compulsion"—the upper echelons of the army, secret police, and party *apparat*. Many of these could lay no claim to skills in a productive sense, but their functions were quite evidently requisites of the Stalinist system.

Under the forceful influence of the Soviet model, the Eastern European states gradually developed patterns of differentiation, in the economic sphere and others, similar to those of the USSR in general outline but generally somewhat less radical in the violence they did to presocialist patterns. Partly, this was a result of the "alien" quality of the imposed revolutions, the questionable legitimacy of Muscovite regimes, and the consequent gradualism of policy in the Eastern European states when compared to the USSR's implementation of its own "authentic" revolution.*

First, the pace and tempo of industrialization in most of the Eastern European states, however rapid, never quite equaled that of the Russia of the "plan era." The Eastern European societies, despite their diversity, were on the average more modern than the Russia of 1917–1928. For all the drive involved, the 1945–1955 period was not as crucial, did not generate such an immediate demand for scarce skills as had the previous Soviet experience, and hence required less of a Stalinist income policy.

Second, the sorts of training and skills which had been so scarce in the pre-1928 USSR, if not abundant in Eastern Europe, were not as rare as they had been in Russia. More people could read and write, more were accustomed to dealing with complex machinery and technical tasks, more were educated to university standards in relevant disciplines than the USSR had inherited or, early on, been able to create. Particular national situations differed, of course: the Bal-

*The two Eastern European states where an authentic domestic revolution *did* take place—Yugoslavia and Albania—have manifested, albeit in different directions, even greater divergence from Soviet patterns, founded in large part on the "native" quality of their regimes. They have also, at various phases, approximated the Soviet experience in the *intensity* of their assaults on certain elements of the old order.

kan intelligentsia was rather small and not technically oriented; the Polish educated classes had been decimated by war. Czechoslovakia, as a more modern nation, had no particular scarcity of educated people equipped to perform the tasks of an industrial economy, at least in the Czech lands. In some measure, different degrees of scarcity accounted for different levels of reward inequality, including a rather egalitarian Czech pattern. As Otto Ulc relates in a humorous but not unserious vein, recounting the words of an official in Prague in 1958:

> The Poles pay their professionals well because they haven't got enough of them. The East Germans have to pay even better so that not all will defect to the West. In our country we abound with intellectuals who, incidentally, have nowhere to flee. Hence we can afford to mistreat them with impunity.[2]

Indeed, the scarcity of the Polish intelligentsia led to quite different results, not only in the economic sphere. The artistic, cultural/humanistic, and scientific intelligentsia (or its surviving members) had not "betrayed" the nation, and there survived, among its numbers, many "progressives." Unlike the prewar capitalists, and in contrast to the treatment accorded many suspicious intellectuals in other Eastern European states, many weathered the early post-1945 years and gained respectable positions in the new Poland. They have been in a position to impose, implicitly at least, many of the old values they still held along with their socialist convictions. As Alexander Matejko observes:

> Mass media, culture, leisure, and education are formally controlled by state and Party officials; but in reality they are run by members of the intelligentsia who impose their own tastes, aspirations, and practical choices upon the masses. The young generation of blue-collar workers and peasants is being socialized primarily to intelligentsia values. Paradoxically, the ideal of being culturally sophisticated and following the examples of the "well-mannered" people who know how to enjoy life has become the latent function of the Communist take-over.[3]

Third, the less extreme experience of agricultural collectivization (and its curtailment in Poland and Yugoslavia) prevented the development of a collective farmer stratum as low on the economic scale as were the Soviet *kolkhozniki*. Village living standards were often lowered—but so were those of urbanites. Gaps can be moderated, inequality made less severe not only by limiting the rewards at the top but also by keeping the bottom from falling too low. This was the outcome in the Eastern European states, whose approach to collectivization generally avoided beggaring the rural population and thus helped spare Eastern Europe the extreme income inequalities of the Soviet Union.

Eastern Europe by the mid-1950s presented a variant of the Soviet pattern of substantial inequalities, justified by the differential "functional significance" of contributions to production (and to compulsion). Living standards remained low for all but the core elite, who enjoyed privileges like those of the Soviet leaders—low enough for less-tamed Eastern European working classes to mount the protests in Plzen, Poznan, Berlin, and elsewhere in the early to mid 1950s. The educated nonmanuals generally earned more than the workers, the workers more than the peasants. The socialist principle of reward according to work was in force: the communist principle of reward according to need had been, as in the USSR, shelved for an indefinite period.

THE STRATA OF SOCIALIST SOCIETIES

Into what sort and number of hierarchical groups—social strata—are socialist societies today divided? This question, though we must answer it before we proceed, is controversial. First, are we referring to categories that may be constructed by an outside observer? If so, then of course we may construct as many as we choose, according to whatever criteria best serve our analytic purposes. But our goal here is to identify strata that have a reality in themselves and are recognized as real by those who make up socialist societies—for nothing else would serve our purposes.

Second, controversy surrounds the appropriate criteria for distinguishing "real" strata. Orthodox Marxian analysis would stress relation to the means of production, and consequent position as exploiter or exploited, as the central criterion. Only groups divided along these lines would be fundamental, qualifying as "classes." Others would minimize this criterion, focusing instead on effective control of political and economic resources, whatever the juridical ownership relations. Still others might see the key less in the ownership or power dimensions normally associated with the word "class" and instead focus on differential distributions of money, education, prestige, breeding, and power (for it is difficult to exclude it) in an attempt to discover groups marked by consistent patterns of location in some or all of these dimensions—strata.

The question is also a polemical one. The greater the emotional baggage one brings to it, the more likely are extreme categorizations, and simple, dichotomous models of social structure. Anticommunists may summarize, appropriately, their *feelings* about the moral status of the systems in question by identifying dichotomies: rulers and ruled, the powerful and the powerless, the rich "new class" of communist rulers versus the masses, little better off than before the revolution. On cooler inspection, they might, however, perceive a more complex set of gradations. Apologists for socialist systems, on the other hand, might not argue that they are egalitarian utopias; but they would emphasize the gradual, "nonantagonistic" nature of differentiated access to scarce goods. They would, however, find it hard to convince an observer, or many socialist citizens, that the distribution of *power* is at all gradual, or that "rich" and "poor" are really inappropriate categories. (Polish workers, who in the 1950s quipped that Polish society was divided into the "proletariat and the Chevroletariat," were scarcely convinced. Nor was Djilas, whose critique of inequalities in the postrevolutionary socialist states gave us the term *The New Class.*)[4]

Questions of socialism's stratification system will remain controversial, whatever we do with them here. Reserving the discussion of power per se until later in this chapter, as well as the different question of social prestige, we will try, simply, to arrive at a reasonably accurate model of stratification, and a workable one for organizing our data. Our path lies in the examination of ways in which previous scholars have modeled the class/stratum structure of a number of socialist states, and in a search for commonalities therein as well as differences we must expect to find.

POLAND: SZCZEPANSKI'S MODEL

A simple yet potentially valuable scheme is Jan Szczepanski's for contemporary Poland.[5] Essentially a four-class model, it may be represented, with its major subdivisions, thus:

I. "Intelligentsia"
 creative intelligentsia
 highly educated professionals (academics, doctors, etc.)
 political officials
 civil servants
 economic management personnel
 routine white-collar functionaries
II. Manual workers
 (incorporating differences by skill levels, sector/branch location, etc.)
III. Peasantry
 independent peasant proprietors living from agriculture
 "peasant-workers" with mixed incomes
 "peasant-white collar employees" (local administration)
 collective farmers
IV. Private entrepreneurs
 (artisans, shopkeepers, etc.)

The order in which Szczepanski takes up the classes, though not explicitly hierarchical, implies hierarchy. Nor are the implications surprising. The intelligentsia, given the abolition of the large landowning classes and the bourgeoisie of presocialist Poland (*mutatis mutandis*, the same scheme could be applied to Hungary), occupy in the absence of competitors generally high positions in prestige and income hierarchies, though with some internal variations. Szczepanski's "intelligentsia" is traditionally Eastern European in that he includes *all* nonmanuals—though not without qualifications about the less advantageous place of the routine white-collar functionaries. But it is also modern in that it includes as well the political and economic leaders of state, Party, and industrial bureaucracies—among them those high in power hierarchies. It is an elite, made up increasingly of organization men.

Szczepanski identifies four hierarchies upon which members of the intelligentsia may be located: first, an economic one that through the imperatives of a modernizing economy generates differences in income and, to some degree, in occupational prestige. Second, a distinct political/administrative decision-making hierarchy exists, overlapping (but only at the top) with the economic hierarchy. Third, a hierarchy of "merit"—perhaps better rendered "attributed significance," or "contribution to socialist construction"—that has shifted from ideological criteria emphasizing "redness" to a focus on expertise—rooted in crucial professions, jobs, and "types of creativity." Finally, a separate hierarchy of education provides a fourth basis for stratification.[6]

Untangling these is not an easy matter, but it does seem that the traditional triad of power, property (at least in the sense of income), and prestige is encompassed here. There is, also, ample scope for status inconsistency within the intelligentsia. The correlations between property, power, and prestige may not be strikingly high. The openly reported salary schedules of government officials, even quite high ones whose large quantum of power is undeniable, are sometimes modest compared to the total income of many members of the "creative" intelligentisa, doctors, and even university professors; their prestige, as we shall see, is often lower as well. On the other hand, one should not be blind to the real lack of power that even prestigious and well-paid professionals experience in a system where it is the least equally distributed commodity.

Less of all these scarce goods comes to the workers and peasants, although of course skilled workers earn more than unskilled, enterprising farmers more than incompetent ones, and medium-holding peasants who work also in the nonagricultural sector (the "peasant-workers") more than those with similar land who lack outside employment. Educational differences may play a role in intraclass distinctions, allowing those with more education to lay claim to life-styles somewhat higher than those of their category. But all in all, workers and peasants can be perceived as groupings clearly set off from even a broadly defined intelligentsia.

Are workers generally superior to peasants? Ideology would dictate yes, but in Poland, as in Yugoslavia, private agriculture complicates the answer. Polish peasants are not the helots of the Soviet collective farms. Indeed, the independence of the peasantry is a consequence of socialist policy, a product of People's Poland—via land reform and the later renunciation of forced collectivization. In socialist terms, Polish farmers are not badly off. But they are, as peasants, carriers of the agrarian past; their numbers are declining. And they are hardly rich, despite the grumblings of urbanites as they pay for their weekly food.

Peasant life has been improved under Polish socialism, but not so much that peasants have, on the whole, overtaken the urban working class on the most critical dimensions of status. However much group mobility the peasantry may have experienced, it is still a deprived stratum (as indicated by the reluctance of peasant sons to inherit their fathers' occupation). Those who have left the land for jobs in cities come off better.[7] A prosperous farmer may eat better, lead in some aspects a more comfortable life, and perhaps even have a higher disposable money income than some urban workers, but on the whole the peasantry occupies a position at the bottom of the new hierarchy, as it did in the old.

Szczepanski also includes "private entrepreneurs" as a separate social grouping. The status of the private-sector artisans and small shopkeepers is a bundle of inconsistencies. Incomes are (reputedly) quite high—but this is a hard-working and heavily taxed group of entrepreneurs. In any case, the high incomes that people in general attribute to the private repairmen, locksmiths, and merchants in clothing, accessories, etc. are not matched by any high prestige. Ideology (which still treats private enterprise as a rather alien if tolerated element in the economy) and populist feelings (fueled by the reputed high incomes and the experience of direct dealing with independent operators who charge what the market will bear for a good or service unavailable from state outlets) combine to emphasize the marginality of the independent in the socialist system.

Szczepanski's scheme seems a sensible, generally comprehensible model of Polish society. Organized around socio-occupational groupings for the most part, it contains also elements of a Marxian class perspective. Intelligentsia and workers do different work, but are similarly related to the means of production, as they are located in the state sector (workers here would include state farm workers—a small category). Peasants and independents also do different work, but both are private, owning their means of production though barred from such hiring of labor as would create "exploitation." (Even the few Polish collective farmers, as collective owners of collectively pooled property, are seen as outside the state sector.) Yet some workers in state industry and private artisans do similar kinds of work, and tilling, planting, and hoeing are similar tasks whether agriculture is individual, collective, or state in setting. No scheme, even a simple one, can fail to reflect such complexities, and none can really cope with them to general satisfaction. Thus, in describing socialist strata/class systems the relative weight to be given to character of work versus relation to the means of production remains an issue.

USSR: KATZ'S MODEL

The USSR's social-structural complexities have for some time defied description by the Stalinist formula of "two nonantagonistic classes" (workers and collectivized peasants) and "one stratum" (the intelligentsia, including all nonmanuals)—a fact finally reflected in the USSR in 1966 at a sociologists' conference in Minsk,[8] where many solutions were offered, and later underlined by a flurry of articles in Soviet journals in the late 1960s and early 1970s.[9] Probably no one has studied this literature more than the sociologist Zev Katz, and it is to be his model of the Soviet stratification system that we turn here.

Katz's scheme identifies six major groups in the Soviet social structure, as follows:

I. The *nachalniks* ("rulers," "bosses")—essentially the governing political class
II. The intelligentsia—the educated specialists in various fields
III. White-collar employees—service and technical nonmanuals of lesser education, essentially what we refer to in this book as "routine nonmanuals"
IV. The workers—manuals, ranging from the highly skilled to the unskilled
V. *Kolkhoz* (collective farm) peasants—including both rank and file labor and the administrative staffs of collective farms
VI. The privately employed—hired and self-employed persons not drawing wages/salaries in the state or collective sector[10]

Four of these six groups are seen as "classes" and two—the white-collar employees and privately employed—as strata, given that they, in Katz's view, lack a sufficiently "characteristic" loading of class determinants. Twelve of these determinants are identified: (1) function in the system (i.e., occupation); (2) relationship to resources—control, formal and informal, over the means of production; (3) relationship to political power—both participation in its exercise and attitudes of authorities toward the group; (4) material rewards; (5) knowledge and skill; (6) prestige; (7) personal relationships within the group—"group feelings" of members; (8) consciousness of common group interests and pursuit of appropriate activities on behalf of those interests; (9) group subculture and "way of life" or value system; (10) presence/absence of specific group organizations and institutions; (11) self-perpetuation arrangments controlling access to group membership over time; and (12) specific sets of relationships with other social groups.[11] While we cannot here summarize the position of each group on all these dimensions, their role should become clearer as we proceed.

Katz makes more explicit Szczepanski's differentiation of political functionaries within the intelligentsia. For Katz, the *nachalniks* are clearly a separate class, although in education, nominal salaries, prestige, and some other characteristics they are on the average not far from the intelligentsia. It is in function—"not production or the provision of an essential service for the population but social control, or the control of men"[12]—variables 2 and 3—that the *nachalniks*, the political rulers, are distinctive. They constitute not one among many strategic elites, but *the* ruling class, the monopolizer of effective power. As a group, they are aware of common interests, ready and able to defend them with coercive and normative resources, and to control entry of candidates to their ranks. These are *apparatchiki* and state officials, from Brezhnev on down to urban and provincial bosses whose power, in Boris Meissner's apt phrase, "rests in the *positions* they hold, while that of the intelligentsia is rooted in the authority and prestige inherent in the *functions* it performs.[13]

This is a major distinction between the *nachalniks* and the intelligentsia. The latter are not, as a class, in the business of ruling, nor have they the access to power and resources of their political overlords. Though often well paid, they are specialists in delimited fields, not generalists given over to power and its exercise. To a certain degree, they enjoy their perquisites on the sufferance of the *nachalniks.* Life-styles, attitudes toward the "good life," and so on will diverge somewhat between the groups, much as they might between American academics and artists on one hand, and lawyers, government officials, etc. on the other. There is, however, significant mobility, both career and intergenerational, between the groups. An individual with critical skills and a bent for the arts of governance might shuttle back and forth between *nachalnik* and *intelligent* jobs during his career. The sons of high *nachalniks* typically become members of intelligentsia—"staff" men rather than "line" political operators themselves (one notes the examples of the sons of Anastas Mikoyan and Andrei Gromyko, both holders of elevated staff positions in the economic and foreign affairs bureaucracies)—a pattern not limited to the USSR.[14]

Less power by far, or chance of achieving it, and less in the way of scarce skills are possessed by the white-collar employees. Literacy—the basic hallmark of this group in the early Soviet period vis à vis most peasants and many workers—is not now the rare coin of the past, and hence it is these routine nonmanuals whose superordinate status in relation to the working class, or "leading" segments of it, is in doubt. Katz rates them low to low-medium in education, income, and prestige, as well as lacking in political clout. All true no doubt, but such a characterization misses what may be an important point. As an *occupational* stratum, this is a predominantly female one. Its female members are less likely to be heads of households and therefore less likely to be the bequeathers of initial status to younger members of the household. *Male* members of this stratum may, on the average, be better placed on all these dimensions, and thus still rank higher than skilled male workers. Whether one stratum is above the other or vice versa is a question that recurs throughout this book at the various points where we address problems at the borderlines of nonmanual and manual work.

Soviet workers are, as workers elsewhere, in some respects a homogenous and in some respects a heterogeneous category. Their wages and skill/education levels vary and "favored" branches of industry are more advantageous locations than light and consumer-goods branches—but elements of life-style and "working-class culture" bind them together in what may be considered a whole.

The *kolkhozniki*, or collective farmers, are distinguished in Marxian "relations of production" terms from the previous groups by their formal status as *collective* owners of property. This "inferior" form of ownership until recently barred them from state pensions, social services through labor unions, etc., which workers enjoyed. On the whole, their position was, and is today despite some changes since the mid-1960s, at the bottom of Soviet society, in their own eyes and those of their urban cousins. To be a "peasant" is little more honorific today than yesterday. (Katz's inclusion of the nonmanual farm administrative staff—the major element of the "rural intelligentsia"—in the *kolkhoznik* category might be questioned: these are scarcely "peasants." But the rural-urban dimension is itself a status dimension—a gulf still yawns between the worlds of city and village in the Soviet Union, and for many purposes a member of the rural intelligentsia—a *kolkhoz* agronomist, a village school teacher—might be considered by the average Soviet citizen to be inferior to an urban factory worker. The quality of rural schools also places children of the rural intelligentsia in a disadvantageous position for maintaining or increasing their occupational status vis à vis their urban counterparts. Low in power, income, and skills and disadvantaged on virtually all of Katz's 12 stratification dimensions, the *kolkhozniki*, especially the farm laborers, form a unified group because of their shared disadvantages.)

Finally, the privately employed make up Katz's last, and in the Soviet context questionable, category. This group's private employment (as domestics, free-lance translators, family members of *kolkhozniki* working *only* on the household's private plot) is the only unifying element. The rewards, security, and work situations are quite disparate, and the privately employed (other than those who work on private farm plots and who thus could be categorized as peasants) amount to little more than 1 percent of the working population, according to Katz's estimates.[15] That a great deal of money is made, and changes hands privately, in the USSR is not subject to doubt—but much of this is illegal and carried on by persons with another "main" occupation. The Soviet economy, unlike the Polish and Hungarian, has made essentially no room for the small category of private artisans and shopkeepers. That the privately employed, spanning legal and illegal, farm and nonfarm work, and various degrees of linkage to the more conventional Soviet economy, should be considered even a "stratum," is doubtful.

In general, Katz's scheme, like Szczepanski's, has its base in socio-occupational groupings, with an admixture of property relations. He goes further in breaking down the broad "intelligentsia as nonmanual" category into two "elite" components distinguished by *type* of function and *power* (*nachalniks* versus intelligentsia proper) and one nonelite stratum, the white-collar employees, separated from both of these by a lesser share of *all* scarce goods. The farm-nonfarm dichotomy divides the workers and peasants, both manual groups, with the latter clearly less advantaged.

We have, then, a hierarchy (for Katz's treatment of the twelve stratification determinants shows that this scheme *is* generally hierarchical) that, like Szczepanski's, *could* be collapsed into the simple "nonmanual-manual-farm" trichotomy frequently employed in past stratification and mobility research. We need not limit ourselves entirely to such a trichotomy, but some of our data will have to be treated in such a manner.

CZECHOSLOVAKIA: MACHONIN'S MODEL

Both Szczepanski's and Katz's schemes draw on conceptions of occupational grouping and "class" in structuring their views of social hierarchies. A quite different approach is that taken by the Czech research team headed by Pavel Machonin in their 1967 large-scale national survey,[16] an approach that generally discarded aprioristic categories, whether occupational, "class," or of any other nature. Instead, the core of the Czech research involved ascertaining the position of individual respondents, consistent or inconsistent, on five stratification criteria, and *then* analyzing the data in search of patterns: groupings of people, of significant size, with similar configurations of status attributes. Such relatively unconventional research yields rather different results, well worth our attention.

The criteria whereon the sample of almost 8,000 male household heads was ranked on separate six-point ordinal scales, were: (1) complexity of work, (2) education, (3) income, (4) life-style (most to least "cultured"), and (5) participation in management—"power" in a rather general sense. Equally weighted, the criteria allow individual scores from a high of 5 to a low of 30—but, of course, equal summary scores, as they diverge from the extremes, may manifest very different configurations of status attributes. The task was to find, in this five-dimensional space, significant clusters of people with similar rankings on the criteria, whether the pattern of a given cluster was consistent or inconsistent across all the criteria.

The analysis (a necessarily complex one, which we cannot summarize here) yielded seven groups—four relatively consistent, three less so, covering 92.1 percent of the sample (high of 1, low of 6):

1. (Median score, *1.6;* % of sample, 4.7)
   Generally specialized nonmanuals with high work complexity, secondary—or university—educations, living in large cities and enjoying a quite cultured life-style; income score ca. 1.4 (over 2,250 kcs. per month), power ca. 2.2
2. (Median score, *2.8;* % of sample, 12.9)
   Specialized nonmanuals, secondary education and complex but generally standardized work, above average in culture of life-style, urbanites with an income score ca. 2.5 (over 2000 kcs.) and ca. 3.9 on power (a significant decrease from group 1)
3. (Median score *4.2;* % of sample, 23.4)
   Skilled and semiskilled industrial workers, frequently living in middle-sized towns; elementary education plus apprentice training; average in cultural level of life-style; income score ca. 3.5 (1,750 kcs.) and 5.0 on power
4. (Median score, *5.3;* % of sample, 28.4)
   Unskilled and some semiskilled manuals, agricultural workers, cooperative peasants and individual farmers, simple manual work; generally elementary education and resident in villages/small towns; average incomes ca. 5.4 to 5.5 (1,250 kcs. and less); no participation in management (power score ca. 5.6 to 5.7)

Three sizable groups marked by particular patterns of inconsistency were also located in the data (the labels in quotes are those of the present author):

5. (% of sample, 8.9) "low status high earners"
   Skilled and semiskilled industrial manuals, below average culture and no management participation (power ca. 5.0); elementary education at best, but with incomes in the 2,000–2,500 kcs. range (score on income ca. 1.8)

6. (% of sample, 9.3) "underpaid nonmanuals"
   Specialized employees and "clerks," performing simple nonmanual work; lower vocational educations (secondary), but above-average culture; low in management participation (power ca. 4.9) *and* low in income (ca. 4.8, 1,300 kcs.)
7. (% of sample, 4.6) "working-class aristocracy"?
   Skilled and semiskilled manuals, low in power (ca. 4.9), but with somewhat higher education (ca. 3.8) than typical for manuals (vs. 4.3 for group 3 and 5.2 for group 4); *very* high incomes (score ca. 1.4) and cultural life-style (ca. 1.8) inferior only to group 1, at ca. 1.6.

Thus, interesting findings emerge from the Czech data-gathering procedures that, while they *include* references to jobs and work (skilled, unskilled, manual-nonmanual, etc.), direct our attention to other elements. We see a fairly flat income curve (the range of raw scores scarcely more than 2 to 1), evidence of Czechoslovakia's degree of economic egalitarianism, but radical discrepancies in power. Group 1's 2.2 stands out from the range for the rest, of 3.9 to 5.6–5.7, and five groups in all (3 to 7) are concentrated at or below 4.9! Such findings remind us that scarce resources of differing types may be distributed in quite different ways in a single society, thus complicating the task of assigning socio-occupational groups a place in a general hierarchy. Nonetheless, the question arises: can these Czech data be accommodated to, or suggest insights into, the nature and placement of socio-occupational strata such as the Katz and Szczepanski schemes are concerned with?

Looking at the consistent groupings (1 to 4), it is not too hard to argue their rough equivalency to a hierarchy of intelligentsia–routine nonmanual–worker–peasant. The intelligentsia (group 1) is weighted toward Katz's intelligentsia and away from the *nachalniks;* as the Czech report tells us, the real power elite was not included in the sample,[17] but there are *enough* of those close to the latter to raise the power scores rather high. Group 2 may include some intelligentsia, but its characteristics in general would seem to indicate a range of routine nonmanual occupations. In this connection, group 6 is also relevant—seemingly a *very* routine sort of nonmanual/clerical work is involved here, with rewards less than those of skilled and semiskilled manuals. In this group we might seek those routine clericals who earn less than manuals but seek compensation in "clean hands and white collar" and a "respectable" life-style. Some confirmation is offered by the life-style score (ca. 2.8), which is well above the group 3 ("working class") 3.8.

Groups 3 and 4 may be taken as our "workers" and "peasants," respectively, despite the presumed presence of some nonfarm unskilled workers in group 4. Here the working class is fleshed out by inconsistent groups 5 and 7, which direct our attention to its heterogeneity. Both are "aristocrat" groups in earning terms compared to other manuals, while their complexity of work is about equally minimal. Otherwise, they diverge. The "low status high earners," of group 5 are proletarian in education and life-style—we may have here simply those who benefit from the high wages of favored heavy industries. The "working-class aristocrats" are even better paid. More notable are their educations—well ahead of group 5 *and* group 3—and their life-style which is, at about 1.8, stratospheric in comparison to the cultural level of other manual workers. About the composition of such a group, one can do little except hazard two tentative guesses. *Some* are likely to be talented deviants of humble origin, whose abilities earn them high pay and whose life outside work, facilitated by a rather high income, is lived in the style of nonmanual strata with which they, in some measure, identify. And some others may be "skidders," sons of presocialist intelligentsia whose educational careers were interrupted in the early days of Stalinism and perforce entered the working class rather than the university. Their inherited cultural advantages and skills, though not allowing resumption of education and consequent job mobility, may have assured them intra–working class success in wage terms and the ability to realize a life-style which early socialization made appropriate for them. From both categories, one might expect substantial mobility of sons into the intelligentsia. The basic familial prerequisites, economic and cultural, seem to be present, and such parents may already identify the intelligentsia as their offspring's destination.

Would similar research in other socialist societies have yielded results like these for Czechoslovakia in 1967? We cannot tell with any certainty, but our efforts to match the categories to socio-occupational groupings suggest that some similarities might be anticipated, in the general picture and in specifics. "Underpaid nonmanuals," the "working class aristocracy," and "low-status high earners" are all frequently noted in discussions of socialist social structure, whatever the country, when writers assure us that the old hierarchy no longer obtains; such groups do indicate points where it may not. The issue, in any case, is not whether the manual-nonmanual income hierarchy obtains perfectly—for it does so nowhere—but to what degree, and where, it remains important. The Czech 1967 research directs our attention to this, as well as to other aspects of the socialist hierarchy.

POLAND: A MODEL OF URBAN SOCIAL STRUCTURE

The final scheme we consider returns us to Poland. This ten-stratum model, literally composed of socio-occupational categories *(kategorie spoleczno-zawodowe)*, was developed by Wlodzimierz Wesolowski and his collaborators for a set of studies of stratification and mobility patterns in three Polish cities—Lodz, Szczecin, and Koszalin—in the years 1964–1967 (studies to which we will have intermittent recourse throughout this volume).[18] This scheme generally encompasses urban occupational structure, excluding rural areas—but is more detailed than the others examined, taking account of complex gradations. (In reporting the distribution of male working populations in the three cities—but only infrequently in further analysis—Wesolowski used subdivisions within each of the ten categories that provided *40* separate groupings.)[19]

1. Intelligentsia—mainly professionals with high education, plus managers of large organizations and independent "creative" persons (artists, writers, journalists, etc.), independent of education: 7 subcategories
2. Office or clerical workers *(pracownicy biurowy)*—middle/lower administrative nonmanuals in industrial enterprises, offices, etc.: 5 categories
3. Technicians—persons with specialized (technical) secondary

educations in a variety of employments, including accountants and paramedical personnel: 4 subcategories

4. Foremen and "brigadiers"—industrial workers in charge of work units: 2 subcategories
5. Artisans *(rzemieslnicy)*—private and cooperative, as well as small private shopkeepers: 4 subcategories
6. "Physical-mental workers"—occupations at the conceptual borderline of manual-nonmanual work; bus drivers, trolley drivers, shop assistants, postmen, etc.: 3 subcategories
7. Skilled workers—4 subcategories
8. Semiskilled workers—4 subcategories
9. Unskilled workers—4 subcategories
10. Others—military and police; residual agriculturalists in city, etc. (generally a small group): 3 subcategories

We have here a set of categories most of which resolve into a fairly simple hierarchy. The "intelligentsia" here is more inclusive than Katz's for it *does* encompass such political power-wielders as may fall into the sample, and less so than Szczepanski's, for it does not include the routine nonmanuals. These latter are subdivided here into office workers and technicians: two groups with somewhat different types if fairly similar levels of education, with differences in the setting of labor, though both are nonmanual, and neither of which really qualifies for inclusion in the intelligentsia proper.

The working class is usefully, here for the first time, divided into three groups by levels of skill (the unreported subdivisions refer to economic branches). The peasantry are absent from this urban scheme, and thus we have a trichotomy of "intelligentsia–routine nonmanual–worker," to which a separate peasant category could be appended in a broader framework encompassing village as well as city.

Most interesting in this scheme are the intermediate groups—4 to 6—whose place in a hierarchy and relation to other strata are hard to specify. An artisan employed by a cooperative is surely in many senses quite similar to a wage worker in industry—but what of the added "proprietor" character of an independent artisan, or even more of a small independent shopkeeper? Foremen, in their supervisory functions, tread the line between management and workers; delegates of the former in a real sense, they nonetheless generally share the background and style of the latter, with whom they are in constant contact on the factory floor. The physical-mental workers perform an amalgam of nonmanual and manual tasks, all highly routine. The critical questions with such groups are where to place them in more summary schemes—are they manual or nonmanual, workers or routine nonmanuals?—and the propriety of drawing conclusions of the sort we tend to draw concerning attitudes, "self-image," etc. once having classified them as nonmanual or manual. These are obvious problems with borderline occupations, and we cannot really resolve them completely. The complexity of modern occupational structures exceeds the reach of the old manual-nonmanual dichotomy. The Polish researchers treated these categories as hybrids, as truly intermediate—and so shall we for some purposes. But, all in all, on criteria other than the nature of work itself, the intermediate strata seem to resemble the working class more than high or low level nonmanuals.

A COMPROMISE MODEL

Thus we have four different views of the structure of socialist societies, all empirically rooted, yet varying in the elements they highlight and in the concrete societies they depict. We cannot and need not reconcile them, but certainly some things should be clear. First, the new hierarchy is different from the old, in that it is emphatically a state-socialist hierarchy, with no sign of the wealthy entrepreneurs and landowners of presocialist times. Second, there *is* a political ruling class, whether we conceive of it as a group separate from the intelligentsia or a specialized (and dominant) subcategory thereof. Third, elements of the old hierarchy are also present. While the social structure may have grown more egalitarian in the allocation of all resources save power, the *ordering* of groups seems more familiar than not, with peasants still at the bottom, workers above them, and an intelligentsia at the top.

Fourth, the organization of these models seems to affirm the old "superiority" of nonmanual to manual work. But this is a matter of some controversy. In *any* industrial society, some manuals earn more than some nonmanuals. Has this gone further in the socialist "workers' states" than elsewhere? If so, does a parallel homogenization or overlap of attitudes and life-styles also occur? The Czech research discussed above cautions us against linking the two together readily. These are questions to be explored later.

The scheme we adopt here is distilled from those we have reviewed, and is influenced as well by two factors: first, the forms in which our data, rich but frequently unsystematic, come; second, our desire to arrive at the most accurate *general* representation of socialist social structure, which will facilitate comparisons among the socialist states and, later on in this book, with nonsocialist countries as well. We settle on the following scheme, adopted as consistent with realities, if not fully representative of the diversities:

1. *Elite or intelligentsia*—encompassing both the political "rulers" and the specialist-creative intelligentsia
2. *Routine nonmanuals*—the residual, nonelite white collar strata
3. *Workers*—manuals outside of agriculture, including artisans whether independent or cooperative
4. *Peasants*—manuals in agriculture, whether independent, collective, or wage workers on state agricultural enterprises.

We have elected what are essentially socio-occupational categories. Our concerns with intergenerational mobility and with the elements of group inequality are generally well served by such a focus. At some points we must settle for a trichotomous model, treating the two nonmanual categories as one. At others, more categories will be in use, to take advantage of more data even at the cost of comparability. These four categories *do* have a reality, recognized by Eastern European and Soviet masses as well as researchers, and should meet our needs both in comparative presentations of data and in describing the structure of stratification in the socialist states.

THE PROBLEM OF PRESTIGE

Prestige, though real enough, is not as tangible a property as money or power. Hence, presumably, attempts to replace an old pattern of its distribution with a new and different one will encounter difficulties. Power is relevant to such attempts, especially as it is used to effect cultural change through control of socialization mechanisms, mass media, and the like—and socialist regimes possess such power. But, pursuing the developmental goals of modernization, these regimes have created occupational structures similar to those in Western societies—structures along which prestige has been allocated in characteristic ways in the West. Has a different prestige hierarchy emerged under socialism, distinguishing these industrial societies and echoing their revolutionary origins?

A tradition of American prestige studies prompted researchers in the Harvard Project on the Soviet Social System to pose this question over twenty years ago. The answer emerging from interviews with Soviet refugees[20] was that the Soviet occupational prestige hierarchy was quite similar to that in Western societies.

One answer, however, scarcely ended the inquiry or terminated interest in differences between capitalist and socialist systems. Sarapata and Wesolowski, in their early investigations of occupational prestige in Warsaw,[21] and Sarapata in his continuing and imaginative work in this field,[22] pointed to intercountry correlations lower between Poland and a sample of Western countries than were intra-Western correlations, suggesting that the major difference lies in a higher Polish rating of many skilled manual occupations, and a lower rating of routine white-collar positions, than is typical in the West. Such a characterization seems to indicate great changes from the presocialist Poland of the deferential, inegalitarian tradition, and raises questions about the possible variation of prestige hierarchies in the other socialist states from those to be found in the West. The USSR is but one socialist country, and the number of occupations "matched" in the early comparative prestige studies was small. Historical diversity might lead us to expect a whole range of patterns among the socialist states, not predictable from the fit of the Harvard Project Soviet data with those for Western societies in the 1950s. Questions, thus, remain.

In a gross sense, the evidence dictates a negative answer to the question, Do occupational prestige hierarchies differ *markedly* from society to society? Treiman's recent and ambitious analysis[23] of data from 53 countries (including the USSR, Czechoslovakia, Poland, and Yugoslavia) concludes that populations in all societies construct *roughly* similar prestige hierarchies, whether those societies be industrial or "traditional" and (though he places less emphasis on this distinction) socialist or capitalist. Socialist societies, he finds, do deviate somewhat from other societies in their patterns of prestige allocation, but not so radically as to constitute a different world. How, then, does the prestige hierarchy look under socialism?

Our situation with respect to data is troublesome but not hopeless. While we have a relatively rich data base for Poland, we lack *any* information on occupational prestige in Hungary. For the Balkans, only Yugoslavia is represented, by two studies.[24] Czechoslovakia—from the Machonin team's study of 1967—yields rather copious data on 50 occupations.[25] Finally, a variety of Soviet studies produced in recent years speak to prestige, though often obliquely. Graduating classes of secondary schools, rather than adults, have generally provided the respondents, and more often than not the "attractiveness" of an occupation—with the diverse baggage such a term contains—rather than its "prestige," has been the subject of inquiry.

Such data are better than none, but they do not, in toto, warrant large tabular arrays, nor a great deal of technical discussion. For our own purposes, we have converted the different scoring techniques and alternatives utilized in the separate national studies into a single 1–100 scale, permitting examination across nations of the range of ratings assigned to different occupations (since a nation in which top occupations are rated in the 85–90 range and the lowest around 10–15 is one more concerned with making status distinctions than one where the range may run up to only, say to 70).

Table 3.1 provides these data. As we see, first of all, the ranges of the ratings vary: while the USSR and Yugoslavia show about half the scale separating the top and bottom-rated occupations (57.2 and 54.6, respectively), Poland's range is much wider, with 78.9 of the 100.0 scale points covered. The sample of occupations for each country varies but not in a way that would by itself account for these results. We have, then, some warrant for asserting that Poles see greater prestige gaps between occupations they rate high and those they rate low than do other socialist citizens— as might have been predicted by one who assumed that the heritage of a highly stratified society is still alive in Poland. Czechoslovakia, on the other hand, has the most egalitarian profile, though we might have expected Yugoslavia to prevail here. Czechoslovakia too is a nation whose modern history lacks the presence of a native gentry with all it implies.

Table 3.1.
Selected Summary Occupational Prestige Indicators, Four States

	Czechoslovakia		*Poland*		*USSR*		*Yugoslavia*	
No. categories	50		51		80		100	
Highest rating	76.0	government minister	86.4	professor	79.5	physicist/medical researcher	72.2	mechanical engineer
Lowest rating	36.8	unskilled laborer	7.5	unskilled farm worker	22.3	bookkeeper	17.6	porter
Highest manuals	60.8	miner	60.6	skilled steelworker	54.1	miner	60.0	auto mechanic
	59.2	combine operator	58.2	miner/electrician	53.3	steel founder	58.7	aircraft mechanic
	58.4	locomotive driver	51.8	machinist	51.7	ship builder	57.8	machine technician
	56.8	lathe operator	51.2	farmer	50.9	sea/river worker	52.3	watchmaker
Lowest nonmanuals	50.4	librarian	33.8	train conductor	29.4	salesclerk	29.2	budget clerk
	48.0	hairdresser	27.1	office clerk	26.3	office clerk	27.5	dispatcher
	48.0	train conductor	25.2	typist	25.5	communal employee	27.0	clerk/typist
	44.0	letter carrier	22.8	salesclerk	22.3	bookkeeper	19.8	messenger
Doctor	69.6		80.5		76.3		71.1	
Professor	72.8		86.4		66.8		71.6	
Lawyer	—		66.3		—		68.8	
Agronomist	—		66.3		48.5		61.1	
High school tchr.	67.2		—		56.4		61.4	
Bookkeeper	—		50.4		22.3		49.0	
Salesperson	—		22.8		29.4		26.4	
Office clerk	—		27.1		26.3		27.0	
Lathe operator	56.8		—		38.2		40.8	
Miner	60.8		58.2		54.1		—	
Unskilled wkr.	—		13.1		—		18.2	
Farmer	—		51.2		—		44.1	
Farm laborer	43.2		7.5		32.6		20.4	

SOURCE: adapted from materials cited in *nn.* 23, 25.

In all the countries, the highest prestige ratings generally go to the sorts of high-level professional occupations rated high in Western countries. Similarly, the lowest-rated occupations are, with the exception of the USSR, in the unskilled manual category. None of this is really surprising—however egalitarian the ideology, one would scarcely expect to find a manual job rated number one in *any* industrial society, nor much other than unskilled manual work at the very bottom.

Overlap exists too; there are some generally nonmanual occupations near the bottom, some manual jobs that range near or into the top third of occupations rated. From this, some have argued the existence of an important socialist breakthrough in the development of a new prestige hierarchy. Yet such an argument may overstate the case, and certainly ignores one major issue. As the table data indicate, the top four manual occupations *are* rated higher than the lowest four nonmanual jobs in each of the countries. But these nonmanual jobs are highly "feminized" occupations, while the jobs that lead manual occupations in prestige rankings are for the most part highly skilled occupations whose incumbents are overwhelmingly male. Assignment of prestige to an occupation can scarcely escape influence by the raters' perceptions of whether the "typical" incumbent of the job is male or female, the likely main earner and head of household or a secondary earner, etc. Sarapata has shown that several routine nonmanual jobs, rated by Polish respondents in 1961, were seen as declining in status and prestige from their levels in 1939;[26] but it has been since 1939, and indeed *in* the socialist period, that the large influx of women into the labor force has intensified, or completed, the feminization of exactly these lower nonmanual occupations. Feminization may have lowered their prestige directly, or a lowering of economic rewards via wage policies may have reduced their appeal for men, thus leading to feminization; both probably played a role. Routine nonmanual occupations may now be lower on the scale than they were in the presocialist period—but to note that this has occurred without taking account of the role feminization has played in the transition is to risk overemphasizing the degree to which socialism has promoted a general equalization in prestige hierarchies. There is strong evidence of a tendency in the socialist states (as elsewhere) to typify certain sorts of work as "women's," and thus to lower its rated prestige and general attractiveness, at least in the eyes of male respondents. Shubkin's studies of occupational attractiveness ratings by Soviet male and female secondary school graduates show, for example, the decrement in attractiveness of work in light, as opposed to heavy industry at any level for males (light industry is traditionally a female preserve). On a 1–10 scale of attractiveness, males and females agreed roughly on ratings for heavy-industry manual workers (4.29 and 4.13) and similar engineers (6.53 and 6.96), but diverged when light-industry workers (2.58 and 4.46) and engineers (3.94 and 5.11) were rated. Male/female divergence is also marked in "highly skilled" jobs in the services (3.49 and 5.27), primary (3.03 and 5.57) and secondary (4.46 and 6.69) education, and such "cultural" jobs as librarian (3.25 and 5.26). Though both sexes rate "doctor" highly, at the level of rank-and-file polyclinic practice, this too is a feminized occupation, and does not receive from males (6.28) the rating it gets from females (8.27). And indeed, as the first figures showed, males will sometimes rate a *manual* job in one industrial branch higher than a nonmanual job in another.[27]

In any case, some closing of the prestige distance between manual and nonmanual occupations has occurred in societies where it cannot be attributed to socialism. In the USA, National Opinion Research Center (NORC) data for 1947 and 1963 both show substantial overlap between the prestige scores of professional, lower white-collar, and manual occupations, and, between 1947 and 1963, a moderate shift upward in the average prestige of blue-collar occupations as against a downward shift in the prestige of clerical and sales occupations,[28] the latter a fair equivalent of the routine nonmanuals in the socialist states, and highly feminized. (The moderation of the American change must be stressed, but it is a change in the same direction as that posited of the socialist states.)

The rather small range of data available here does not facilitate systematic comparisons among the socialist countries, but some points may be advanced. Poland, where the range of ratings is wide, also gives some hint of a continuing elitism in the gap between the rating for the highest manual specialty and that score which tops the scale. Czechoslovakia and Yugoslavia, for which tradition would predict a more egalitarian hierarchy, show smaller gaps. Their highest-scoring manuals rise closer to the top of the whole hierarchy than is the case in Poland.

On the other hand, "farmer" scores as well in Poland as in Yugoslavia—not quite the result we might have predicted. Here, reasoning can scarcely go beyond the ad hoc. It may well be that the farmer's score in Poland reflects public assessments of the positive impact of land reform under socialism (since farm laborers, presumably landless, score only 7.5) in creating independent farmers, as well as the somewhat inaccurate perception that Polish farmers are rich. (Sarapata found in 1961 that 72 percent of his respondents saw farmers rising in prestige in comparison to 1939.)[29] There might also be a certain pride, generalized throughout the population, that Polish farming remains private and therefore unlike the Soviet example, which Poles in general have shown no great desire to follow. Yugoslavia's private farmers achieve a score almost two-thirds of the way to the top of the hierarchy—not unreasonable in a society traditionally peasant-egalitarian in character, but where the thrust of social change in the last generation has emphasized the rapid development and dominance of a modern sector and the relegation of the village to the world of the past.

All in all, no really satisfactory appraisal of the structure, dynamics, and variety of prestige hierarchies in the socialist countries is possible at this time. Hence, we have given the topic a brief discussion here, rather than attempting to stretch data and speculation to cover enough issues to warrant a chapter. But this is by no means to say that we know nothing useful. It appears fairly evident that socialist states, in a global perspective, are not especially deviant from their nonsocialist counterparts (a point Kapr, in his presentation of the 1967 Czech data, emphasizes).[30] The somewhat higher rating of some manual specialties is a clear, but also a moderate difference. Also, much of the way prestige is allocated seems similar. Better-educated persons with better jobs tend to be more critical, less ready to grant prestige to given occupations, than the less-educated,[31] just as in the United States.[32] This means, in concrete terms, that more education and a better occupation leave one less ready to rate a given occupation as a "good job"—both for oneself and for one's children. To an American factory worker, a "good job" for his son may not mean the professions or an executive career alone (though he will think these good) but also a steady job in a strong unionized plant with minimal chances of layoffs and maximal opportunities for overtime. To see his son in such a good job may content him; for the manager of his plant, for a lawyer, professor, or physician, such a prospect for a son would be no occasion for contentment. There is no reason to expect socialist parents to differ greatly in their perceptions. For our purposes, it is enough that we know this much, and therefore can be reasonably certain that upward and downward occupational mobility mean, in the currency of prestige, much what they do in the West.

A NOTE ON POWER

We have considered power only intermittently thus far in our discussion. Like prestige, power is difficult to measure precisely. Even allowing for this, the effects of the differential distribution of power are quite palpable in socialist sociopolitical systems, and their place in the structure of stratification demands our attention.

No one denies that power is unequally distributed in socialist society, not even those whose job it is to celebrate socialist democracy. But the matter, when taken up at all, is handled very carefully, with many circumlocutions. "Power," it seems, is so tied in Marxian rhetoric to the notions of illegitimate exploitation, private ownership, and antagonistic interclass relations under capitalism that the term, except when used in the sense of "worker-peasant power" in the "dictatorship of the proletariat" period, is avoided more often than not. Words like "management" and "administration"—less naked in their references to the unequal resources at peoples' command—are preferred instead.

The Soviet sociologist Shkaratan uses such words to explain that there are those who rule and those who take orders, and that there is a difference between them:

> in order to participate in administration, one must be competent, that is one must possess definite knowledge and skills. But obtaining these presupposes a certain level of education, the presence of free time, and also general culture. Meanwhile, by virtue of the general conditions of existence, different groups of workers have different general and professional preparation, dissimilar time which they

can devote to participation in administration and, finally, different needs for participation in administration.

Therefore, under socialism, along with the equal right for all to participate in administration, there is still preserved a certain inequality between groups of workers in factual utilization of that right.[33]

In essence, "any cook" *cannot* run the state, despite Lenin's early, and soon abandoned, characterization of the tasks of governance.

Such polite language hardly does justice to the concentration of power in socialist societies of the Soviet type, however; and to assert this is not to score polemical points, to be "antisocialist," but simply to recognize realities. "Groups of workers" do indeed differ in their management participation—the vast majority are the objects of regulation in their life in and out of work, with no institutionalized means of effective political input. A very small minority sets policy, makes regulations, and gives orders. A tightly centralized, hierarchical Party-state executive "spine" runs through a socialist society, renewing itself by internal promotion and controlled recruitment. Over these, and over the whole process of politics, the public has no effective control. The "elections" of single-slate candidates to formal legislative bodies scarcely provide it. The judiciary is not independent, the state-controlled press is no watchdog, the countervailing forces of voluntary political associations, organized pressure groups, and the legal right of the citizen to challenge governmental decisions—variously available to citizens in the admittedly imperfect Western democracies—all are absent. "Politicking" and interest brokerage exist—but all at a very high level, with the effective actors constituting but a miniscule proportion of the population.*

To say all this, however, is to say nothing new. What concerns us here is the proper place of power, in the basic Weberian sense of one's chances to realize one's objectives against the will of others, as a variable in the general scheme of socialist stratification.

Some would argue, perhaps, that power is the *only* relevant

*Yugoslavia, here, must again be allowed as an exception, if an uncertain and unstable one. If the "self-management" system is not all it promised to be, it is a reality far beyond similarly called "workers' councils," "production conferences," etc. elsewhere in the socialist world.

stratifying variable: that the opposition between the rulers and mass is crucial, the single important dimension of inequality, and that the others—income, prestige, life-style, etc.—are essentially irrelevant. Such a position implies that we should treat power as a universal solvent. The accuracy of such a view is doubtful—there is evidence aplenty that power, critical though it be, does not dissolve other stratification variables.

A different view admits the relevance of other stratification criteria, but sees these as dependent upon power. A person high on the power scale will also according to this view enjoy high income and material perquisites, high prestige, an elevated life-style. The question here is, does power allow the monopolization of nonpower resources, too? Can we predict from high prestige or income a high quantum of power?

Finally, for some purposes, one might treat power as one variable among the rest—no more, no less—assuming for analytic purposes that its distribution does not necessarily imply the distribution pattern of other properties, nor that they imply its distribution.

The position we take here, as earlier comments have indicated, differs somewhat from these:

1. Power *is* an important variable in socialist stratification patterns, one which is exceedingly skewed in its distribution. As the 1967 Czech survey reported, on a 1 to 6 high-low scale of power (seen as participation in management, already a loose measure) only group 1—containing 4.7 percent of the sample—even scored above the midpoint, at 2.2. Other groups ranged from 4.9 to ca. 5.7 (which for practical purposes means the absence of power)—these results from a sample that admittedly did not include the presumptive holders of "real" power at all. Evidence from investigations by Arutiunian of collective-farm work forces in the USSR, based on questions about whether they exercised influence on the "affairs of their production collective" and on "the resolution of important questions in the collective,"[34] shows work leaders and "specialists" much less likely to answer in the negative than rank-and-file personnel. (Interestingly enough, over three regions and three different types of enterprise—collective farm, state farm, and other offices and enterprises—the range of "leaders and higher specialists" who also

felt that *they* had no influence ranged from 8 to 20 percent, suggesting that many of these, too, frequently feel powerless compared to those who set their plans and work conditions.)

2. Those who possess a great deal of power *will* command a goodly share of other resources—but these are more likely to be of the material sort than imponderables like prestige. While the wielders of real power are not evident in stratum-related income statistics (being merged there, to the degree that they are respondents at all, with the intelligentsia), their material benefits are undoubtedly large. For all that may occasionally be said about the best-selling authors, artists, etc. who earn more than major party functionaries and cabinet ministers, the latter are scarcely dependent on their already high salaries. The various perquisites of office include many material benefits that are not part of official salaries, but real nonetheless—all the way to living on an "open account" for those at the very top. That some national leaders choose to live modestly and others more lavishly has nothing to do with the fact that all could, if they wished, live on a rather grand scale.

Less certain is that power commands prestige or esteem. While the Czech sample of 1967 rated "minister" highest in prestige among 50 occupations, Poles in the ongoing research by Sarapata rated the same position much lower—8th of 29 occupations.[35] Soviet research, not surprisingly, has not inquired into prestige ratings of such occupations. Indeed, cabinet minister is itself a relatively modest power position, an executive role meshed in a hierarchy directed by the politburos or presidia of the national communist parties. No research, to my knowledge, has asked respondents to rate "Party secretary" on its prestige as occupation. Significantly, perhaps, lower-level power occupations (those that involve the means of compulsion as against means of production)[36] are also rarely rated. Policemen, whether civil or political, are not often exposed to respondent judgments, although it is with these that the public will be most familiar. (In the Sarapata-Wesolowski research, civil "policeman" was rated 23rd of 29 occupations in prestige by Warsaw residents, and 24th of 50 in the 1967 Czech research.) All in all, power is an uncertain guarantee of prestige, which may explain the frequent exclusion of such positions from prestige studies.

3. Power, on the whole, is not well calibrated with other indices of status (income, prestige, education, etc.). By this we do not mean a lack of correlation, but only that one can proceed from the bottom well up the ladders of income, education, and prestige without advancing similarly in terms of power.

If this is true, we should expect that a graphic, pyramidal representation of a population on the power dimension would show a much steeper pattern than pyramids of income, prestige, education, etc. And such, indeed, seems to be the case. Brokl, the member of the Machonin research team to whom it fell to deal with this issue most explicitly,[37] shows exceedingly steep distributions of power among the respondents to the 1967 survey, with an extremely small percentage of the population falling in the first or second of the six categories of power,[38] while fully 61.25 percent of the respondents score 6 (the lowest possible score) and are "only simple objects of power."[39]

Brokl is meticulous in his explication of the limits of his research methods, and it is well to add two points here. First, admittedly the sample did not include the "highest level of positions, which are in their own way the pivotal ones."[40] Thus, the top score of 1 on the power scale is inclusive enough to encompass persons whose power is little compared to the holders of higher positions not interviewed. Second, "power" in the Czech research was an aggregate, encompassing both "authority" *(pravomoc)*, or role in "industrial-professional management," and "influence" *(vliv)*, or participation in management through election[41] (the latter being the area wherein Communist Party slates are approved, run for, and "win" important posts, and thus the area with more directly political content). The researcher anticipated a steeper distribution of authority than of influence, since the number of ranked positions in economic organizations is limited, whereas the politicized system can generate any number of part-time "elective" positions. But the findings were quite the reverse. In the pyramid of authority, 51.67 percent of the respondents were located at the bottom, having none; but fully 69.87 percent shared in absolutely no influence.[42] Influence, the more "political" of the two species of power, is, interestingly, less strongly correlated with other elements of status than is authority.[43]

Czech society in 1967, then, showed power to be a resource outside the grasp of the majority of people, even when it was defined quite broadly. Power went with nonmanual origin and status rather than manual, with formal education rather than the on-the-job training ex-proletarians have received, and with income. But the important point here is that numerous persons who had elevated educational, occupational, and income status were still objects, rather than subjects, of power. Power was scarce enough that the simple fact of Party membership did little to confer it. While one could reasonably predict that an individual whose "power" was an established fact would be a Party member, power *among* Party members was distributed very unevenly, according to many of the same criteria as operated in Czech society as a whole.[44]

Nothing really comparable to the Czech research is available from other socialist states. Yet, what we know of the basic similarities in socialist political organization—similarities for which Moscow acts as guarantor—would lead us to expect similar patterns elsewhere. Power—not so much in the sense of having subordinates to order about in the course of a workday but rather as a "piece of the action," a share in decisions on national or regional priorities (such as citizens of democracies enjoy, albeit in a small way, when they choose to cast a vote for one party or another)—remains beyond the vast majority of socialist citizens. As Paul Hollander says of the USSR, the economically middle-class citizen enjoys no commensurate advantage in political participation or influence. He is "as much excluded from the political decision-making process" as are the lower economic and educational strata.[45] Mobile the citizens may be on other dimensions, but mobility on these is no guarantee that increments of power will follow. Not that the other dimensions are unimportant—in fact, the unavailability of power seems as likely to enhance the relevance of education, income, status, and consumption as not. People who have much of these are probably more satisfied than those, similarly powerless, who have less of them. The lack of credible prospects for access to power may intensify the competition for the other scarce resources by which socialist citizens can differentiate themselves from one another.

4. Power, in its pervasiveness and in the very broad set of uses to which it may be put in the socialist states, is *most* critical to

stratification in that the narrow circle of holders of nationally effective power can determine a good deal (but not all) of the structure of rewards, and control access to those rewards. It can, within broad limits, manipulate the system of stratification itself.

This is not a new idea. Geoffrey Gorer, in an unfortunately largely overlooked 1962 essay on "The Danger of Equality,"[46] makes several relevant points. Noting that complex societies need, at a bare minimum, a hierarchy of power, he argues the theoretical possibility of a single-value, single-hierarchy society based on power alone. Democracies he sees as honoring a multiplicity of values (including power), thus supporting multiple hierarchies. This diversity diffuses among separate hierarchies a more general social power, preventing the specialists in political and military power from gaining a total monopoly. Dictatorships, feudal and theocratic states he views as essentially single-hierarchy societies, though power in them be held under different mantles of legitimacy. Our point: in the socialist states, the "power" (political) hierarchy dominates all others. The tops of the other hierarchies, the "functional elites" of culture, education, and the like, are at the command of the political elite. The exchanges of income and day-to-day security for expertise and services taking place between political and functional elites are not really reciprocal, not *equal*: the political elite is in a position to set the terms. This ability, covering the whole work force, from research scientist through rank-and-file worker to collectivized peasant, means that the political elite can determine in large part the place of a given occupation (and, indeed, a given incumbent) in the material hierarchies of stratification, though somewhat less in the prestige hierarchy.

More directly relevant are Goldthorpe's arguments in his well-known essay, "Social Stratification in Industrial Society."[47] Critical of the Kerr, Dunlop, et al. notion of "industrialism" as a phenomenon with universally similar consequences, he characterizes the similarity of the Soviet and Western industrial stratification structures as a "phenotypical" resemblance, arguing that the USSR and the Eastern European states are "genotypically" different. The core of the difference is the influence a monistic or "totalitarian" political order exerts, which might as readily create patterns of stratification different from as similar to those produced by the free play of market forces in the West. Hierarchical differentiation thus is "an instrument of the regime. To a significant degree stratification is *organized* in order to suit the political needs of the regime; and, as these needs change, so too may the particular structure of inequality."[48] Goldthorpe (understandedly in a 1964 essay) cited changing needs that seemed at the time to have moved the USSR from the inegalitarian income, inheritance, and tax structure of Stalin's time to Khrushchev's egalitarian populism of the late 1950s and early 1960s (reductions in the security of the bureaucratic and managerial elites, reforms in access to education, lessening of income inequalities, etc). That not all of these have stood the test of time in the Brezhnev-Kosygin period does not alter the sense of Goldthorpe's conclusion that the USSR, despite familiar patterns of inequality, is not class stratified in the sense true of the West (echoing here the treatment of the continuing state omnicompetence through Tsarist and Soviet regimes noted in the preceding chapter).

The structure of inequality in the socialist states did not simply grow—it is partly a product of tradition, of historical experience that cannot be readily manipulated by socialist regimes; partly of the "market" and its reflections of scarcities; but also—significantly—of *design*, imposed by socialist regimes on society. Power, the least-dispersed resource, is what permits this imposition.

But the hierarchy of power, though it dominates, does not subsume the other hierarchies of income and prestige. The phenomenon Dahrendorf noted, that there is "many a compensation" for those who do not share in the exercise of power in modern Western European society, that this compensation takes the form of "second chances" in economic, educational, and other hierarchies,[49] applies to the socialist states as well. Though the power hierarchy is more dominant there than in the West, the design it has imposed leaves some room for achievement and mobility along other dimensions. And there is tension as well between the designs power attempts to impose and the tendency of persons to strive for reward and status and to secure these against the exercise of that power. As Zygmunt Bauman puts it, two principles of hierarchy—"officialdom" and "class"—coexist under socialism. The first reflects the force of state power to manipulate the distribution of resources in society, to delimit individuals' freedom of action. The second derives from the fact that, because even under socialism there is a market in labor (persons are not "tied" to their jobs) and because work is rewarded with money (rather than a centralized rationing of all goods), there are elements of autonomy, choices individuals can and do make. Each individual is located somewhere on each hierarchy; each tries in various ways to increase his advantages and *secure* them. Money gained by favorable location in the class hierarchy is used in an attempt to gain goods or status officialdom controls, while the resources of a person high in the hierarchy of officialdom are used to secure the material benefits that go with a favorable market position in terms of the criteria of class hierarchy.[50]

This tension seems inherent in the structure of socialist society, and thus likely to persist, with power, property, and prestige intertwined but not quite synchronized, and with individuals constantly attempting to achieve the synchronizations, the consistency, they desire. These things understood, the socialist hierarchy becomes more comprehensible, leaving us ready to deal with the phenomena of mobility through it in the chapters to follow.

Chapter Four

Socialism, Revolution, and Mobility

. . . One of the immediate aims of the leaders of the socialist states was to reach the level of more advanced capitalist countries in industrialization, urbanization, development of communications, and mass education. *All these processes imply an increase in social mobility in socialist countries as well as elsewhere,* and since they were induced by social revolutions we can therefore postulate a plain causal relation between social revolution and—this increase of social mobility. *But it is the 'social-economic expansion' and not the revolutionary introduction of a socialist order which can be considered a necessary condition of this increase. Increased mobility of this type could have been accomplished also if the capitalist system had persisted: it could have been done, e.g., with the help of schemes like the Marshall plan.*

—Stanislaw Ossowski, 1957

From villages and little towns, they come in carts
to build a foundry and dream out a city,
dig out of the earth a new Eldorado.
With an army of pioneers, a gathered crowd,
they jam in barns, barracks, and hostels,
walk heavily and whistle loudly in the muddy streets:
the great migration, the twisted ambition.
With a string on their necks—Czestochowa cross,
three floors of swear-words, a feather pillow,
a gallon of vodka, and the lust for girls.

. . . .

The great migration building industry,
unknown to Poland, but known to history,
fed with big empty words, and living
wildly from day to day despite the preachers,
in coal gas and in slow, continuous suffering,
the working class is shaped out of it.
There is a lot of refuse. So far, there are grits.

—Adam Wazyk, "A Poem for Adults," 1955

MOBILITY IS, in many senses, drama. For any individual with aspirations, succeed or fail, it is one of life's dramas, and for the most career-oriented, the central drama. It also sometimes achieves the status of national drama. The socialist states, in propaganda and literature as well as in the statistical chronicling of economic development, have treated it thus. The emergence of peasant societies into industrialism, the creation of new cadres of intelligentsia, administrators, and technicians—these, as well as the revolutionary downfall and dispersal of old elites, are all products of mobility. Farmers move to the factory, as do yet more of their sons. Workers, the "revolutionary mass" behind the political vanguard, study, master unfamiliar skills, and become technicians, administrators, and the like. Their sons and daughters, and peasants' children as well, face hitherto inconceivable career prospects as under the aegis of the new regime, and in the schools and universities it creates and multiplies, they form themselves into the new intelligentsia of the socialist state.

This is the national drama, expressed in media ranging from poetry and cinema to prose and poster art. It revolves mainly around occupations and occupational mobility. One may, of course, conceive of mobility along other dimensions—economic, educational, prestige—but today these are mostly connected with occupation, as its causes, consequences, or corollaries. Occupation is central. In the advanced capitalist world, except for that small number of persons with sufficient inherited resources to live as they like, occupation determines, at least better than any other characteristic, one's place in society. In the socialist states, where work is, according to the Marxian dictum, "man's material and moral necessity," this is even more true: political control and the absence of inheritable wealth in large amounts guarantee that occupation is preeminent in determining access to most of those things that men find desirable and gratifying.

Social mobility is a sensitive political phenomenon in socialist states. On the whole, the claimed "high" rates of mobility are seen as good, a benefit of socialism. The rise of workers and peasants, the building of a new intelligentsia, the sundering of automatic linkages between social origin and destination are seen as progressive, a realization of the new society.

Yet mobility also calls attention to the tension between the values of achievement and equality in their socialist forms. Of those who pride themselves on socialism's approximation to a society of merit—the performance principle—others of a more egalitarian bent can ask, as we saw earlier, Is not mobility important because the goods that men desire are *still* quite unequally distributed, because men, for themselves and their children, hope to rise and fear to fall? Marx himself thought little about mobility per se. It is, as many have argued, a dissociative process with respect to origins, and thus antithetical to the formation of "class consciousness," to the transition from *klasse an sich* to *klasse für sich* that lay at the center of Marx's concerns.[1] He provides little guidance in dealing with the question. The socialist leaders have not, however, been totally without answers. With the precedent of Lenin (and Stalin as well) they rely on the formula that identifies socialism as a "transitional phase" on the road to communism. If the operative principle of communism remains "from each according to his abilities, to each according to his needs," under socialism it stands as "from each according to his abilities, to each according to his work," legitimating unequal access to scarce goods until communist abundance is achieved, and thus legitimating aspirations to more important work and greater rewards.

Thus, mobility of worker and peasant sons into the intelligentsia continues to be seen as upward mobility. What does this suggest about the ultimate consequences of revolutions made on behalf of the working class and, derivatively, the peasants?—the rather paradoxical situation wherein the working class, still exalted in political rhetoric, is called upon to take pride in its "central" role in socialist society, but at the same time to feel paternal pride when its children manage to *leave* the working class. The major problem, as many socialist sociologists recognize, as that Soviet and Eastern European socialism, like other "isms," is a captive of history and the problems it imposes.

Marx attended little to the crucial situational factors his followers faced in the Russia of 1917, and later in Eastern Europe in 1945: poverty, destruction, scarcity, and backwardness. For much the same reasons that impel other nations faced with the problem of backwardness, the socialist states pursued rapid economic development. Once political control was assured, *development*, rather than the construction of a new egalitarian society, became priority number one—a necessary precondition to the new society. Development produced mobility. Not surprisingly, it did less to promote equality of reward and condition. Differentiation of reward was used to enlist those who competed for and were mobile into vital and expanding sectors and, in a sense, to punish those who did not compete, or did and lost. What there was of "equalization" came mainly as a consequence of development, through the expansion of the more desirable nonmanual and nonfarm sectors, affording more room for worker and peasant sons to move up. Otherwise, the tension between equality and the rewards and costs of differential achievement remained.

These historical circumstances deserve some further comment. Hardship, scarcity, and speed characterized the waves of development, in the USSR in the 1930s and in Eastern Europe in the late 1940s and through the 1950s, that evoked much of the mobility we will later examine. In some other states, development was preceded by the culmination of gradual accumulative processes and by gradual rises in standards of education and skill. But typically socialist economic development began in the wreckage of war, a wreckage of societies and economies that for the most part had been irregular performers, often nearly stagnant before the war, and generally poor by European standards.

The emphasis on forced savings and rapid accumulation combined with these low starting points to produce low living standards in the early years of socialism. The impact was felt especially strongly in urban areas. A Warsaw worker's real income, measured by the space, food, and clothing he could buy, was less than in the late years of capitalism—and thus it was through most of the socialist bloc (as it had been in the USSR, where the termination of the New Economic Policy and the onset of "plan era" industrialization at the end of the 1920s heralded a decline in the living standard it would take a generation to make good). Upward mobility takes on new meanings under such circumstances. Staying in the same place as a worker meant an objective decline in welfare for many in comparison with their previous lives. Professionals and intelligentsia who came over to serve the new regimes did better, but their welfare declined too in comparison with the standards of presocialist low-growth economies. The *sons* of workers and intelligentsia, inheriting their fathers' positions, did not inherit all that had hitherto gone with them.

Such declines in welfare threaten destabilizing political consequences. In large measure, however, the socialist states were spared these, not only because of the regimes' firm grip on the ultimate instruments of coercion, but because, *through* mobility, the membership of these groups became fluid, and standards of comparison changed. Some Warsaw or Budapest workers of 1950 might look back with nostalgia on a better life without a "worker's state," but many could not, since they were ex-peasants or sons of peasants at the terminus point of a mobility experience that profoundly changed their lives. The old working class became a minority among the new. And for the new, despite the poverty of city life, the change was generally for the better. Village life they knew to be even meaner and more laborious, and they lacked in any case the reference point of the old working class.

Similarly, upwardly mobile workers and workers' sons who donned white collars and occupied desks did not inherit the material privileges and perquisites of the old intelligentsia and managerial groups. But what they achieved was more than their old lives had given them in income, prestige, and—for some—power. The old intelligentsia was a drop in the ocean of the new, and their standards were largely irrelevant to those who had just arrived in the wake of revolution.

The gains one might make by farm to factory or manual to nonmanual mobility were small by the standards of the affluent West. From its vantage point, the general "grayness" and depression of living standards might make life seem egalitarian, if grim. But those gains *were* critical to those within the socialist system, who could much more readily perceive the new hierarchies of access to scarce values that were emerging. Insofar as socialism appealed to and raised expectations, it was fortunate in being able to meet many of them through the mobility processes it fostered. Life indeed was grim—Wazyk's poem, a section of which heads this chapter, was scarcely an ode to joy. But the young peasants it describes, impressed into the building of the Nowa Huta "steel city" near Krakow, were getting their first taste of regular wages and something approaching city life—an accomplishment. Riots in Poznan and elsewhere indicated that not all were always satisfied with such accomplishments, but on balance the mobility born of socialist economic policies was an important *political* fact, cushioning the impact of falling living standards and an inegalitarian system of reward at a time when the new regimes could count on few ideologically committed adherents.

The mobility of the early socialist years remains, then, a sensitive aspect of history: the positive side of a situation whose negative facade was shortage, scarcity, and the gray life. And, to the degree—quite considerable—that scarcity is still a hallmark of life in the socialist states, mobility and the distribution of opportunities for it remain pressing issues.

How are the *sources* of a high claimed rate of mobility to be regarded? This too is an issue in the socialist states. The socialist revolution, in all but Czechoslovakia, preceded the rapid economic development that facilitated mobility—and thus can in a sense take credit for it. But do particularly socialist principles *continue* to play a distinct role in the dynamics of mobility, by promoting a specifically egalitarian distribution of opportunity? Or does one think of the mobility attendant on economic development in a "secularized" manner, as a process similar to that expected in any rapidly developing economy?

The last sentence of the quotation from the late Polish sociologist Stanislaw Ossowski that begins this chapter expresses the "secular" view. Socialism brought "social-economic expansion," but expansion, not socialism, accelerated mobility. The necessary condition of expansion, or economic development, could as readily have been supplied under different political auspices: as Ossowski suggests, the Marshall Plan. All this is quite simple, even trivial. Yet the fate of Ossowski's sentence is an interesting index of the sensitivity mentioned above, for to my knowledge it has never appeared in Poland. Delivered in a paper at a Western conference in 1957, the sentence disappears from the 1968 Polish-language edition of Ossowski's works, to be replaced by the following innocuous, noncontroversial, and rather vague substitute: "The introduction of the socialist order through revolution and the accompanying social-economic expansion is a necessary condition of this growth.[2] Otherwise, the passage remains the same, and the sense is there—but, posthumously, Ossowski was deprived of the ability to cross the t's and dot the i's. This suggests the political constraints that form an important, if sometimes forgotten, element in the working environment of sociologists in the socialist states, and the reluctance of some to see socialist mobility patterns viewed in such an un-ideological manner.

DATA: FORM, QUESTIONS, AND INTERPRETATION

Our basic intergenerational mobility data for the socialist countries come in the form of seven tables, or "transition matrices," depicting the experience of six countries as measured in national surveys ranging in dates from 1960 to 1973. On the whole simple in design, they are what some scholars have called "first-generation" studies, specifying the respondents' occupations at the time of the survey, and the fathers' occupations at (with one exception) an unspecified prior point in time. They take the form here either of 3 × 3 (nonmanual, worker, peasant) or 4 × 4 (elite, routine nonmanual, worker, peasant) matrices.

The glaring omission in our mobility data is the Soviet Union itself, with a population larger than that of the rest of the socialist countries combined. Unfortunately, no nationwide study of mobility has been conducted in the USSR (or if it has, it has neither been published nor even circulated in any accessible form). And the mobility data collected on postwar Soviet emigrés by the Harvard Project on the Soviet Social System, while still interesting, are now quite old, and marked by the atypically successful composition of the sample.[3]

Mobility studies based on subnational, generally urban samples, though interesting and available for some Soviet cities as well as for some in Poland and elsewhere, are not very useful for the purposes of this chapter.[4] A tendency to study urban samples is understandable in societies undergoing modernization and urbanization at a rapid pace, but such studies contain large numbers of unrepresentatively successful persons of peasant origin, tell us nothing of those who stay in the countryside, and in general depart in many ways from the mobility patterns of national societies as a whole.

There are many methodological and analytic problems in interpreting such data that have already been dealt with at some length by Duncan,[5] Blau and Duncan,[6] Lopreato and Hazelrigg,[7] Boudon,[8] and others. It is not our object here to add to or recapitulate these discussions: however, some cautionary words are in order, especially for readers whose interests generally lie outside the area of mobility studies. First, we should note that while our *main* concern is with intergenerational mobility (differences in fathers' and sons' occupations), all the tables in this first set (tables 4.1 to 4.7) contain intragenerational or "career" mobility as well. Ideally, in measuring intergenerational mobility, one wants to isolate the effect of social origin (father's occupation) on son's occupational attainment, independent of the son's own exertions *after* commencing a work career. The best approximation would be son's first job and father's job at the time of son's career entry (or father's main occupation if he retired or died prior to son's career entry): but we lack such data in all cases save Hungary and Bulgaria. Thus, for now, we confine the comparisons to our most general tables, wherein "intergenerational" mobility is composed of (1) "true" intergenerational mobility—changes between social-origin category and the respondent's career-entry category, and (2) intragenerational mobility accomplished between time of career entry and time of the survey. The differing "weights" of intragenerational movements within intergenerational mobility, broadly defined, will be clarified to some degree in our consideration of the Bulgarian and Hungarian data (tables 4.8 to 4.12).

Second, though we use "generational" throughout our discussion as the term of convenience, it is unfortunately a very loose one. Neither sons nor fathers are "generations." All our studies are relatively unspecific on the age range of respondent sons, and a sample where age ranges from 20 to 60 encompasses diversity beyond the broadest definition of a single generation. Sons' reports of father's occupations produce a distribution of fathers that cannot be considered an accurate picture of a national occupational distribution at some previous point in time. Indeed, large national surveys with loose age restrictions incur the risk of including pairs of fathers and sons in the same sample. A 25-year-old factory worker may report his 48-year-old father as currently a peasant, and that 48-year-old, also a respondent, will answer "peasant" for *his* father, the 25-year-old's grandfather, somewhat distorting the portrait of father-son mobility the researcher seeks. (That some of this occurs in the very large Polish national survey there is little reason to doubt.)

Thus, our tables will contain a mix of different "typical" experiences. The oldest respondents in a sample, assuming that the pace of economic development at the period of *their* career entry was slow, had relatively small chances to be mobile at that point. Much of their observed mobility, then, will be intragenerational in a strict sense. Young respondents' mobility will be more likely that of a strict intergenerational type. But these may have substantial career mobility ahead of them, which only a later study would reveal. (The possibility also arises that those who appear to be "inheritors" of fathers' status—and hence "immobile" on the main diagonal—have been mobile twice or more in the past, leaving the father's category at career entry or later but returning to it by the time of the survey.) A national sample, if atypically young or old, will provide a distorted picture of the processes that interest us. Indeed, the vast majority of national mobility studies extant and available for cross-national comparison, whether from East or West (including the majority of the Western studies we utilize in the last section of this chapter), suffer from all these difficulties. But, as S. M. Miller has observed, "we must choose between using shaky data or no data."[9] Our choice is obvious.

Other problems arise. For purposes of broad comparability with overwhelmingly males-only studies conducted elsewhere, it would be better to have data here for males only. Some of our samples, however, are mixed sex. Given the differences between the occupational distributions of males and females in socialist as well as nonsocialist states, inclusion of females alters the outcome picture. In discussions of each national sample, account is taken of this as far as possible, even if at times it is no more than to caution the reader.

A desire to ensure comparability has caused us, on occasion, to use less than the whole of our information. While the original tabular data for some countries provide us only with a trichotomy of nonmanual, worker, and peasant, other countries yielded a profusion of categories. These latter we have collapsed to the four-category classification of elite, routine nonmanual, workers, and peasants in this section, and for the purpose of summary measures calculated later, to 3 × 3 form. We have already argued the utility of the four-category classification for socialist societies. This does not, of course, mean that is is perfect. But for the most part, it seems as good a vehicle for facilitating comparison across the socialist countries, and between socialist and nonsocialist states, as any scheme we are likely to develop.

A final, important point: the next section discusses gross mobility patterns, without separating the effects of development-induced changes in the occupational structure from those of "circulation mobility" not directly attributable to development. This may reduce its interest for sociologists primarily interested in precise measurement of mobility, in "state of the art" analytic techniques and their application. But, rather than inviting them to pass over it to the following section, it seems worthwhile to stress the importance of structural mobility, though it be often slighted in current research.

Insofar as certain kinds of mobility are desiderata to aspirants and other kinds to be avoided as degradation, the degree to which a society facilitates the one and limits the other may be regarded as an important part of its total "performance," with implications for mass satisfaction, willingness to accord legitimacy to a political-economic system, and hence, for systemic stability. The main mode of such facilitation is economic development. The "structural demand" it generates causes, as readers will see, the preponderant amount of upward mobility (manual to nonmanual, farm to nonfarm manual) in any society. To control for international differences in structural demand in order to arrive at measures of "circulation" mobility alone, at estimates of the openness of the structure, is reasonable for many purposes and crucial for some. But to focus, as some do, on circulation alone is to disconnect economic development from mobility and to risk underemphasizing the main determinant of the volume of mobility.

One might make the point differently. Let us imagine "Ruritania," a classic, but in one sense improbable, Eastern European state of the presocialist period. Ruritania's occupational structure is 65 percent peasant, 25 percent workers and artisans, 10 percent nonmanuals. Now Ruritania, a somnolent backwater with no real development and hence a stable occupational structure, is improbably idyllic in that social origin there has virtually nothing to do with determining one's career chances. In other words, virtually no structural mobility takes place* as one generation succeeds another, but as much circulation mobility exists *as the unchanging social structure will tolerate.*

The sons of Ruritanian peasants can comfort themselves with the knowledge that their chances of entering nonmanual jobs are equal to those of workers' sons and even to the chances of nonmanuals' sons to "inherit" those positions. One hopes the knowledge provides comfort, because it is about all the comfort most will receive. As long as Ruritania's nonmanual sector amounts to only 10 percent of the total, only 10 percent of those peasant sons can expect to end there. They may derive some psychological gratification from the fact that nonmanual sons face the certainty that most of them—90 percent—will circulate downward, something that distresses those nonmanual sons, each wondering whether he will be the one in ten to avoid a fall. But, with so *few* nonmanual sons to begin with, most of them will disappear into the peasant mass before the rustics can take any gratification in seeing the scions of privilege laid low.

Ruritania is not on any map. But it does help demonstrate that equality of opportunity will be small consolation in a society where people seek something better: peasants' sons, the regular hours and cash income of the factory worker; workers' sons, a place in the white-collar world; the sons of nonmanuals, retention and improvement of that status. Rapid economic development and the structural changes it creates will better serve their individual purposes than egalitarian but unchanging Ruritania, even if their developing economy accommodates a substantial element of hereditary influence so that nonmanual, worker, and peasant sons have unequal chances of success. In the end, what is important is that they achieve their desires; whether the pretext is "structural" or "circular" mobility matters little. In looking at the data, it is well to remember that our tables are populated by *real* people, to whom the final results of their countries' performance in promoting chances for advancement are what counts: results determined primarily by the level and pace of

*We simply ignore here the problems that fertility differentials among the occupational strata may cause—but let us assume that Ruritania is atypical enough to avoid these too.

economic development, rather than by various degrees of imperfect approximation to equal opportunity.

FATHERS AND SONS: MOBILITY OBSERVED

The Bulgarian data (table 4.1),* gathered by researchers at the Scientific Research Institute of Statistics, are based on a 3.0 percent sample of employed men and women as of November 1, 1967. (Sample proportions were projected onto the employed total, accounting for the large *N*'s.) Though seven categories were initially reported, the data permit reorganization only into a most basic mobility table, a tripartite classification of nonmanuals, workers, and peasants.

Bulgaria's heavily peasant past is reflected in the marginals on fathers' occupational categories, with a substantial industrial transformation evident in the son/daughter distribution. This transformation is compounded of a high rate of intergenerational inheritance for those of worker origin and an apparently *very* high outflow rate for peasant offspring into the worker category. A cautionary note: wage-earning agricultural manuals (who work on state as opposed to cooperative farms) are classified here as workers rather than peasants. There is no way to recover data on them from the original data, but other evidence suggests that a correction factor of about 13.9 percent (subtracted from the current worker totals in each cell and added to the corresponding peasant cells) would not be out of line.[10] Such an operation, assuming similar composition by origin (inflow)

*In this table, as well as in the mobility tables that follow in this chapter, the structure is as follows: the *top* row of figures attached to a given origin category (i.e., father as nonmanual, peasant, etc.) are outflow percentages, to be read across; these show the occupational destinations of the children of such fathers. The non-decimal figures of the middle row are the "raw" numbers in each cell; read across, they total to the number of fathers in a given origin category (whose percentage of the total of fathers is expressed in the figure in parentheses); read down, they total to the number of sons, or sons and daughters, whose destination is in that category (their percentage of the total of offspring is expressed in the parenthesized figures at the bottom of the table. Finally, the third row of figures attached to each origin category, to be read *down* only, give inflow percentages: that is, the proportions of offspring of different social origins who make up a given category at the time of the survey. These are totalled in the *top* row of the "total" figures at the bottom of each table. Hence, in 4.1, for example, 54.3 percent of the offspring of nonmanual fathers themselves have nonmanual jobs; these same people, 11,597 in number, make up 22.2 percent of *current* nonmanuals.

of the peasantry, would leave approximately 7 percent more peasant offspring in their origin status, and reduce their outflow to the worker stratum proportionally. This would probably be a more accurate representation of Bulgaria in 1967, but because of the uncertainty in our additional information, we have not constructed an adjusted table.

Bulgaria appears to be a classic case of transformation of a Balkan peasant society. The shift from the land to nonfarm pursuits is a major process however we assess the data, while the more modest movement of worker and peasant children into the nonmanual sphere is still considerable, given the starting point. Finally, the growth of the nonmanual stratum, from 6.7 to 16.3 percent of the whole, signals structural demand for outside recruitment. More than three-fourths of the current nonmanuals are of worker or peasant origin.

Czechoslovakia, as table 4.2 shows, is a very different case. These data, collected in 1967 as part of the nationwide survey of Czechoslovak social structure under Machonin and his research team,[11] were made available later in a limited, mineographed edition, and originally appeared in a 10 × 10 matrix. They probably refer to men only.*

One sees again a quite mobile society, with striking changes in the marginals. But both origin and outcome distributions point to the uniqueness of the Czechoslovak case in Eastern Europe. Less than 40 percent of the fathers are peasants, and almost half are workers. Outflow reduces the peasant share among sons to less than 15 percent. Movement of peasant and worker sons into both "elite" and routine nonmanual categories is substantial, as is peasant outflow into a large and growing working class. Czechoslovakia is a society with a quite developed starting point that maintained a high rate of structural mobility thereafter. The very high outflow of peasant and workers sons into the elite, compared with Hungary, Poland, and

*The current author only had short-term access (from a scholar who was not Czech, and in a country other than Czechoslovakia) to these data in the source cited. The source itself (see source note to table 4.2) is a "restricted" two-volume work printed in only 600 copies. While the repressive internal politics of the post-Dubcek period account for the suppression of much research, it is paradoxical that these data, as we shall see, show Czechoslovakia to be a highly mobile society that also scores high on measures of equal opportunity.

Table 4.1.
Intergenerational Mobility, Bulgaria (1967)

Father	*Son/daughter in 1967*				
	1	*2*	*3*	Total	
1 Nonmanual	54.3	42.4	3.4	100.1	
	115,797	90,486	7,161	213,444	(6.7)
	22.2	5.2	0.8		
2 Worker	22.6	69.8	7.6	100.0	
	187,737	581,031	63,591	832,359	(26.0)
	36.1	33.3	6.8		
3 Peasant	10.1	49.8	40.2	100.1	
	216,909	1,073,028	866,547	2,156,484	(67.3)
	41.7	61.5	92.4		
Total	100.0	100.0	100.0		
	520,443	1,744,545	937,299	3,202,287	
	(16.3)	(54.5)	(29.3)		

SOURCE: adapted from Atanas Atanasov and Aron Mashiakh, *Promeni v sotsialnata prinadlezhnost na zaetite litsa v Bulgariia* (Sofia: Nauchnoizsledovatelski institut po statistika, 1971), pp. 31–32. Nonmanual: employees; Worker: worker, cooperative artisans, independent artisans; Peasant: members of collective farms, private cultivators. "Others" excluded.

Table 4.2.
Intergenerational Mobility, Czechoslovakia (1967)

Father	*Son in 1967*					
	1	*2*	*3*	*4*	Total	
1 Elite	62.7	8.4	27.6	1.3	100.0	
	141	19	62	3	225	(6.0)
	16.3	5.2	3.2	0.6		
2 Routine nonmanual	38.6	14.5	45.4	1.6	100.1	
	96	36	113	4	249	(6.7)
	11.1	9.8	5.7	0.8		
3 Worker	24.7	11.2	59.1	4.9	99.9	
	440	200	1,054	88	1,782	(47.9)
	50.7	54.6	53.6	16.9		
4 Peasant	13.0	7.6	50.3	29.1	100.0	
	190	111	737	426	1,464	(39.4)
	21.9	30.3	37.5	81.8		
Total	100.0	99.9	100.0	100.1		
	867	366	1,966	521	3,720	
	(23.3)	(9.8)	(52.8)	(14.0)		

SOURCE: adapted from Ceskoslovensky Vyzkumny Ustav Prace, "Intergeneracni mobilita v profesionalni sfere," in *Socialni a profesionalni mobilita pracujiciho obyvatelstva CSSR* (Bratislava, 1972), p. 78. Elite: specialist employees; Routine nonmanual: clerks and other employees; Worker: skilled worker, semiskilled worker, unskilled worker, independent worker outside agriculture; Peasant: agricultural worker, manual worker in cooperative farm, independent worker in agriculture.

Table 4.3.
Intergenerational Mobility, Hungary (1973)

Father	*Son in 1973*					
	1	*2*	*3*	*4*	Total	
1 Elite	54.4	29.8	14.1	1.6	99.9	
	166	91	43	5	305	(2.0)
	17.2	4.2	0.6	0.1		
2 Routine	24.9	40.6	30.5	4.0	100.0	
nonmanual	172	281	211	28	692	(4.5)
	17.6	12.8	2.7	0.7		
3 Worker	7.1	20.4	61.5	11.1	100.1	
	395	1,134	3,420	617	5,566	(36.1)
	39.8	51.3	42.8	14.6		
4 Peasant	2.8	7.9	48.8	40.5	100.0	
	247	698	4,313	3,580	8,838	(57.4)
	25.4	31.6	54.0	84.7		
Total	100.0	99.9	100.1	100.1		
	980	2,204	7,987	4,230	15,401	
	(6.4)	(14.4)	(51.8)	(27.4)		

SOURCE: adapted from Rudolf Andorka, "Tendencies of Social Mobility in Hungary: Comparisons of Historical Periods and Cohorts" (paper for the Conference of the Research Committee on Social Stratification, International Sociological Association, Geneva, 1975; Budapest, 1975; mimeo.) and Andorka, "Social Mobility and Education in Hungary: An Analysis Applying Raymond Boudon's Models," *Social Science Information* 15, no. 1 (1976), 64–65. Elite: executives, managers, professionals; Routine nonmanual: other nonmanual; Worker: skilled workers, semiskilled workers, unskilled workers, independent artisans/merchants; Peasant: peasant; "Others" excluded.

Table 4.4.
Intergenerational Mobility, Poland (1972)

Father	*Son/daughter in 1972* 1	2	3	4	Total	
1 Elite	42.4	24.5	30.0	3.1	100.0	
	949	548	671	69	2,237	(3.2)
	14.2	7.4	2.2	0.3		
2 Routine	27.9	30.6	38.4	3.1	100.0	
nonmanual	846	927	1,164	94	3,031	(4.4)
	12.6	12.5	3.8	0.4		
3 Worker	12.1	15.5	63.7	8.7	100.0	
	2,952	3,782	15,541	2,123	24,398	(35.1)
	44.1	51.0	50.4	8.6		
4 Peasant	4.9	5.4	33.7	56.0	100.0	
	1,952	2,152	13,427	22,312	39,843	(57.3)
	29.1	29.1	43.6	90.7		
Total	100.0	100.0	100.0	100.0		
	6,699	7,409	30,803	24,598	69,509	
	(9.6)	(10.7)	(44.3)	(35.4)		

SOURCE: adapted from Krzysztof Zagorski, "Changes of Socio-Occupational Mobility in Poland: Selected Methodological Issues and Preliminary Findings" (Warsaw: Central Statistical Office, 1974; mimeo) pp. 20–21.
Elite: managerial and administrative personnel, managerial staff in technical and productive fields, other engineers and technicians, specialists in nontechnical fields of a higher level, other specialists in nontechnical fields, specialists in agriculture and forestry;
Routine nonmanual: administrative and office workers, nonmanual workers in transport and communications, nonmanual workers in trade and nonindustrial services;
Worker: foremen and related, industrial and related workers, construction and related workers, "laborers for different simple works," manual workers in transport and communications, manual workers in trade and nonindustrial services, nonqualified service staff, workers of unclassified occupations, workers "on own account" in industrial, construction and related occupations, workers "on own account" in other nonagricultural occupations, outworkers and agents;
Peasant: agricultural laborers, individual farmers, fishermen ("Others" excluded).

Table 4.5.
Intergenerational Mobility, Romania (1970); Estimated Data

Father	*Son in 1970*					
	1	*2*	*3*	*4*	Total	
1 Elite	70.3	21.6	8.1	—	100.0	
	26	8	3	—	37	(3.3)
	17.4	4.9	0.6	—		
2 Routine nonmanual	52.6	30.9	16.5	—	100.0	
	51	30	16	—	97	(8.7)
	34.2	18.4	3.5	—		
3 Worker	13.8	23.6	57.3	5.3	100.0	
	34	58	141	13	246	(22.0)
	22.8	35.6	30.5	3.8		
4 Peasant	5.2	9.1	41.1	44.6	100.0	
	38	67	303	329	737	(66.0)
	25.5	41.1	65.4	96.2		
Total	99.9	100.0	100.0	100.0		
	149	163	463	342	1,117	
	(13.3)	(14.6)	(41.5)	(30.6)		

SOURCE: adapted from Honorina Cazacu, *Mobilitate sociala* (Bucharest: Editura Academiei Republicii Socialiste Romania, 1974), pp. 82, 110, 196, 267–68. Elite: technical employees with higher education, other employees with higher education, free professions, businessmen and traders; Routine nonmanual: technical employees with secondary education, service employees with secondary education; Worker: unskilled workers, skilled workers, cooperative artisans, private artisans; Peasant: farmhand, private farmer, state farmer.

Table 4.6.
Intergenerational Mobility, Yugoslavia "I" (1960)

Father	*Son/daughter in 1960*				
	1	*2*	*3*	Total	
1 Nonmanual	67.3	22.1	10.6	100.0	
	495	163	78	736	(8.5)
	30.0	5.9	1.8		
2 Worker	27.9	58.3	13.8	100.0	
	488	1,020	242	1,750	(20.1)
	29.6	36.8	5.6		
3 Peasant	10.7	25.5	63.8	100.0	
	666	1,586	3,969	6,221	(71.4)
	40.4	57.3	92.5		
Total	100.0	100.0	99.9		
	1,649	2,769	4,289	8,707	
	(19.0)	(31.8)	(49.2)		

SOURCE: adapted from Vojin Milic, "General Trends in Social Mobility in Yugoslavia," *Acta Sociologica* 9, nos. 1–2 (1965), 120.

Table 4.7.
Intergenerational Mobility, Yugoslavia "II" (1962)

Father	*Son in 1962* 1	2	3	Total	
1 Nonmanual	66.3	26.1	7.6	100.0	
	63	25	7	95	(13.8)
	35.6	9.4	2.9		
2 Worker	26.1	64.7	9.2	100.0	
	37	93	13	143	(20.8)
	20.9	34.8	5.3		
3 Peasant	17.1	33.0	49.9	100.0	
	77	149	225	451	(65.5)
	43.5	55.8	91.8		
Total	100.0	100.0	100.0		
	177	267	245	689	
	(25.7)	(38.8)	(35.6)		

SOURCE: adapted and approximately reconstructed from data reported in Lawrence E. Hazelrigg, "Cross-National Comparisons of Father-to-Son Occupational Mobility," in J. Lopreato and L. L. Lewis, eds., *Readings in Social Stratification* (New York: Harper and Row, 1974), pp. 469–93. (N = 689 in this reconstruction differs slightly from original reported N = 682.)

Table 4.8.
Intergenerational Mobility, Bulgaria (1967);
Father's Occupation, Son's/Daughter's First Job

Father	*Son/daughter at first job* 1	2	3	Total	
1 Nonmanual	52.6	42.3	5.1	100.0	
	112,035	90,123	10,758	212,916	(6.7)
	24.3	6.6	0.8		
2 Worker	19.7	69.8	10.5	100.0	
	163,746	580,305	87,450	831,501	(26.0)
	35.5	42.6	6.4		
3 Peasant	8.6	32.1	59.3	100.0	
	185,064	690,822	1,278,387	2,154,273	(67.3)
	40.2	50.7	92.9		
Total	100.0	99.9	100.1		
	460,845	1,361,250	1,376,595	3,198,690	
	(14.4)	(42.6)	(43.0)		

SOURCE: Atanasov and Mashiakh, *Promeni* (cited in table 4.1), pp. 51–52.

Table 4.9.
Intragenerational Mobility, Bulgaria (1967); First Job, Current (1967) Job

First job	*1967 job* 1	2	3	Total	
1 Nonmanual	81.3	16.5	2.2	100.0	
	386,991	78,672	10,428	476,091	(14.7)
	72.3	4.5	1.1		
2 Worker	8.8	84.7	6.5	100.0	
	121,242	1,172,622	90,519	1,384,383	(42.7)
	22.7	66.4	9.6		
3 Peasant	1.9	37.3	60.7	99.9	
	26,763	515,493	838,926	1,381,182	(42.6)
	5.0	29.2	89.3		
Total	100.0	100.1	100.0		
	534,996	1,766,787	939,873	3,241,656	
	(16.5)	(54.5)	(29.0)		

SOURCE: adapted from Atanasov and Mashiakh, *Promeni* (cited in table 4.1), pp. 95–96.

Table 4.10.
Intergenerational Mobility, Hungary (1962–1964)

Father	*Son in 1962–1964* 1	2	3	4	Total	
1 Elite	56.8	24.4	16.6	2.2	100.0	
	130	56	38	5	229	(1.9)
	16.3	4.7	0.7	0.1		
2 Routine	28.8	35.8	33.3	2.0	99.9	
nonmanual	128	159	148	9	444	(3.7)
	16.0	13.3	2.5	0.2		
3 Worker	8.7	17.0	65.5	8.8	100.0	
	342	669	2,574	344	3,929	(33.1)
	42.8	56.1	44.2	8.5		
4 Peasant	2.7	4.2	42.2	50.9	100.0	
	199	309	3,070	3,704	7,282	(61.3)
	24.9	25.9	52.7	91.2		
Total	100.0	100.0	100.1	100.0		
	799	1,193	5,830	4,062	11,884	
	(6.7)	(10.0)	(49.1)	(34.2)		

SOURCE: adapted from Rudolf Andorka, "Social Mobility and Economic Development in Hungary," *Acta Oeconomica* 7 (1971), 28, and Andorka et al., *A tarsadalmi mobilitas torteneti tendenciai* (Budapest: Kozponti statisztikai hivatal, 1975), statistical appendix. Elite: executive, intellectual; Routine nonmanual: other nonmanual; Worker: artisan, skilled worker, semiskilled worker, unskilled worker, office attendant, day-worker; Peasant: peasant; "Others" excluded.

Table 4.11.
Intergenerational Mobility, Hungary (1962–64);
Father's Job in 1938, Son's First Job

Father	*Son at first job* 1	2	3	4	Total	
1 Elite	46.3	30.0	22.9	0.9	100.1	
	105	68	52	2	227	(1.9)
	26.1	9.2	1.0	0.0		
2 Routine	17.1	36.5	42.6	3.8	100.0	
nonmanual	76	162	189	17	444	(3.7)
	18.9	21.8	3.8	0.3		
3 Worker	3.2	9.2	74.5	13.2	100.1	
	125	365	2,948	521	3,959	(33.1)
	31.1	49.2	58.5	9.0		
4 Peasant	1.3	2.0	25.3	71.4	100.0	
	96	147	1,848	5,228	7,319	(61.3)
	23.9	19.8	36.7	90.6		
Total	100.0	100.0	100.0	99.9		
	402	742	5,037	5,768	11,949	
	(3.4)	(6.2)	(42.2)	(48.3)		

SOURCE: adapted from Andorka, "Social Mobility," p. 29, and Andorka et al., *A tarsadalmi*, statistical appendix, cited in table 4.10.

Table 4.12.
Intragenerational Mobility, Hungary (1962–1964);
First Job, Current (1962–1964) Job

First job	*1962–1964 job* 1	2	3	4	Total	
1 Elite	84.7	9.3	5.8	0.3	100.1	
	337	37	23	1	398	(3.3)
	41.2	3.1	0.4	0.0		
2 Routine	29.0	57.6	12.1	1.3	100.0	
nonmanual	220	438	92	10	760	(6.3)
	26.9	36.2	1.6	0.2		
3 Worker	3.8	12.1	74.8	9.3	100.0	
	196	618	3,813	472	5,099	(42.6)
	24.0	51.1	64.7	11.6		
4 Peasant	1.1	2.0	34.3	62.5	99.9	
	64	116	1,962	3,576	5,718	(47.8)
	7.8	9.6	33.3	88.1		
Total	99.9	100.0	100.0	99.9		
	817	1,209	5,890	4,059	11,975	
	(6.8)	(10.1)	(49.2)	(33.9)		

SOURCE: adapted from Andorka, "Social Mobility," p. 30, and Andorka et al., *A tarsadalmi*, statistical appendix, cited in table 4.10.

Romania (see below) is, of course, conditioned by the fact that these data show an unusually large "elite," a category seemingly based, to judge by its original label, heavily on educational criteria. Again, we cannot unfortunately do anything about the nature of the data, but we should remain aware that *this* elite is perforce less exclusive, less socially distant from the other strata, than is the case in the data for other countries. Even were the table collapsed to 3 by 3 form, yielding an undifferentiated nonmanual stratum, the modernity that distinguishes the Czech case would remain, however. As we saw from the earlier discussion on interwar social structure, and as these figures partially confirm, Czechoslovakia did not need a socialist revolution to build an industrial society.

Hungary (table 4.3) presents a middling picture. Neither developed to the Czech level nor quite a peasant society in the Balkan sense, it combines elements of both to some degree. These data were derived from a 1973 study conducted by the Hungarian Central Statistical Office, involving surveys of 0.5 percent of Hungarian households. Respondents, male heads of household, specified their fathers' occupations in 1938.

Traditional Hungary's social structure is transformed through the outflow of peasant sons into nonfarm manual work and the forging of new elite and nonmanual classes largely through recruiting sons of manual origin. The working class grows from about one-third to one-half of the total over the thirty-five years involved, while the peasantry's share declines from well over half to less than one third. Elite retention of status is rather pronounced, and most sons who slip from it are caught by the lower white collar ranks. Sons who originate in the lower white-collar stratum are somewhat more likely to descend to manual work than they are to rise to the elite. There is more room for them in the former stratum. In terms of inflow, the effects of economic development and the growth of a nonmanual sector are clear: 65.2 percent of the elite and 82.9 of the routine nonmanuals originated in the worker and peasant strata. But most workers' sons remain workers, four out of ten peasant sons peasants. If the latter are mobile, the movement, in the great majority of cases, is an exchange of farm for factory.

Poland's data base is largest. The data in table 4.4 were collected in a December 1972 survey of the economically active population, men and women, aged 15–69. A two-stage stratified probability sample of 0.5 percent of this population netted a total, before our deletion of the "other" category, of 72, 179, or almost 91 percent of the planned sample size. Zagorski's preliminary report of findings, the only one available to this author at the time of writing, unfortunately does not give separate matrices for men and women, but some of the effects of this are predictable.

The picture of mobility and change in Poland conveyed by the table is, in some respects, similar to the Hungarian data. Outflow of peasant offspring is what might be expected, given the inclusion of somewhat less mobile women in the Polish data: Polish peasant children became workers *less* often and stayed peasants more than their counterparts in Hungary. Conditions of various sorts make men readier for the transition to the urban factory world than females. Among worker offspring, the greater outflow into the elite in Poland may reflect not only the larger size of the Polish elite, but also the "empty space" created by elite daughters, who fail to retain this occupational status as often as do their brothers. Allowing for the inclusion of daughters, the elite inheritance rate of 42.4 percent need not be interpreted as low in comparison to Hungary.

Allowing for all this distortion, Poland and Hungary still show persistent similarities that echo their prerevolutionary social histories. Peasant to nonmanual mobility is quite moderate in both, while worker to nonmanual is similar, involving roughly one-quarter of the persons of worker origin. But this outflow, given the size of the origin categories, "proletarianizes" the nonmanual ranks, elite and routine, in both societies: between two-thirds and three-quarters of the elite, and over 80 percent of the routine nonmanuals, are of "toiling" origin.

The origin of our Romanian data (table 4.5) is peculiar enough to necessitate modifying "Romania" with the adjective "estimated." The findings, as reported by Cazacu, are from a study, apparently of 1970, conducted by the Center for Sociological Research of the Academy of Social and Political Sciences. Male family heads, 25 years old and over, made up the sample. Rather than one, national sample, however, it is in fact two: Bucharest, the capital, provided 919 respondents, and the rural commune of Calugareni, 197. We have thus taken liberties with the data, combining the samples and weighting them according to the urban and rural proportions of the 1970 Romanian population (40.8 and 59.2 percent, respectively).[12] Now Bucharest is not "urban Romania," nor presumably is Calugareni its quintessential rural counterpart. But this weighting does produce a "synthetic quasi-national" study, moving us somewhat closer to our objectives.

Elite sons inherit in seven of ten cases, showing a remarkable staying power, while for routine nonmanual sons mobility into the elite is more frequent than status inheritance. Especially regarding the elite, these figures are in some measure artifacts of the unconventional sample: *no one* of elite origin appeared in the Calugareni (rural) sample, so we are dealing here with sons of elite origin *all* of whom have either inherited or achieved residence in Bucharest. It seems likely that most, in fact, are native to the capital and less likely to have faced risks of losing fathers' status than sons of provincial elites. (A more diversified sample, with some second-class towns included, should have yielded *some* elite and white-collar sons descending into the peasantry, and more into nonfarm manual work.)

Still, the general inheritance of nonmanual status is impressive: virtually 86 percent of the sons of nonmanual fathers also hold nonmanual occupations. The relatively late date of the study shows the results of a decisive turning away from an agricultural role for Romania and rapid industrial development. This, as well as the peculiar sample, helps account for the high outflow of workers' sons into nonmanual employment, and movement of peasant sons that shows more who leave than stay—most, predictably, swelling the ranks of the workers. This stratum almost doubles in size and proportion of the whole between the generations, while the peasant component is reduced by more than half. Inflow figures show an almost proletarianized elite (48.3 percent of worker and peasant origin; given the Bucharest bias in the data, which favors inheritance, the nationwide figure must be over 50 percent), and domination of nonmanual ranks in general by those whose origin lies elsewhere. Worker and peasant sons make up 63.1 percent of the current nonmanuals. While all the qualifications warrant our continued treatment of these data as an estimate of Romanian patterns, the patterns are much what one would expect of a Balkan society in rapid transition.

Yugoslavia provides our last case, as well as some further questions and complications. Previous treatments of mobility that have included Yugoslavia have used the data gathered in the April 1960 pilot population census, as reported by Milic.[13] These data, however, are problematic. In the light of the full 1961 census, the mobility subsample (N = 8,707) of 1960 overrepresented current urbanites and underrepresented peasants, leading Milic to conclude that the "source data, consisting of a disproportionate share of the more mobile urban population, overstates the true amount of social mobility in Yugoslav society."[14] The sample also, unfortunately, includes both working males and females over 20, as well as their dependents (classified by the occupational category of those who supported them). From the point of view of our interests, these data are scarcely ideal.

An alternative source, used by Hazelrigg,[15] is a sample of 682 males collected in 1962 by the International Institute for Social Research (IISR) in an investigation mainly concerned with nonmobility issues. This has the virtue of being confined to males alone, albeit within the limits of a rather small sample. Hazelrigg cites the deficiencies of the 1960 pilot census subsample as the reason for using the IISR data,[16] but it is not really clear that these provide an unambiguous improvement in terms of representativeness. As we shall see (tables 4.6 and 4.7) though Milic concludes that his data overstate mobility, the IISR data yield a picture of an even more mobile society, only two years after the pilot census. Some of this, no doubt, is due to the greater mobility of males—but *how* much? Statistical yearbook figures based on census data are of little help here, and for now the best course would seem to be to report both "Yugoslavia I" (Milic) and "Yugoslavia II" (our rough reconstruction of the IISR data) separately.

Both tables reflect, in fathers' marginal distribution, the heavily peasant background of Yugoslavia—the Balkan character it shares with Romania and Bulgaria. Indeed, allowing for the extra eight years of development time in Romania as against Yugoslavia II, these males-only data show, in their peasant-son outflow, quite similar patterns. Both sources also indicate roughly a doubling of the size of the nonmanual sector. (This change is more marked in the Milic data, probably due to the heavy recruitment of women into the routine nonmanual posts. Nonmanual inheritance remains high, as does the direct inheritance of worker status, although with respect to the latter, the greater growth and larger final share of the working class in the males-only data [Yugoslavia II] facilitates greater peasant outflow *into* the working class as well as a higher rate of inheritance by working-class sons.)

This, then, is our assortment of national data, evidencing the common effects of development and the persistence of differences traceable to diverse takeoff points. Substantial shifts in the marginals for all six countries point to the changes in "structural demand" that are a *sine qua non* for large-scale mobility. None of these countries, from initially developed Czechoslovakia to the Balkan states at the other end of the spectrum, has failed to experience substantial mobility. Yet as the starting points were different, so also are the outcomes. The share of those in agriculture at the time of the study ranges from a low of 14.0 percent in Czechoslovakia to a high of 49.3 in Yugoslavia I, while the nonmanual component also ranges widely, from Czechoslovakia's 33.1 percent to Bulgaria's 16.3.

All the foregoing tables provide an unspecified mix of mobility experiences. Though they portray intergenerational mobility in a broad sense, a good deal of their content may be intragenerational or career mobility, accomplished after an entrance into the work force in the same occupational category as one's father. Fortunately, data for two of our countries—Bulgaria and Hungary (an earlier 1962–1964 study of which the 1973 study was essentially a replication)—allow us to break down this process into two steps: from father's occupation to respondent's first job, and from the latter to respondent's current occupation.

Table 4.8 yields the Bulgarian figures on social origin versus first job. Its similarity to table 4.1 is evident at first glance. The distribution of nonmanual offspring is almost identical across the two tables, as is that of persons of worker origin. Thus, the vast majority of the stability and mobility evident earlier in these two categories is truly intergenerational. Many nonmanual children entered the labor force in manual jobs, and nearly one-fifth of the manual children entered in nonmanual occupations. The largest divergence is in the peasant category. Roughly 60 percent of peasant children took first jobs in that same stratum, but only about two-thirds of these remain there in 1967, most having moved into nonfarm manual work as industry, mining, and other secondary-sector opportunities developed. An intragenerational table should show quite moderate career changes for the nonmanual and worker strata and more marked mobility for the peasants.

Table 4.9 provides "first job" to "1967 job" data. As we see, those who started as nonmanuals or workers are extremely likely to be in the same category. The intragenerational downward mobility of "first job" nonmanuals is very moderate compared to the incidence of intergenerational skidding. While some who began as workers fall into the peasantry, it seems certain that a goodly number of workers' offspring who began their own work as peasants have restored themselves to blue-collar ranks. This is suggested not only by the fact that while 10.5 percent of worker offspring (table 4.8) began their careers as peasants, only 7.6 percent (table 4.1) remained in that category in 1967—probably providing enough mobiles to counterbalance the 6.5 percent of those who began as workers but became peasants—but also by the figures in row 3. Almost 40 percent of those who began work as peasants now have moved into blue-collar jobs, with a small number making the ascent into nonmanual work. (Similarly, a goodly share of the nonmanual offspring who had fallen as low as the peasantry in their *first* jobs have "restored" themselves by 1967.) In Bulgaria, for the most part, the distance between fathers' and childrens' occupations, as measured in these 1967 data, was covered when those children took their first jobs. A partial exception which focuses our attention squarely on the major social transformation of Eastern Europe, measured by the numbers involved, is the pattern for peasant children. The son or daughter of a peasant had roughly one chance in three of becoming a worker by 1967.* Here, both inter- and intragenerational mobility have been

*These figures do not reflect the correction factor discussed earlier in connection with the Bulgarian data, and thus in some measure exaggerate the numbers of places available in the nonfarm manual or worker stratum since they do not (for such an operation here is even more difficult than in table 4.1) shift state farm workers to the peasant category.

important: continuing economic development has posed relatively constant career contingencies for young peasants.

A comparable data set for Hungary (tables 4.10, 4.11, 4.12) yields somewhat different impressions. Table 4.10 is a "general" intergenerational matrix, the product of the 1962–1964 study that the 1973 study replicated.[17] As a comparison with table 4.3 will indicate, it is rather similar overall to the later study, and we are compelled to use it here as a base since first-job and intragenerational data from the 1973 study are not yet at hand.

As a comparison of table 4.11 (father in 1938, son at first job) with table 4.10 shows, the initial placement of the respondents was generally markedly less advantageous than their positions in 1962–1964. More of elite and nonmanual sons began in the manual ranks than remained there later, while elite sons slipped into routine nonmanual work more often, and sons of routine nonmanuals ascended to the elite much less often in taking first jobs than in their subsequent job attainment. Conversely, only 12.4 percent of worker sons had a first job in the nonmanual sector, and only 3.3 percent of peasant sons. By 1962–1964, 25.7 and 6.9 percent, respectively, had achieved such jobs—roughly double the earlier proportion. The changes are much greater than those reflected in the Bulgarian data. We should thus expect fewer immobiles along the main diagonal of table 4.12, and those data confirm this. More workers improve their career lot by entering nonmanual work (15.9 percent, versus 8.8 percent in Bulgaria) and a somewhat larger share moves into farm work. All in all, 10 percent fewer workers remain in their first-job stratum in Hungary than do in Bulgaria. Though career-length retention of status is slightly greater for Hungarian nonmanuals and peasants than for their Bulgarian counterparts, in the total picture (based on a 3 × 3 collapsing of the Hungarian data) 70.3 percent of the Hungarians and 74.0 percent of the Bulgarians are located on the stable main diagonal of these first job to current job tables.

These patterns, then, are somewhat distinct. Comparable data for the other nations, which would allow us to assess the *range* of inter/intragenerational combinations in the broad intergenerational data we possess for the six socialist states, would be welcome. Lacking them, we can only emphasize for the reader the fact that mobility data of the sort used here, though they describe a gross form of "intergenerational" mobility, will contain a quantum of intragenerational or career mobility as well, one that cannot be specified in the absence of other data. That quantum will vary depending on the age structure of the population and on the balance of structural demand and its changes during the period before first-job attainment and the succeeding career period—phenomena on which data have been only rarely available.

Finally, we need address the problem of the *mechanism* of occupational status transmission. How do elite fathers ensure the inheritance of their status by a disproportionate number of their sons? How do skidders lose it? What is provided to some sons of humble origin that allows *them* to rise that is not provided to the majority, who thus remain in the stratum of origin, or at best are mobile within manual ranks, from peasant to worker or from unskilled to skilled worker?

History provides many examples of the sorts of resource whose command ensures elite inheritance and whose lack bars one from advancement: lineage itself; the direct purchase of position and prerogative for one's children; capital bequeathed that allows a son to establish himself in a manner that reproduces father's status if not his particular occupation; finally, cultural characteristics, breeding, and style that mark one as a person nurtured appropriately and thus "fit" to live a privileged adult life. However, the modern world seems to rely increasingly, in conferring status, on another mechanism, independent of though often related to these other resources—formal education. Insofar as the occupational world of the nonsocialist West grows more bureaucratized, with less competitive room for individual entrepreneurship, "success," it is argued, increasingly depends on the possession of educational credentials certifying one for entrance to the occupational hierarchy at an advantageous level. In the socialist world, a greater bureaucratization operates in combination with the abolition of concentrations of private, inheritable wealth to give education an even greater significance in the process of status attainment. Thus, we might expect that (1) elite sons inherit parental status through the appropriate education, while skidders will be marked by a lack of such education; and that (2) a prerequisite of long-distance upward mobility (from peasant or worker origin to elite status) will be a level of education uncharacteristically high for the stratum of origin.

In the face of many quantitatively sophisticated studies of the relation of education to occupational and general status attainment that have appeared in recent years,[18] we have little available by way of data to test our expectations. But the data we have—derived from the 1962–1964 and 1973 Hungarian mobility surveys (tables 4.3 and 4.10, above)—are of rather good quality and allow us to address two questions squarely. How central *is* education in the process of intergenerational status transmission or attainment? And, how much, if anything, does father's occupational status per se add to a given son's occupational attainment, when that son is compared with a peer of similar educational level but different social origin?

Table 4.13 provides the sort of information we need. The earlier four-stratum classification is used here to locate sons in 1962–1964 and their fathers in 1938. As we see, father's occupational status has a great deal to do with education attained by the son. More than half of elite sons graduate from the university, and another third complete the classical academic high school curriculum and receive the diploma. Routine nonmanual sons attain university education less than half as often: still, more than half of their number attain either degree or diploma. (This "diploma," or *erettsegi*, was in prewar Hungary a ticket of admission into polite society—just as in Poland, various privileges [officer status if one joined the armed forces, access to the franchise and the right to stand for election to the National Senate, and membership in the intelligentsia] were attached to the attainment of the *matura* after graduation from the classical lyceum.)[19] Conversely, among worker and peasant sons, attainment of *either* educational or credential is much less frequent (with a large drop in attainment between workers and peasants as well). These figures seem to confirm more general perceptions of relationships of social origin to education: unequal distribution in the parental generation of education, status, economic resources, "culture," etc. leads in the next generation to differences in resources, values, preparation, and attitudes relevant to chances for continued study in virtually all societies we know.

The "university degree" rows tell us clearly that such education is

Table 4.13.
Occupational Outcomes of 1962–1964 Sample, Hungary; Sons, by Fathers' 1938 Occupations and Sons' Educational Levels

Father	Sons' education (%)	Sons' occupations, 1962–1964				
		Elite	Rtn. nonman.	Worker	Peasant	Other
Elite						
Under 6 yrs.	—	—	—	—	—	—
6–7 yrs.	3.5	—	—	78.9	10.5	10.5
8 yrs.	6.7	18.9	48.6	18.9	13.5	—
9–12 yrs.	2.0	—	18.2	81.8	—	—
Diploma	33.6	29.2	49.7	20.0	1.1	—
Univ. degree	54.2	83.2	7.4	8.4	1.0	—
Routine nonmanual						
Under 6 yrs.	1.2	—	—	53.8	23.1	23.1
6–7 yrs.	13.9	—	17.0	74.1	7.5	1.4
8 yrs.	20.7	4.1	31.5	61.6	1.8	0.9
9–12 yrs.	7.8	6.1	37.8	52.4	3.7	—
Diploma	34.6	27.7	57.8	14.0	0.5	—
Univ. degree	21.8	80.9	16.9	2.2	—	—
Worker						
Under 6 yrs.	15.0	0.4	3.9	76.2	17.1	2.4
6–7 yrs.	36.1	0.6	5.6	79.6	13.1	1.1
8 yrs.	27.2	2.2	18.0	73.6	4.7	1.5
9–12 yrs.	5.0	6.2	39.4	52.6	0.9	0.9
Diploma	12.1	22.0	58.5	18.3	0.6	0.6
Univ. degree	4.6	88.2	7.3	3.3	—	1.2
Peasant						
Under 6 yrs.	28.7	—	0.7	34.1	64.1	1.1
6–7 yrs.	52.6	0.5	1.7	43.3	53.5	1.0
8 yrs.	13.4	3.2	8.2	61.4	25.1	2.1
9–12 yrs.	1.3	10.3	36.1	38.6	13.9	1.1
Diploma	2.4	24.6	57.4	12.2	5.8	—
Univ. degree	1.6	82.5	12.5	4.3	0.7	—

SOURCE: adapted from Rudolf Andorka, *A tarsadalmi atretegzodes es demografiai hatasai. II. Magyarorszagon* (Budapest: Kozponti statisztikai hivatal, 1970), p. 98 (worker and peasant panels); pp. 198–206 (elite and routine nonmanual panels).

an extremely strong mechanism of elite inheritance, indeed close to a necessary one, and an equally powerful mobility escalator for routine nonmanual, worker, and peasant sons. University graduates of worker origin were in fact slightly more likely to enter the elite than similar-credentialed elite sons were to inherit, while peasant-son graduates slightly outstripped lower nonmanual sons in entering elite ranks with the degree. Once possessed of higher education, worker and peasant sons were less likely to skid to manual work than were elite sons with higher education. (The latter's 9.4 percent rate of such downward mobility would seem to reflect the 1962–1964 detritus of politicization of career access in the early postrevolutionary years: see "Perspective: Presocialist Mobility," below.)

Lacking a university degree, one's chances of entering the elite, whatever one's social origins, fall precipitously. This is true for sons of the elite as well as those of lower origin. Within the bounds of this sample at least, higher education is *the* transmission mechanism for elite occupational status.

The cash value, so to speak, of the "diploma" (a category that includes *uncompleted* higher education) for elite access seems a bit higher for the two nonmanual categories than the two of manual origin. However, elite sons who *only* attain this educational level are in a risk situation—they fall more often into manual ranks than do similarly educated worker and peasant sons. (Interestingly, this outcome parallels Blau and Duncan's findings for their sample of U.S. males in 1962,[20] wherein men with college education *short* of graduation generally suffered high risks of skidding below their fathers' status attainments. Of course those paternal attainments, relatively high, as with our elite Hungarian fathers, were among the main reasons their sons had spent time in the university environment to begin with.) Otherwise, the diploma operates, with about the same results for routine nonmanual, worker, and peasant sons, in providing access to nonmanual work in general.

Strikingly different, however, is the value of a bare 8 years of schooling. Relatively few elite and nonmanual sons are limited to this level of attainment. But for those who are, it still suffices to keep 67.5 percent of elite sons out of manual work, and does the same for 35.6 percent of nonmanuals' sons. It works not nearly so well, as the figures show, for worker and peasant sons, who rarely cross the manual-nonmanual boundary with it.

Especially interesting is the fate of those elite sons who received 9 to 12 years of schooling (although here the *N* is so small as to make arguments perilous). This shortfall is disastrous for them, but not for routine nonmanual, worker, and peasant sons. For the latter two groups, it provides a substantial increment of job attainment over the 8-year category. It is likely that the 9 to 12 category, evidently made up of those who failed to graduate from high school, signals a serious precareer failure for elite sons, the prelude to a long downward skid.* For worker and peasant sons, however, attainment of this educational level is more in the nature of a real accomplishment which, if not so striking as a diploma or degree, nonetheless distinguishes them from their original peers.

The comparable 1973 data (table 4.14) demonstrate, first, the persistence of a strong connection between origin and education—sons of elite fathers remain much more likely than others to receive a university education. All four strata have increased in the percentage of sons receiving such certification. The worker and peasant strata increases are much larger proportionately than those of the two nonmanual groups, but their absolute numbers are still quite small.

The degree remains an entry ticket for the elite—and, as in the 1962–1964 data, works slightly better for university-educated peasant and worker sons than for those sons of routine nonmanual and elite fathers who are more likely to receive it. The slight decline in percentage of degree-holders achieving elite status in three of the four strata is most probably an artifact of a slightly narrower definition of the 1973 elite.

Across the board, the diploma and incomplete higher education show less value in 1973 than in 1962–1964. Fewer so certified enter the elite from all four strata, and more finish in the manual strata. But the situation has worsened more for worker and peasant sons

*Again, one cannot discount the probability that these are politically induced skidders—sons of the "old elite" unfortunate enough to have been barred from further education in the early postrevolutionary years, and never managing to recoup their lost positions.

Table 4.14.
Occupational Outcomes of 1973 Sample, Hungary;
Sons, by Fathers' 1938 Occupations and Sons' Educational Levels

Father	Sons' education (%)	Sons' occupations, 1973				
		Elite	*Rtn. nonman.*	*Worker*	*Peasant*	*Other*
Elite						
Under 6 yrs.	0.3	—	—	100.0	—	—
6–7 yrs.	0.9	—	—	100.0	—	—
8 yrs.	6.2	—	36.8	47.4	15.8	—
9–12 yrs.	5.2	—	62.5	37.5	—	—
Diploma	26.9	17.1	61.0	22.0	—	—
Univ. degree	60.3	82.6	13.0	3.3	1.1	—
Routine nonmanual						
Under 6 yrs.	4.4	—	19.4	58.1	19.4	3.2
6–7 yrs.	9.6	—	23.9	65.7	9.0	1.5
8 yrs.	17.6	3.3	20.3	67.5	6.5	2.4
9–12 yrs.	8.2	7.0	43.9	43.9	1.8	3.5
Diploma	34.6	10.3	72.3	14.9	2.5	—
Univ. degree	25.6	77.7	19.0	2.8	0.6	—
Worker						
Under 6 yrs.	9.5	—	2.4	74.7	22.9	—
6–7 yrs.	23.7	0.3	8.3	74.2	16.1	1.1
8 yrs.	38.8	0.6	11.8	74.5	11.0	2.1
9–12 yrs.	4.3	2.9	27.5	63.3	5.0	1.3
Diploma	17.4	9.1	63.0	25.2	2.4	0.3
Univ. degree	6.4	78.1	19.4	1.9	—	0.5
Peasant						
Under 6 yrs.	17.9	0.3	0.5	38.8	60.3	0.2
6–7 yrs.	39.2	0.2	3.8	46.2	49.1	0.7
8 yrs.	33.1	0.6	7.3	61.7	27.7	2.7
9–12 yrs.	1.9	1.7	20.3	60.6	12.2	5.2
Diploma	5.6	8.0	58.0	26.1	7.2	0.8
Univ. degree	2.3	88.5	9.1	1.9	0.5	—

SOURCE: adapted from Rudolf Andorka, "Social Mobility and Education in Hungary: An Analysis Applying Raymond Boudon's Models," *Social Science Information* 15, no. 1 (1976), 64–65.

than for those of the elite or of routine nonmanual origin, and elite sons are now *less* likely to descend into manual work than are manual-strata sons to remain there, with the diploma.

The value of 8 years' schooling also has declined, precipitously for elite sons but markedly so for the other strata too. Chances for elite entry at this educational level, whatever one's origin, are small indeed. As insurance against a manual occupation for elite sons, it has ceased to work—32.4 percent of sons so educated were in manual work in 1962–1964, while 63.2 percent fall here in the 1973 data. Worker and peasant sons at this educational level are less likely to be upwardly mobile in 1973 than in 1962–1964. Finally, in the 9–12 year category, some interesting changes occur. Elite sons whose education stops here now retain nonmanual status at a greatly increased rate (but the *N*, though increased, remains a small one). Changes in outcome are modest in the routine nonmanual origin stratum, but favor remaining in nonmanual strata. No longer do 9–12 years do much for worker and peasant sons, however. As their access to the diploma and to university education has increased, their chances of attaining either level of nonmanual job with one level less schooling have decreased markedly—peasant sons, for example, achieved nonmanual occupations in 46.4 percent of the cases with such educations in 1962–1964. In 1973 only 22.0 percent do so.

What, then, do these data indicate? First, that education *has* been central in the process of status inheritance and attainment. Whatever one's social origin, higher education provides access to the elite, and is near-essential to inheritance for those born in the elite. Similarly, low education (7 years or less) locks one into manual work whatever one's origin. Generally, increments in education are matched by increments in occupational attainment, and comparisons of the figures give some reason to argue that educational levels below university are losing value as the supply of university graduates grows.

Second, these data give no firm indication that high status of origin adds *much* to occupational attainment when education is held constant. Elite sons with university degrees, in fact, skid to manual work more often than equally educated persons from the other three strata in both data sets; but this echo of politics is less evident in the 1973 data. Routine nonmanuals' sons, however, do turn educational levels below university degree to somewhat better account than worker and peasant sons in the quest to remain or rise above the manual-nonmanual line. (Here one cannot discount the possibility that they are using other "origin resources.") Generally, these data contain some anomalous instances of lower social origins benefiting, and higher origins hurting career attainments. We get something less than a clear picture of delayed effects of parental origin (those not absorbed when educational level is controlled) that have been noted by scholars in, inter alia, Great Britain and Sweden.[21] This is not to say that such effects do not exist in Hungary—for there is other evidence that they do[22]—but that they seem to be moderate and difficult to detect or infer within the context of our four occupational categories.

Finally, one additional qualification: we have treated educational attainment here as if it preceded occupational attainment—just as Western studies generally treat similar data. This assumption is generally accurate—but not always, in socialist or in Western data. Some of the educational attainment here has fostered career mobility, probably most marked in the case of many peasant and worker sons whose first jobs were in field or factory and whose subsequent education made them mobile. With this, there is no problem, as long as we understand that, here as earlier, some intergenerational mobility registered in the table was in fact intragenerational. Others, though, are likely to have inhabited a given occupational category longer than they have possessed appropriate educational credentials. This is likely in the case of some (but by no means necessarily a majority) of the current elite of worker and peasant origin, whose job status, conferred on political grounds, was later justified by the advanced degree: much in the manner that upward-mobiles throughout history, ascendant on some important dimensions but lacking other typical characteristics of their new status, have sought to supply the latter in the interests of status consistency (as well as job retention).

How likely are these Hungarian data to typify the general relationship of education to intergenerational occupational mobility in Eastern Europe and the USSR? Some of what they reveal finds echoes in bits of data from other countries. (For example, a Soviet study in Leningrad revealed that, holding education constant at the level of secondary school graduation, young people with one or two parents in intelligentsia occupations were most likely to secure nonmanual jobs, while those of similar education but of working class or routine nonmanual parentage took manual positions.)[23] But it is difficult, really, to go much beyond the level of an educated guess. The Hungarian data presented a picture of higher education, and also complete academic secondary education, as rather scarce commodities. The two nonmanual strata where such educational levels were relatively common made up a quite small proportion of the population, compared to the worker and peasant strata, where such education was a rarity.

Scarcity, however, is relative. In some states, where higher education on the whole would have been scarcer than in Hungary, less than a university level education might still provide a good chance of access to elite jobs, especially for those from strata where higher education would be extremely atypical and secondary schooling a considerable attainment. In Romania, data from the Cazacu study cited earlier show, for example, that current elite members drawn from worker and peasant strata possess a degree in 34.0 and 34.8 percent of the cases, respectively, while elite inheritors and those who have risen from lower nonmanual backgrounds have higher educations in 56.4 and 51.7 percent of the cases.[24] Though Cazacu's data do not permit systematic comparison with Hungary, they suggest that in the less-developed socialist states, with an insufficiency of university-educated persons to staff the elite, the next lower level of education retains a cash value that would be lower in a society where the supply was greater. In a context of much less scarcity (such as we may presume Czechoslovakia to have been) it is possible that educational levels below complete university degrees (e.g., the classical secondary school diploma) proved less valuable, providing fewer at such levels with an entrée to the elite. (Given the large size of the Czech "elite" in our mobility data, however, it would be hard to confirm this, even if we had educational data comparable to those on Hungary.)

Some evidence is at hand that formal education is comparatively more crucial to occupational attainment in socialist societies than elsewhere even where the supply of educated manpower is large. The 1967 Czech national survey also provided information for a larger sample (N = ca. 13,215) on the correlation between educational level and "complexity of work"—an indirect measure of occupational status. Over three generations, this correlation increased from .412 for the respondents' fathers, to .579 for the respondents themselves, to .675 for the currently employed offspring of those respondents;[25] evidence of its increasing salience in occupational attainment. Comparison of the path coefficients linking respondent's education both to first job and to current job, for Blau and Duncan's sample of U.S. males, Broom and Jones's 1965 Australian study, and the 1967 sample of Czechs shows that in both cases, the Czech coefficients are greatest: .557 versus .440 (USA) and .410 (Australia) for education—first job; .507 versus .384 (USA) and .290 (Australia) for education—current jobs.[26] This provides some basis for arguing that the linkage of education to occupational success is probably greater in socialist than in nonsocialist systems. Despite a growing bureaucratization in the latter, noneducational resources relevant to occupational attainment, while perhaps declining, are still more available than under socialism (and indeed, as developed Western societies move toward overproduction of the highly educated, may become increasingly relevant).

"DEMAND" AND "EXCHANGE"

Thus far our discussion has focused on gross mobility rates, making no attempt to distinguish mobility necessitated by changes in the occupational structure from mobility attributable to exchange or circulation—intergenerational movement of the sort that presumably speaks to the "openness" of opportunity structures, *whatever* the degree of economic development. Nor have we provided any sort of summary statistic that, in one number, can tell us to what degree the weight of prior history determines current occupational distributions—i.e., the degree to which the sons' pattern can be explained by reference to the distribution pattern of their fathers.

Here, we employ two measures to make good the deficit. Both are simple, in two positive senses. First, they are readily interpretable: the values vary within clearly established limits, from 0.0 to 1.0. Second, they are relatively well suited to our data, where individuals are placed in relatively broad occupational categories rather than

Table 4.15.
Measures of Immobility and Dependence, Socialist States.

	I_B	$\bar{r}^2$
Bulgaria	.79	.091
Czechoslovakia	.63	.084
Hungary	.71	.101
Poland	.75	.155
Romania	.81	.178
Yugoslavia I	.74	.151
Yugoslavia II	.79	.133

classified by compound indices of status involving measurements of income, education, and occupational prestige.

The first measure, the "immobility index" developed by Boudon,[27] assesses the amount of "circulation" or "inheritance" in a matrix, independent of changes in occupational distributions evoked by economic development. The phenomenon directly measured here is inheritance, or stability: thus, higher values of the index I_B indicate less circulation and lower values, more. The limits of 0.0 and 1.0 would then indicate, respectively, maximum possible circulation—the "equal opportunity society" like our hypothetical "Ruritania"—and a complete lack of free circulation (in societies scoring 1.0).

The second measure, Beck's mean squared canonical correlation $\bar{r}^2$,[28] while it does not completely exclude the impact of changing occupational distributions between the generations, yields another useful summary statistic: the percentage of the variance in sons' occupational destinations explained by a linear combination of fathers' occupational distribution and a similar combination of sons' destinations. Simply stated, it is a measure of the degree to which the pattern of one generation is explained by the pattern of the previous generation.

Table 4.15 reports the values of these measures for the socialist samples (all values calculated on 3 × 3 tables—nonmanual, manual, and farm). As we see, there is rather little variation in the openness of the opportunity structure across the socialist states, as measured by the I_B values. The seven-case average is .75, while elimination of the "extreme" Czech case raises this to .77. There is, however, no real reason to eliminate it. Within the context of this measure, Czechoslovakia *is* registered as a more egalitarian society than the rest in terms of openness to mobility, upward and downward. What the figures tell us, on the whole, is that about three-quarters of those in socialist societies who *could* be intergenerationally mobile, given the occupational structures of their societies, are not (while the comparable Czech immobiles amount to about two-thirds). The question of whether "capitalist" societies do "worse" or "better" will be addressed below, when we return to consider these values in a comparative context.

The values for $\bar{r}^2$ look a bit different. These, it will be recalled, reflect changes in the occupational structure as well as circulation. Czechoslovakia's low score (8.4 percent of the variance is explained here, versus 12.9 for the socialist states as a whole) is a combined product of the openness registered in the I_B values, its advantageous starting point as the deviant, "developed" case in Eastern Europe, and a high gross mobility rate. Bulgaria's value, almost as low, is in fact too low, reflecting again the "mobility" created by the inclusion of state farm workers in the worker rather than peasant category, which overstates the outflow of a group drawn predominantly from peasant families. The other countries appear more similar, especially if one takes into account that the inclusion of women in the Polish data probably exaggerates inheritance vis à vis the Hungarian data. Similarly, the males-only Yugoslavia II sample shows less variance explained than the mixed-sex population of Yugoslavia I.

In all, and allowing for the many qualifications, historical differences among the socialist states do find some moderate if ambiguous echo here. Czechoslovakia, an industrial state by any definition, is a high-mobility society. Hungary and Poland, allowing for the effect of women's inclusion in the latter sample, seem somewhat more mobile and open than the Balkan component—Bulgaria, Romania, and Yugoslavia. Though arguments from such data as these must be tenuous indeed, the figures suggest that development may have more to do with circular as well as gross mobility than do differences in value systems. That Czechoslovakia leads here is no surprise, but that Poland and Hungary, the historical "gentry" states, should seem somewhat more open than the "egalitarian" peasant societies of the Balkans is more remarkable. Possible unmeasurable effects of development that may in an indirect way influence openness make one cautious here—it would be much better to have data on Yugoslavia for the early 1970s, for example. In any case, the differences we have found do not appear very large. Is there then a common, "socialist" pattern reflected in these indicators? There may be, but we must forego answering this question until we address, in the last part of this chapter, the comparable data for nonsocialist societies.

PERSPECTIVE: PRESOCIALIST MOBILITY

Do the rates of mobility achieved under socialism radically exceed those of the same societies before the onset of socialist regimes? That mobility under the new regimes has exceeded that of the presocialist 1920s and 1930s we may readily assume. The sustained, and on the whole successful, committment to economic development in the socialist period would guarantee this. Yet how large has the increase been? How immobile and closed were these societies before their revolutions? What evidence, if any, is there of specific political impacts on mobility which would suggest that changes in patterns were not simply functions of economic change? Finally, has socialism, independent of the changing occupational structure, made these societies more open? Have we, in other words, evidence that increases of whatever magnitude in structural mobility have been accompanied by increases in circulation or exchange mobility?

We know remarkably little about all of this, and the small Western literature on socialist mobility has hardly come to grips with these questions at all. Such as it is, that literature has suggested that such changes in mobility as have occurred under socialism are heavily, indeed almost exclusively, determined by economic development. Feldmesser, dealing in a 1953 article with the transrevolutionary "persistence of status advantages" in the USSR, argued convincingly that while the chances for persons of worker and peasant strata to reach nonmanual jobs did increase after the revolution, and accelerated massively with the economic development of the Plan Era, they increased because of the new space created by this transformation, and "*not at the expense* of those of nonmanual origin."[29] This does not mean that the Revolution was not expensive for a portion of the prerevolutionary nonmanuals. These, Feldmesser estimates, were intragenerationally downwardly mobile into manual ranks by 1926 to the total of about 10.0 percent.[30] A 90.0 percent "persistence" of this sort of advantage across the revolution sounds rather conservative. If the time frame were moved backward twenty or thirty years, what would we have found? Of nonmanuals working in, let us say, 1900, what proportion had suffered reverses in their careers by 1915 that placed them among the manuals? What proportion of manuals' sons entering the labor force between 1900 and 1915 started in nonmanual jobs? Ten percent? Five? One? We simply do not know—and lacking the knowledge, it is quite difficult to assess the impact of revolution on mobility, as opposed to the effects of economic development.

Socialist writings, understandably enough, picture the old societies as economically stagnant, hierarchically closed, low-mobility social systems. There are elements of both truth and propaganda in such characterizations, but most of all they are imprecise. The stagnation, closed nature, and restricted mobility of a society at one point in time can only be appreciated against measures of these characteristics in the same society at another point in time. And whether a society presents an "adequate" number of career opportunities depends not only on objective measures but also on what opportunity structure the members of that society view as adequate.

What might we expect in, say, a thirty to forty year period encompassing the twilight of an *ancien régime,* a revolution and its upheavals, and later an embarkation on the path of rapid economic development? Low intergenerational and intragenerational mobility in the old society? *How* low? Societies that are in their "twilight" do not necessarily know this, nor behave as we might expect. Both Tsarist Russia in the years after 1890 and Hungary in the late 1930s were experiencing rapid economic change that may have provided a base for rates of mobility that, if recorded, might belie any general characterization of stagnation.

What does a "revolution" do? If it leaves much of the old elite in their places, the old clerks and desk workers at their jobs, can it be a revolution? Surely it must rid itself of some: but do they appear at their new destinations in mobility data, or simply disappear? What can the revolution do *rapidly* for its constituency of workers and peasants? Promote them all to nonmanual work? Scarcely; but if not all, how many can be thus promoted?

Postrevolutionary economic development, as we have already seen, creates a good deal of mobility as peasants move into industry and the expanding intelligentsia and white-collar strata draw, as they must, on external recruits among peasant and worker offspring. But such developments are compatible with at least two outcomes: a final purging of the intelligentsia and lesser nonmanual categories of all old regime "holdovers" and their children, the gap to be filled by more of the "new men"; or, given the continuing need for manpower, the continued use of the holdovers, as well as their well-prepared offspring. It is, in essence, a political question, and politics decides it. Which alternative have socialist regimes adopted?

Answers to such questions are not easy. Revolutions, after all, are a messy business, and while their consequences are of great sociological interest, by themselves they do not generate much sociology. Our data thus far date from times well after the revolutions, when sociological research began to reemerge in situations of much greater social stability. Prerevolutionary data are even less to be expected, since research on mobility is itself generally an enterprise of the post–World War II period.

It is, then, gratifying to find that we do possess one data set that corresponds to some of our need, allowing us to examine mobility patterns in Hungary over a period from 1930 to 1973. The Hungarian National Statistical Office, in the national census questionnaire of 1930, included questions about the occupation of the male respondent's father, and followed the same procedure in the census of 1949. We have, thus, data crude in form but national in scope on intergenerational mobility for points fifteen years prior to, and four years after, the onset of socialism in Hungary. (In a somewhat rougher form, the 1949 data including both males and females were utilized in Miller's 1960 comparative analysis of mobility,[31] which provides some of our comparative material on Western societies in tables 4.20 through 4.26, below. These 1949 data were restructured to separate males and females, and reanalyzed in a somewhat different fashion than here by Dr. Rudolf Andorka of the Central Statistical Office, Budapest. Most of the original large tabular data sources,

Table 4.16.
Intergenerational Mobility, Hungary (1930); Census Data

Father	*Son in 1930* 1	2	3	Total	
1 Nonmanual	65.7	31.0	3.3	100.0	
	62,526	29,541	3,110	95,177	(3.6)
	38.9	3.0	0.2		
2 Worker	9.6	79.9	10.5	100.0	
	71,156	590,607	77,748	739,511	(27.6)
	44.2	60.1	5.1		
3 Peasant	1.5	19.7	78.9	100.1	
	27,235	362,613	1,455,445	1,845,293	(68.9)
	16.9	36.9	94.7		
Total	100.0	100.0	100.0		
	160,917	982,761	1,536,303	2,679,981	
	(6.0)	(36.7)	(57.3)		

SOURCE: adapted from Rudolf Andorka, "Historical Comparison of Hungarian Social Mobility, 1930–1963, by Means of Census Data and Retrospective Life Histories," (Budapest: Central Statistical Office; mimeo., n.d.), p. 4. Nonmanual: nonmanual; Worker: day worker, industrial worker, commercial worker, transport worker, artisan, shopkeeper, office attendant; Peasant: peasant; "Other" and "Pensioner" categories excluded.

including the males-only data in table 4.17, are unfortunately available as yet only in Hungarian.)[32]

In addition, the Central Statistical Office's 1962–1964 and 1973 studies (tables 4.3 and 4.10 above) collected complete occupational histories from their respondents, and these, in combination with the 1938 base point for father's occupation, allow a slightly different measurement of mobility over time for those in the sample who were working in 1938, or joined the work force later and were still employed in 1962–1964 or 1973. These data, adapted here for our use, allow us to compare sons' 1938 occupations with those of their fathers in 1938, and again sons' 1949 occupations with those of their fathers in 1938. The 1930 and 1949 census data, which provided only one undifferentiated nonmanual category, are presented in 3 × 3 tabular form, with "others" removed and other small changes, while the later surveys allow a 4 × 4 presentation.

Table 4.16, then, provides the census data of 1930. These show a mix of immobile and negative outcomes. Upward mobility of peasant and worker sons into nonmanual occupations is minimal, while less than one peasant son in five has moved into nonfarm manual work. For the working class, downward movement into the peasantry was somewhat more likely than an elevation into the white-collar ranks, while the sons of nonmanuals lose their place in about one-third of all cases, mainly falling into the working class. The impression of "immobility" is, of course, most clearly conveyed by these outflow figures. However, in *inflow* terms, the nonmanual stratum of 1930 is 61.1 percent of manual origin—hardly a hereditary stratum. These figures, in fact, compare favorably with inflow figures cited by Lipset and Bendix in 1959 from a large study in Germany in the late 1920s, and suggest that for some purposes, "backward" Eastern Europe's mobility patterns were not drastically divergent from the West's.[33]

Changes in the marginals are moderate, with the share of nonmanuals increasing from 3.6 to 6.0 percent, and similar changes in the other categories. The 1930 data reflect, it seems, the impact of two forces: a fairly substantial economic growth rate before World War I, when Hungary commanded the not inconsiderable resources of its part of the Hapsburg Empire, and the subsequent reversals of that war, the territorial changes that left only a "rump" Hungary and contributed to the economic stagnation of the 1920s. Many of those who are mobile in these data would probably have appeared in the same cells in a 1917 study, and are among the older persons counted in the census—especially those who are upwardly mobile.

The 1949 census (table 4.17) shows Hungary in the infancy of revolution, and is remarkably similar to the 1930 data in the impression it conveys. There is slightly more downward mobility. Nonmanuals inherit father's status 1.5 percent less often, while entering peasant ranks more often than in 1930, though still very rarely. Peasants' and workers' sons' chances of attaining nonmanual jobs are increased, although again the total proportion so mobile from such origins is small. The marginal distribution of fathers by occupational category changes very little from 1930, while the distribution of sons changes slightly more. Mobility has increased, but not very much. Hungary in 1949 is again the product of diverse and contradictory historical processes. The stagnation of the depression in the earlier 1930s gave way to rapid industrial growth later in the

Table 4.17.
Intergenerational Mobility, Hungary (1949); Census Data

Father	*Son in 1949* 1	2	3	Total	
1 Nonmanual	64.2	30.0	5.8	100.0	
	86,086	40,235	7,776	134,097	(4.7)
	31.0	3.7	0.5		
2 Worker	16.0	72.2	11.8	100.0	
	127,531	577,071	94,685	799,287	(27.8)
	45.9	53.7	6.2		
3 Peasant	3.3	23.6	73.1	100.0	
	64,162	457,614	1,415,766	1,937,542	(67.5)
	23.1	42.6	93.3		
Total	100.0	100.0	100.0		
	277,779	1,074,920	1,518,227	2,870,926	
	(9.7)	(37.4)	(52.9)		

SOURCE: adapted from Rudolf Andorka et al., *A tarsadalmi mobilitas torteneti tendenciai* (Budapest: Kozponti statisztikai hivatal, 1975), pp. 52–53, and Andorka, "Historical Comparison" (cited in table 4.16), pp. 9–10. Nonmanual: nonmanual; Worker: unskilled workers in industry, unskilled in commerce, unskilled in transport, skilled workers in industry, skilled in commerce, skilled in transport, office attendants, self-employed in industry, in commerce, in transport, other self-employed; Peasant: agricultural worker, small farmer, medium farmer; "Unknown" and "Pensioner" categories excluded.

decade as Hungary's economy geared itself to Germany's. The economic upturn continued through a good part of World War II, but the war finally brought devastation to the economy, especially the industrial sector. Postwar reconstruction had compensated for much of this damage by 1949, as the figures attest, but little further economic development had yet taken place. (A subcategory of workers, those specifically in industry, as the original data show, had grown only from a 55.5 percent share of the total in 1930 to 55.6 percent in 1949.)[34] A new political order prevailed, but its impact, reflected dimly in the slightly increased downward mobility of nonmanual sons, is hard to assess without separate classification of elite and routine nonmanuals. Land reform, by 1949, had had its own impacts—the status of many peasant sons who appear immobile here in fact was altered as they moved from landless to small-farmer status. Changed also for a time were the lives of some working-class sons who left urban employment (where their grip had been precarious), and, spurred by the reform, returned to the land, in greater proportions than in 1930. Such movement would decrease with the agricultural collectivization soon to come. Overall, the 1949 data show the seeds of a new society, but little more.

From a different angle, we can trace the changing mobility patterns from 1938, through 1949 and 1962–1964, to 1973, in data from the two surveys of mobility conducted by Andorka and his colleagues of the Central Statistical Office. Table 4.18 gives occupations of sons in the 1962–1964 study who were working in 1938, and the occupations of their fathers in the same year. While the retrospective nature of these data should caution one against making precise comparisons, it is notable that the sons' occupational distribution here is more modern than the 1930 census data, while in comparison with similar marginals for the 1949 census, these 1938 figures reflect an economy almost as developed: slightly fewer nonmanuals, all in all, but a smaller share of persons in agriculture and a larger share in the nonfarm manual sector than is the case in 1949. In terms of

Table 4.18.
Intergenerational Mobility, Hungary (1962–1964 Sample); Father's Job in 1938, Son's Job in 1938

Father	*Son in 1938* 1	2	3	4	Total	
1 Elite	56.0	25.7	18.3	0.0	100.0	
	98	45	32	0	175	(1.5)
	25.5	6.8	0.6	0.0		
2 Routine	22.3	37.4	37.2	3.2	100.1	
nonmanual	99	166	165	14	444	(3.8)
	25.8	25.0	3.3	0.2		
3 Worker	3.4	9.3	80.4	6.9	100.0	
	117	320	2,784	240	3,461	(29.4)
	30.5	48.3	54.9	4.2		
4 Peasant	0.9	1.7	27.2	70.2	100.0	
	70	132	2,087	5,397	7,686	(65.3)
	18.2	19.9	41.2	95.5		
Total	100.0	100.0	100.0	99.9		
	384	663	5,068	5,651	11,766	
	(3.3)	(5.6)	(43.0)	(48.0)		

SOURCE: adapted from Andorka et al., *A tarsadalmi mobilitas* (cited in table 4.17), p. 66. For composition of categories, see table 4.10.

economic development, 1938 was a rather good year. The reader will note that if this 4 × 4 table were compressed into a 3 × 3 form, the total nonmanual inheritance would, at 65.9 percent, be quite similar to the 1930 and 1949 census data. However, the likelihood of a worker's sons joining the peasantry is less here, while peasant sons' chances of attaining nonfarm manual work are greater than indicated in either the 1930 or 1949 censuses.

The separate classifications of elite and routine nonmanuals in this and the following tables demonstrate the differences in chances for mobility of the two nonmanual categories. Elite sons inherit in more than half the cases, while one-quarter take lower nonmanual positions, and the remainder, less than one in five, enter the working class. Of these, the vast majority become either artisans or skilled workers according to the original data—15.4 percent of the total of elite sons, or 84.4 percent of such sons whose destination is the working class.[35] Lower nonmanual sons fare worse—almost twice as many fall into manual ranks as ascend to the elite—but all in all well over half retain a place in the nonmanual strata, and almost one in four attains elite status. Their chances of elite entry thus are roughly six and a half times those of workers and twenty-five times those of peasants. For the routine nonmanuals sons who enter the working class, the destination therein is similar to that of elite sons: 78.8 percent become either artisans or skilled workers.[36]

In 1949, a different picture emerges (table 4.19). Some have now entered the working world who were dependents in 1938 and thus not in the previous table, increasing the *N* slightly. In collapsed 3 × 3 form, this table would show 68.2 percent of nonmanual sons inheriting their fathers' status: higher than 1930 and 1949 census data and higher than the same group in 1938, scarcely evidence of revolutionary "leveling" at first glance. Elsewhere, figures for workers' sons' status inheritance and downward mobility into the peasantry are similar to the 1949 census data, while peasant mobility into nonfarm manual work is greater. The most marked changes, however, are evident in comparing figures here for total peasant and worker outflow into nonmanual work with those in the 1930 census, and with the parallel data for this group in 1938. About two and a half times the 1930 proportion of peasants' sons, and almost twice that of sons of workers, are mobile into nonmanual jobs in 1949.

Table 4.19.
Intergenerational Mobility, Hungary (1962–1964 Sample); Father's Job in 1938, Son's Job in 1949

Father	*Son in 1949* 1	2	3	4	Total	
1 Elite	48.3	29.8	18.5	3.4	100.0	
	99	61	38	7	205	(1.7)
	19.2	6.7	0.7	0.1		
2 Routine	27.6	36.1	31.8	4.5	100.0	
nonmanual	123	161	142	20	446	(3.8)
	23.9	17.7	2.8	0.4		
3 Worker	4.9	13.2	70.3	11.6	100.0	
	188	508	2,700	444	3,840	(32.3)
	36.5	55.8	52.5	8.3		
4 Peasant	1.4	2.4	30.6	65.6	100.0	
	105	180	2,263	4,858	7,406	(62.3)
	20.4	19.8	44.0	91.2		
Total	100.0	100.0	100.0	100.0		
	515	910	5,143	5,329	11,897	
	(4.3)	(7.7)	(43.2)	(44.8)		

SOURCE: adapted from Andorka et al., *A tarsadalmi mobilitas* (cited in table 4.17), p. 67. For composition of categories, see table 4.10.

Between 1938 and 1949, the mobility increase for these strata is on the order of 150 percent. There *has* been, then, a change for the better in the peasant and worker mobility patterns between 1938 and 1949, and a good deal of it has involved career mobility of sons who started lower than their 1949 destinations.

Elite sons fare notably less well in 1949 than in 1938. Now less than half retain the fathers' status, more are in lower nonmanual jobs, and 3.4 percent are in the peasant category. Some elite sons have lost their 1938 positions, and others entering the work force later are placed lower than they might have been in 1938. There *has*, then, been a moderate casting down of old regime people, even though the size of the elite category has expanded absolutely and proportionately since 1938. Expansion in size, combined with the exchange mobility of political upheaval, has begun in fact the transformation of the elite. In 1938, it was composed predominantly of nonmanual sons (51.3 percent), elite sons occupying a 25.5 percent share. By 1949, elite composition has shifted in favor of the new men from the working class and peasantry—56.9 percent, while hereditary elite sons now make up only 19.2 percent.

Sons of routine nonmanuals on the whole suffer few revolutionary reverses. A slightly larger proportion winds up in agriculture, but on the whole, less descend to manual work in 1949 than in 1938, while more than one in four achieves elite status. Lower white-collar progeny seem beneficiaries of the revolution, rather than victims, though hereditary members of the category are clearly a minority of the total. In 1938 they, with their downwardly mobile colleagues from elite families, were less than one in three, by 1949, they are less than one in four (24.4 percent). Without the downwardly mobile elite sons, they made up 25.0 percent in 1939 and a minimal 17.7 percent in 1949. Peasant and working-class sons in large numbers have flowed into this expanding clerical stratum.

The evidence of revolutionary changes is here, then, but it does not overwhelm. The indicators of elite displacement or demotion, of purging of the servitors of the *ancien régime*, are clear but modest. Yet, of course, 1949 marks only the beginning of certain processes whose impact might have been more evident in a hypothetical table for around 1953. Political terror launched by the trial of Laszlo Rajk in 1949 and guided in the early 1950s by Rakosi removed large numbers of highly placed and middle-level functionaries from their posts, demoting some and sending many others to prison or exile (one estimate places the number of the latter, as of March 1953, at around 150,000 or about 1.5 percent of the total Hungarian population).[37] Were such upheavals visible in mobility tables, we might expect to see more impressive figures on demotion of those in the 1962–1964 study whose fathers were members of the 1938 elite. Thus, 1949 should not be taken as demonstrative of the full impact of politics on Hungarian mobility, but only as suggestive of the direction that events very probably took in the years that followed.

The next data set, for sons in 1962–1964, we have seen already in table 4.10. In the context of the earlier history revealed in the last two tables it evidences something of the old order restored, in the careers of sons of 1938 elite fathers. The elite inheritance and mobility pattern in 1962–1964 is more similar to that of 1938 than to that of 1949. Once again, more than half the elite sons are in their fathers' stratum, with fewer to be found among the lower nonmanuals. We may presume, and with good warrant,[38] that some elite sons, after a lower start, have intragenerationally recovered their fathers' status, while some younger sons of the 1938 elite, who entered the work force only in the late 1950s and early 1960s, did so not only with the certification and credentials that dictated elite placement, but also at a time when political prejudices against such backgrounds had abated.

This restoration, however, has not occurred at any great cost to the mobility of worker and peasant sons. The clear, if moderate, enhancement of their chances for mobility into elite or routine nonmanual positions between 1938 and 1949 has, because of economic development and the need for new cadres, grown further. As opposed to 1949, in 1962–1964 a worker's son enjoys a 77.6 percent better chance of entering the elite and 28.8 percent improvement in access to routine nonmanual jobs, while peasant sons' parallel opportunities have been enhanced by 92.9 and 75.0 percent, respectively.

Our final data set is that displayed earlier in table 4.3: the distributions of working males in 1973 by their fathers' 1938 occupations. A retrospective look at those data will show that, for this sample (which is not the same as that we have followed through the last three tables), little change has occurred except for persons of peasant origin. Slightly fewer elite sons inherit (54.4 versus 56.8 percent for the 1962–1964 data)—partially, and perhaps even wholly, as a result of a somewhat narrower definition of "elite" in the 1973 study.[39] On the whole, fewer elite sons skid to manual work (15.7 percent) than in 1962–1964 (18.9 percent). Fewer sons from routine white-collar background enter the elite, but since the direct inheritance rate in this stratum rises more, proportionately to the decline in elite access, in comparison with the 1962–1964 sample, their rate of descent into manual work lessens. Workers' sons suffer slightly decreased mobility into the elite, but for them, as for routine white-collar sons, this can be explained by the stricter definition of the category. There are fewer immobiles in the worker category as more sons move into lower nonmanual work and also into the peasant category.

Here we confront a case of factory to farm mobility that cannot for general purposes be interpreted as "downward." The 1973 excess of worker sons entering the peasant category is arguably a result of the changing job profiles on the cooperative farms themselves. Increasingly mechanized, and since 1968 freed by the reforms of the New Economic Mechanism to diversify into various light-industrial and service lines (taking up the slack of seasonal underemployment), the cooperative farms now afford real opportunities for the energetic and enterprising whose skills fit the *non*agricultural labor needs of the cooperatives. Rises in procurement prices and wages have also contributed to the transformation of the farms from stepchildren of the economy to viable and productive units, wherein the average annual income matches or exceeds the average for workers in industry—though work-hours are longer.[40] Thus for some a move from factory to farm in post-1968 Hungary has been economically advantageous.

Finally, the sons of peasants enjoy an increase of mobility chances almost as great as the change that took place between 1949 and 1962–1964 for the other sample. This time, the expansion of both the routine nonmanual and the worker stratum plays an important role, providing peasant sons with the most marked improvement in mobility prospects of all four strata, when we compare 1962–1964 with 1973. Excepting the peasants, however, the changes are moderate over this decade, and many of them are attributable to a changed definition of the elite in the 1973 data.

Thus has been the experience of Hungary, before and after its revolution. A society of limited mobility in 1930 owing to the lack of economic development prerequisites, it had changed rather little in this respect by 1949, owing to a continued deficit of structural mobility. However, as the figures showed, *in* 1949 and against the weak trend of upward structural mobility, some sons of the 1938 elite had lost their places. The figures suggest that the politics of the time did affect the mobility pattern, creating some circulation mobility that otherwise would not have occurred. The amount is modest: the "exploiters" sons have not been cast down in great numbers; but 1949, as noted earlier, probably marks the beginning of a process rather than its high point.

It should be interesting to examine these data with an eye to establishing the course of circulation mobility through these years.

We have seen that the fortunes of elite sons have improved from their low point of 1949—a restorationist tendency but one that involves relatively few people. The chances of peasant and worker sons to improve their lot need not have suffered, however, from these elite-inheritance tendencies: has circulation mobility increased or decreased over time?

There is some tendency for scholars to argue that circulation is on the decline in the socialist states. Frequently they cite in evidence the all-too-clear inequities in access to a resource so critical as higher education. Yet this focuses on access to the elite, and ignores other parts of the picture. If "truth" be defined by the indicators used earlier, the true picture seems in fact to be the opposite. When we calculate I_B on the four data sets (reduced to comparable 3 × 3 form), we arrive at

1938/1938	.86
1938/1949	.80
1938/1962–64	.78
1938/1973	.71

indicating an *improvement,* albeit small, in equality between 1949 and 1962–1964 as well as in the earlier period, and a further improvement in the decade most recently covered. Is it possible that we lose critical information in dealing with the collapsed version of the tables? This we can ascertain by analyzing the same tables in 7 × 7 form (the largest format that allows complete categorical comparability among the four data sets, since the 1973 data are reported in fewer categories). We get

1938/1938	.659
1938/1949	.634
1938/1962–64	.631
1938/1973	.558

which again points to the same conclusion. Along with the acceleration of gross mobility rates, there is an increase in circulation, suggesting that as structural mobility increased in Hungary, there developed as well a more open structure of mobility opportunities. It should be noted, however, that Andorka, using a somewhat different sort of procedure than employed here to separate structural and circulation mobility, arrives at a somewhat different conclusion with respect to any significant increase in circulation mobility over time.[41]

It is thus probably dangerous to reify too much the results of such measures. "Controlling" for changes in the marginals, the procedure upon which indices such as the one used here are based, is tempting—but it is difficult to get away from the reality those marginals express. As Blau and Duncan have observed, many such techniques yield results that still "rigorously imply" the marginals.[42] But the performance of Hungarian society, as recorded in the tables—the opening of opportunity for peasant and workers sons, the improvement of elite inheritance chances after the 1949 low—is a fact; for most purposes, the central fact.

Can the Hungarian experience be generalized to other socialist states? In a narrow sense, the answer must be an automatic no, since we have not the comparable data to make any firm judgements. But less systematic evidence does point to similarities between aspects of the Hungarian experience and patterns of revolutionary mobility in other states.

Polish data, for example, indicate a certain amount of precipitous upward and downward career mobility in the early years of socialism, with displacement of the old professionals. Top industrial management was especially fluid. One sample study shows 84.0 percent of enterprise directors possessed of higher education in 1945, a figure that declines to 36.2 percent in 1949, and to 19.7 percent in 1952.[43] In 1945, only 12.0 percent of directors were of "worker origin" (presumably, "origin" here refers to resondent's previous stratum or that of his father—the two frequently the same). In 1949, 53.7 percent were drawn from this category, and 62.2 percent of directors were of worker origin by 1952.[44]

Such figures indicate substantial displacement of industrial elites in the period of social revolution: intragenerational downward mobility for them (though many were shifted horizontally to less sensitive but still responsible posts outside production),[45] and likely blockages to status inheritance for their children, leading to lower starting points in the occupational hierarchy.

But few things last forever. Thus, we have also evidence from 1955–1962 of a process of "reproletarianization" of workers who had been promoted to nonmanual, administrative positions in the 1945–1955 period: according to one estimate, 85.6 percent of these career-mobile manuals were sent *back* to the bench.[46] Due to the clear oversupply of nonmanual functionaries in Polish industry at the time, not all of these were replaced. But while many vacancies were no doubt subsequently filled by worker and peasant sons who had by this time received the requisite education for their positions,[47] others were probably taken by offspring of the presocialist intelligentsia who, as in Hungary, might now enter careers at a point commensurate with their educations, or rise from positions in which politics had confined them.

Much of this seems to recapitulate elements of the Soviet experience in the somewhat comparable period of the 1920s. This decade was marked by the phenomenon of *vydvizhenie*—the promotion to supervisory positions, direct from the ranks and often without much special training, of workers and peasants. Sometimes displacing a bourgeois manager with a new "red director," sometimes simply filling spaces in a new political-supervisory hierarchy with a politically reliable "son of the masses," the *vydvizhenie* process was an early legacy of the revolution. But, much as their Polish counterparts a generation later, these career-mobile Soviet citizens suffered high rates of attrition from their nonmanual positions. As Feldmesser noted, between 1924 and 1928 seven central agencies of the USSR and RSFSR governments had at various times a total of 130 *vydvizhentsy* on the payroll; at the end of the period only 74 remained. In one RSFSR province, 306 persons were elevated in the *vydvizhenie* process between January and June 1928: 111 of their predecessor *vydvizhentsy* were dismissed at the same time. Dismissals outnumbered promotions in some districts.[48] Even so "red" a regime had to reckon with the costs of promoting the politically reliable nonexperts to functions they could not discharge. "The vydvizhentsy came in by the thousands, and by the thousands they returned to their old jobs. . . . The new bureaucrats could not match the skill and experience of the old, and the regime still insisted that its administrative offices function effectively."[49] The writ of *vydvizhenie* ran only so far—the consolidation and economic imperatives of industrialization terminated it in the early 1930s. In the first ten years of revolutionary Russia, through the late 1920s, representatives of the old order who remained in the country suffered many reversals—intelligentsia, merchants, nobility, military officers, landlords, clergy, and civil servants lost dignity, perquisites, and often their lives. Their children suffered discrimination in the quest for higher education. Yet most who remained, to judge from general evidence as well as the former Soviet citizens studied by Feldmesser, retained nonmanual posts, many at high levels.[50] The 1930s saw their children admitted again to higher education without any administrative obstacles comparable in strength to the cultural, educational, and economic advantages they enjoyed over the worker-peasant masses. A great increase (again, assuming a low rate of prerevolutionary mobility) would come in the access of workers' and peasants' children to nonmanual occupations.[51] But, as in Hungry and in Poland, it would come *with* economic development, as its corollary, and not because of great disadvantages imposed on their contemporaries of nonmanual origin.

In summary, it seems, both on the data and the logic of events, that revolution has its greatest *initial* impact on intragenerational mobility. Some elite representatives of the old regime are cast down, and some workers are promoted from the factory bench to supervisory positions. Such processes are most intense in the sphere of directly political positions, and less so elsewhere.[52] Both demotion and promotion processes will have some permanent effect. Some members of the old elite, even if young enough to reenter their previous work, do not rise again as the political climate moderates; some *vydvizhentsy* hang on to their posts. But many make a second move restoring original status.

Short-term intergenerational effects will likely involve two changes from the prerevolutionary status quo. Sons of the old elite or bourgeoisie may find, for a time, the doors of the higher educational institutions they normally would have attended closed to them. Hence, their placement at first job will be lower than it otherwise would have been. But some, making a virtue of necessity, will take jobs as workers, establishing a social status different from that of their parents, and then compete successfully for entrance to higher education.[53] While they have prior education and socialization going for them, governmental policy will also open wide the doors of educational opportunity to "real" workers and peasants—both the offspring who have not yet settled into work in these strata and those a few years older who may now be admitted under social quotas to higher education. Graduating, they will be placed in the middle to lower supervisory-administrative ranks of political and economic hierarchies. Over the longer term, their members will transform the composition of the elite.

The socialist revolution, then, leaves a legacy. That legacy, in its most political aspects, is still most visible in a state like Yugoslavia, where an authentic domestic revolution catapulted many young peasants, persons in their twenties in the civil war period, into the political elite as Tito's Partisans triumphed—"an opportunity never to be repeated for those of peasant origin to get on the escalator of social and political mobility on a large scale."[54] The first, most markedly political phase of revolution affects the posts of sheer *power* more than any others, thus touching "somewhat narrow spans of occupations,"[55] but very important ones.

The early phase aside, the fullness of the revolutionary legacy becomes apparent only as economic development accelerates. Then, mobility matrices tend to take on the shape one might expect in any society undergoing such rapid change, whatever its political coloration. Peasants come to the factory, workers' children rise to fill posts in the growing bureaucracies, sons of the white collar classes, cashing in on their advantages, assert a firmer grip on their fathers' status. Some apparent distinctiveness remains: highly visible examples of humble origin persons in the political elite (though far fewer in the scientific and technical elite), the majority worker and peasant offspring make in the nonmanual sector as a whole. But whether socialist revolutions write a whole new rule book on social mobility is doubtful, and the answer requires an examination of socialist performance against that of nonsocialist states.

PERSPECTIVE: MOBILITY IN SOCIALIST AND CAPITALIST SOCIETIES

How do the mobility patterns of socialist states, in both their structural and their circulation components, resemble or differ from those of nonsocialist countries? *Are* there distinctly socialist patterns at all? If so, are they marked across a whole range of different types of mobility, or confined only to some? Evidence in this section from twelve nonsocialist national studies (nine European nations plus Australia, Japan, and the USA), most of them familiar to students of mobility, allow us to attempt some answers to these questions.

In line with our earlier argument that gross mobility rates indicate important phenomena, worthy of attention even though they be mainly attributable to structural change rather than circulation, we look first at gross national figures. Table 4.20 summarizes upward and downward flow: sons of manual fathers moving to nonmanual work (first column) and sons of nonmanuals moving to manual work (last column). The two center columns give, where available, separate figures for outflow from worker and farmer/peasant categories into nonmanual occupations.

A first glance yields little except an impression of similar diversities in the first column. Socialist manual to nonmanual mobility runs from 13.5 to 29.0 percent, a range of 15.5 percentage points, while the nonsocialist range, 20.9 percentage points, stretches between a low of 9.9 percent and high of 30.8. Doubts about the quality of the Finnish data and hence the 9.9 figure may warrant eliminating it, giving us a nonsocialist low extreme of 17.1 percent and narrowing the range to 13.7 percentage points. All in all, the socialist countries average a manual to nonmanual rate of 18.6 percent against 23.8 percent for the other countries, excluding Finland.*

This gross examination of upward mobility leaves the socialist experience looking rather unexceptional. One can, of course, speculate that the scheduling of the studies is relevant here—that a similar set of Western studies conducted later in time, closer to the mid-to-late 1960s average for the socialist studies, might show some declines in manual to nonmanual mobility. Lacking longitudinal data, we can say little about this. But we *can* explore the possibility that the heavy *farm* component in the fathers' generation in Eastern Europe acts as a brake on the total manual to nonmanual mobility there, as opposed to the situation of the nonsocialist countries,

*Here we have treated Yugoslavia I and II as separate cases. When they are averaged together (16.9), the average socialist rate rises to 18.9. Taking Yugoslavia I alone, it falls to 18.5; with Yugoslavia II alone, the rate increases to 19.3.

Table 4.20.
Basic Indicators, Intergenerational Occupational Mobility, Socialist and Nonsocialist States

	Manual to nonmanual	*Worker to nonmanual*	*Farm to nonmanual*	*Nonmanual to manual*
Bulgaria	13.5	22.6	10.1	45.8
Czechoslovakia	29.0	35.9	20.6	38.4
Hungary	17.2	27.5	10.7	28.7
Poland	16.9	27.6	10.3	37.9
Romania	20.0	37.4	14.3	14.2
Yugoslavia I	14.5	27.9	10.7	32.7
Yugoslavia II	19.2	26.1	17.1	33.7
Australia	27.2	31.0	19.0	41.0
Denmark	24.1	—	—	36.8
Finland	9.9	11.0	9.0	36.1
France	22.0	27.8	17.2	35.0
Great Britain	24.8	—	—	42.1
Italy	17.1	24.9	11.8	26.7
Japan	23.7	—	—	29.7
Netherlands	19.6	—	—	43.2
Norway	23.7	25.8	22.1	35.4
Sweden	27.4	29.7	17.7	32.9
USA	30.8	36.1	22.5	30.5
West Germany	20.9	22.3	18.5	32.3

SOURCE: socialist states from tables 4.1 to 4.7, above; Denmark, Finland, Great Britain, Japan, Netherlands, Norway, and West Germany adapted from S. M. Miller, "Comparative Social Mobility," *Current Sociology* 9, no. 1 (1960); Australia adapted from L. Broom and F. L. Jones, "Father-to-Son Mobility: Australia in Comparative Perspective," *American Journal of Sociology* 74, no. 4 (1969); France adapted from M. Garnier and L. Hazelrigg, "Father-to-Son Occupational Mobility in France: Evidence from the 1960s," *American Journal of Sociology* 80, no. 2 (1974); Italy adapted from Joseph Lopreato and Lawrence E. Hazelrigg, *Class, Conflict, and Mobility: Theories and Studies of Class Structure* (San Francisco: Chandler, 1972), p. 380; Sweden adapted from Gosta Carlsson, *Social Mobility and Class Structure* (Lund: Gleerup, 1958), p. 93; USA adapted from Peter M. Blau and Otis Dudley Duncan, *The American Occupational Structure* (New York: Wiley, 1967), p. 95.

better-developed on the average. Blue-collar nonfarm sons ("workers") are mobile into nonmanual jobs in 29.2 percent of the cases in the socialist average, and 28.2 in the nonsocialist sample (again excluding Finland), averaging *only* those seven countries where nonfarm and farm manuals are separated. Here, then, the gross rates are close—indeed, virtually identical.

In both types of society, as previous research leads one to expect, outflow rates to nonmanual for farm sons are lower than for their blue-collar counterparts. The socialist average is 13.4,* that of the nonsocialist countries (grouped as above) 18.4, indicating the greater ease with which the peasant/farm–origin stratum can be evacuated when its size is the relatively modest one of a modern society. Among socialist countries, such a condition is met only by Czechoslovakia, but by many more of the nonsocialist states. The gap between worker and farm outflow is larger in the socialist than in the nonsocialist states, the ratio being 1 to .65 in the latter and 1 to .46 in the former. It is, then, an important historical and developmental characteristic of the socialist states that their heavy farm-origin sector acts to moderate their total manual to nonmanual mobility in comparison with the rates in the nonsocialist industrial states. The blue-collar workers of socialism, taken alone, enjoy parity on the whole with their Western counterparts in prospects for ascent to nonmanual occupations.

Shifting our attention to downward, nonmanual to manual mobility reveals other elements of interest. Despite the development that, in changing marginal distributions, demands upward mobility, nonmanuals' sons in Miller's 1960 exploration of comparative data showed greater tendencies to descend than did manual sons to rise.[56] Our data show a similar phenomenon. On the average, 33.1 percent of nonmanuals' sons are downwardly mobile, while 35.1 are in the eleven nonsocialist countries. (Given the nature of the Romanian data, which understate nonmanual to farm mobility, we would probably be warranted in excluding its suspiciously low 14.2 percent, yielding then a 36.2 percent average for socialist countries.) There is nothing particularly "socialist" about these figures, nor should their significance be overemphasized. First, those downwardly mobile from nonmanual ranks come from a much smaller stratum of origin than those upwardly mobile from manual to nonmanual. As rates, figures on the percentage of men with original advantages who skid may seem impressive. But taken as percentages of the total populations of the tables, they are much less so. Second,

*Again, treating Yugoslavia as two cases. Averaging them (13.9) yields 13.3; using I or II alone, respectively, gives 12.7 and 13.8 percent.

the nonfarm manual sector expands in most of our tables at a rate no less impressive than that of the nonmanual sector, creating more space for skidding sons of nonmanuals to occupy. In the socialist countries, this is especially so of the skilled sector of the blue-collar work force, and it is here that most skidding nonmanual sons come to rest.

A critical type of mobility is the outflow from various strata into the elite, with its implied consequences of access to scarce goods in the domains of prestige, property, and power (see table 4.21). Outflow patterns are quite diverse, both between origin strata and between the socialist and nonsocialist countries. Elite inheritance, as we see, is a rather strong tendency throughout, though the ranges, affected as they are by the size of the second generation elite, are wide.*

Outflow from nonelite strata into the elite is generally modest, though rather higher for the socialist countries on the whole. Where such outflow is quite high (as in Czechoslovakia, Australia, and the USA), we face rather well-developed societies in which the receiving elite stratum is itself quite large.

The advantage of blue-collar over farm sons in elite access is quite manifest in the socialist data, and evident though less so in the nonsocialist cases (though here Italy shows even chances and West Germany in 1955 a slight edge for farm-origin sons). The greater gap in the socialist countries is explicable: according to the standards of their own societies, cultivators were relatively worse off in Eastern Europe than in the West. The presence of some farm *owners'* sons in the Western data makes for a farm stratum with some advantaged people—but the lack of a substantial middle-farmer category in presocialist Eastern Europe as well as in the contemporary states makes for a farm stratum whose disadvantage in mobility competition is more readily predictable.

Turning to inflow figures, we see the consequences of revolution and economic development in sharp focus. The composition of current elites by social origin rather clearly distinguishes the social-

*Indeed the socialist range of 27.9 percentage points between Romania and Poland is most likely an "artifact." The peculiar nature of the Romanian estimate seems to minimize elite skidding, while the inclusion of daughters in the Polish data should minimize inheritance.

Table 4.21.
Mobility from Various Strata into Elite, and Inflow Coefficients for Elite

		From					*Inflow*				
	Size of elite (%)	*Middle*	*Manual*	*Farm*	*Worker*	*Elite inheritance*	*Middle*	*Manual*	*Farm*	*Worker*	*Elite inheritance*
Czechoslovakia	23.3	38.6	19.4	13.0	24.7	62.7	11.1	72.6	21.9	50.7	16.3
Hungary	6.4	24.9	4.5	2.8	7.1	54.4	17.6	65.2	25.4	39.8	17.2
Poland	9.6	27.9	7.6	4.9	12.1	42.4	12.6	73.2	29.1	44.1	14.2
Romania	13.3	52.6	7.3	5.2	13.8	70.3	34.2	48.3	25.5	22.8	17.4
Australia	22.0	34.5	15.5	12.2	17.0	43.7	20.4	53.9	13.3	40.6	28.3
Denmark	3.3	4.6	1.1	—	—	31.6	59.5	17.7	—	—	22.8
France	7.0	11.8	2.0	1.7	2.3	43.9	43.9	19.4	8.3	11.2	36.7
Great Britain	7.4	8.6	2.2	—	—	44.8	33.6	18.7	—	—	47.7
Italy	2.8	5.8	0.5	0.5	0.5	40.0	43.2	13.5	8.1	5.4	43.2
Japan	11.7	15.1	6.9	—	—	38.5	20.1	43.4	—	—	36.5
Netherlands	11.1	11.5	6.6	—	—	53.3	23.8	41.8	—	—	34.5
Sweden	6.7	18.3	3.3	2.0	4.5	54.5	34.0	41.0	13.0	28.0	25.0
USA	21.0	38.6	12.2	3.8	18.3	51.6	27.5	44.1	5.7	38.4	20.8
West Germany	4.8	8.6	1.8	2.0	1.6	53.8	45.8	26.1	11.1	15.0	28.1

ist from the nonsocialist countries. Persons of farm origin compose, on the average, 25.5 percent of the current socialist elites, and those from a working-class background 39.4, as against 9.9 and 23.1 percent for the nonsocialist elites. Thus, moderate outflows from the worker and peasant strata, when viewed as inflow coefficients in an elite, show a major impact. Elite expansion is, of course, nearly universal: even in the nonsocialist countries, inheriting elite sons never manage to hold even half the places in the current elite. But they are in no case swamped by the new men from below to the same degree as in the socialist elites. While the inheriting sons' lower limit is 20.8 percent for the West (the USA in 1962) this is still higher than the *largest* such figure for socialist societies (Romania's probably inflated 17.4 percent).

Persons of lower white-collar origin (our routine nonmanuals, the West's "middle classes" and so labeled here) benefit from their location on the upper side of the manual-nonmanual line and their consequent proximity to the elite stratum. Sons of this stratum are more likely than those of any other save the elite itself to enter the elite (36.0 percent for the socialist countries, 15.8 for the others). (The small size of the "middle class" as origin category in the socialist countries moderates the inflow consequences; socialist elites are no more "middle class" in origin than they are "hereditary." In the other countries, as the figures show, the more moderate outflow rates from larger middle classes have a much more marked impact on elite composition.) The outflow differences are quite large, and *do* reflect a difference in the career prospects of middle-class sons, attributable to their scarcity value in the socialist states. The only Western states that approach or exceed their outflow rates are those of the largest elites—Australia and the USA.

We return, again, to the skidders (table 4.22), this time distinguishing between elite and routine nonmanual origins where the data permit. Predictably, few nonmanual offspring skid so far as the farmyard; and, in the comparatively large farm sectors of the socialist states, skidders represent only an infinitesimal proportion. The impact of skidders is rather more pronounced in the nonsocialist countries, where the receiving farm sector is generally smaller, but the outflow figures too are somewhat higher, suggesting the possibil-

Table 4.22.
Downward Mobility: Elites and "Middle" Classes

	Outflow					*Inflow*			
	Elite to middle	*Elite to worker*	*Elite to farm*	*Middle to worker*	*Middle to farm*	*Elite to worker*	*Elite to farm*	*Middle to worker*	*Middle to farm*
Czechoslovakia	8.4	27.6	1.3	45.4	1.6	3.2	0.6	5.7	0.8
Hungary	29.8	14.1	1.6	30.5	4.0	0.6	0.1	2.7	0.7
Poland	24.5	30.0	3.1	38.4	3.1	2.2	0.3	3.8	0.4
Romania	21.6	8.1	—	16.5	—	0.6	—	3.5	—
Australia	21.7	28.3	7.1	41.4	4.7	7.7	7.5	10.3	4.6
Denmark	57.9	(10.5)		(38.2)		(0.4)		(38.2)	
France	42.5	11.6	2.1	37.4	2.3	1.5	0.7	21.0	3.6
Great Britain	37.3	(17.9)		(48.8)		(2.3)		(22.5)	
Italy	47.5	10.0	2.5	25.5	3.2	0.7	0.2	12.3	1.6
Japan	34.6	(26.9)		(31.6)		(4.7)		(7.7)	
Netherlands	22.4	(24.3)		(49.2)		(2.5)		(16.2)	
Sweden	32.7	9.4	3.4	30.1	7.9	0.6	0.5	8.0	4.4
USA	22.5	24.7	1.2	29.2	1.6	4.2	1.3	8.7	3.2
West Germany	28.8	15.0	2.5	30.7	3.1	0.7	0.4	15.6	5.2

Table 4.23.
Stability and Outflow of Elite Sons; Averages and Ranges for Socialist and Nonsocialist Countries

	Socialist countries	*Nonsocialist countries*
Elite stable	57.5	45.6
(range)	(27.9)	(22.9)
Elite to middle	21.1	34.8
(range)	(21.4)	(36.2)
Elite to manual (all)	21.5	38.5
(range)	(25.0)	(24.9)
Elite to farm	1.5	3.1
(range)	(1.8)	(5.9)

ity that for some nonmanuals the acquisition and operation of a farm may signal some advancement in personal and familial welfare.

For nonsocialist elites, short-distance downward mobility, into the middle class, generally is predominant over other forms of skidding—the exceptions here being the two states (Australia and the USA) where the elites are quite large to begin with. Czechoslovakia's large elite and quite small routine nonmanual stratum produces a similar but even more extreme pattern. Skidders from these three large elites face greater prospects of joining the blue-collar work force than of taking a nonmanual job at a lower level. Even here, however, they fade from sight in their destination stratum, dissolved in the large numbers of hereditary manuals.

The middle-class sons in nonsocialist states face substantial risk of entering the manual workforce: a ten-country average of 38.5 percent skid to worker or farm status, and their inflow impact among the nonfarm manuals, if not large, should by no means be thought inconsequential. Their socialist counterparts skid thus somewhat more frequently (41.0 percent, excluding the Romanian data which understate outflow to farming; including these produces a 34.9 percent average).

In which type of society do elite sons have a better grip on fathers' status, and in which type is skidding, when it occurs, likely to be more precipitous? Table 4.23 provides the relevant data. First, as the comparison of the average figures and the ranges between countries indicates, it is difficult to speak of clear patterns at all, in either socialist or nonsocialist countries. But, on the whole, elite sons inherit more frequently in socialist societies than in the others. (The problems with the socialist data, for these purposes, are in some measure self-canceling: Poland's data, including women, underestimate elite inheritance, while Romania's probably more moderately overestimate it; the Czech elite's size does not seem to foster inheritance nearly so much as it magnifies elite access opportunities for those from other strata.)

The sizable Western middle classes catch more skidders than the smaller comparable strata of Eastern Europe—though here the lack of separate recognizable patterns is quite clear, as the ranges exceed the averages. On the whole, however, a much larger share of elite sons skid to manual work in the nonsocialist states than in our four socialist countries, and more as well into farm occupations. Paradoxically or not, elite sons enjoy better guarantees of status maintenance in four postrevolutionary states surveyed between 1967 and 1973 than in ten nonsocialist countries studied between 1949 and 1964.

Earlier, we noted that the large farm-origin segment of the socialist samples acted as a brake on total manual to nonmanual outflow. But peasant sons and daughters are far from immobile—it is simply that for the most part their outflow is into the nonfarm manual sector. Worth strong emphasis here is the contribution such mobility makes to the total mobility in the socialist as opposed to the nonsocialist states. Table 4.24 gives relevant comparative figures.

The first column shows the proportions of socialist working population from farm origins who are mobile into nonfarm manual, mainly industrial work; the proportion is much larger than that in the nonsocialist states and is partly a reflection of the size of the stratum of origin. The second indicates the proportion of all mobile persons who fit the farm-to-factory category. Here we see that about *half* of all intergenerational mobiles fall into this category in the socialist countries, and closer to one-third in the others. Column 3 uses as a base all *upwardly* mobile persons, the figures indicating that if we know nothing of a socialist citizen other than that he is an intergenerational upwardly mobile, *we will be right more often than wrong in guessing that he is the working-class son of a peasant*

Table 4.24.
Impact of Farm-to-Nonfarm Manual Mobility

	Farm-origin mobiles into nonfarm manual work as:			
	% of N	*% of mobiles*	*% of upward mobiles*	*% of farm-origin mobiles*
Bulgaria	33.5	65.5	72.6	83.2
Czechoslovakia	19.8	35.7	41.5	71.0
Hungary	30.0	54.1	61.9	81.9
Poland	33.7	45.1	53.5	76.6
Romania	27.1	51.2	55.0	74.3
Yugoslavia I	18.2	49.2	57.9	70.4
Yugoslavia II	21.6	48.4	56.7	65.9
Australia	9.3	22.0	31.5	67.9
Finland	10.1	28.0	53.9	70.0
France	12.6	31.7	45.1	67.9
Italy	15.8	42.8	54.8	74.9
Norway	14.0	31.8	42.4	58.1
Sweden	17.6	37.7	46.9	70.1
USA	16.2	34.0	41.0	71.1
West Germany	10.3	28.1	41.2	67.6

father. Making the same guess in the other countries will leave us with more errors than right guesses.

Finally, while the large size of the peasant-origin stratum in all the socialist countries but Czechoslovakia renders the chances of farm sons to leave farming not particularly advantageous versus those in other countries, once we *know* that such a person is mobile, we can make roughly the same predictions as to his destination: an average of 74.8 percent of the mobile sons of farm origin in the socialist countries, and 68.5 percent in the others, join the blue-collar work force.

Thus, rates of gross mobility based on dichotomous manual-nonmanual classifications do not necessarily inform us of what the modal experience of mobiles is. Moving from manual to nonmanual work is important. But no less important is the transition wherein son, as father, continues to work with his hands, but makes the move from the seasonal and weather-regulated rhythms of rural life to the "artificial" schedules, different rhythms, and more certain monetary returns of factory work. In the socialist states, the latter has been the modal experience, and is related, in subtle and not-so-subtle ways, to the nature of socialist political and social life.

The similarities and differences observed here are products of a compound of factors, some of which are extraneous but, as in other comparative studies of mobility, impossible to control completely. The *time* of a study may be significant: a generally better developed Western state studied earlier in time (e.g., 1950–1955) will be more similar, in its "fathers' generation" distribution, to a socialist society whose sample was drawn later in time, while simultaneous studies would underline the difference in origin distributions that strongly affect gross mobility rates. The precise definition of strata is a persistent and nearly insoluble problem in comparative studies. It is less critical in the case of rough nonmanual-worker-farm trichotomies as we often use here, but much more so in dealing with cross-national differences in the composition of, and inflow and outflow rates for, strata such as the elite or middle class. A *large* elite of the Australian, Czech, or U.S. variety is simply not as exclusive, not as sealed off from other strata as a small one. Yet, given the essentially occupational definition of our strata, nations with differing occupational structures will have elites of different sizes. Insofar as this can be "controlled for" in secondary analysis, it is mainly by persistently reminding the reader of the pitfalls of too facile interpretations—as we have tried to do here.

The human experience of mobility does not take place under any set of controls, and thus this comparative discussion of gross mobility rates should provide some insight into that experience, East and West, worth digesting. But before departing from the topic, we return to the measures used earlier, and add another, in an attempt to get a final, summary view of the comparative openness of opportunity structures, power of the fathers' occupational distribution in determining that of their sons, and a clear idea of the balance of structural and circular mobility in socialist and nonsocialist states.

Table 4.25 restates the I_B and $\bar{r}^2$ values for the socialist states, adding this time the comparable values for the Western nations (all based on 3 × 3 tables). The ranges on the I_B index are not too dissimilar: .18 separates Czechoslovakia from Romania among the socialist states, .14 Australia from Italy in the Western sample. On

**Table 4.25.
Measures of Immobility and Dependence,
Socialist and Nonsocialist States**

	$\bar{I}_B$	$\bar{r}^2$
Bulgaria	.79	.091
Czechoslovakia	.63	.084
Hungary	.71	.109
Poland	.75	.155
Romania	.81	.178
Yugoslavia I	.74	.151
Yugoslavia II	.79	.133
Australia	.64	.140
Finland	.67	.186
France	.73	.216
Italy	.78	.249
Norway	.69	.134
Sweden	.67	.118
USA	.67	.113
West Germany	.71	.193

the whole, and perhaps indicating that a relatively open opportunity structure is a frequent companion of industrial modernity, the nonsocialist countries are as a whole more egalitarian (an average I_B of .695 versus .746 for the socialist countries). But our Western studies are on the average older than the socialist cases: would an updating show another trend? This is hard to say. Our most recent Western studies (Australia, France, Italy) are scarcely similar. In fact they bracket the range for the West. Many questions must then remain open; but for now, the data give us no warrant to argue that circulation mobility is greater under socialism than in the nonsocialist world, that socialist social structure is more open for both potential risers and sinkers.

A different picture is outlined by the values of $\bar{r}^2$ for the two samples. The fathers' occupational distribution explains more of the variance in the sons' (almost 17 percent) in the nonsocialist states than in the socialist ones (almost 13 percent), and there is much less overlap on this index. The weight of heredity among the socialist cases is heaviest in Romania, but four of the nonsocialist countries

(Finland, France, Italy, and West Germany), or half of their total number, register higher values yet. The Western values, again, might look different if the temporal parameters of the Western studies were more similar to the socialist studies; but the relatively low values for the socialist states *are* clear testimony to the mobility induced by rapid economic development. The differences here between the two sets of nations are of a middling sort—one could readily say "as much as" or "as little as" about the difference that separates the means. Such judgments the reader may make for himself.

Another mode of approach, not yet used in this chapter, provides perhaps the most convenient method of summarizing these data (especially for persons who find the statistical measures rather bleak), while at the same time directly separating the mobility generated by structural change from that attributable to circulation alone. This is simply a matter of taking the 3 × 3 variants of all our mobility matrices as base points, and then constructing alternative 3 × 3 tables wherein the sons' distribution does not differ from that of the fathers—as Hazelrigg did in a recent (1974) study.[57] Such alternative tables are arrived at by a simple, but lengthy, iterative process of successive adjustments—labor-intensive for a person, an easy matter for a computer.[58] The alternative table, preserving the fathers' marginal distribution, otherwise gives us the mobility data as they would be if no structural change had taken place.

Table 4.26 reports the different rates. This is a remarkable set of figures, in two senses. First, comparing the rates here with their real counterparts in table 4.20 brings home the dominant role of structural mobility. Without it, scarcely one manual son in twenty could achieve a nonmanual job in the socialist states, while close to two-thirds of nonmanual sons would lose, rather than inherit, that status. Even any moderate approximation to such a situation would have had profound implications for social unrest and instability in regimes that imposed economic and political privations on their subjects in the process of "socialist construction." These figures, then, highlight the critical function of mobility in the political sphere, suggested earlier in this chapter.

Second, the figures serve to highlight differences between the socialist and nonsocialist states that seem to inhere in their social

Table 4.26.
Basic Mobility Indicators, National Data Adjusted to Eliminate Structural Changes

	Manual to nonmanual	*Worker to nonmanual*	*Farm to nonmanual*	*Nonmanual to manual*
Bulgaria	4.6	11.1	2.0	64.0
Czechoslovakia	6.5	14.1	4.1	65.6
Hungary	4.3	8.3	1.8	61.0
Poland	5.3	10.7	1.9	64.4
Romania	4.2	12.7	1.4	30.6
Yugoslavia I	5.3	14.2	2.8	57.6
Yugoslavia II	8.2	17.5	5.3	51.6
Australia	18.9	23.2	9.4	52.5
Denmark	27.3	—	—	33.0
Finland	6.7	—	—	47.1
France	17.6	29.0	6.4	37.3
Great Britain	24.8	—	—	42.1
Italy	10.8	20.1	4.3	34.8
Japan	15.4	—	—	42.1
Netherlands	19.0	—	—	44.3
Norway	12.5	16.4	9.5	50.7
Sweden	10.4	15.0	5.8	56.3
USA	15.7	22.0	5.8	49.5
West Germany	15.1	18.4	9.8	38.4

structures, and that do not seem likely to be altered. As we see, the Western states, by and large, are "better" places to live if "better" be a function of limited risks of downward mobility and increased chances of upward mobility. There would be plenty of downward mobility in the nonsocialist nations if they were not developing, but less than in the socialist states if *they* were not, while the chances of upward mobility would be generally much greater. These figures, derived from an assumption of structural stasis, reflect both the impact of more modern Western social structures at the starting point (more nonmanual and worker positions, less farm slots) and some perhaps marginal advantages in "equality of opportunity" *narrowly* defined, in the Western countries. There is no compelling reason to expect that the historical/developmental gap they portray will be closed in the foreseeable future.

Thus we end a lengthy—perhaps too lengthy—exploration of a large amount of data. A page or two of conclusions might seem called for here, but such of them as the reader cannot already anticipate are left to the last chapter. In any case, we are not yet done with mobility. The data here speak eloquently to some concerns but they are mute on others. The anticipations, aspirations, and preparation for mobility in the socialist states today are the subject of the next chapter.

Chapter Five

Contemporary Mobility: Aspirations, Barriers, Outcomes

> . . . A manual worker's child today has on the average at least nine to ten times less chance to become a professional than a child of a university trained person or a manager . . . [who] has on the average at least twenty times less chance to become a manual worker than a manual worker's child.
>
> —S. Vrcan, *Praxis* (1973)

> Years ago, times were hard, but all the young people wanted to go to the university, they were willing to study hard for it. Now, it's different . . . my son, he could try harder, maybe go and get a degree. But he says he can get a good factory job, and make money *now*, and that's what he wants. . . .
>
> —Conversation with a Moscow taxi driver (1969)

MOBILITY TABLES, and the data they contain, portray the past—a record of advancement and decline, success and failure, already written. They are, in a sense, historical documents. But the successes and failures, realizations and abandonments of aspiration of the adolescents and young adults who are, in today's socialist societies, just entering the mobility competition are still prospective. We cannot chronicle their future success and failure, but we cannot ignore the factors that will influence them. This chapter focuses on the formative effects of the diffent social strata of their origin, the resources and collective self-images of those strata, and how these determine degrees of readiness for competition, aspirations (mainly educational) and their initial realization. Even with a great deal of such information, we cannot foresee mobility outcomes in any detail. Much depends on the sorts of structural changes or stability that economic development or stagnation will produce. What we can hope to arrive at is some understanding of the goals young people are motivated to pursue, why different categories of young people show similarities and differences in motivation, and how motivation and performance are related.

STARTING POINTS

The social world of the socialist countries has changed in shape, in the relative weight of various strata in its composition; but the strata themselves persist. There are fewer peasants and more industrial workers today than in the past: the latter category has grown at the expense of the former, and still shows signs of its origin. The nonmanual strata too have changed. Increasingly, the "intelligentsia" is composed of persons, relatively young persons, who have not only been educated under the socialist system but were born into it. Decreasingly but still to a significant degree, the composition of both elite and routine nonmanual strata reflects the periods of rapid growth, when external recruitment of urban and rural manuals filled opening spaces in the ranks.

For a hypothetically "mobile" person, the stratum in which he is born and in which he undergoes many formative experiences is in effect his starting point. A low point leaves room for much upward mobility, in the abstract sense that most change must be for the better. But it may be, in the concrete, quite disadvantageous, for those characteristics that make it a low stratum may include shortages in the attitudes, motivations, and knowledge necessary if one is to become even a credible competitor for higher status, better occupations, and greater rewards. A middling point places one closer to the top, but opens the prospect of a fall as well. A starting point at or near the top creates the possibility of a real fall, since positions in the higher strata are less plentiful. But as a rule it will confer resources that create a probability of status inheritance, or that at least tend to moderate substantially the distance one will travel downward from father's status.

These observations, derivable from many sources on mobility in nonsocialist societies, apply also to socialist systems. We will examine three different starting points—the village-peasant level, the urban industrial level, and the world of nonmanual urban work—showing *how* they apply today, and how the social changes of the last thirty years have modified their application.

THE VILLAGE WORLD

Writing about the village and its place in the broader social framework of the socialist states is largely a matter of emphasis. One can argue that, despite impressive economic growth, large-scale mobility from agricultural to nonagricultural work, and a diversification of rural occupational structures, a large gap remains between the village and the city, even after thirty years of socialism. Conversely, one can claim with full warrant that the yawning chasm that placed villager and urbanite in distinct physical and mental worlds in the period before socialism has narrowed markedly under it.

There is ample enough evidence to support either of these assessments. As an environment within which one internalizes ideas of what constitutes status, within which aspirations and plans grow, and as a staging-point from which one moves into the world of work, the village is closer to the city than in the presocialist past, yet still far enough removed to give both aspirations and fulfillment a particular flavor. This applies equally well in those countries where agriculture has been collectivized, in imitation of the Soviet precedent (Bulgaria, Romania, Hungary, Czechoslovakia) and in those (Poland, Yugoslavia) where the development of collective agriculture has been minimal.

The villages of presocialist Russia and Eastern Europe possessed relatively uniform and clearly articulated images of "the good life," "success," and the sort of achievement entitling an individual to claim the respect of his fellows. The criteria were, by and large, oriented to production rather than consumption—an image of "the good farmer." Status in the traditional village, according to one Czech source, was largely a matter of the number and quality of livestock, the produce yield, and the equipment of the farmstead.[1]

Clearly associated with prestige and entitlement to deference was the size of one's landholding; gradations from relatively large to minimal holdings were a recognized part of the social geography of the village, with the landless laborer at the bottom. Occupations related to but outside agriculture (grain milling, lumbering, etc.) fit into the village hierarchy only with some ambiguity, so strongly was it concentrated on farming as the normal activity of man. Relatively prosperous villagers who engaged in such occupations might use their excess resources to acquire more land and thus better define their place in the village hierarchy.[2]

The village was far from unworldly. Material possessions mattered a great deal. But rarely, and then mainly on ceremonial occasions, was this importance transformed into display. For everyday purposes, asceticism rather than hedonism (for those few who had a real choice between the two) in the use and enjoyment of material goods seems to have been the mode.[3] Status had, however, multiple if subtle modes of expression. As an ethnographic study of the Hungarian village of Atany reports, "parade harness" for horses, or an extra light carriage for use on special occasions, distinguished the relatively well-to-do peasant farmer from the humbler villagers. With wheat the staple of all diets, the quantity of fats and meats added distinguished the prosperous landholder from the person with a minimal plot and the landless laborer—"One who does not stick a pig is a real pauper." Within general conformity to peasant modes of dress, the prosperous could distinguish themselves with an extra, "good" broadcloth suit, while the common folk made do with one only. Moderate differences in the size and equipment of essentially similar houses provided one more cue to the owners's status.[4]

There is little of conspicuous consumption of all this; even display items in the villages were utilitarian. Such consumption, insofar as it developed at all in the presocialist periods, was an urban phenomenon, and even in the city, far removed from the blue-collar workers' world. Given the localized perspectives and the general poverty of village life when compared to the urban environment, "style" in the generally accepted sense was unattainable. The physical isolation of the worlds of city and village—most pronounced in Russia and the larger Eastern European states, but still marked where village and city were geographically close—rendered such "urban" concerns and criteria irrelevant in the countryside.*

If the village had its own standards for allocating status, different from those of urban folk, the same was true of the sphere of job aspirations and mobility orientations. As general concepts, these were scarcely part of the village mentality at all. For most, the village life was the only conceivable one. Peasant sons waited to inherit a portion of their father's land, even though division threatened to leave each with a parcel too small to sustain a family. Even the landless, with no hope of inheritance, found it hard to conceive of a future outside the village and agriculture. "Mobility," as an investigator of data from Polish peasant autobiographical memoirs of the 1930s concludes, meant progressive mastery of *farming* skills, advancement to more responsible farming jobs, rather than moving into some other occupational track.[5] Prospects in the nonagricultural sphere were few in Tsarist Russia, and in most of Eastern Europe hardly more promising in the typical periods of economic stagnation. The lack of skills applicable outside agriculture limited the jobs to which a migrant peasant, or peasant sons, could realistically aspire in the urban economy. Apart from such economic barriers, tradition itself—regard for one's elders and their opinions—militated against the development and persistence of nonrural aspirations. Sanders, in his classic study of the Bulgarian village of Dragalevtsy, notes the peasant parents' lack of enthusiasm for education, and their concern lest it turn their children aside from "proper" concerns to which such education was seen as irrelevant. While the children Sanders observed showed a desire to study, "many parents killed this enthusiasm. They either sent their children to tend the cattle, or, if the student gave lessons as an excuse for not doing some task, the parent said, "You don't need all that stuff from books."[6]

For all these impediments, the villages of Russia in the late nineteenth and early twentieth centuries, of Eastern Europe in the 1920's

*Of course, we are dealing here with the village as a *peasant* milieu. Landowning nobles in Russia, Poland, and Hungary, and other rich landowners, might spend a portion of the year away from the city on their estates, with an accompanying display of a very different standard of living. They were not, however, part of village life, and it seems as likely that their periodic appearances did as much to underline the gap between classes, and between the city and the village, as to bring them in any way closer together.

and 1930s, did experience outward mobility. But the move from agriculture to employment elsewhere was initially experienced, by many who made it, as necessary migration rather than upward mobility. The Russian peasant who left the land to work as a craftsman or to seek a job in industry was motivated mainly by necessity—a deficit of land, and taxes which demanded that someone in the household seek wage-earning nonagricultural employment. Conditions in the factories were not such as to make him feel that he had improved his status[7] by migration to the alien worlds of St. Petersburg or Moscow. A generation later, in interwar Eastern Europe, it was again the poor and the landless who were forced out of the village. Given the opportunity to farm an adequate plot, they for the most part would likely have stayed. The urban jobs to which they might aspire—in domestic service, unskilled labor, etc.—were irregular, low paid, and strange to people whose psychological compass did not really extend beyond the village. The city, for many, was a place of uncertainty—it could not beckon.

Still, some were hopeful as they left the countryside. There were those, such as the inhabitants of the *puszta* whose lives Illyes described, for whom any change seemed for the better: to them, Budapest in their imaginations "gleamed afar like a wonderful fairy palace shining high above the curse-ridden morass of the pusztas."[8] And from the villages, people like Lajos, the peasant protagonist of Laszlo Nemeth's 1936 novel *Guilt,* went to the suburbs of Budapest, the one area with some demand for unskilled labor, in hopes of finding work in construction. His reactions after landing a short-lived job as an unskilled building worker are valuable for what they reveal of the confrontation between his own simple world and that of skilled craft. We see him at work:

> From time to time, he stole a glance into the adjoining room where the carpenter was measuring off planks on a trestle. The man had big, bushy eyebrows, and as he bent over the board with his pencil and folding rule, he looked extremely learned. Even the thick hair protruding for his ears seemed to shroud the profound knowledge in his brain in its bush depth. It must be wonderful to be learned—thought Lajos, casting looks of deep respect at the man and his work.[9]

Like hundreds of thousands of real peasants, however, the fictional

Lajos found that work is short in hard times, and that finding one's place in the urban economy is difficult, as if the "whole town must have conspired against people from the village."[10]

Socialism and the economic revolutions it brought, in Russia after 1928 with the Five-Year Plans and collectivization, in Eastern Europe after World War II, changed the picture of the traditional village radically. "Pull" and "push" factors came into operation, accelerated mobility, and eventually changed the status structure of the village itself. An extensive economic growth policy created the "pull" of an unprecedented demand for factory hands. Urban life, alien though it had been, finally offered *opportunity*—money, secure employment, even regular hours. Collectivization, pursued to its conclusion everywhere except Poland and Yugoslavia, provided for many the necessary "push." Inheritance of a farmstead, in the old sense, became impossible, while compulsory free deliveries, low fixed procurement prices, and the oppressive organizational framework of the *kolkhoz* and its counterparts elsewhere served to drive many more from the land. In Poland and Yugoslavia uncertain prospects in the countryside plus a vastly more promising urban labor market generated much the same effect: private farmers began to find sons reluctant to inherit and assume the duties of proprietorship.

With increased mobility out of agriculture, the hitherto-divided status systems of city and village began to merge. It became realistic to compare urbanite and village dweller on the same scale, since their worlds were no longer sealed off from one another. The result was predictable—a decline in the attractiveness of farming under the new social system, and a general discontent with the farmer's lot, both in countries with "deferential" and those with "egalitarian" traditions.

The contemporary village, then, is mobility-oriented. Adults in farming see their status as low, and believe (in general accurately) that others view it so. The Polish sociologist Pohoski reported several surveys in the later 1950s in which farmers rated their incomes quite low and their prestige "average"; when asked how *non*farmer Poles regarded them, approximately two-thirds answered "low" or "very low."[11] Arutiunian's research in various Soviet rural areas on ratings of job attractiveness and on jobs respondents would most like to have allowed the construction of an ideal, as opposed to real, rural occupational distribution. Occupations classified in the "intelligentsia" and "employee" categories, peripheral to agriculture itself, are rated by far the highest, while unskilled, unspecialized manual work, in which the majority of the rural work force is engaged, rates extremely low. Arutiunian's survey of farms in the Krasnodar region, for example, shows 10.8 percent of the work force in intelligentsia and employee positions, and 64.4 percent in semiskilled and unskilled general manual work. Were respondents' wishes to come true, the first category would swell to 63.0 percent, while the semiskilled and unskilled category would shrink to 15.6 percent.[12] There is little status in being a collective farmer.

Nor is there much money. Generally, the incomes of farmers have lagged well behind those in the industrial sector. This in itself may be a sufficient reason for downgrading the farmer's status, but the general quality of rural life itself is important as well. In both Hungary and Czechoslovakia, where economic policy has raised the money incomes of farmers to a rough equality with those of urban workers, assessments of the status and attractiveness of farming are on balance no higher than elsewhere. Hungarians are still reluctant to see their offspring follow them into farm work, and in the prosperous Czech village of Komarov, despite the opportunities, the young are inclined to leave.

> These young Czechs seem to care little for the heavy outdoor work involved in farming or the episodic distribution of free and work time inherent in much of agricultural production. But least of all are they willing to give up the lifestyle that a city has to offer despite its inevitable inconveniences, which in most cases are considerable.[13]

No longer, then, does the older generation exercise a conscious braking force on the young, seeking to keep them on the land. In Zerovnica, a village in Slovenia, Winner reports a reluctance of many informants to see their children leave, balanced by a realization that the search for less hard life is, after all, rational and to be expected.[14] In Orasac in Serbia, Halpern's investigations show peasant parents, though reluctantly, accepting their children's nonagricultural plans as a shedding of "old ways, no longer valid."[15] Rosko's survey of 943 parents on 132 cooperative farms in Slovakia

(1965–1966) showed that, of about the three-quarters who *would* recommend future paths to their school-age children, only 40.7 percent wished to see their sons in agriculture, and 19.7 percent their daughters—and most of these only after further education. The remainder wished to see their offspring leave farming and receive further education before assuming a nonagricultural job.[16] In Romania, a similar survey ($N = 15{,}412$) focused on parental desires concerning their children's schooling beyond eighth grade. While farm parents were less committed to this than intelligentsia and working-class parents, fully 77 percent desired continued education for their children—a clear if indirect indication of a desire to see them leave the farm for a career elsewhere.[17]

Nor, of course, do the young show any great disposition to remain on the land. Data gathered by Soviet researchers speak most eloquently to the motivations of young migrants, for the USSR still manifests the largest gap between urban and rural living standards, opportunities, and satisfactions. F. N. Rekunov, interviewing eighth and eleventh graders (graduating classes) in rural schools in the Sverdlovsk area and in the Siberian region of Transbaikalia, found only 8 and 7 percent, respectively, of the eighth grade graduates intending to enter agriculture, while 13 and 10 percent of the eleventh grade graduating classes, presumably with less opportunity to defer entering the labor force and a more realistic vision of job openings, intended farm work. Much larger numbers actually were forced to work in agriculture, but doing so is felt by most to be "a personal drama, a dashing of hopes."[18]

The village, then, is situated differently in socialist society than in the presocialist period. In orientation, it is more open to influences from the outside, more *au courant* with criteria of status and prestige which are largely a product of the dominant urban world. A peasant is still a peasant, but no longer does he, or his son, assume that the latter will automatically inherit that status.

URBAN BLUE COLLARS: THE WORKERS' WORLD

The large mass of nonagricultural wage workers in the USSR and Eastern Europe is largely a product of socialist commitments to industrialization. It is therefore difficult to contrast the contemporary working-class world with its presocialist counterpart, as differences of scale are so large. The presocialist working classes of Russia and Eastern Europe were small and mixed: a core of skilled workers, adjusted to the urban environment, and a larger, fluid category of semiskilled and unskilled, mainly of rural background, who flowed into and out of the cities as economic conditions dictated.

Socialist industrialization demanded a large and permanent inflow into the nonagricultural sector, which only the peasantry could provide. The old urban proletariat (its economic condition worsening in the early years of "socialist construction," as allocations from national income for consumption were severely curtailed) was in Zygmunt Bauman's words, "dissolved in a vast mass of peasant migrants, to whom the living conditions they met meant a genuine improvement on the standards they had known. The urban environment, with all its deficiencies was incomparably better than anything they had experienced so far in the thick of the 'idiocy of the rural life.'"[19]

The *contemporary* working class is still close, chronologically and in a sense psychologically, to the peasantry, and thus perhaps inclined to utilize it as a reference group of sorts. How do workers evaluate their social position vis à vis the other strata?

Nowak, in a 1961 study of 2,167 Polish urban males, provided some answers to this question. Asked to rate their "social position" on a scale ranging from "very low" (1) to "very high" (7), skilled workers averaged a self-rating of 3.25, and their unskilled counterparts 2.65. These averages reflect choices by 45.1 percent of skilled and 66.4 percent of unskilled workers of the alternatives "lower than average, low, and very low." Certainly, such data bespeak a moderate self-assessment on workers' parts—hardly consciousness of being the "leading class" in a socialist order. Yet Nowak's data also indicate that among these workers, those who inherited this status from their fathers and thus can contrast their status directly with that of workers a generation before often feel that there *have* been improvements over time in social position. Of skilled sons of skilled workers, 39.0 percent felt that their position had improved, as against 18.6 percent who saw it worsening; parallel figures for second-generation unskilled workers were 31.2 percent versus 12.5

percent (with the remainder in each case uncertain that much change had taken place at all).[20]

Further indications of the worker's self-placement may be gathered from the refugee interview data of the Harvard Project on the Soviet Social System. These data are a decade older than Nowak's, but reasonably well fitted for general comparison because of that fact: Nowak reflects socialist Poland at about age 16, the Harvard data the USSR at 20–22—the pre–World War II Soviet society.

These data, as presented by Inkeles and Bauer, place the worker between the routine white-collar employee and the peasant on most major dimensions. In response to a question asking respondents to identify strata that received "less than they deserved" from society, workers were so identified more often than intelligentsia and routine white-collar workers but less often than peasants by respondents of all four categories, including workers themselves.[21] Similarly, workers' sons under 21 in 1940, and hence near the start of their careers, aspired to the same status in 40 percent of the cases, while half of peasant sons wished to achieve worker status, and only 13 percent were willing to continue in farming. (Only 3 percent of workers' sons aspired to farm work.)[22] Both strata viewed the worker's position as better than the peasant's. In summary ratings of job satisfaction[23] and satisfaction with pay,[24] workers generally fell between routine nonmanuals and peasants, with *skilled* workers equally or marginally overlapping the nonmanuals and the unskilled much closer to, but still placing themselves well ahead of, peasants' self-ratings.

The industrial worker, it seems, reads his place in the distribution of status and societal benefits much as the worker would in nonsocialist industrial societies. In an urban world, he is exposed to visible evidence of the managerial, administrative, and professional-technical strata above him. For all the poster art, workers know they follow rather than lead. On the other hand, except when grumbling over food prices and fantasizing tremendous profits for the growers, the worker knows well that his condition is much superior to that of the peasant: and the peasant world remains a real reference point for his assessment of self.

Not surprisingly, then, workers' feelings about their children inheriting their status differ somewhat from those of peasants. More working-class than peasant fathers, it seems, would be content to see their sons take up the same occupation. L. A. Margolin, in a study of workers and their children in the medium-sized Soviet city of Nizhnyi Tagil, reports that worker fathers are frequently satisfied to see their sons become workers as well. Their aspirations for their sons involve higher skill levels, cleaner work, intrastratum mobility rather than exit from it entirely.[25]

There is some evidence also of the foreshortened time perspectives, limited ability to delay gratification, and other components of "working class culture" familiar to students of stratification in the United States and Western Europe, which limit parental expectations. On the basis of numerous interviews, one Hungarian scholar noted: "Quite a few [working-class parents] were tempted by the possibility of earning money fairly early. Why go to school? He can become a good worker without further schooling and will earn money earlier and for a time he will get more, too, than a young man with a special diploma."[26]

Hungarian working-class parents do in some measure act on such convictions. To their influence must be ascribed at least in part the fact that only one-third of the children of skilled workers go to academic secondary school, while the rest learn trades in vocational institutions. Parents view academic secondary and higher education as "a path which is expensive and risky and the results of which are 'doubtful.'"[27] Given the immediate benefits of another earner in the household, many are quite ready to see a son in the factory before his eighteenth birthday.

But this is scarcely the complete picture. Hungary, indeed, may be something of an extreme case, with an educational system still structured much like the presocialist system (and in this resembling Poland), and thus formidable in appearance to working-class parents. Yet, for many such parents, and for their children, even if a worker's life is not seen as a disaster, a move up and out *is* a desideratum. Evidence here is diverse, but points clearly to higher aspirations in the working class.

In the Romanian study cited earlier, 88 percent of working-class parents desired that their children continue education into the ninth year. While many of these no doubt thought of a trade or vocational school, others saw academic high school as a path to advancement for their offspring.[28] A later Romanian study, investigating the career plans of 513 high-school students in six heavily industrial cities (where a substantial number, though not necessarily the majority, of students should be of working-class background) found only 1 percent ready to go "into production" upon graduation! Fully 87 percent aimed at a higher-education institution, and therefore a career outside the working class.[29]

In Yugoslavia, Mihailo Popovic observes that, while most adult workers may be content with their own lot (which, considering the heavily peasant origin of the contemporary Yugoslav working class, would represent significant upward mobility), they wish on the whole to see their children in nonmanual occupations. While 89 percent of workers in a 1959 inquiry were themselves content, 86 percent wished to see their children move up into the ranks of administrative employees.[30]

A 1963 survey of 15,000 Hungarian households sheds further light on parental aspirations—what careers, manual or nonmanual, they intended for their children. Workers seemed less than eager to see their children succeed them. Fathers who were skilled workers intended that their children enter nonmanual ranks in 57 percent of all cases, leaving 43 percent who, presumably, could seek working-class jobs with paternal approval. More moderate but still ambitious were unskilled workers, who in 34 percent of cases intended that their offspring enter nonmanual jobs.[31] Such expressions are not, however, easily reconciled with earlier indications that working-class children seem to be drawn *away* from the type of education that leads to such jobs, a discrepancy indicating the gap between long-run wishes, which may be cheaply entertained, and short-run contingencies where costs are clear.

On the whole, the picture of working-class mobility orientations is a mixed one. Elements of striving combine with elements of satisfaction with one's lot. A substantial number of the working class seem roughly satisfied with the general quality of their lives, or at least hold convictions that effort will not greatly improve their lot, nor their children's educational efforts *their* future lot.

CLEAN HANDS AND WHITE COLLARS

The world of nonmanual work is a diverse one, united in the end only by the work its inhabitants do not do. Its two district strata—the elite (or intelligentsia, taken broadly) and the routine white-collar employees—deserve separate discussions, though they are linked in several ways.

The elite is a broad category. It includes not only the "classic" intelligensia of the arts, sciences, culture, and the free professions, but also the managers of factories, the government and Party bureaucrats, the engineers and designers who work in industry. The workaday worlds of such groups are different. Their power and command over resources varies, as do their levels of education. But, given what previous chapters have shown, one might expect that members of the elite will be commonly conscious of an elevated place in the system, expect deference on the basis of their power, position, or expertise, and take measures to ensure that their descendants maintain this status.

Rather different is the position of the lower white-collar stratum, the eternal target of socialist anti-bureaucrat satire. This too is a mixed category, including lower-level supervising personnel (office managers, etc.) as well as rank-and-file processors of paper—clerks, typists, and the like. Should we expect that lower white-collar workers, like their Western counterparts, experience status anxieties especially vis à vis skilled workers at the top of the blue-collar hierarchy? Should we expect a high valuation of nonmanual work per se, even at modest salary, as the distinguishing mark elevating the white-collar father above the skilled worker whose individual pay packet may be equal or larger? Or, might we find that many are willing to see their offspring *enter* better-paid manual jobs, that the ideological exaltation of the working class has overcome the traditional sensitivities of the lower nonmanuals, leaving them free to follow simple economic calculations? Perhaps, but it should be noted that the ecology of their work situation places many lower white-collars in more contact with the intelligentsia than the setting of blue-collar workers does. It is, then, possible that the value placed on nonmanual work is enhanced by contact with the intelligentsia who demonstrate a more desirable status, a goal to be reached. It also seems likely that such contact provides cues and encouragement to aspire, if not for one's own career, then certainly for the future of one's children.

What are the realities? A goodly range of data, first of all, suggests that the contemporary intelligentsia values its place in society and does all it can to ensure that offspring will inherit the status of their parents. Parental resources, economic and cultural, are mobilized to rather good effect in an academic merit system, in pursuit of the appropriate credentials for the children.

The Soviet students of mobility Rutkevich and Filippov put the matter squarely in terms of "meritocracy."

> Socialist society has an interest in the selection of people who will bring the maximum benefit in the future as qualified specialists. . . . But it is well known that the level of preparation for matriculation depends not only on [a person's] natural abilities, but also on the material and cultural level of the family in which he grew up, the level of instruction in the school where he studies. . . . Thus, in otherwise equal circumstances, those have the best chance of entering higher educational institutions who came from more comfortable families, and especially those families where the parents' education level is higher; from large cities . . . etc.[32]

And, as N. A. Aitov observes, on the basis of studies in various cities in the Tatar ASSR, the intelligentsia, with their higher educational level, "provide much more help to their children in their studies, especially in senior classes, than do workers."

> If the parents have a high educational level, then the children, from very earliest childhood, are as a rule infused with a striving toward an intelligentsia profession. In other words, a *special psychological situation* is created. [Emphasis added.][33]

Another Soviet study, conducted in Estonia by M. Kh. Titma, concludes that intelligentsia parents have a profound impact on their children's values relating to expectations from work, professions that are acceptable or unacceptable, and other components of career orientations and aspirations.[34]

From the other socialist states come similar indications of the elite's consciousness of position and determination to see it passed on. Julia Juhasz observes that "the child breathes in culture and the demand for culture as soon as he begins to think"[35] in the households of Hungarian professionals. Parents of the intelligentsia stratum, indicating their plans for their children's careers in a large national survey, were willing in only 11 percent of the cases to see any of their children in manual work, while 68 percent wished an exclusively intelligentsia career for all their children.[36] In Morea's similar study of parental aspirations in Romania, only 1 percent of parents with higher education were willing to see their children terminate education at the eight-year level, and thus forsake an intelligentsia career.[37] The potency of home-infused cultural vitamins is evident in the enrollment profiles of Bucharest academic institutions that stress and require elements of "creativity." The Architecture Institute, the Music Conservatory, and the Fine Arts Academy in 1973 drew, respectively 53.0, 48.6, and 36.5 percent of their students from intelligentsia backgrounds (in the case of the conservatory, the figure includes children of white-collar workers as well).[38] These figures indicate overrepresentation of the intelligentsia stratum, and indeed an overdraft of Bucharest residents, ranging from 76.8 to 65.0 percent of the total enrollment. The two go together, to a degree: the capital city acts as a magnet holding those for whom higher education is a family trait, as well as retaining first-generation graduates who show no desire to return to the provincial life from which they rose.

Data from various studies show the intelligentsia possessing a high estimate of their own status. Nowak's survey of Polish cities revealed exactly 50 percent of those with intelligentsia occupations rating themselves very high, high, or above average in social position, versus 6.9 percent for skilled manuals.[39]

Limited but interesting data from Hungary—whose heritage, like Poland's, is one of a culturally legitimated inegalitarianism—strongly suggest that value is placed, not only on current intelligentsia status, but also on its being part of one's background; that hereditary intelligentsia may look down on *arrivistes*. Susan Ferge reports a study in various institutes of the Hungarian Academy of Sciences that found researchers of professional and clerical origin rating themselves "higher than average" on a prestige scale 1.5 times as often as their colleagues from worker and peasant backgrounds. The latter, though they had traveled a greater social distance and did see themselves as achievers, apparently reacted to the attitudes of their "better-born" colleagues. As Ferge puts it, "they may feel that in their environment they do not rank quite as equals."[40] As another Hungarian researcher observes, "culture" is a commodity critical to full acceptance in the intelligentsia, yet one not to be gotten through education alone. Its lack divides the newly arrived from those who have been there for more than their own generation, and finds expression in the conviction of some current intelligentsia whose fathers were also of the stratum "that too many of their colleagues have risen from below."[41]

Do such attitudes not hint at a measure of insecurity on the intelligentsia's part, a feeling that their status and benefits are either too conditional, insufficient, or both? Nowak's 1961 data certainly seem to point to this direction for Polish male intelligentsia. Of those whose fathers were also of the intelligentsia, 39.3 percent felt that the social position of the stratum had declined, while only 21.5 percent felt it had risen (this, somewhat paradoxically, against an almost even division—31.2 versus 33.7 percent—among the routine nonmanual sons of routine nonmanual fathers over whether their stratum had fallen or risen, respectively, in social position).[42]

Some of this malaise is, surely, attributable to the conditions socialism has imposed. The "compression" of the economic reward structure (which, even if it has not radically altered the hierarchy itself, has changed the distance between its ranks), the worker-peasant rhetoric, the tighter and more restrictive organizational network within which the intelligentsia function in socialist society, have all had effects.

Further evidence gives some insight into the complex interplay of reality and perception that underlies convictions about one's relative status. Table 5.1 presents data on 917 respondents in a study conducted in two Polish cities—Koszalin and Szczecin. Respondents are divided according to whether their stratum membership is inherited or "achieved" by intergenerational mobility (the latter, of course, implying downward mobility for some incumbents of all but the intelligentsia stratum). Three indicators—income levels, satisfaction with one's general material situation, and satisfaction with one's income as related to one's job—allow us to examine real versus perceived value of rewards. Several points are interesting. First, "inheritors" of intelligentsia and white-collar status enjoy better

Table 5.1.
Real Income, Self-ratings of General Material Situation and Income, by Occupational Stratum and Mode of Recruitment; Szczecin and Koszalin, Poland

		Real income (zl./mo.)		*Material situation*			*Income*	
		2,000 or less	*4,000 or more*	*good, v.g.*	*average*	*poor*	*satis.*	*unsatis.*
Elite	"I"	3.6	25.0	64.3	7.1	28.5	17.9	82.1
	"A"	10.4	13.4	75.4	7.4	19.2	24.6	75.4
Routine	"I"	24.3	9.4	67.6	12.2	20.3	37.8	62.1
nonmanual	"A"	31.9	2.2	69.9	11.0	19.0	34.9	64.6
Skilled	"I"	41.2	—	55.8	13.2	30.9	32.3	69.1
worker	"A"	39.5	0.5	46.1	20.2	33.2	31.2	68.2
Unskilled	"I"	59.5	—	49.3	11.4	39.2	34.2	66.8
worker	"A"	68.1	0.8	30.1	15.9	53.1	23.8	76.1

SOURCE: adapted from Antonina Pilinow-Ostrowska, "Ruchliwosc zawodowa i jej konsekwencje," in Wlodzimierz Wesolowski, ed., *Zroznicowanie spoleczne* (Wroclaw, Warsaw, Krakow: Wydawnictwo Polskiej Akademii Nauk, 1970), pp. 367–69.

incomes, on the whole, than "achievers" of such status. Proportionally, only about a third as many hereditary intelligentsia as achievers of this status fall into the lowest category, while inheritors in general reach the highest category almost twice as often as do the achievers. But despite their advantages, the inheritors are, as the figures on ratings of income and material situation show, less satisfied than their counterparts who came from other strata. Routine nonmanuals rate their material situation generally higher than does either category of manual worker, suggesting that we be wary of assuming too much about the impact of the alleged blue-collar–white-collar income overlap. More interesting, however, is the level of satisfaction with the income received, relative to the job position. Here, virtually two-thirds or more in every category are dissatisfied, but the intelligentsia, by far the highest paid, are most dissatisfied. All in all, these data tend strongly to support the observation of Wlodzimierz Wesolowski, who noted evidence of "dissatisfaction among circles of the intelligentsia because they consider their salaries as comparatively too low and not in correspondence with their knowledge and training (as compared, for instance, to that of unskilled or semi-skilled workers)."[43]

The intelligentsia is an important category, and in a broad sense its self-assessment and appraisals of its children's prospects are matters of concern to political leaders, who need its services yet are unwilling to provide the intelligentsia with autonomy. The resources of the intelligentsia are considerable, and while willing to buy some compliance from them through various concessions, the regime still guards its control prerogatives. A major resource of the intelligentsia is the general culture it possesses, the competence at abstraction it often passes on to its offspring. Thus, a strain toward inheritance of status, *especially* when, in recent history, it has meant offspring of presocialist "bourgeois" intelligentsia passing into the new socialist intelligentsia, is a matter of political sensitivity. Orthodox communist responses to the Prague Spring and the Warsaw student disturbances of 1968 have played on the dangers of inheritance. The Soviet sociologist N. A. Aitov, writing in 1970 and specifically mentioning Poland and Czechoslovakia, argued that the "old intelligentsia" reproduces itself through higher education, warning of their "antisocialist moods" and susceptibility to inflammation by "imperialist propaganda."[44] *Rude Pravo,* the Czech party daily, took the same line, and in addition warned those who had risen from humble backgrounds that they "ought never to forget" that socialism had "made it possible for them to study and make their way up the ladder."[45]

Whatever the phraseology, the concerns *are* real. The Czech intelligentsia of the 1960s did resent its material position. The radical leveling of the Czech income structure left them, as well shall see in more detail in the next chapter, disadvantaged in relation not only to counterparts in the West but also to the intelligentsia of the other socialist countries.[46] A part of the economic package of the 1967–1968 Czech reform movement was aimed at further stimulus though more differentiation of income, and the intelligentsia was bound to benefit from it.[47] But none of the reaction to the reformers' "assault on socialism" since 1969 has reduced the privileges of high Party and state officials.

The problem of inheritance of intelligentsia status has in recent years assumed a new dimension, as the parents' generation is increasingly made up of those who received higher education under socialism—the first-generation "socialist" intelligentsia. One can scarcely attack these as representatives of the old regime, and indeed the state does rely on their progeny, well prepared as they are for further schooling. Yet hereditary qualities are still anathema to propagandists and publicists who stress the openness of the opportunity structure under socialism. One of the most interesting attempts to resolve the problems was that of the Soviet researcher M. N. Rutkevich, reporting a study of the social origins of intelligentsia ("engineering–technical workers") in one Soviet factory.

> Above all, the fact commands attention that the portion of engineering-technical workers coming from specialists' families, *i.e.*, "second-generation intelligentsia," is very small—from 3 percent of the older specialists to 7 percent of the younger. This [share] grows somewhat as one looks at younger groups—but less rapidly than the share of specialists in the general population! Moreover, even at present among the employed population, specialists constitute about 10 percent, so that the share of engineering-technical workers, coming from the intelligentsia, is less than the share of intelligentsia in the whole population![48]

What Rutkevich overlooks, of course, is that none of these mid-1960s data speak to his point. The years after World War II saw immense growth in the size of the "technical intelligentsia" in the USSR—and these people were in large measure upwardly mobile, since there were no parent strata sufficient to supply the demand. Thus a low share of inheritors among older intelligentsia cadres is hardly striking (and in any case one should recall that the old intelligentsia distributed some of its offspring to privileged strata outside the engineering-technical intelligentsia). Among the younger, the share, though twice as high, is still small—but much of the current intelligentsia in the USSR and in the Eastern European countries has not yet seen its children complete schooling and enter the labor force. Certainly there is no evidence of a closure of the intelligentsia to all but those born into considerable cultural and economic privilege, but Soviet data of recent years do show tendencies for the most prestigious intelligentsia occupations to be mainly the preserve of those of intelligentsia and white-collar parentage.[49] On the whole, it seems that the socialist intelligentsia will be successful at replacing itself over the long run—passing on its advantages to a large number of its children, though not barring access to the talented who emerge from humbler strata. However, as long as regimes continue to view such inheritance as a "problem" worthy of sharp comment from time to time, the intelligentsia will retain an awareness of its somewhat exposed, though privileged, position.

What of the self-assessment of routine nonmanuals? Here, we can once again turn to Nowak's study of urban males in Poland. Those whose fathers were also in this stratum, as we saw earlier, are just about evenly divided over whether their social position has improved or worsened. But among male routine nonmanuals whose fathers were peasants, unskilled workers, or skilled workers, their convictions are heavily in favor of their upward mobility (65.4, 72.0, 61.7 percent, respectively) as against those who feel that a routine nonmanual destination has meant skidding from parental status (15.0, 2.0 and 17.3 percent, respectively). On the seven-point scale of social position, the routine nonmanuals rated themselves at a 3.78 average, versus the earlier-noted 3.25 and 2.65 self-ratings of skilled and unskilled workers.[50] All this suggests strongly that routine nonmanuals tend to place themselves hierarchically between the intelligentsia and the working class, and thus that routine nonmanual parents are likely to view their children's entering manual work as degradation; and perhaps, any but an intelligentsia career of some type for their sons (if not their daughters, so many of whom will be absorbed in the heavily feminized stratum of their origin) as a lack of achievement.

Similar conclusions may be drawn from Hungarian data. In the study conducted by the Central Statistical Office, only 21 percent of the routine nonmanuals were willing to see *any* of their children enter manual occupations, while 55 percent aimed at intelligentsia work for all their children.[51] Data that would be comparable to these are lacking for the other countries, but one can judge, from earlier evidence of the large number of workers and peasants who would like to see their children rise, that the white-collar strata in Romania, Bulgaria, Yugoslavia, and Czechoslovakia must not be too different. Even lacking the "traditional" Polish and Hungarian elitist ethos, these societies have absorbed the lessons of economic development and the implications of a modern division of labor sufficiently to perceive that the balance of rewards, psychic and economic, lies with those who do not toil in field or factory.

Still, some researchers contradict this view, pointing up some of the ambiguity of the routine nonmanual's place in socialist society. In another study of Polish routine office workers, male and female, in 1960, Lutynska reports a tendency for her 2,617 respondents to place themselves, independent of sex or position within the office, between workers and foremen. Educational level plays a role, with those possessing only primary education placing themselves below the workers; and those with secondary or more education locating themselves above the foremen. The type of workplace also seemed relevant, with office workers in factories tending to rate themselves below workers, while those in social or cultural institutions placed themselves above foremen.[52]

It is difficult to judge these against other findings. Lutynska is vague, despite her reference to little difference between the sexes, on the composition of her sample;[53] if it is representative, it is likely to be rather heavily female, as is the routine nonmanual stratum in general (with economic effects that will be treated in the next chapter), and thus tilted toward less supervisory and more routinized work, which females seem to monopolize within it.

Data yet to come may help to resolve some of these ambiguities. What does seem likely in any case is that the office workers, technicians, etc. who make up the routine nonmanual stratum have a good mental picture of the stratification hierarchy, in no way inferior in its accuracy to that of the intelligentsia. Although they rate it higher, they may well be less satisfied with their own status than even some workers may be with theirs, since their aspirations and perceptions of the top make their frame of reference different from the worker's. Clearly, they are at pains to distinguish themselves from the working class, and eager to move closer to an intelligentsia jealous of its own status. As one Polish researcher found, "the technician likes to be called engineer, and says he belongs to the technical-engineering group, whereas the engineer is inclined to stress his superiority to the technician."[54]

Do routine nonmanuals, in societies where ideology seems to place them below the skilled working class, manage to close this gap between themselves and the intelligentsia? Some observers of socialist stratification strongly doubt it, among them Frank Parkin, who sees little career promotion for such persons in the socialist states, contrasting this to Britain and other Western states where "clerical employment is often regarded as the bottom rung of a ladder which leads to junior managerial positions," and concludes that "they cannot really be regarded as forming the tail-end of a professional middle class in quite the same way" as in capitalist societies.[55] Perhaps so: but as Hungarian career mobility data (table 4.12, above) show, 29.0 percent of those males whose first job fell in the routine nonmanual category had, by the time of the 1962–64 survey, assumed elite jobs, versus only 3.8 percent of those whose first jobs had been as manual workers. Would Western rates for such career mobility be all that much higher? Soviet data for selected locales also suggest a rather high rate of career mobility into higher-level jobs from an entry point as a routine nonmanual; such evidence need not indicate that there is a direct route, a "ladder" whose span takes one from routine nonmanual work at the bottom to an elite position at the top, but it does raise the possibility that, especially among males, entry into the workforce as a routine nonmanual rather than as a worker signifies that one may see himself as "passing through," and likely to be attempting to gain the requisite further education for advancement in the somewhat easier circumstances of combining study with nonmanual rather than manual work.[56]

MOBILITY COMPETITION

We know something now of the characteristics of social strata as starting points for mobility at the socialist states. The strata, for these purposes, may be seen as collections of households whose adult members (parents) are characterized by certain attitudes and values relevant to the eventual success or failure of their children in the competition for scarce and desirable goods that underlies the processes of mobility. Depending on its economic, social, and psychic resources, a family fits its offspring for the competition in a more or less effective manner. The result may be a strong stimulus to strive for the heights—in some elite families, with a confidence that one is "naturally" fit for high-level work and that one possesses the resources to achieve it. It may be, on the other hand, an image of the world of work that is vague, limited in perception of competition or readiness to enter it, and a consequent acceptance that one will do the same kind of work as one's parents.

Families, however, do not dominate this socialization process entirely. The school now reaches larger proportions of the younger Soviet and Eastern Europe generations than was the case before socialism, and has an impact separate from though moderated by parental input. Schools teach knowledge, but they also socialize, inculcating particular images of the desirable and undesirable. They carry a rather uniform set of modern urban values and attitudes to national student bodies whose familial and environmental access to these may be quite diverse and unequal. Schools, to the degree that they succeed, can be expected to produce aspirations of a relatively uniform sort in students whose resources, whose chances of achieving those aspirations, are quite divergent.

Schooling is also the major avenue of mobility. It prepares, facilitates, "teaches," but also sifts and selects. A basic education of the elementary variety may still suffice, as it does in many industrial societies, for a basic job—unskilled or semiskilled manual work. But such jobs are the stuff of few people's aspirations. Failure to go further in the educational system may bar access to jobs that are seen as desirable. We saw, in the previous chapter, something of the impact of education for those whose mobility is already a matter of record. Now we turn to the role of education in recent or contemporary mobility processes, to examine the aspirations produced in youths by the combination of familial starting points and earlier schooling, their realization or denial in later schooling, and the factors influencing these outcomes.

ON THE PERFORMANCE OF DIFFERENT STRATA

Our data are, as usual, limited but also useful, and with appropriate qualifications provide some base for international comparisons. The researches of the Soviet sociologist V. N. Shubkin, much of which yet remain to be published, are of particular interest. These concentrate on an early but critical point in Soviet career development—the point of graduation from secondary (ten-year) school. What are the immediate plans of tenth graders, and to what extent are they fulfilled? How does social origin influence plans and fulfillment? Readiness to go into full-time work at the average graduating age of 17 implies a lack of any strong mobility orientations—at least those that involve leaving a working-class origin. Plans to combine work and study (by way of part-time evening courses) are more ambitious, but also ambiguous. The dropout rate from such courses is quite high. Plans to continue full-time study do show evidence of some ambition. Perhaps not all who plan to continue into higher education or further specialized secondary schooling have great aspirations, but those who *do* have them will be found here. Table 5.2 provides data from Shubkin's 1963–1964 research in the Novosibirsk region, combining the urban center and rural outlying areas, with plans reported before graduation, and real outcomes assessed the following autumn. Modeled after Shubkin's procedures was the 1965 Polish research conducted by Boiarskaia, whose data are reported in the lower panel of the table. Boiarskaia uses a different set of origin categories than Shubkin, a set more natural to the Polish context; her respondents are elementary school (seven-year) graduates, for whom continuing education does not yet mean higher education, and are for the most part rural youth, living in rural areas and attending rural schools in the Pulawy district, whose center is a medium-sized industrial town. The samples, thus, do not match, but they both help in addressing questions of interest.

The most striking impression is the near-universality of educational aspirations. The overwhelming majority of graduates desire to continue their studies, while the number ready to enter the labor force ranges from small in the Soviet Union to infinitesimal in Poland (a difference to be expected given the different ages of the two groups). If initial parental input differs greatly by stratum, we have evidence here suggesting that the school moderates the differences to produce a relative homogeneity of educational aspiration. But, from the evidence of parental aspirations earlier in this chapter, there is little reason to think that the parental inputs in the very basic sense of defining further education as desirable vary all that greatly by stratum. More likely, what we face here is a leveling and equaliza-

Table 5.2.
Post-Graduation Expectations of Soviet Secondary-School, and Polish Elementary-School Leavers, and Real Outcomes, by Social Origin (USSR 1963–1964; Poland 1965)

	Aspirations			*Outcomes*		
	Work	*Work/study*	*Study*	*Work*	*Work/study*	*Study*
USSR						
Urban nonmanual	2.0	5.0	93.0	15.0	3.0	82.0
Rural nonmanual	11.0	13.0	76.0	42.0	—	58.0
Worker, industry and construction	11.0	6.0	83.0	36.0	3.0	61.0
Worker, transport and communications	—	18.0	82.0	55.0	—	45.0
Peasant	10.0	14.0	76.0	90.0	—	10.0
Poland[a]						
Intelligentsia	—	2.4	96.4	—	1.4	97.2
Skilled worker	0.9	6.5	92.6	6.2	2.1	83.5
Unskilled worker	1.6	6.3	88.1	11.5	5.3	75.2
Peasant-worker	2.4	6.6	87.5	8.2	7.8	80.9
Peasant	7.4	7.0	80.1	30.0	6.0	60.0

[a]Polish figures do not add up to 100%; missing is original category "other/NA"

SOURCE: adapted from V. N. Shubkin, "Molodezh vstupaet v zhizn'," *Voprosy filosofii,* no. 5 (1965), and from M. Boiarskaia, "Problema vybora professii sel'skoi molodezh'iu," in G. V. Osipov and J. Szczepanski, eds., *Sotsial'nye problemy truda i proizvodstva* (Moscow: "Mysl'," 1969), pp. 102–4.

tion of aspirations[57] wherein parents and school play complementary roles, or at least wherein parents do not actively resist the new lessons the school teaches.

There are, however, some differences in levels of aspiration, and they run in the direction one would anticipate. Children of Soviet urban nonmanuals (intelligentsia and routine white-collar) overwhelmingly vote for further full-time education, as do their Polish counterparts (intelligentsia children). The two Soviet manual worker categories and the Polish workers and peasant-workers are behind here, but no great gap separates them from the intelligentsia. Comparatively least committed to further education are peasant children, yet any notion of traditional orientations toward immobility is dispelled by the fact that they too, by a more than 3 to 1 ratio, orient themselves toward further education.*

The critical differences are found in the success ratios of the different strata. In the USSR study, these are particularly marked. Almost 9 out of 10 of the children of urban nonmanuals who desired to continue full-time education did so. The successes of rural nonmanual and urban workers' children were much less, while peasant children desiring higher education met with disaster: 10 percent went on, while 76 percent desired to do so, and the 10 percent who initially intended to enter the work force were joined by 80 percent more of the total. For most of these, except for the possibility of later mobility into and within the urban working class, the race has been run, and they have finished out of the money.

At the less critical juncture between elementary and secondary education, the Polish sample shows less wholesale violation of expectations (quite natural, since the supply of places in secondary education in Poland is better synchronized with the level of demand than is the supply of places in higher education in the USSR). Still, success in attaining one's aspirations comes much more readily to children of the intelligentsia (indeed, they overfulfill their target) than to children of workers and peasants. Among the peasants, 3 out of 10, *or four times as many seventh-grade graduates as wished to do so*, enter the work force, most of these presumably on their parents' farms.

Reference was made above to the important rural-urban dimension in this process of mobility and selection, independent of the occupational status of parents, While our data do not allow us to control for this, table 5.3, which regroups some of Boiarskaia's data and adds comparable data from the Leningrad region, gathered by another Soviet researcher, should still be of interest. Vodzinskaia's

*The "rural nonmanuals" in Shubkin's data are an interesting case—their orientation toward continued full-time education is no stronger than that of the children of peasants (manuals in agriculture). We can be rather sure, however, that (1) the admixture of intelligentsia in the white-collar category in the rural areas is quite small, and that (2) the figures reflect, independent of this, the underprivileged status of the Soviet rural population, of whatever level. Given the large gap between city and village in educational facilities, cultural amenities, etc., the urban-rural axis is important in differentiating both aspirations and their fulfillment.

Table 5.3.
Post-Graduation Expectations of Soviet Secondary-School, and Polish Elementary-School Leavers, and Real Outcomes, by Urban-Rural Background (USSR 1964–1966; Poland 1965)

	Aspirations			*Outcomes*		
	Work	*Work/study*	*Study*	*Work*	*Work/study*	*Study*
USSR						
urban	1.3	12.5	86.2	14.0	12.8	69.3
rural	10.3	32.8	56.9	48.3	10.3	39.7
Poland						
urban	4.0	7.9	87.4	8.2	5.4	81.7
rural	6.1	6.5	83.6	21.9	6.2	67.1

SOURCE: adapted from V. V. Vodzinskaia, "O sotsial'noi obuslovlennosti vybora professii," and M. Boiarskaia, "Problema vybora professii sel'skoi molodezh'iu," both in G. V. Osipov and J. Szczepanski, eds., *Sotsial'nye problemy truda i proizvodstva* (Moscow: "Mysl'," 1969), pp. 41, 54, 99–100.

Soviet data are grouped according to the location of the secondary school attended—in Leningrad or in the rural areas surrounding—which also provides an indication of the students' residences. Boiarskaia's respondents all attended schools classified as rural; the "urbanites" are those who lived in the city of Pulawy itself. In both cases, outcomes are similar; urban children, whether the products of urban or rural schools, have somewhat higher aspirations, and see them fulfilled more often than rural children.

The processes that differentiate aspirations and also separate those of similar aspirations into winners and losers continue to operate, with more critical effect, in the higher reaches of the educational system. The evidence of general underrepresentation of worker and peasant offspring, and overrepresentation of youth of nonmanual and especially intelligentsia backgrounds in socialist higher education, is well discussed, and incontrovertible. Figures that showed offspring of nonmanuals in Poland occupying 45.4 percent of the places in higher education as against their 17.8 percent of the total population, and even more skewed parallel figures of 56.2 and 17.7 percent for Hungary in the earlier 1960s, no longer surprise one, and indeed the Soviet sociologist N. A. Aitov admits that in the socialist states as a whole, intelligentsia offspring are overrepresented by 2.5 to 3.0 times in the ranks of higher educational institutions.[58]

Having accepted the general fact of overrepresentation, however, we also find that within higher education, there is stratified access to various institutions and specialties. Americans readily distinguish the differences between Harvard and Yale and small state colleges. The British are still attuned to the distance between Oxbridge and the "redbrick" (and more recently "plateglass") universities. Poles, Russians, and others, for some similar and some different reasons, have many of the same perceptions of their own situations, and undergo sifting processes with somewhat similar outcomes. Table 5.4 derives from three studies: a Polish investigation of the social composition of student bodies in Warsaw higher educational institutions; a similar Soviet study in the city of Sverdlovsk (limited to members of the first-year class); and a Soviet study conducted in several institutions in the Baltic republics of Latvia and Lithuania.

The institutions in each panel have been ordered, as far as possible, to ensure comparability with those in other panels. Also, based on the author's unsystematic but I think reasonably accurate impressions of how students view the relative prestige of different types of institutions and specialties, the ordering in each panel is by prestige and difficulty of admission.

As we see, half to well over half of the students in polytechnics and medical schools are from nonmanual backgrounds—overrepresenting these groups even if one assumes that the student populations are drawn from the urban locales of the institute themselves, where one would expect a large number of nonmanual households. The academic demands in these institutions, their concentration in hard sciences, distinguish them from the economics, pedagogical, and agricultural institutes, which have on the whole more mixed student bodies. The case of agricultural institutes is particularly interesting. While peasant offspring are better represented here than in any other kind of institution, nowhere do they approach a majority. This attests both to the difficulties peasant offspring face in attaining a place in higher educational institutions and perhaps to the low attractiveness of any, even "modern" agricultural pursuits, which will leave them working in the countryside. But does the

Table 5.4.
Social Backgrounds of Students in Higher Educational Institutions, Poland and USSR, by Type of Institution

	Nonmanual	*Worker*	*Peasant*
Poland (1965)			
Warsaw University	59.6	21.6	8.0
Technological University	58.2	25.4	11.4
Medical Academy	66.4	13.9	9.5
School of Planning and Statistics	56.0	26.4	10.5
College of Agriculture	40.5	23.0	27.0
USSR (Sverdlovsk, 1968)			
Ural State University	52.5	43.7	3.8
Polytechnic Institute	64.4	34.1	1.5
Medical Institute	72.0	26.8	1.2
Economics Institute	47.3	49.5	3.2
Pedagogical Institute	56.2	41.8	2.0
Agriculture Institute	22.5	43.1	34.4
USSR (Baltic area, 1968)			
Latvian State University	47.7	40.6	11.7
Riga Polytechnic Institute	51.8	41.9	6.3
Riga Medical Institute	56.0	31.8	11.2
Daugavpils Pedagogical Institute	38.2	37.0	24.8
Liepaja Pedagogical Institute	27.8	49.0	23.2
Kaunas Agricultural Academy	26.6	38.4	35.0

SOURCE: adapted from Wieslaw Wisniewski, "The Academic Progress of Students of Different Social Origin," *Polish Sociological Bulletin*, no. 1 (1970), p. 136 (Polish data); M. N. Rutkevich and L. I. Sennikova, "O sotsial'nom sostave studenchestva v SSSR i tendentsiiakh ego izmeneniia," in *Sotsial'nye razlichiia i ikh preodolenie* (Sverdlovsk, 1969), p. 51 (Sverdlovsk data); Mervyn Matthews, "Soviet Students—Some Sociological Perspectives," *Soviet Studies* 27, no. 1 (1975), p. 91, citing "Sotsial'nye aspekty obrazovaniia," *Uchenye zapiski Latviiskogo gosudarstvennogo universiteta*, vol. 158 (Riga, 1970), p. 20 (Baltic area data).

nonrural student majority in these institutes testify to any desire on their part to contribute their services to the countryside? Scarcely. The point is that *any* degree is seen as useful and desirable, and the urban graduates of agricultural schools, matriculating there for the most part because of failure to gain entry to more prestigious schools, will (as will many of those who graduate from pedagogical institutes) generally seek jobs outside these specialties as soon as possible, relying on the general power of the degree, on the status of graduate, to make them more attractive in the labor market.

Perhaps surprisingly, the nonmanual dominance is not most marked in the universities that head each of the three lists, nor (except in Warsaw) is the peasant contingent the smallest in these institutions. Are the universities, then, more open in admissions policies? In a special, nonprogrammatic sense, yes. That is, the universities, as distinct from the other institutions, are composed of different faculties (departments), which are of different sizes and show very different enrollment profiles. In the Ural State University in Sverdlovsk, for example, nonmanual-origin students make up 67.2 percent of the difficult and limited-size physics faculty, and workers' children only 27.2 percent. In chemistry, the comparable figures are 71.8 percent and 21.6 percent. This is generally true of the hard sciences. On the other hand, the history, philosophy, and journalism faculties, all more ideological in content and evidently less intellectually demanding, have somewhat different profiles, with workers' children making up, for example, 52 percent of the journalism students.[59] The slightly more balanced social mix in universities, then, is a product of their more diverse structure, which provides offerings at different levels of difficulty with different degress of attraction for the nonmanual children who lead in the competition for university entrance.[60]

OBSTACLES TO MOBILITY

Differences in the performance of social strata in the educational segment of mobility competition are evident. They are scarcely unique to the socialist states, but they still warrant some discussion.

The most disadvantaged milieu is that of the rural village, despite all the progress it has made. Here, the obstacles to educational achievement come under four headings: parental attitudes and resources, village social structure, village education, and competing loyalties.

Parental attitudes are, as we have seen, not the obstacles they once were. As a path to something better for their children, education has acquired an almost talismanic quality in peasants' eyes. But here one major problem arises: for all their enthusiasm, peasant parents *understand* very little about the educational process, about how parental inputs can promote educational success. To lack such understanding is to lack critical resources. Thus while in a Hungarian village school both parents and teachers may threaten poor pupils with the prospect of a future in agriculture if their academic performance does not improve,[61] positive concrete steps are rarely taken to encourage that success. Judit Sas's investigation of Hungarian rural communities provides some interesting illustrations: for one, the historic pattern of heating only the kitchen in peasant households, and concentrating all family activities there in colder months, is still followed by many villagers with multiroom dwellings, leaving their school-age children with no place to study. There is no compelling reason why a bedroom could not be heated, except that it is "often incompatible with the village conventions and with the value system of saving."[62] Similarly, Sas found that less-educated villagers (who make up, of course, a large percentage of rural populations), while they will discipline children for disobedience to parental authority, generally do not make poor school performance a matter for discipline, as do middle-class families.[63] Lacking an understanding of the calculus of effort and outcome, their response to children's educational difficulties is generally fatalistic. These difficulties reflect a low level of general culture, of the fact that the rural adults still lag in educational level. But beyond lies the peculiar composition of the village itself.

Village social structure, compared to that of the city, is still relatively homogeneous. Most of the adult population engages in agriculture—some exclusively, others combining small plot farming with a nonagricultural job—while some reside in the village but are fully employed outside agriculture. The variance among the different socialist countries is marked in this respect, but in general the village lacks the occupational heterogeneity of the city, especially the admixture of intelligentsia the city provides. A village youth's exposure to different models of adult occupational roles is thus somewhat restricted, and his picture of the variety of the occupational structure limited. Perhaps more critically, the village social structure guarantees that the social composition of elementary schools will be heavily weighted toward students whose parents' educational levels, and command of resources to promote their children's progress, are low. Such an environment is weak in stimulation. For a talented peasant child, who might profit from the challenge of a more mixed school, it retards progress. The evident similarities between this line of reasoning and the burden of parts of the "Coleman Report" in the American context are confirmed somewhat by the research of the Budapest sociologist Susan Ferge. Ferge found that in *urban* schools, a high proportion of students from intelligentsia background ("students who are closer to the culture of the school") had a general uplifting effect on the academic performance of schoolmates whose families were less advantaged.[64] Homogeneous working-class urban schools, and *a fortiori* rural schools with their heavy peasant bias, can scarcely provide such opportunity.

All this would have effect even if rural schools possessed good equipment, committed and enthusiastic teachers, and parity in other respects with urban schools, But this is not the case, and rural education itself is a third obstacle to mobility. The low quality and underprovisioning of rural schools in the USSR is proverbial, and already too well documented to require further comment here.[65] The problem is similar in other socialist countries, even though the rural-urban school gap is not so great in the more compact states.[66] A rural child is quite likely, and an urban child quite unlikely, to undergo several years of instruction in a classroom where one teacher must divide time between several grades—reminiscent of the American "one-room schoolhouse" (the physical reality in many Soviet villages). The teacher who stands before the class is likely to be there unwillingly, because of a lack of better opportunities. No less than other trained manpower, teaching personnel in the socialist states much prefer the city to the village. In the USSR, where first-job assignments on completion of higher education are semicompulsory, 569 young teachers arrived, in a seven-year period in the 1960s, in a rural area of Sverdlovsk province; 639 left in the same period.[67] In Hungary in 1970, 4,014 secondary teaching positions, mainly in the villages, were available: candidates who manifested any interest numbered only 2,789.[68] School teachers in Poland are produced in university pedagogical faculties, and also by a swifter process in pedagogical institutes (similar to the traditional American "normal schools"). In the teaching market, the university graduates generally can command urban teaching positions. The institute graduates, with less training, are relegated to rural schools.[69] Often reluctant and disgruntled, they are ready to contribute further to the self-reinforcing cycle of rural educational disadvantage.

Finally, competing loyalties counterpose long-run abstract wishes for children's advancement via education to short-run perceptions of economic necessity in two ways, one specific to the rural life, one shared in some measure with the urban blue-collar world. First, agricultural work, whether on family farms in the predominantly still-private agriculture of Poland and Yugoslavia, or on the private household plots in collectivized systems, remains an area in which unskilled work is useful. School-age children, then, can be and frequently are used as extra hands in the family enterprise, setting up the competition between farm chores and schoolwork familiar in many areas throughout the world.[70]

The generally low incomes of peasants in the socialist countries induce a tendency, also present to a degree in the urban working class, to view younger members of the family as future extra earners, whose potential should be actualized at minimum age for leaving school. The deferral of earnings involved in lengthy education will not be accepted in many peasant families. The need for extra income may be especially strongly felt among the peasantry since, until quite recently in most states, they did *not* receive state pensions and many social benefits that urban workers did; aging peasant parents were the future dependents of their children. Long-run parental aspirations for their children may thus conflict with medium and short-run perceived necessities.

In this context, we should note that the relatively small differences between the aspiration levels of peasant youth and those of other strata do not mean no difference—that peasant youth necessarily aim at intelligentsia or nonmanual jobs just as frequently as do the children of current nonmanuals and industrial workers. Shubkin's Soviet data, for example, exclude the significant, if declining, numbers of peasant youth who were not completing secondary education at all, but instead entering the farm or, less likely, industrial labor force. Other data and impressions indicate that Soviet peasant youth aspire to places not so much in the nonmanual sphere as in urban industrial work of some kind,[71] and we may readily assume that some of the 76 percent who, in table 5.2, wished to continue their studies aimed not at the university but at specialized training in preparation for a skilled manual job.

Similarly, the aspirations of peasant students in Boiarskaia's Polish study are not completely clear from their desire to continue education. Their aims may be much more modest than those of skilled workers' or nonmanuals' children, but still such as to require schooling beyond seven years. As Adam Sarapata has demonstrated, peasant youth, in rating the attractiveness of a large variety of occupations, are rather *less* attracted to those that require the time and energy investments of a higher education than are similar youth from nonmanual and working-class backgrounds.[72] It would not be surprising to find that peasant youth view the university as a formidable prospect. The relatively high success rate of peasant students, once admitted to Polish and Yugoslav universities, indicates to some degree how selective their admission is, how much of an overachiever a peasant youth in a university has become.[73]

Obstacles to mobility in the working-class milieu seem to be much the same as among the peasantry, only less in magnitude. In their own histories of intergenerational and career mobility, many workers are still rather close to the peasantry. While the educational level of adult urban workers is higher than that of peasants, it is much lower on the average than the average level of education to which working-class children must aspire if they are to advance themselves beyond their parents' positions. The parents, while viewing education as desirable (although, as we noted above, with some reservations about whether the long university training is in the end more promising than the acquisition of a skilled trade), can offer little by way of stimulation and help to their children in their studies.

Low educational levels, monotony of work, and the flavor of proletarian city life combine to produce, as we observed earlier, elements of a "working-class culture," with many problems and pathologies similar to those in the West. It is from the urban working class, in the USSR and in Eastern Europe, that a disproportionate amount of negative phenomena—crime, delinquency, alcohol abuse—arise,[74] diverting some youth from accepted mobility channels. This is especially true in the unskilled stratum (which is far from disappearing) where living accommodations, dress, and "way of thinking as a group," in the words of two Polish writers, "above all brings to mind the pre-war proletariat."[75] The patterns of working-class adult leisure show little that is stimulating and much that, if absorbed by children, is conducive to a "killing time" attitude. Conversations with workers and artisans in one Polish town, focusing on their leisure activities, produced answers like the following: "I'm fond of going out, taking a walk, having a pint of beer and a chat with buddies," and "I've got no favorite occupation [hobby]. What can a man with two grades completed be interested in?" One wife summarized a common experience of working-class women: "My husband goes after vodka and sports."[76]

From such families, even if they offer generalized support for children's schoolwork, little specific help can be expected. One Hungarian investigator, interested in why workers' children rarely attended academic high schools or the university, found parents responding in good-willed helplessness. "I cannot help, for I do not know enough. It is up to the school to teach the child." "I do not have the heart to torture him with study. I let him play or tell him to go and get some fresh air instead. If he's done his homework, he does well, if not he brings home a bad mark. Am I to blame?"[77]

To place the full burden on working-class culture is, however, to go too far. We will see in the next chapter that working-class families are economically disadvantaged versus intelligentsia families, and also frequently so versus routine white-collar families when the income per capita within a household is taken into consideration. We should then emphasize here, despite generally held impressions, that education is *not* free in socialist countries. True, tuition is free, and students receive stipends, pegged sometimes to need as well as to academic performance. But stipends rarely provide enough for maintenance, especially if the student must travel to another city for higher education and rent a room in lieu of receiving scarce dormitory space. (Students from villages and small towns may even have to relocate to a regional center for full *secondary* education.) Students whose parents cannot supplement their stipends are in a much worse position than those who can draw on such resources. For working-class (and peasant) families then, the costs of "free" education involve not only a deferral of income, but also include current out-of-pocket expenditures that many such families cannot make, or that, as a result of long habit, they are unwilling to make. As Mikolaj Kozakiewicz puts it, "the very readiness to spend money on education is itself a cultural factor"[78]—here, the economic and cultural conditions of working-class and peasant life intertwine. Finally, as we shall see below in more detail, the size, density, and equipment of working-class households compare unfavorably with the accommodations of intelligentsia *and* lower white-collar strata. Overcrowding and cramped space render even more difficult the educational progress of a working-class child who, throughout the socialist world, finds himself in a school system that is, for all its revolutionary embroidery, *very* traditional in its academic demands and heavily reliant on homework.

All in all, then, children of parents who have relatively high educational levels, and who thus tend toward more prestigious occupations and higher incomes, have a better chance in the educational system: in access to it, and in remaining in it. The differential dropout rate in socialist primary and secondary schools is proverbial. Entering cohorts in the first year of primary school are, of course, "representative"—but the picture is gradually altered until, by the time eight to ten years have elapsed, the surviving cohort has lost, disproportionately, children of peasant and worker background, while the offspring of nonmanuals have come to assume their typical overrepresentation, before the competition for college entrance really begins. Various studies also indicate the dependence of school grades on parents' education and occupational levels.[79]

Thus, the many inequalities which result from the operation of the performance principle in the adult world of work have their impact on the young. It is understandable that many argue that this should not be the case, that, as one Yugoslav writer put it, the "position of pupils in the system of education must not depend on the status of their parents, even if that status derives from the principle of distribution according ot the results of labor."[80] But such an imbalance of advantage seems to be, as the experience detailed here indicates, an equally inescapable concomitant of capitalism *and* socialism in their contemporary forms, and one which only an inconceivable degree of regimentation could eliminate.

Is it appropriate to talk of obstacles to mobility, or to status inheritance, for young people who come from the intelligentsia and lower white-collar milieus? In an absolute sense, yes; the shortage of places in higher education clearly affects the percentage of aspirations fulfilled among these groups as well. Not all, despite their initial advantages, manage to secure a seat in the lecture halls. But the overrepresentation of both these groups (moderate among lower white-collar sons and daughters, quite marked among intelligentsia children), which intensifies through secondary education and into higher education, makes it more appropriate to talk of relative advantages, and their persistence across generations. For the intelligentsia, these are obvious. For the lower white-collar stratum, they seem to involve advantages in family size, in ratio of earners to total family members, and consequent higher per capita incomes than among skilled blue-collar families. Products not of chance but at least partly of design, these differences suggest that white-collar families conserve and mobilize their resources in a way much less characteristic of the upper reaches of the working class, and more on the order of the choices an intelligentsia household would be likely to make.

Thus, the general elite/intelligentsia–routine nonmanual–worker-peasant hierarchy sketched earlier in this book makes itself felt in aspirations and early successes and failures of socialist youth as they enter the competition. Social changes born of socialism have had a marked effect in homogenizing educational and career aspirations (though they have not completely done away with differences in their levels), and in making education available to the mass of youth. But they have done less to alter the patterns of differential access and achievement whereby the hierarchy, though its component parts be closer together today than ever before, still reproduces itself.

CHAPTER SIX

The Stratification of Incomes

The first and foremost problem of the construction of communism is not how to distribute justly but how to create an abundance of material values.

—M. Sakov, 1960

Upon seizing power, one segment of the movement's adherents begin to live off the revolution, instead of living for it. . . . They usually attempt to justify their position by claiming that the sum total of the privileges . . . is only a "trifle" as compared to the national income. First of all, however, all privilege in a backward country seems many times greater psychologically than in a wealthy one; and secondly, these privileges are hardly "trifles" in a moral-political sense.

—S. Stojanovic, *Between Myths and Reality* (1973)

GETTING AT economic inequality in the socialist states is no easy matter. The question of the differential distribution of material rewards is a sensitive one. Official discourse, even in countries like Poland, Hungary, and Yugoslavia, where such matters are rather openly discussed, very rarely employs such words as "rich" and "poor." Western specialists on socialist economies do not, of course, fear such words, and they have tackled squarely, over the years, many fundamental problems of income distribution, equality and inequality, under socialistm. Data have been and remain a major problem. One encounters statistics so fragmentary one wonders why the government censors did not simply turn down the whole rather than letting the unfortunate economist publish such trivialities; income distribution curves have been published virtually without labeling or numerical base points and thus necessitated elaborate detective work and "code-cracking" by the energetic investigator;[1] and there are other tantalizing, incomplete examples.

With such data constraints, Peter Wiles seems quite correct in claiming, in his attempt to compare American, British, Soviet, and Polish income distributions, that "all compendious formulae to describe an income distribution are thoroughly misleading."[2] Here, we will not attempt to deal with the stratification of incomes in "compendious formulae" at all. Our approach may strike some as simple-minded, indeed repetitive, but it is not without rationale. The questions that interest us diverge somewhat from those economists so often answer in Lorenz curves and Gini coefficients. The main focus of interest here is inequality not between individuals but between strata—the same strata we have identified previously. Answers to our questions are not so easily summarized in compendious formulae.

We try, in the succeeding sections, to give serveral concerns their due. The first deals with some aspects of inequality and distribution in (very rough) economists' terms, while the second specifies some sociological questions to address to income data. The third deals with income differences among socio-occupational strata, and the fourth with the slippery topic of the very affluent in socialist countries. The fifth section, drawing on elements in earlier ones, deals with the evidence for and against one assumed outcome of socialist revolution—the equalization or inversion of economic advantage across the traditional borderlines of manual and nonmanual work.

ON WHAT ECONOMISTS LOOK AT

One of the most common economist's instruments for dissecting the pattern of economic advantage and disadvantage in a society is the "quantile." It is of quantiles—most frequently deciles or quartiles—that tabular and graphic expressions of income distribution are generally composed. Quantiles let us know what proportion of total income is claimed by the best-off x percent of income receivers, what by middling groups, what by the lowest. It is here that we begin, reminding the reader that we are, as yet, far from addressing the question of *who* is poor or rich, or *what kind* of people they are.

Table 6.1 provides a start: quintile data on income for four social-

Table 6.1.
Income Distribution, Quintile Data, Selected Countries, 1960s

	Czecho-slovakia (1964)	*Hungary (1962)*	*Poland (1965)*	*Yugo-slavia (1964)*	*Austria (1962)*	*West Germany (1964)*	*France (1962)*
1	1.000	1.000	1.000	1.000	1.000	1.000	1.000
2	.744	.676	.649	.608	.622	.627	.485
3	.633	.519	.506	.482	.481	.508	.369
4	.511	.407	.396	.373	.383	.403	.292
5	.390	.264	.258	.262	.231	.224	.174
Percent of all income to (1)	30.5	34.9	35.6	36.7	36.8	36.2	43.1

SOURCE: adapted from Jiri Vecernik, "Problemy prijmu a zivotni urovne v socialni diferenciaci," in Pavel Machonin et al., *Ceskoslovenska spolecnost: sociolgicka analyza socialni stratifikace* (Bratislava: Epocha, 1969), p. 298.

ist states in the early-mid 1960s, and three capitalist countries. Here we have used a somewhat unconventional format to maximize information without constructing a large table. The table provides the shares of the fifth through second quintiles as decimalized percentages of the first, "richest" quintile, the top 20 percent of the population, and in the final row the percentage of total income going to that top 20 percent (from which readers interested can calculate the percentage of income going to each succeeding quintile). The data, adapted from a Czech source, indicate several interesting points. First, they indicate that socialist states are generally more egalitarian in income distribution than are capitalist states, judging by such figures as these: the richest quintile receives a smaller share of the total, and the poorest quintile a larger one (although the Yugoslav and West German top quintiles do overlap). Among the three capitalist countries, France's figures show it by far the most unequal, while Austria and West Germany are rather closer to the rough pattern of Hungary, Poland, and Yugoslavia. Second, Czechoslovakia is quite evidently more egalitarian than the other socialist states: its richest fifth claims quite a bit less of total income than the corresponding quintile in its socialist neighbors, and consequently each successive quintile is less disadvantaged versus it than in the other states. In fact, the poorest quintile receives an amount equal to

Table 6.2.
Decile Ratios, Workers' and Employees' Earnings,
Socialist Sector, Various Socialist States

	In 1960s	*1970*
Bulgaria	2.4 (1967)	—
Czechoslovakia	2.4 (1959)	2.4
Hungary	2.5 (1960)	2.6
Poland	3.1 (1960)	3.2
Romania	—	2.3
USSR	3.7 (1964)	3.2

SOURCE: adapted from Peter Wiles, "Recent Data on Soviet Income Distribution," *Survey* 21, no. 3 (1975), p. 33.

39.0 percent of the richest; much better than the poorest quintiles in the other socialist states, who have to settle for little more than 25 percent.

While such data are useful, decile ratios provide a convenient single figure to characterize a nation at various points in time. Table 6.2 provides some such ratios for earnings of workers and employees. These, as such things go, indicate a comparatively modest degree of inequality. With one exception, the ratios change little if at all over time; with *two* exceptions, they are quite similar in magnitude across the array of states. From these data, the USSR has clearly moved toward a more egalitarian distribution, but from a past point so inegalitarian that it still remains more so than the other countries. (Calculations from 1934 and 1956 data show Soviet decile ratios of 4.15 and 4.4, respectively,[3] indicating a degree of inequality not distinct from the developed capitalist economies of the time.) The USSR and Poland are both somewhat more inegalitarian in their distributions than the other countries listed.* with the USSR evidently on the move and Poland's pattern fairly stable. (Calculations on the distribution of gross wages in Poland, for example, give a decile ratio of 3.1 in 1970, and 3.0 in 1972.)[4]

Separate historical courses, such as those taken by the USSR and

*The absence of Yugoslavia here is unfortunate, since its more market-oriented economy makes it an interesting case.

Czechoslovakia, caution us against taking any degree of *current* similarity as indicative of a common experience over time with respect to income distribution and levels of compensation for various occupations, in policy or in fact. The USSR's experience, as noted earlier at various places in this box, has been one of marked inequality through much of its history. From Lenin's early counsel that the pay of Party functionaries should be no greater than that of a skilled worker, the Soviet Union had moved, with Stalin's denunciation of wage-leveling at the beginning of the 1930s, to an acceptance of large differentials: between manual and nonmanual work, between skill levels in industry, and between more and less favored branches. A large literature[5] has been devoted to tracing the dynamics of Soviet income distribution; the major findings may be conveniently summarized here:

1. Inequality increased in the period after 1930 (the beginning of planned socialist industrialization), exceeding even that which existed during the NEP period when a good deal of capitalist enterprise was tolerated.
2. Inequality probably peaked around the beginning of World War II. Certainly the 1956 decile ratio noted earlier in the text does not represent the *peak* of inequality, though it is an increase over 1934.
3. Since 1956, the movement has been toward less inequality—a rather steady process that marked certain gains in equalization by 1959, more by the early 1960s, and substantial further gains since then.[6]

The change has involved both "secular" (in the sense of nonideological) and, perhaps, normative factors. The first is itself linked with success of overall socialist development. Two scarce capacities—literacy and manual skill—had become much more abundant by the 1950s, permitting a reduction of the differential between the earnings of workers and those of the technical intelligentsia, and a reduction of the average compensation of routine clerical personnel to a point below that of the workers' average. Within the working class, pay differentials by skill were moderated through increases in minimum wages. Skills, too, became more widespread. But this leveling was scarcely the outcome of a disappearance of unskilled jobs. It was their persistence, as Yanowitch notes, that further spurred equalization. Such jobs, undesirable as they were, *had* to be filled, and the reluctance of workers with higher skills than such jobs required made an upgrading of their pay levels—a reduction of the tariff on skills—"a desirable policy."[7] This reasoning applied also to moves in the late 1960s to increase the economic welfare of the collective farm peasantry—the perpetual orphans of the Soviet economy—who had ceased to be a surplus category, and whose younger members showed strong desire to leave the countryside for jobs in industry and construction.

On the normative side Peter Wiles has argued that a strain toward consistency with two elements in socialist ideology also prompts the egalitarian thrust of recent times. First, "egalitarianism," though not announced as such, is now being pursued after its long Stalinist deferral. Second, the "simple Marxist bias in favor of manual labor,"[8] long an element of the ideology, has been given more play. Whether such normative forces are really at work in the USSR, and to what degree, is not certain—and in the nature of the case, probably not ascertainable. Events in the last decade do not rule out their operations, although another author stresses the *lack* of any egalitarian rhetoric accompanying these economic changes.[9]

Very different has been the experience of Czechoslovakia—in Wiles's words, "the only Communist country to be governed by genuine proletarians with genuine feeling that Communists ought to favor directly the manual worker."[10] (One might object somewhat—was Novotny, with whom he identifies this policy, genuinely proletarian? *He* lived rather lavishly. Wladyslaw Gomulka, on the other hand, presided over a markedly less egalitarian Poland from 1956 to 1970 but, it seems, lived quite modestly himself.) Whatever the authenticity of leadership conviction, Czechoslovakia has been indeed at the egalitarian pole of the socialist continuum, or so it has convincingly appeared to foreign and socialist analysts alike.

Czech egalitarianism, which we have noted in earlier chapters, occasioned critical comment both outside and inside the country to the degree that it seemed "extreme." As one American scholar of Czech birth wrote in 1961:

> While a certain reduction of the prewar disparity between the wages of manual workers and the salaries of managerial and technical personnel was undoubtedly justified, the opposite is true of the

extreme to which the rulers of communist Czechoslovakia have resorted. It is hardly justifiable on moral, social or economic grounds to pay an engineer, who had to study long years to obtain his diploma, only some 30 percent more than a manual worker with no more schooling (beyond compulsory school attendance) than after-work apprentice school.[11]

By the early to mid-1960s, as we saw in chapter 1, reform economists such as Ota Sik were also arguing the dysfunctions of wage egalitarianism, while the research on social structure conducted by the team headed by Pavel Machonin yielded similar conclusions. These were reflected in the 1968 "Action Program" of the Czechoslovak Communist Party:

levelling has spread to an unheard of extent . . . it puts careless workers, idlers and irresponsible people to advantage as compared with the qualified, the technically and expertly backward people as compared with the talented and those with incentive.[12]

What had happened to Czechoslovakia to produce this egalitarianism, so frequently played as a political card by the Novotny leadership in appeals to the workers, so frequently criticized before and during the Prague Spring by reformers who aimed at a simultaneous democratization of political life along with increased economic differentiation?

First, a certain amount of egalitarian sentiment was diffused broadly among the Czech working class—more so perhaps than elsewhere in Eastern Europe. Socialist and labor movements had operated freely in the interwar years, among a literate, articulate, and generally highly skilled working class, and had an impact on belief and ideology all the greater for the lack of historical elitism, *before* the onset of Soviet-style socialism.

Second, Czechoslovakia was, by the standards of the late 1940s, by and large a modern industrial society—far from the USSR of the "plan era" and thus far from the need for Stalinist wage policies. Skill and literacy were simply not scarce enough to command high prices, especially in an economy that was being driven into a extensive-growth pattern that deferred the development of new varieties of skill and expertise that *would* be scarce and costly. Czechoslovakia could afford an egalitarianism the less developed socialist states seemingly could not.

Third, there is reason to believe that Czechoslovakia, given its political complexion, *needed* an egalitarian income policy for stability. Well into the 1960s it remained, in the view of most observers, the most unreformed, "Stalinist" polity among all the Soviet client states. Novotny's Stalinism may be seen as an attempt to keep the lid on the only socialist country that had been a functioning democracy in the interwar years. Too many remained who remembered democracy, whose political socialization reflected it, to risk even halting "liberalization" and the threat to centralized power it would represent. Hence, the trade-off: for the democracy and freedom of expression that had been lost, and whose loss was *felt* by all, there was offered an equality of material status made possible by the relative prosperity of the country. As one writer puts it,

> just because the country was *already* industrial, it could use egalitarianism to compensate for the *other* deformation and buy off popular discontent in some measure, and postpone though "extensive" expansion that stagnation which, in the end, was the inescapable penality of the "egalitarian-bureaucratic" syndrome.[13]

Economics was a convenient sop. One may recall that the "good soldier Schweik" was a person who knew how to adjust. Not excessively greedy, he was happy with the little he had, as long as no one else had much more. This is what the Novotny regime aimed for, and, until the economic reverses of 1963, the policy worked rather well, keeping the Schweiks of the 1950s and earlier 1960s quiescent. This, too, was the diagnosis of the philosopher Ivan Svitak, whose words (from a 1968 speech) are quoted here:

> Another characteristic feature of this totalitarian dictatorship was that, for twenty years, internal political crises were avoided so long as there was something that could be reduced in price. And it must be said that this suited our people fine; it was enough for them.
>
> The regime survived at the expense of economic effectiveness. It made it possible for one to work less and worse for more money. It insured the legal and economic equality of a laborer with a university professor. Thanks to this, no noticeable opposition appeared in Czechoslovakia, even during the last decade, when our economic difficulties were growing. The State was led to bankruptcy, helped by the taciturn discipline of the controlled but thrifty citizens. . . .[14]

Thus, we have seen the extremes, and though historically, "egalitarianism" has been a highly variable commodity among the socialist countries, it seems generally accurate to say that the income distributions in the rest of Eastern Europe never reached, in the socialist period, the inegalitarian peak they attained in the Soviet Union nor the equality of Czechoslovakia.[15] By and large, by the standard methodologies of economics, socialist countries *do* manifest greater equality in the total distribution of individual incomes than do Western states. We may allow for many problems of comparability here, as well as the lack of opportunities for personal capital accumulation and investment, and question the meaning of the precise answers economics provides, but we can expect that both painstaking comparative studies[16] and such sources as United Nations comparisons[17] will continue to yield such conclusions.

Who, what sort of people, receive more and less economic reward under socialism? Answering this question will take us, soon, back to the four categories (elite/intelligentsia, routine nonmanuals, workers, and peasants) we have already employed, but another group basis of differentiation requires some attention first, since it crosscuts the occupational strata that form the major focus of this book. This is the differentiation of reward between *sectors* of the economy and between *branches* of industry.

Intersectoral differentials, reflecting differences in average rewards accruing to work in industry, construction, transport, trade, communications, agriculture, health and education, etc., are found in all economies, socialist or nonsocialist. Their socialist form reflects the impact of differences in labor-force composition, resource scarcities, levels of technology and skills—common to other types of economies—as well as "normative" decisions influenced by socialist ideology, perceptions of national need, and the weight of developmental history under socialism, which must have significant impact in systems so structured that the government sets wage and salary schedules centrally.

Thus, some common, socialist patterns exist: relatively high rewards for work in construction, which remains a priority sector in nations with perennial housing deficits and commitments to policies of growth, as well as rewards above the total-economy average for those in industry and, often, in transport. Conversely, as the early locus for forced savings to finance industrial growth, as an area where labor and its availability is somewhat less controllable, and finally as a sector low in skill and high in the risks imposed by nature, agriculture has remained low in reward.

So too, on the whole, have been the education, health, and related sectors. Here, socialist planners have banked, not unsuccessfully, on the relevance of psychic rewards to offset the relatively low compensation of sectors that provide employment for a large body of females of high and medium qualifications. Employment in trade at the retail level and in other consumer services suffers a double burden: however necessary, trade remains an ideological stepchild whose "productivity," even under fully socialist auspices, is in doubt, and draws heavily on unskilled female labor. Its rewards are, correspondingly, low. These general patterns are evident in Table 6.3.

Indeed, with the exception of Yugoslavia, whose intersectoral pattern diverges from the more "orthodox" socialist economies, the service sector as a whole receives rather short shrift in the economies of the USSR and Eastern Europe—a function of the priority assigned to "productive" sectors and an apparent decision by socialist planners to place the burden of supplying services on the consumers themselves.[18] The outcome of such a decision is reflected starkly in the constant complaints about services in the socialist press, and in their cause, the atrocious quality of those services, especially in the retail/consumer sectors, throughout the socialist world.

Intersectoral differentials mean that workers or employees of equal skill and qualification will earn more, or less, depending on the sector in which they make their livings. The same is true of industrial workers and employees, according to the branch of industry in which they work. At certain points, interbranch differentials in average wages bulk large enough so that, as some Soviet data indicate, manual workers in an exceptionally well-paid branch may average more earnings than specialists (engineering-technical personnel) in branches of lower priority and reward.[19] Thus, the more extreme interbranch differentials provide the base for a certain amount of the overlap between manual and nonmanual earnings which we shall be examining throughout this chapter. Summarizing a picture whose detailed presentation would detain us too long, it suffices to say that heavy industry, now as in the past, retains a priority in socialist planning. Extractive industries and metal fabricating are the sources of "producer goods" and the place of employ-

Table 6.3.
Monthly Average Earnings, Workers and Employees, by Sector, 1964 and 1973

	Bulgaria		*Czechoslovakia*		*Hungary*[a,c]		*Poland*[a]		*USSR*		*Romania*	
	1964	*1973*	*1964*	*1973*	*1964*	*1973*	*1964*	*1973*	*1964*	*(1971)*	*1964*	*1973*
Industry	102.6	101.5	105.9	100.2	100.5	99.9	107.8	101.5	111.5	109.5	104.0	99.1
Construction	121.8	116.1	113.6	111.8	103.8	107.8	116.3	122.7	117.6	122.6	106.1	111.0
Agriculture[b]	87.3	93.0	86.4	94.9	85.7	95.9	81.4	NA	78.4	84.4	90.5	95.2
Transport	111.5	114.2	113.5	115.1	99.3	104.6	101.5	103.6	113.4	114.4	98.7	104.0
Communications	82.6	89.1	88.7	88.1	—	—	—	—	81.4	78.8	92.6	85.2
Trade	88.1	90.1	83.1	84.7	88.2	91.3	81.4	82.0	72.9	77.0	86.5	88.4
Education	92.1	96.0	88.1	95.1	—	—	91.8	90.7	73.0	85.3	97.7	101.3
Health	85.5	89.2	81.3	97.4	96.2	99.9	79.4	86.0	87.1	73.8	92.4	94.9

(Average for whole economy = 100.0)

[a]"Transport" row combines transport and communications. [b]State-sector agriculture only.
[c]"Health" row combines "administration, health, and cultural institutions."

SOURCE: 1964 figures adapted from United Nations, Secretariat of the Economic Commission for Europe, *Incomes in Post-War Europe: A Study of Policies, Growth and Distribution* (*Economic Survey of Europe in 1965*, Part 2) (Geneva, 1967), ch. 8, pp. 66–67, ch. 12, p. 14; 1973 figures adapted from national statistical yearbooks.

ment of large numbers of skilled, well-rewarded (and predominantly male) workers—the proletarian core of industry. At the other end of the spectrum, as an examination of any number of statistical yearbooks will show, are the light industries producing goods destined immediately or indirectly for personal consumption—textiles, clothing, leather and footwear, food processing. These branches tend to be more feminized, with the lower rewards that planners seem to attach to such industries by virtue of their lower priority, and perhaps as well as by virtue of the unspoken conclusion that women are generally secondary earners and therefore *can* be rewarded on a lower scale. Just as the service sector as a whole underperforms, the shoddy quality, scarcity, and high prices of clothing and footwear in socialist countries seem to bespeak the low place in the wage hierarchy occupied by their producers.

Socialist wage-setting, for branches and sectors, is a complex process, taking into account needed skills, the arduousness of labor and work conditions, and so on.[20] But it also involves those normative elements noted above, whose imposition in a centrally controlled economy, made possible in the last analysis by a monopoly of power, gives a particular character to the reward hierarchy. As we have noted already, these differentials cut across our categories of intelligentsia, lower nonmanual, and worker, with some effect. While the figures in table 6.3 submerge the gaps between factory directors and unskilled labor, it *is* the case that a director of a plant in the consumer sector will generally earn less than his counterpart in a complex metallurgical plant, and that skilled and unskilled workers will also show differences in reward depending on their branch/sector locations.

What drives, or draws, a person to one branch or another? We cannot go much beyond generalities here, and without forgetting that *some* centralized information services and labor-recruitment mechanisms still exist within the generally unregulated socialist labor market, we might suggest that accidental and contingent elements play, together, an important role—much like the forces, *mutatis mutandis*, that Jencks argues are important in explaining occupational and economic outcomes in the USA:

> chance acquaintances who steer you to one line of work rather than another, the range of jobs that happen to be available in a particular

community when you are job hunting, the amount of overtime work in your particular plant, whether bad weather destroys your strawberry crop. . . . [21]

This is not, of course, the total picture. Beyond the factors that determine the initial branch or sector in which one finds work, the problem of job-switching or "labor turnover," a massive one in the USSR and scarcely less in some of the Eastern European states, calls to attention a number of factors: climate, regional differences in levels of wages for similar work, the amenities of large urban over rural or semi-rural locales, and even differences between cities in this respect, all of which evoke intersectoral mobility in socialist workforces. Many of these factors are, in the particular forms they take, rather peculiar to socialist states, and play a lesser role in the United States of which Jencks writes. While they have been dealt with by other scholars,[22] and fall largely beyond the scope of class and stratum differences on which this book concentrates, it is well to remind the reader here that some of these factors, especially differences in amenities and in the provisioning and "prestige" of life in major cities like Moscow, Warsaw, Budapest, etc., and life as lived in second-rank cities and towns or the countryside, form a distinct dimension of the inequality that socialist citizens experience in their daily lives.

Economists deserve, no doubt, an apology for the brevity with which their concerns and questions have been treated here; those with more sociological and political interests, however, may be now be impatient to get on to the rewards of the socio-occupational strata that cut across the branch and sectoral boundaries just discussed. Of these rewards and their differences, previous chapters have already given some indication, but it should be worthwhile to specify some of the areas and questions about the rewards of different strata that call for attention and treatment from the perspectives of sociology and political science.

ON WHAT SOCIOLOGISTS SHOULD LOOK AT

Socialism is "about" equality—historically. But socialism, in its Soviet and Eastern European manifestations, has also been "about" economic growth and development. It triumphed not in the developed economies of the West where Marx expected it, but in areas backward by comparison. Thus it has been faced with the problem of stimuli—how to make people do a certain sort of work, make them do it well, and make them do a lot of it. Stimulation and equality were not readily reconcilable, and the conflict between them, as we have seen it emerge, was not one for which socialist doctrine was well prepared:

> the whole tradition of socialist thought, including its Marxian wing, had long been imbued with the vision of eliminating the income inequalities associated with capitalism. While there were differences within this tradition with respect to the timing and the extent of the increased equality expected under socialism, there was nothing in socialist thought to suggest that the new society would ever require a widening of income inequality among workers.[23]

Over time, the inequality born of earlier struggles has moderated and socialism has settled into certain distributive patterns, which look rather egalitarian in comparison to the rest of the industrialized world and also to the early years of socialism. What are these patterns, as they are reflected in the relative economic standing of socio-occupational strata? What questions need we ask to understand them?

The first, an essential one, concerns the *working class*, the manual workers. This is the class collectively exalted in propaganda and poster art, the class which, it is frequently claimed, has benefited most from socialism, seeing the rewards of many of its members exceed the rewards of the routine clerk and "desk-jockey." How well are workers rewarded in comparison to the other strata? There are some reasons to expect that workers should be a highly rewarded group indeed. But there has already been evidence that they see themselves as a "middling" stratum in esteem and reward: should we expect this to be borne out by their relative rank in the socialist income hierarchy? The skills and educational levels of workers, after all, are no longer in very short supply. What need, then, for any special premium on them, as against other occupational strata?

In numbers, the elite or "intelligentsia" is small compared to the working class. Knowing nothing of the history of the socialist period, but only the ideology of revolution, we might expect the intelligentsia, tarred with the brush of collaboration with the capitalists and bourgeois, to have been cast down in symbolic and economic degradation, consonant with the ascent of the "toilers" to a favored place in the system. But, in fact, matters have not been so clear, as the data on mobility have shown. In the years of postrevolutionary reconstruction and industrialization drives, the scarcity of technological and managerial talent dictated incentives and rewards out of line with the ideologically shaky position of old-regime holdovers. The Soviet Union relied for years on its "bourgeois specialists."[24] The Eastern European regimes, by and large, did the same.

Rewarding these holdovers could be rationalized as necessary. Today, however, the intelligentsia is itself overwhelmingly a product of socialism—educated and, increasingly, born under it. The socialist intelligentsia is, as we have seen, heavily composed of the upwardly mobile. Are they then close to their origins? More egalitarian and less likely to desire material reward disproportionate to that received by workers? And thus, rewarded relatively modestly by the state for their efforts? (One need recall here too that the intelligentsia are no longer so scarce as they once were.) For many in this category, the job is a vocation, with a good deal of intrinsic interest and nonmaterial reward: are these a trade-off for modest material compensation? We have seen already that the intelligentsia are not all happy with their state, but the question remains: how much do they make?

Our interest extends to the peasants, and to routine white-collar employees as well. Information on all of these categories will reveal hierarchies in the average wages of real people in the pages that follow. (Unfortunately, the data are frequently drawn from less than national samples; they will also represent, generally, averages of strata across the branches and sectors which, as we have seen, do make a difference.)

Other data will take us beyond individuals' average earnings by occupational stratum, and into the composition of households and the per capita incomes of their members. Here we can search for familial responses to socialist income policies, which may reorder the priorities expressed in those policies, as well as for the effects of redistributive mechanisms such as family allowances. The main determinant of total household income may well be the income of the main earner, usually the male head of household. But his economic status, and that of his spouse and dependents, is more a function of their per capita income, whose composition is more complex. Two men in the same plant—one a senior clerk in the office, the other a skilled worker on the floor—may have roughly equal pay packets. The high degree of women's employment makes it likely that they both have working wives—but of what sort? "Advantageous" marriage will serve to upgrade economic status, and a "poor" one to depress it. Also, although the number of earners in a household generally increases with household size, it does not increase at a constant rate. Decisions made by spouses about number of children, readiness to assume responsibility for aged relations, etc. will largely determine the earners-to-dependents ratio, and hence the per capita economics of the household. One should note that it is the per capita, rather than the absolute, household income that greatly affects the daily life and the prospects of younger members of the household: the degree of current need to be balanced against long-term advantages as parents formulate their attitudes, and their children's, toward advanced education.

THE DIFFERENT INCOMES OF DIFFERENT STRATA

We begin with table 6.4. We have made some compromises with the gaps in data in the national statistical yearbooks, while taking advantage of what they offer. Hence, the first three occupational groupings are groupings within industry alone. Among nonagricultural sectors, it is only industry for which intelligentsia (generally "engineering-technical employees"), the routine white-collar ("administrative" and "clerical" personnel), and manual workers' average earnings are separately reported. Given the centrality of industry and its impact on total national average earnings, we are not badly off with these figures. Our peasants are close to, but not quite, the "real thing"; this category is made up of manuals in state agriculture (except for Czechoslovakia, where the only figures were combined ones for all employed in state agriculture). These, then, are not the individual peasants of Poland and Yugoslavia nor the collective or cooperative farmers of the other countries. The latter's incomes are nowhere near so well reported, and are more variable.

Table 6.4.
Average Pay, by Occupational Category: Intelligentsia, Routine Nonmanuals and Workers, All in State Industry; "Peasants" (Workers in State/Socialist Agriculture)

	1960	*1965*	*1970*	*1973*
Bulgaria				
intelligentsia	142.1	145.0	140.3	132.1
routine nonmanual	93.8	100.3	102.5	95.5
worker	100.0	100.0	100.0	100.0
peasant	92.1	84.7	86.2	91.5
Czechoslovakia				
intelligentsia	116.8	120.2	121.6	120.4
routine nonmanual	77.0	77.1	81.8	81.3
worker	100.0	100.0	100.0	100.0
peasant	79.2	85.5	95.0	98.1
Hungary				
intelligentsia	157.2	155.1	150.7	142.4
routine nonmanual	94.8	96.0	96.5	92.4
worker	100.0	100.0	100.0	100.0
peasant	NA	88.1	100.0	94.1
Poland				
intelligentsia	156.7	161.0	150.0	144.3
routine nonmanual	105.1	108.0	102.8	100.1
worker	100.0	100.0	100.0	100.0
peasant	NA	72.0	75.0	77.5
USSR				
intelligentsia	150.9	145.9	136.3	134.1
routine nonmanual	82.1	84.4	85.5	84.5
worker	100.0	100.0	100.0	100.0
peasant	57.7	71.2	75.4	76.5

SOURCE: adapted from *Statisticheski godishnik NR Bulgariia 1974*, pp. 68–69, 155; *Statisticka rocenka CSSR 1974*, pp. 135, 253; *Hungarian Statistical Yearbook 1973*, pp. 151, 242–43; *Rocznik Statystyczny 1974*, pp. 234, 321; *Narodnoe khoziaistvo SSSR 1922–1972*, pp. 350–51.

Still, the state farm figures do not, on the whole, make agriculturalists look *worse* off than they are—for the most part, their incomes are higher than their collective counterparts, and more stable than their independent smallholder counterparts as well.[25]

The table reveals several things:

1. Measuring equality by the distance between extreme strata, it seems that all the countries have become more egalitarian over the period reflected here; the USSR has been particularly notable in this respect.
2. The relative welfare of farmers has generally improved, and especially in Czechoslovakia and the USSR.
3. The intelligentsia's rewards are far from symbolic; they are decisively the best-paid group, and *most* so in the two countries whose presocialist traditions dictated quite differential rewards—Poland and Hungary.
4. The routine white-collar employees are in a seemingly ambiguous and unstable, but not bad situation in Bulgaria; in Czechoslovakia and the USSR their status seems depressed indeed; they do best in Poland—where consistently if decreasingly they are favored over the workers—and not badly in Hungary.
5. Workers on the whole have not done badly, though farm incomes approach theirs ever more closely in Czechoslovakia and Hungary; their overtaking of the white-collar employees everywhere but in Poland indicates that the manual-nonmanual income overlap requires serious discussion.
6. Czechoslovakia is the most egalitarian state, with almost punitive leveling of intelligentsia incomes, and a holding of routine white-collar incomes below those of state agriculturalists; Poland the least egalitarian.

We have, thus, some preliminary and general answers to questions raised in the previous section. If socialism has squeezed the ends of the income distribution together, the working class today still enjoys (as it has in the past) more rewards than the peasantry, and less (again as in the past) than the intelligentsia. If there has been a real change, it has been in the relationship of manuals to the *lower* white-collar strata, a point for later, and extended, discussion.

Another kind of data allows us to see the distribution of nonmanuals and manuals (outside agriculture) across a number of income

Table 6.5.
Average Monthly Earnings of Manuals and Nonmanuals; Poland 1962–1963

zl. per month	*1962 (males only)*		*1963 (males and females)*	
	Manual	*Nonmanual*	*Manual*	*Nonmanual*
to 1000	10.5	3.3	17.9	6.7
1001–1500	23.6	15.8	24.3	26.2
1501–2000	27.0	24.3	24.7	26.3
2001–2500	18.8	20.9	15.9	16.3
2501–3000	10.2	14.3	8.5	10.4
3001–3500	5.0	8.6	8.7 (3001 and over)	14.1 (3001 and over)
3501–4000	2.4	4.9		
4001–4500	1.2	2.7		
over 4500	1.3	5.2		

SOURCE: 1962 data from Adam Sarapata, "Stratification and Social Mobility in Poland," and 1963 data from Wlodzimierz Wesolowski, "Changes in the Class Structure in Poland," both in *Empirical Sociology in Poland* (Warsaw: Polish Scientific Publishers, 1966), pp. 44, 27, respectively.

categories. Table 6.5 provides Polish national data from the early 1960s. Such figures are frequently used in support of claims about egalitarianism—what they show is, to some degree, a matter of debate or definition. In the 1962 data for males only, there are few manuals in the top three income categories—but they are not entirely excluded. Still, in each category, the male nonmanuals (including both intelligentsia and routine white-collar) are much more heavily represented. The ratio of the proportion of nonmanuals in the three top categories to the manuals' proportion is 2.16 to 1. Nonmanuals are not absent from the two lowest income categories, but manuals are there in are greater amount. The ratio for the lower (up to 1000 zl. per month) category is 3.18 to 1 in favor of the manuals, and 1.79 to 1 for the two categories combined.

The addition of women (1963 data) changes things markedly, if not drastically. Though it is a year later, adding women to men in both manual and nonmanual categories shifts the center of gravity lower in the income scale in general. More importantly, *adding women reduces the earnings profile of nonmanuals more than it does that of the manuals.* Given that women *are* paid less than men in general, the larger shares of the total in lower income categories, and smaller shares in higher, is to be expected. But the ratios also look more egalitarian with women than without them. Between nonmanuals and manuals in the top income categories, the ratio is 1.62 to 1 (versus 2.16 to 1 for men alone) and between manuals and nonmanuals at the bottom, 1.28 to 1 (versus 1.79 to 1 for men alone). Our job categories, manual and nonmanual, are of the grossest sort. If the inclusion of women has this effect here, what effect would their inclusion or exclusion have in a more precise comparison, between the routine nonmanuals and skilled manuals at the blue-collar–white-collar borderline? We will touch upon this question several times again, before dealing with it at length in the last section of this chapter.

Meanwhile, we can go into some further detail on income by socio-occupational group, using data for Hungary, Poland, and the USSR that go beyond the four-stratum breakdown of table 6.4. Table 6.6 provides data from a nationwide Hungarian survey and a series of studies in 1964, 1965, and 1967 in three Polish cities. (The Soviet data are given separately, in table 6.7, because of their somewhat different occupational classifications.) There are similarities across the nations and cities. Among these *male household heads,* skilled workers do better than unskilled workers consistently, and very much better in Hungary. The gaps between the intelligentsia and the routine nonmanuals (the clericals, and the category of "professional nonmanuals" [Hungary] and technicians [Poland]) are marked. Where the worlds of white and blue collar confront each other, however, the patterns differ. The Hungarian skilled manual averages about 18 percent more than his clerical counterpart. In Poland the picture is different. Male clericals make *more* than male skilled workers, somewhat less than foremen—those who straddle the manual-nonmanual line—and also less than artisans. (The latter is largely a private-enterprise group with incomes less controlled than those in other categories.) These data seem to point to a skilled-worker ascendancy in Hungary (against the bottom of the nonmanual ranks) and a lack of such in Poland; a presence and an absence of overlap. (Of course, these index numbers reflect means for the

Table 6.6.
Average Incomes, Male Household Heads, Poland and Hungary

	Poland				Hungary, Nation, 1963
	Koszalin 1964	*Szczecin 1964*	*Lodz 1965*	*Lodz 1967*	
Intelligentsia	190.4	163.3	195.6	206.4	201.0
Professional nonmanual	—	—	—	—	152.1
Technicians	153.7	137.3	145.2	156.2	—
Clericals	141.0	123.3	129.2	129.0	123.3
Foremen, etc.	141.3	125.6	144.7	137.0	—
Artisans	148.5	134.0	144.9	143.7	—
Physical-mental workers	110.7	106.5	106.7	111.1	—
Skilled workers	118.3	119.7	111.3	116.2	145.4
Semiskilled workers	102.6	100.4	104.0	105.0	119.5
Unskilled workers	100.0	100.0	100.0	100.0	100.0
(Unskilled worker = 100.0)					

SOURCE: adapted from K. M. Slomczynski and K. Szafnicki, "Zroznicowanie dochodow z pracy," in Wlodzimierz Wesolowski, ed., *Zroznicowanie spoleczne* (Wroclaw, Warsaw, Krakow: Wydawnictwo Polskiej Akademii Nauk, 1970), pp. 164 ff., and Hungarian Central Statistical Office, *Social Stratification in Hungary* (Budapest: CSO, 1967), pp. 38, 43.

Table 6.7.
Average Monthly Earnings, Workers and Employees: Machine Construction Industry, Leningrad; Industrial Workers and Employees, Tatar ASSR (3 Cities)

	Leningrad	*Kazan*	*Al'met'evsk*	*Menzelinsk*
Managers, etc.	177.3	222.6	283.5	244.9
Scientific-technical employees	130.3	212.6	232.6	323.7
Skilled mental workers	112.6	150.4	177.6	184.1
Other mental workers	85.7	102.6	123.1	115.9
Physical-mental workers	132.3	132.7	183.8	207.1
Skilled manual workers	123.1	135.4	152.3	140.2
Skilled machine operators	110.3	134.3	182.2	161.3
Unskilled manual workers	100.0	100.0	100.0	100.0
(Unskilled manual worker = 100.0)				

SOURCE: adapted from O. I. Shkaratan, *Problemy sotsial'noi struktury rabochego klassa SSSR* (Moscow: "Mysl'," 1970), p. 404.

groups. There is always some overlap, but what concerns us here is how things are on the average.)

Our Soviet data (table 6.7) are derived from O. I. Shkaratan's studies in Leningrad (a sample of workers in the machine-construction industry) and the Tatar ASSR, where the industrial labor forces of three cities provide the data.

For our purposes, the first two categories may be conveniently thought of as equivalent to the intelligentsia; "skilled mental workers" is harder to grapple with, but on balance is probably closer to routine white-collar, while "other mental workers" obviously refers to lower white-collar. Physical-mental worker is quite different from its Polish counterpart, while the "worker" categories are all reasonably clear. Here we find substantial variation between the cities and samples, mainly a product of marked divergencies in the absolute pay levels for the index group—unskilled manuals. (Their pay in the three Tatar cities is, respectively, 75, 64, and 59 percent of Leningrad's.) Given the large Soviet regional variations, the cultural-developmental distance between Leningrad and Tataria and the different labor force profiles of the three Tatar cities, these figures are readily understandable. But the common aspects of the four samples are interesting as well.

We see, first, that the bottom of the nonmanual hierarchy—the "other mental workers"—is uniformly overtaken, and by a significant amount, by skilled manuals and skilled machine operators, and, in Leningrad, even by the unskilled manuals. In Leningrad, the skilled manuals' average earnings also exceed those of skilled mental workers, while the latters' earnings fall below those of skilled machine operators in Al'met'evsk. All in all, one who sought evidence of a "revolutionary" reversal of the nonmanual-manual earning hierarchy, a situation the opposite of Poland's, might be convinced that he had found it here. But one need recall, for future reference, that these Soviet figures include *both males and females*.

Now we shift the focus, from individual income to per capita income in the household of different socio-occupational strata. This allows us to see "inequality" not only generated by one earner's income versus another's, but as the outcome of familial decisions, which may move the patterns of income distribution by occupational category further in the direction laid down by state wage and

Table 6.8.
Per Capita Incomes, Households, Poland and Hungary

	Poland		Hungary,
	3 cities 1964–1965	Lodz 1967	nation, 1963
Intelligentsia	168.6	175.9	186.6
Professional nonmanual	—	—	154.9
Technicians	143.5	144.3	—
Clericals	132.2	124.8	145.0
Foremen, etc.	129.2	126.4	—
Artisans	—	122.0	—
Physical-mental workers	112.4	104.4	—
Skilled workers	107.9	110.0	132.6
Semiskilled workers	107.6	102.5	114.7
Unskilled workers	100.0	100.0	100.0
(Unskilled worker = 100.0)			

SOURCE: three-city data adapted from K. M. Slomczynski and K. Szafnicki, "Zroznicowanie spoleczne: podstawowe wyniki," in Wesolowski, ed., *Zroznicowanie spoleczne;* Lodz data from same authors, "Zroznicowanie dochodow," pp. 174–75, and Hungarian data from *Social Stratification,* all cited in table 6.6.

salary policies, or in the opposite direction. As Peter Wiles has observed, if "rich earners have or acquire more dependents, then the work of the welfare state is being done for it."[26] If they do not, obviously, the outcome is different.

We return to the Hungarian and Polish data sources of table 6.6 in table 6.8. In all cases, shifting to a per capita classification reduces the distance between the extremes. But, examining the middle, the relationship of clerical workers' households to those of skilled workers, we find that

1. In Hungary, the advantage of the skilled worker disappears—the gap is reversed, and the average per capita income in the nonmanual's household rises above that of the skilled manual.
2. In Poland, where the clericals enjoyed a slight advantage over the skilled manuals in basic individual earnings, the gap widens. In the averages for the three cities in 1964–1965, the advantage of the clericals increases, while the gap between them and the intelligentsia decreases markedly; they achieve per capita incomes higher than those in artisans' and foremen's households

Table 6.9.
Per Capita Monthly Incomes, Households of Workers and Employees in Leningrad Machine-Construction Industry

Managers, etc.	117.0
Scientific-technical employees	118.8
Skilled mental workers	110.5
Other mental workers	102.5
Physical-mental workers	103.0
Skilled manual workers	106.1
Skilled machine operators	96.1
Unskilled manual workers	100.0
(Unskilled manual worker = 100.0)	

SOURCE: adapted from Shkaratan, *Problemy* (cited in table 6.7), p. 420.

as well. (In the 1967 Lodz sample, the changes are more moderate, but still there.)

These data cannot tell us why these changes occur—but the answer must lie in differences in the incomes of the working wives of these male household heads, to the advantage of the clerical husbands, and/or fewer dependent mouths to feed in clerical households.

Shkaratan's data in per capita form (table 6.9) show first a radical leveling in the Leningrad figures. The extremes are much closer together than in Polish and Hungarian data. Two things have happened here, it seems, one of which confuses the issue and one of which tells us something. First, it is quite probable that the categories are *not* quite the same as in table 6.7. In the original Russian, they differ slightly from one table to the next, and such a reshuffling might produce a more egalitarian picture. Given that the original data show very little variation in average family size or in number of family members with income, and thus little variation in earner-dependent ratios, something of the sort must have taken place.

On the other hand, there is very probably a reality here. It is, in continued contrast to the Polish and Hungarian figures, a product of the fact that both males and females are in these Leningrad data. There is every reason to assume (see below) that those underpaid "other mental workers" of table 6.7 were overwhelmingly women. But in table 6.9, earners in different categories are reporting per capita income in "their" households, whether they are the heads or not. Thus, the female "other mental workers," generally second earners, are reporting the advantages accruing from the higher earnings of their husbands. Conversely, the leveling down of managers' and scientific-technical employees' salaries, *to the degree that it is real and not the product of a reclassification of categories,* is quite probably caused by their marriages to women who, perforce, earn much less than they do. The effect of sex differences in earnings is manifested, however dimly, in these data. While our concerns here are not focused on discrimination or differentials in reward based on sex, these *do,* as we shall show here and later, play a role in the overall structuring of inequality as evidenced in standard income data.

First, we need emphasize that women are concentrated in sectors and branches where incomes are low. One can, fairly confidently, predict low rewards from high feminization, and high feminization from low rewards: an observation summarized in table 6.10, which presents correlation coefficients linking the two for sectors in socialist economies. As evident, the correlations are decidedly negative (all are significant at the .01 level, save Romania's and Yugoslavia's

Table 6.10.
Correlation Coefficients,[a] Percentage Women in Sector of Economy and Average Earnings in Sector (1973)

	r	No. sectors
Bulgaria	−.802	11
Czechoslovakia	−.940	7
Hungary	−.984	4
Poland	−.755	11
Romania	−.442	9
USSR	−.723	12
Yugoslavia	+.518	8

[a]All except Romania and Yugoslavia significant at .01 level.

SOURCE: national statistical yearbook data for 1973.

positive* one). In general, one can say that the more women in a sector, the lower the average pay.

These figures, though of the grossest sort, are indicative. More detailed data demonstrate more clearly that women are essentially absent from the high-income categories in the socialist countries and overrepresented in the low categories. Figures for Poland in 1972, distributing workers and employees across ten income categories, show the lowest category for the socialist economy as a whole containing only 1.5 percent of men, as opposed to 9.5 percent of the women. Adding together the three top categories (since women are so few in the top category that they are not reported at all) yields the following shares of men and women: economy total, 6.7 versus 0.4 percent; industry, 7.9 versus 0.1 percent; construction, 11.7 versus 2.6 percent; trade, 2.2 versus 0.1 percent, and health, social welfare, and physical culture, 4.1 versus 0.4 percent.[27]

Hungarian figures for the state sector in 1972 convey a similar impression. In the two lowest of seven categories fall 0.3 percent of all men in industry, versus 1.6 percent of all women. In construction, the comparable figures are 0.3 for men and 0.9 for women, while in trade 0.4 percent of men fall in these two categories versus 1.8 percent of women. The "top" of this Hungarian distribution (3,001 and more *forint* per month) is not a very exclusive category, but only 4.7 percent of the women in industry achieve it (versus 40.3 percent of men)—while the comparable female-male proportions in construction and trade are 13.6 versus 42.6 and 11.8 versus 38.8 percent, respectively.[28]

Figures for the state industrial sector in Czechoslovakia over three years underline the generality of this pattern across socialist states, and its stability over time. In the lowest of five income categories fell

*The Yugoslav exception is one that, for various reasons, may be partially disallowed: women dominate less the sectors in which their representation is heaviest in Yugoslavia than in the other socialist states, forming the majority in only one of 8 sectors there (versus 4 in the USSR, 5 in Bulgaria, 3 in Czechoslovakia, 2 in Hungary, 6 in Poland, and 3 in Romania). Though their representation is highest in the two best-paid sectors, governmental administration and cultural-social activity, the pay of males in these sectors is quite high in Yugoslavia, and probably creates an impression of female advantage that would be dispelled by figures for women alone. Yugoslavia, a Balkan society with a (relatively) low female participation rate in the labor force, is probably not so deviant as these figures indicate, although it would be foolish to dismiss its anomalous quality here as totally illusory.

0.7 percent of men, versus 3.5 of women, in 1959. In 1964, with average wages up, the comparable figures were 0.1 and 0.6 percent, while in 1966 they equalled 0.1 and 0.5. In the fourth and fifth categories combined fell 16.7 percent of men, and only 0.7 percent of women, in 1959; in 1964, 27.0 and 1.4; and in 1966, 32.5 percent of men and 2.2 percent of women. (In the top category women do not appear at all until 1966; then only 0.1 percent of them attain it.)[29] Later research in 1967 by the Machonin team found women virtually absent from top income levels in and out of industry, owing partially to a diversion of female labor into what was regarded as "typical women's work."[30]

At the risk of anticipating the basis of the argument on the manual-nonmanual income overlap that completes this chapter, we can extend further the treatment of women's wages and their relevance in the overall pattern of income stratification, using data from Czechoslovakia and Hungary. In Czechoslovak industry in 1967, average earnings for all workers, male and female, were 1,609 kcs. per month; for "engineering-technical" employees, 2,288 kcs., or 142.2 percent of the workers' average; and for "administrative" employees, 1,452 kcs., or a 90.2 percent share of the average worker's earnings[31] (the latter two categories the equivalents of "intelligentsia" and "routine white collar" in table 6.4). The same source yields base pay (smaller than total earnings) for the two nonmanual categories, by sex, and also their sex composition. In table 6.11, we index base pay of male and female nonmanuals to average earnings of the worker category. First, we see that males enjoy a vast preponderance in the intelligentsia category, while females have a parallel lopsided dominance in the routine nonmanual stratum—confirmation of the high index of feminization argued earlier. This does much to account for the overlap of workers' pay with that of lower white-collar ranks, since males' basic pay in lower white-collar jobs exceeds workers' average earnings. Workers' average earnings also exceed the base pay of female intelligentsia by slightly more than 10 percent. Women, to the degree that they dominate an occupational stratum, "disadvantage" it—but men in the category do considerably better than women. (We have here a trade-off in the data. Were women eliminated from the "workers' average earnings" category, its value would rise. So, however, would the values of our nonman-

Table 6.11.
Base Pay of Male and Female Nonmanuals (Intelligentsia and Routine Nonmanual),
Industrial Workers' Average Earnings, and Sex Composition of Nonmanual Categories
(Czechoslovakia, State Industry, 1967)

		Base pay	*Composition of category (%)*
Intelligentsia:	male	119.3	85.2
	female	89.1	14.8
			(100.0)
Routine nonmanual:	male	105.2	14.6
	female	75.8	85.4
			(100.0)
Industrial worker: average earnings		100.0	

SOURCE: adapted from Augustin Kudrna, "Diferenciace v odmenovani," *Planovane hospodarstvi*, no. 9 (1968), pp. 2, 5.

ual categories if we had their average *earnings*, rather than base pay. If our figures were all sex-specific and measured exactly the same things, would we find more, or less, manual-nonmanual overlap? No absolute answer is possible, but it is probable that such figures would still show that the aggregate disadvantage of lower white-collar employees versus the whole working class, or the skilled workers alone, has its roots in the extreme feminization of lower white-collar occupations.)

Hungarian data for 1959 (monthly average earnings by sex, for "managers and engineers-technicians," "other employees," skilled, semiskilled, and unskilled workers) support this. Average earnings of males in the "other employee" category—2,045 *forints* per month—exceed those of skilled (1,923), semiskilled (1,558), and unskilled (1,342) male manual workers. But these three latter categories *all* exceed the average earnings of female routine nonmanuals (1,322 forint), who are likely to make up the solid majority of all "other employees."[32]

Finally, although we do not have data from Shkaratan's Leningrad study on the sex composition of his machine-construction personnel, one can make "ball park" estimates from 1970 census figures on employment by sex for the RSFSR.[33] This takes us far from Leningrad, including the rest of Russia, and Siberia as well, but not so far as to make such estimates pointless. Suffice it here to say that the "managers" category (table 6.7) is unlikely to contain more than 15 percent women, while scientific-technical employees would include no more than 40 percent, the majority of these falling into lower, routine classifications such as draftsman. "Skilled mental workers," and "other mental workers," are likely to be respectively, feminized to about 75 and 95 percent. (The closest general Russian term to the last category, *deloproizvodstvennyi personal,* might be translated more literally as "paper-processing personnel." In 1959, women up 94 percent of this category, in the RSFSR, while in 1970, their share had climbed to 97 percent.)[34] Conversely, those categories of physical-mental workers, skilled manuals, and skilled machine operators, against whose earnings indices the lower white-collar groups look disadvantaged, are overwhelmingly male—less than 10 percent of the first two categories, and less than 30 percent of the last, should be made up of women.

None of this is unique, however, to socialism. An inspection of the relevant data in the national statistical yearbooks of advanced Western states will also show the pattern—male manuals do tend to overtake the average earnings of female nonmanuals, though they rarely overtake male nonmanuals in aggregate figures. The point is that socialism has not escaped this relationship.

To shift focus: incomes depend not only on what people earn at work, whom they marry, and what those spouses earn. They also depend on state welfare provisions, taxes, family allowances, etc. To these we have thus far given little attention—truthfully, a whole treatise on socialist welfare economics would be necessary to handle the topic fully, but such is neither the scope nor purpose of this book. We can, however, address some questions, and provide some answers backed with observations on people's behavior.

Individual income taxes, first of all, play little role in redistribution, with their relatively low maximum rates and only moderate progressiveness. Other rationales are more important, the main one probably the reduction, across the board, of earnings that frequently creep higher (through bonuses and premiums for the overfulfillment of relatively low plan targets) than initially allowed for in national income and consumption planning.[35] Socialist economies suffer chronically from the problem of too much money "chasing" too few goods. Though the income tax system is (to widely varying degrees) adapted to the number of an earner's dependents, it does little to affect per capita income figures.

Family allowances, almost by definition, *are* aimed at per capita income. If the "rich" continue to have fewer children than the "poor," then allowances per dependent child should have some equalizing effect—and indeed they do. But all in all, it too is moderate, and certainly no spur to fertility. In 1964 allowances for *three* children amounted to percentages of the average *individual* gross wage as follows, by country: Poland, 15; Hungary, 20; Bulgaria and Romania, 25; and Czechoslovakia, 30. In none of the socialist states did even combined allotments for *six* children reach parity with the total wage of *one* average earner. In Czechoslovakia, they came closest (84.6 percent) while in the USSR they reached only 19.9 percent of this figure.[36] The equalization effect on the whole seems quite moderate, and people behave as if it is. Purposeful restriction of fertility *is* the norm in the socialist countries. Commentary and reportage in the socialist press, as well as the observations of demographers, economists, and sociologists indicate that "extra" children—generally meaning a second or at most a third child, are perceived as a real threat to plans for household consumption.*

Blue-collar families have marginally more children than white-collar, but they are scarcely responding to the invitations of family allowances. Much more likely, this is an effect of less sophistication in the use of contraceptive techniques, less capacity and inclination to plan fertility, and other deficiencies in managing and structuring the household. Even then, the sizes of intelligentsia, lower-white-collar, and workers' households diverge only moderately. Under such circumstances, few relative gains through income taxes and family allowances amount to much concretely. In Czechoslovakia

*This seems especially the case with what is, for most socialist families, the largest single possible purchase—a private automobile. In societies where only a very small minority have their own homes, the purchase of a car, at a price often well more over average earner's annual income, is an important event economically and for the status car ownership symbolizes. It is a matter for planning and prolonged saving (one does not buy by installments). It is no exaggeration to say that families face the choice, frequently, between a second child and a family car.

(1964) a household with only one child, a nonworking mother, and a father-breadwinner with "high" wages would feel the combined effect of tax-cum-allowance in a subtraction of 15.0 percent of the *average gross wage.* a family with *six* children, "nonworking" mother, and husband with "low" wages would *benefit* to a total of 82.0 percent of the average gross wage.[37] Czechoslovakia was the most egalitarian state in these matters, yet a penalty of 15 percent of the *average* wage for a family whose head earns *high* wages is hardly unbearable. And, while allowances adding almost the sum of the average wage to a single below-average earner's pay may double it, they will still be inadequate for a decent life for a family consisting of eight members. Six-child families were allowed for in the economists' calculations, but they are not part of the reality of family life in the socialist countries. Even were family allowances exceedingly generous, they would not include and could not guarantee appropriate services and adequate housing for such families.

What of in-kind benefits, of the much-publicized free education and medical care? These, all seem to agree, are important—indeed, general education and medical care have been extremely popular with the public as accomplishments of their socialist governments. About medical care, one could argue that the effects are, by their very nature, equalizing—to large families, presumably, more care is distributed than to small. But more will be said of the utilization of free health services later. With respect to education, we may add some comments here to those in the last chaper that dealt with stratified access to it. Education is also one of those benefits of which members of different groups, all equally entitled, may choose to partake unequally; and in a sense this is quite all right. The problem here is not so much with elementary or secondary as with higher education. Just as in Western countries, insofar as higher education is financed out of total national income, its overutilization by children of already-privileged households involves transfer payments from the poor to the rich. And, while the authors of a comprehensive United Nations study argue that students from less affluent socialist families are more likely to benefit from government living-expense stipends than are the more affluent, and that the use of "heavily subsidized dormitory facilities" is more to the benefit of out-of-towners, mainly peasants, than to urbanites,[38] they overlook several things. Stipends are *not* high, and often inadequate without parental supplements; they are, furthermore, generally pegged as much to academic performance as to need. Dormitory facilities are, indeed, subsidized, but in many university cities they are very much in deficit, and some who need such space are driven into the private and expensive market of rented rooms. With respect to medicine, as we shall see in the next section, the same quality of general service available to persons of low and average income is available to the affluent as well. However, they do not necessarily use it, opting instead for private, paid consultation and treatment; or they may enjoy access, by virtue of position, to a whole elite network of medical services and institutions closed to the general public.

Differences by occupational strata in family composition will have a great deal to do with the final structure of per capita income stratification. Insofar as family heads, and other adult members of the family, show capacities for planning, and actualize those capacities, they can effect changes in the economic status of household members. We can do no better here than to review the conclusions of a 1967 United Nations study, generally confirmed by more recent observations.

1. With increases in family size, total family income tends to increase, as do the number of earners; but the number of dependents increases even more rapidly.
2. Thus, with total size increases, the ratio of earners per family member declines, and with it the per capita income within the household.
3. "Nonwage" income (social benefits and payment of various sorts) *does* rise both in absolute amount and as a percentage of all income as size of household increases. But, given the very marked decline of per capita income from earnings as that size increases, the total compensatory effect (though no doubt welcome to those who benefit from it) does not appreciably reduce the absolute income spread. In sum, without such nonwage income the dispersion of per capita incomes, *already* quite wide, would be even wider.[39]

All this tends to emphasize the degree to which even marginal fertility differentials between manual and nonmanual households will disadvantage the more fertile manual families. Beyond these general conclusions, it is also usually the case that as per capita income rises, the proportion of total family income contributed by working members *other* than the household head rises, except in households where the per capita income is *quite* high. There, where the head's income must itself be quite large, its proportion rises again.[40] This does not mean that the income level of a household head is not a useful predictor of the levels of other earners—especially the spouse, as the typical first auxiliary earner. In fact, as Soviet data convincingly demonstrate, earnings of second earners tend to increase with the head's earnings—although this increase lags in proportion to the increase of head's earnings.[41] The same, judging from the evidence on marriage patterns provided in the next chapter and from the generally high activity rate of women, would seem to be the case in the Eastern European countries as well.

A whole other set of questions involves us with the structure of total work-related incomes (as opposed to average "earnings") and the magnitude of differences among these. Relevant data are generally quite elusive. The amount of premiums and bonuses paid to workers and employees at different levels and in different sectors and branches, the availability and value of opportunities for extra work and such, are not so easily assessed. In fact, the *only* detailed consideration of these problems by socio-occupational categories appears in the investigation in the Polish city of Lodz in 1967, some data from which we have already seen.[42] The study (whose generalizability is uncertain, although similarities of socialist economic organization make it unwise to treat them as unique) showed (1) a strong correlation between basic pay levels and the magnitude of premiums and bonuses. These, while they increase everyone's income, do *not* reduce inequality (even where it might be expected, as between skilled workers whose output is quantifiable and routine nonmanuals whose work is generally *not* so easily measured). (2) A marked difference in opportunities for extra work; while 24.5 percent of the intelligentsia in the 1967 Lodz study reported they had such work, this was true of only 6.2 percent of skilled workers and 3.3 percent of the unskilled. Even lower white-collar workers, at 6.5 percent, did marginally better here than skilled manuals.

The outcome is stretching of the income scale of our occupational groups. In table 6.4 above, we presented the *gross* wage index for the

1967 Lodz categories, with intelligentsia averaging 207 as against the 100 base for unskilled workers. *Net* wage figures, reflecting taxes, reduce this ratio, in a predictably modest manner, to 198 to 100. *Total* income, calculated as net wages plus premiums, bonuses, and extra-work earnings, leaves the intelligentsia with 240 as against the unskilled workers' 100. Lower white-collar workers also improved their situation in relation to skilled manuals, moving from a 129 to 116 gross wage ratio to 141 to 121 for *total* income. Thus is the hierarchy structured.

Although, one must add here, it is not *entirely* structured. Another major influence on the distribution of goods, services, and money in socialist economies—maddeningly resistant to any precise measurement, and unfortunately one which, for that reason and those of space, we can only note here—is the existence of the "second economy," characterized by Gregory Grossman in its Soviet variant as a "vast and varied set of activities," covered in no official statistics, "where production and exchange often take place for direct private gain and just as often violate state law in some nontrivial aspect."[43] There are "second economies" as well in the Eastern European states; and in all the socialist societies, their operations (whether one focuses on unreported "moonlighting," bribery, engaging in prohibited trade, or straight forms of economic crime) add exotic but undefinable variations to the picture of economic stratification thus far presented. Suffice it here to say, just as one might of the distribution of economic reward in any large Western society, that there exist hidden sources of wealth and profit in the shadows of the economy, that many seemingly modest earners in fact generate much more income than appears or is ever likely to appear in official statistics, and that many of the better-off are *much* better-off than their reported incomes or an inventory of their stock of consumer items in *open* view would indicate.

THE SPECIAL INCOMES OF SPECIAL GROUPS

Most income distribution statistics give us a vague picture of the bottom, and an even worse picture of the top. In a capitalist economy, "top" earnings figures frequently understate or ignore interest, capital gains, stock options, and other benefits such as expense accounts. This is all well known, and not controversial. But in a socialist economy, standard measures also fall well short of identifying and specifying the material advantages of the affluent and the very affluent. We have already seen that the intelligentsia, whose basic pay is relatively high, enjoy premium and bonus income that further increases their advantages. They also have readier access to extra work than other strata, opening the gap even wider. But none of these are so exotic as are some of the benefits of the extremely affluent, the upper levels of the managerial, political, scientific, and artistic elites—benefits beyond money, which place them in special positions of access to scarce goods and services.

"Special" compensation outside the normal level of salary has a long history under socialism, with its roots in early Soviet history. These were years of great scarcity, which affected the population as a whole but not all parts equally. A general rationing system remained in effect into 1935 (by which year the effects of Stalin's antiegalitarian policies were making themselves strongly felt in basic pay packets), a system where money could not buy everthing. But within this system, other advantages could buy disproportionate amounts of goods and services. These advantages were themselves strictly rationed within the elite in an administrative pecking order. The memoir literature of the period confirms the access to luxury items enjoyed by privileged strata of the population through special distribution networks—for example, the recollections of a woman whose father advanced swiftly in the secret police ranks, and was seconded to the foreign ministry:

Father's new position made us one of the most favoured families in Moscow. His appointment had been approved by the Seventh Department of the N.K.V.D. who made all the high appointments in the Soviet Union. As well as the wooden villa, we were given a five-roomed Foreign Office flat just outside the Red Gate metro station. We were also given a special Kremlin ration book which enabled us to buy the finest food from the Kremlin Gastronome near Lenin's library. This special ration book also entitled us to have cooked food sent from the Kremlin kitchen. The servants would back a complete dinner, soup, chicken, meat and ice cream in special containers. In addition to his salary from the Foreign Office, Father as a reserve N.K.V.D. official, received a State pension of 500 roubles a month. He was allowed six weeks on the Russian Riviera, the Crimea, and in

Caucasia, all expenses paid. Another privilege was that Moscow publishers, four times a year, sent us a list of their new books. We could buy as many as we wanted at reduced prices.[44]

Nadezhdha Mandelstam, widow and biographer of the poet Osip Mandelstam who died in the Great Purge, reflects on a period when the couple's joint fortunes improved, as Mandelstam moved from newspaper employment to another position that enabled him to enjoy some of the perquisites of favored creative artists.

On the *Moscow Komsomol* M. was paid so little that his month's salary went in a few days. In this country, the privileged have always been rewarded not through their pay envolpes, but by means of unofficial handouts—cash in sealed envelopes, special rations, the privilege of using "closed" stores, etc. There were times when even M. received favored treatment. From 1930 until his arrest in May 1934 we were able to buy our supplies in a luxurious "closed" store. . . . During our *Moscow Komsomol* days, we had to live on our salaries.[45]

Mme. Mandelstam's mention of "sealed envelopes" pinpoints one of the most interesting and egregious de-equalizing phenomena of Soviet economic life. High-level party and state officials, managers of critical factories and enterprises—it is impossible to say how many, and in exactly which categories of the elite—received, in the years when the basic wage-salary distribution was already extremely inegalitarian, a monthly cash "supplement." The dissident Roy Medvedev describes it here:

the disgraceful system of "packets" (*pakety*) was introduced in the higher state and Party institutions. Each month almost every high official would receive an envelope or packet containing a large sum, often much higher than the salary formally designated for his post. These payments passed through special financial channels, were not subject to taxes, and were kept secret from the rank-and-file officials at the institution.[46]

The impact of such a supplement at the upper extremes was, of course, great. Had we figures on elite basic incomes during the Stalin period, knowledge of the packets would require us to multiply them, conservatively, by two. To *double* high and not heavily taxed income with funds from outside normal accounting channels, and also to provide privileged access to goods unknown to the general population, is to widen greatly, with minimum visibility, the gap between the masses and the favored few. The packet system, it seems, was abolished or greatly curtailed sometime after Khrushchev's 1956 denunciation of Stalin,[47] but has been replaced by a new and almost equally effective system.

The "special stores" go back to the early days of the Soviet regime as well, and have long served the purpose of making available to the elite both imported food and consumer durables, and Soviet-produced items absent or in short supply in the regular retail outlets. Today's special stores are divisible into three basic types, according to one student of Soviet elite lifeways:[48] first are the "closed distributors" (*zakrytye raspredìteli*) that serve the upper elite echelons in a given area, and are "disguised," unstorelike in appearance—admission by pass only. Second, "restricted outlets" exist in regular department stores, etc., where goods may be ordered by those with licensed access. Finally come the "foreign currency shops," with whose hotel divisions foreign tourists in large Soviet cities often come in contact. Listed in descending order of exclusiveness, these outlets provide important components of the Soviet elite's material advantages.

How "special" are the special stores? The answer must be, very, on two counts: the assortment of goods available and the pricing structure. Foreign goods—durables, appliances, clothing, specialty foods, liquor, cigarettes—completely unavailable in "open" Soviet stores are available to the patrons of the special system. Soviet goods, whether food items or durables such as refrigerators, televisions, etc. that are available either not at all or only after prolonged waiting periods of months or years to the nonprivileged consumer are also stocked. (Some high-quality domestic food items, such as black caviar, have been virtually unavailable to normal consumers, since so much of the total is exported. No such shortage exists for the privileged.) Not *all* food items or consumer durables are restricted to the special outlets; but this is where the pricing mechanism enters. Western goods are sold at very low prices, and Soviet goods also—the Soviet goods, in fact, for around one-quarter of their price in the open market.

Prices in these stores, both for durables and food items, are listed in rubles—but normal, "soft" rubles cannot be used at all such stores. Foreigners with access to such stores (the "third-tier" foreign currency shops are open to diplomats, correspondents, exchange scholars, etc., in a city like Moscow) use their hard currencies directly, benefiting from the "cut" ruble prices of the goods, at the normal exchange rate. Soviet patrons use special currency—variously called certificate, *valiuta,* or foreign-currency rubles. These are gotten in exchange for convertible currency (such as Soviet advisers abroad, diplomats, correspondents, etc. may earn *or as a regular component of one's pay.* The "elite" (again, how many we do not know) receives some of its pay directly in these special rubles. The exact amount will vary with status, as may the price one pays for the goods. In effect, some members of the Soviet elite recieve a portion of their pay *in* hard currency, while the workers are barred from legal access *to* it. Interestingly enough, the prices on goods in special stores reflect the outside world's assessment of the value of the ruble. In 1969, the ruble was valued at the "official" exchange rate of $1.11; the value set on it in the West ranged from about 20¢ to 25¢, and prices on goods the author noted then reflected a 25-cent ruble. A foreigner using Moscow's large hard-currency *gastronom* (food store) would find that a one-ruble item so priced cost him $1.11; but on the open retail market, the same item, if available, cost between 4 and 5 rubles. The middle-privileged Soviets with whom one rubbed elbows in the store were getting the equivalent of four to five rubles from each of their special rubles.

All this, touching as it does a relatively small proportion of the population, may strike the reader as somewhat inconsequential. Two points should be made in reply.

First, the lowest level of special stores in large Soviet cities are quite evident to the nonprivileged public. They will never see the closed distributor on Granovsky Street in Moscow, where people of Central Committee level and up may shop, but lesser special stores are not nearly so concealed. I have seen "regular" Muscovites try to enter the largest of the special food stores, not realizing at first that its well-packed shelves were off limits, being gruffly sent away by a guard at the door. The contrast between what is available even to the moderately privileged and to the common folk is more evident today than before, and may have strong implications for perceptions of social justice.

Second, to dismiss access to special foods and underpriced durables as insignificant in measuring systemic inequality is to fail to understand how depressed Soviet consumption standards are. One is rarely told at the Moscow *gastronom* that reasonably priced, good-quality meat is unavailable. But it is not uncommon that large Soviet cities, with populations over half a million, are simply *without* meat for periods of months,[49] and suffer other interruptions in basic supply as well. The privileges of the middle-rank Soviet elite would not impress one who lives at Western middle-class levels—but they are a league away from the shabby life of the Soviet mass, and that is the relevant comparison.

As with retailing, so with other things; the members of the elite, to a greater or lesser degree, live in a world where nouns are preceded by the adjectives "special" or "closed." They lunch and dine in special restaurants attached to their work organizations, with better food and lower prices than on the outside. The elite of Moscow and other large cities enjoy country houses (*dachas*) at subsidized low rents—some receive them for permanent residence. The *very* highly placed might even have two or three *dachas*. The lower elite ranks take vacations at low prices in *sanitoriia* restricted to persons of status. If not *dachas*, they are less crowded and better provisioned than the places run by trade unions for the workers. A stay in one may even be gratis, since some functionaries receive free vouchers to cover vacation expenses.

Economists frequently note the redistributive or "equalizing" effect of free medical care, and in some sense correctly. Unpaid physicians' services and low-priced prescription drugs are important, and have long been regarded as a plus factor.[50] But the quality of these standardized services is not very high, and long waits and overcrowding are edemic. It is no surprise, then, that there exists a network of special, closed hospitals and medical services for the elite. The qualifications of personnel, the lack of long waits, and conditions for in-patients all elevate this system high above the common one.

Much of what has been said here about the USSR applies to Eastern Europe as well, with some modification. Certainly, "special" arrangements exist throughout the area and, as a general rule, *anything* is more useful than the national currency in making purchases.

But for certain reasons, the spheres of the special people and the mass seem less tightly sealed off one from another than in the USSR. First, consumer goods are generally of higher quality, and available in better assortment, in the better-developed Eastern European countries than in the USSR. The standards of Bulgaria and Romania are close to the Soviet, but Hungary, Czechoslovakia, and Poland as well have devoted somewhat more attention to everyday goods, while Yugoslavia has for a long time understood that people do not live on slogans alone. More is available for money alone, and in Poland and Hungary at least, government interest in hard currency has led to toleration of its possession (however acquired) by the man in the street and readiness to see him spend it in open hard-currency stores. The goods assortment does not vary so much (though prices do) between stocks purchasable for local and hard funds. Thus, nonelite persons with sources of foreign money or carefully husbanded savings *can* buy things their Soviet counterparts cannot. There are shortages aplenty, and reasons for complaint about quality and service, but shopping in Warsaw, Budapest, or Prague is still a very different matter from Moscow or Leningrad, as the huge lines often found in Moscow in front of the "Wanda" and "Leipzig" stores, selling Polish and East German goods respectively, attest, and Eastern Europe in this respect is a rather pale reflection of its large neighbor.

A pattern of housing allocation that favors the already favored, and keeps their outlay to a very low proportion of income, has been a part of elite life in Eastern Europe, as in the USSR. But increasingly, housing in Eastern Europe has moved in the direction of becoming a market item. The *purchase* of non-standard housing reflecting one's earnings and savings is facilitated by a variety of means. In the USSR competition still centers largely around the allocation of larger and better-located state apartments, while in Eastern Europe more movement has occurred in the direction of self-financed cooperative housing. In the suburbs of Warsaw or Budapest (particularly the latter) those with sufficient funds and access to construction materials can build a detached house, often of Western European standard. Supply of materials and labor is still the bottleneck. The people in this "market" possess a good share of the excess purchasing power that has troubled socialist economic planners. In recent years their chances to break through the bottleneck, to spend it, have multiplied, thus underlining their distance from the masses.*

Another important factor is the heightened access of Eastern European elites to the West—especially the scientific, cultural, and academic intelligentsia. Yugoslavs and Poles in particular are likely to spend more time in Western Europe and North America than their Soviet counterparts, and the economic benefits of such activity are substantial. A lecture tour, a temporary "advisory" position, a visiting academic appointment all produce hard currency, which its earners may bank in their own accounts for future trips, and for facilitating domestic consumption. The Pole or Yugoslav who seeks to buy a home-produced *Polski Fiat* or *Zastava* can do so without a prolonged wait, and pay quite an advantageous price, if he enters the market with dollars, francs, or marks rather than *zloty* or dinars.

Perhaps all this seems a bit heavy on the side of gossip and rumor. Certainly, there are elements of these—but none that seem to me unfounded. Impressionistic materials are much of what we have to deal with, since the lives of the elite are not "public property" as they often seem to be in the West. The information gaps are many. Words such as "elite" and "rich" are banned as descriptions; no public information exists on salaries of high functionaries, nor on elite lifestyles—no *Who's Who*. Nor is the socialist press prone to image-building or "celebrity" coverage. (The Soviet housewife is indeed supplied with women's magazines, but she gets no recipes or advice from Mrs. Brezhnev therein, and knows no more about her than we do). Nor are there any elite-style publications that might afford nonelites some vicarious access to the upper reaches. (Were there a *Town and Country* available in the socialist countries, it would likely be a journal devoted to industry and agriculture!)

*How far this has come from the old days of critical housing shortages, when even the intelligentsia seemed to be crammed into tiny apartments, is evident in Hungary, where residential construction according to owner's specifications has produced embryonic upper-class neighborhoods in the hilly Buda section of Budapest. Another fruit of the consumer emphasis in Hungary's wide ranging economic reform (the "New Economic Mechanism," which commenced in 1968) has been the rapid growth of summer cottage settlements around Lake Balaton and in other resort areas—this to the point where the author found in 1974 on a Budapest newsstand a special magazine of the "*House and Garden*" variety devoted to the design and furnishing of such cottages. A long way, indeed, from the asceticism of the "heroic" years—and about as inconceivable a decade earlier as *Better Homes and Gardens* would be in Moscow today.

That the elite-mass distance *is* important and sharply felt is manifest in Soviet and Eastern European literature (not all of it published at home), which is rich in perceptive vignettes of the confrontation between the meanness of life for the average person and the privileges of the favored. In Ladislav Mnacko's novel, *The Taste of Power,* the divorced wife of a recently deceased Slovak political figure, a woman who found the advantages of marriage to a "hero" different from her expectations when she had fought side by side with him as a partisan, confesses:

I couldn't live the way he wanted me to. It made me feel shy and ashamed. What use was a servant to me? How did that sort of life fit in with what we'd been fighting for? I didn't want to have anything that other people couldn't have. I felt all the time I was betraying something. What earthly difference was there between us and the pre-war bosses? We lived on the fat of the land while other people had ration cards.[51]

The attractions of even modest (by Western standards) consumer goods during the grim years of the 1940s and 1950s find reflection in the Hungarian writer Tibor Dery's portrayal of the widow of a high old regime official, one of a group waiting for "Mrs. V.'s" husband, a nationally acclaimed writer, to finish his death agony in "A Gay Funeral." Politically "out," she is nonetheless courted by the company for the access she provides to things otherwise unavailable.

Of all those present it was she who rested on the relatively most secure financial basis; her daughter had married an American air force officer and now sent her a regular stream of "IKKA" parcels, coffee, cocoa, rum, Gillette blades, nylons, and in separate packages, second-hand clothes which she sold, through an intermediary, to the wife of a cabinet minister. The coffee, cocoa and rum were taken off her hands by Mrs. V at prices somewhat higher than the market ones.[52]

Other examples abound. In the short story "Long Journey" by the Pole Stanislaw Dygat, the protagonist Marion lives a humdrum life of "quiet desperation" in a crowded apartment with wife and two children. He borrows the apartment of well-fixed acquaintance Alfred, who is off to Brussels for a conference. Alfred assumes he wants it for an assignation with a mistress, but the truth is simpler—he simply cannot take life at home anymore.

As he opened the door of Alfred's apartment, his hands trembled and his throat was dry. Quickly, he took off his coat; ran, smiling, into the room; flung out his arms and took a deep whiff of air. The room was quiet. A scent of lavender and English cigarettes still lingered in it. It was full of postcards from foreign places and of articles, everyday articles, which are unknown in Poland. Gaily, he began to dance until, completely exhausted, he had to sit down in an armchair. He reached for the phone and spoke into the humming emptiness:

"Service? Director Jack Brown of Alabama speaking. Reserve two seats on the plane to Rome tomorrow. If Gina Lollobrigida asks for me, show her upstairs. I am not at home to anyone else. . . ."

He put down the phone and picked it up again:

"Director John Brown of Alabama speaking. Send up supper for two. Whiskey, champagne, lobsters, caviar. . . ."[53]

Marion's problem has as much to do with family as with longings for status, and his response is somewhat comic, but the description of Alfred's apartment underlines the gap between have and have-not.

In a striking vignette of upper-class life, Solzhenitsyn's *The First Circle* counterposes a dinner party at apartment of the prosecutor Makarygin to the gloom and poverty of Soviet life under Stalin. While most of Moscow in 1949 lived one *family* to a room, sharing kitchen and bath with numerous neighbors, Makarygin's place,

which aroused the envy of the whole Entry No. 2, but which the Makarygin family itself found too small, was made up of two adjoining apartments, whose connecting walls had been taken down. Therefore it had two front doors, one of which was nailed shut, two baths, two toilets, two hallways, two kitchens, and five other rooms.[54]

Two Bashkir maids, one "their own servant," the other "borrowed from neighbors for the evening," can barely cope with the twenty-five who come to celebrate the award of an Order of Lenin to the prosecutor. His wife knows that her "carpets and tablecloths are important tokens of prosperity," and is especially proud of her crystal—much of it confisticated by court order in the 1920s and 1930s from convicted persons with *ancien régime* connections, and sold "in the distribution centers open only to officials of the courts," such as her husband.

One old acquaintance, invited out of a feeling of duty, threatens to spoil the evening. This "tedious friend," a social inferior who lives in the provinces, corners the Makaygin's daughter with a lengthy talk on how Party activists' children in her area "were on a special list, so that there was always enough milk for them, and all the penicillin shots they needed." Perhaps making such a point of these modest privileges bores Alevtina Nikanorovna, the hostess.

Alevtina Nikanorovna looked at it this way: Whoever had status was assured of good health. All you had to do was telephone some famous professor, best of all some Laureate of the Stalin Prize; he would write out a prescription and any coronary occlusion would instantly disappear. You could always afford to go to the best sanitarium. She and her husband were not afraid of illness.[55]

The privileges of the elite under socialism differ from those of capitalist elites in many ways. Economic status cannot be inherited in the same sense, since it is rooted not in accumulated capital but in official position and status that cannot be passed on automatically. But status *is* often transferred to the next generation, effectively enough, through education and connections. Children of the visible top political elite, though they do not inherit their father's mantles, often wind up in elite staff positions, still heavy with privileges. Tenure in such positions, however, for them and for the less elevated but still comfortably privileged, is at the pleasure of those who hold real power, and the strictly private resources that allow the rich in capitalist systems to enjoy privileged lives *whoever* is in power, to participate in or withdraw from public life at will, are not theirs to command.

Thus, socialist privilege is somewhat caste-like, despite the upward mobility by which many still achieve it. In a capitalist system, money can buy just about everything. Socialism, however, allocates rewards according to bureaucratic position. In the long run, "cash income" is less important than one's place in an elaborately stratified and administratively controlled pecking order, in some senses still reminiscent of the structure of privilege in the Tsarist autocracy. This departure from socialist ideals is quietly tolerated by the masses, to whom it seems, perhaps, only to be expected. Dissident intellectuals, more used to counterposing promise to reality, find it more galling. Their comments, like those of the Polish emigré writer Leopold Tyrmand, are often acerbic.

When he is sick of his own apartment, a member of the upper class has at his disposal the so-called houses of creative work for musicians, writers, journalist, etc. These are for the most part old palaces transformed into confortable *pensions*. The rates are low in relation to current market prices and the food supply comes from special sources. When a country is going through one of its periodic food crises and long lines are forming in front of stores in the cities, the representatives of the upper class go en masse to the houses of creative work where no restrictions threaten them and they can write poems in peace about equality and brotherhood, the abundance of good under socialism, and the hunger of exploited colonial peoples.[56]

The place and privilege of elites in all modern social systems is a matter today of controversy, a question on the agenda of an age that increasingly links equality with justice. Whatever regimes may do to repress and contain, the socialist elites cannot but raise similar questions, since the presence and persistence of such clearly privileged strata in countries still far from affluence belies the egalitarian promises socialism made.

Clearly, in abolishing old elites socialism has created its own. It is now appropriate to assess, drawing on what has gone before, its fulfillment of another strongly implied promise—the destruction of the traditional hierarchy that has exalted work with one's head over work with one's hands, and to reward the latter equally, or better, for its contributions to the production of man's necessities.

THE MANUAL-NONMANUAL INCOME OVERLAP: MYTH AND REALITY

The distinction between manual and nonmanual work has been durable, employed as a general way of organizing perceptions and as a reference point by students of occupational mobility and stratification. There are, however, problems in its use. The increasingly complex occupational structures of industrial societies produce positions that do not fall clearly on either side of the line. As Duncan noted over a decade ago, the distinction

ordinarily is said to revolve about the difference between "head" and "hand" work. This difference is hardly absolute. It is not clear, for example, that a stenographer uses her "head" any more, or her "hands" any less, than a compositor (typesetter). She does, of course, work in an "office" rather than a "shop." Perhaps equally relevant is the fact that training for her job is likely to have been acquired as part of her formal education, while that of the craft printer may have been gained via apprenticeship.[57]

The same, of course, is true of socialist countries. Yet this is hardly the major difficulty. While traditionally this *horizontal* distinction was presumed (in general correctly) to have a clear *vertical* referent as well (the subordination of manual work *in general* to nonmanual work in income and prestige terms), students of stratification no longer find this so clearly the case. There is first the matter of the decreasing scarcity value of the literacy and computational skills that made the difference in the past. History has also witnessed, in the West, the vastly increased impact of labor organization in the blue-collar sector, a major force in improving economic compensation and ensuring employment security, which has allowed the wages of substantial numbers of workers to pass the income levels of "clerical and sales" personnel. The direct prestige advantage accruing to white collar and clean hands has attentuated as well. As Hodge and his collaborators noted, in the United States a comparison of the results of the 1947 NORC study of occupational prestige with the 1963 study indicated a net upward shift in the rated prestige of all blue-collar (nonfarm) groups, while two of the three white-collar categories ("managerial" and "clerical and sales") suffered a net decline.[58]

Socialist countries have claimed the same sort of changes, attributing them directly to revolutionary transformation. In this view, socialist revolutions have inverted the traditional hierarchy, finally and deservedly placing the *skilled* manual worker, at least, above the routine clerks and officials of the lower nonmanual strata, in income *and* prestige terms. These claims are suffused with a rhetoric of "justice"—the notion that the workers, engaged in producing things, are in fact more valuable to society than the processors of paper, and that the casting down of the latter from advantages in income and prestige they previously enjoyed is a matter of just deserts. Once out of the early post-revolutionary phase, arguments that the intelligentsia's rewards should be or have been lowered to those of the skilled worker generally cease (in any case there is too much counter-evidence for such arguments to be credible). But the assertion that the routine nonmanuals have been so leveled is a constant theme.

Western students of socialist stratification patterns have, more often than not, seemingly accepted the truth of the factual, if not the moral, claim. Frank Parkin, especially, appears to argue (basing his assertions on some of the data utilized here) that the manual-nonmanual line, as a major division, has lost much of its relevance. Favoring a general hierarchical ranking of (1) intelligentsia, (2) skilled manuals, (3) routine white-collar, and (4) other manuals, he asserts that

> we cannot represent the reward structure of socialist society as a dichotomous class model on exactly the Western pattern, since there is much less of an obvious "break" between manual and non-manual positions. The lower non-manual categories in socialist society could not be said to enjoy the same kinds of status, material, and social advantages over skilled or relatively well-paid manual workers as do their counterparts in capitalist society.[59]

Mervyn Matthews, characterizing the position of the routine nonmanuals in the USSR, takes the same tack, noting evidence of their generally low salaries. He "would expect a good proportion of them to be in the urban poor, and have the same style of life."[60] Zev Katz, another analyst of Soviet stratification and mobility patterns, says of the lower white-collar workers that their "income, prestige, and education are low-medium to low"[61] and generally leaves it at that.

David Lane dissents from Parkin's position, citing some of the Hungarian income data introduced here earlier, as well as evidence that white-collar workers *do*, at least in Poland, enjoy greater "fringe benefits" than manuals. In his view, Parkin's location of the major division (skilled versus unskilled) "must be treated with some scepticism."[62]

None of these authors, however, pays much attention to the blue collar–white collar question *other than* in the terms in which it is posed in typical socialist sources. They seem little concerned with the difference of individual and per capita household income, or with the sex composition of various occupational categories (although Parkin makes a passing reference to the latter in one essay,[63] and Lane, in a 1976 book which came to hand as this work was in its final stages, does focus on the per capita figures for the

1963 Hungarian data, coming to conclusions rather similar to those drawn here.)[64] Yet the sex compositions of strata, as we have indicated, are very important in general assessments of economic stratification, and especially so in dealing with this question.

Many authors, it seems, have too readily acceded to "obvious" implications of data in Soviet studies, especially, without examining them carefully. One such study, not cited by any of these authors, may serve to make the point. Kamovich and Kozlovskaia deal with a factory labor force in the Sverdlovsk region, distinguishing workers, "employees" (lower nonmanual) and engineering technical personnel ("intelligentsia"). Their data indicate only very modest differentials in the educational levels of workers and employees (both far below the engineering-technical level), but marked differences in monthly wages. Only 6.0 percent of the workers fell into the lowest (66–80 rubles per month) wage category, but 27.7 percent of the employees did so. At the other extreme, only 0.6 percent of employees made over 160 rubles per month, while 41.1 percent of the manual workers did. At first glance, such figures are impressive proof of the economic ascendancy of the manual worker over the clean-handed but unspecialized desk worker. But one should attend carefully when, almost as an afterthought, the Soviet authors note that 95.5 percent of the "employees" in the factory are women.[65]

That they are should not be surprising, given the evidence of current female employment we have seen, and the persistent patterns that push them toward such occupations. (A large Polish study of persons getting their first job in 1971, revealed that 53.5 percent of the women entering work were concentrated in four categories,* all of which seem to promise relatively low rewards, while only 11.1 percent of the males entered such categories. Taking the "clerical and administrative staff" category alone, the figures show 14.4 percent of first-job women entering it as against 2.9 percent of the men. Meanwhile, 55.7 and 8.3 percent of the men entered "industrial workers and similar" and "construction workers and similar," as against 29.5 and 0.9 percent of the women. These figures highlight the pattern that leads to pronounced male dominance in the more

*Categories were "other nontechnical specialist," "trade and nonindustrial service," and "unskilled service staff," and "clerical," as above.

skilled realms of manual work—as they must have dominated in Kamovich and Kozlovskaia's factory).[66] Any informed discussion of whether the manual-nonmanual line is an important divider, one is inclined to conclude, must take account of facts like these.

The point is that it makes little or no sense to assess progress toward "equality," or inversion of manual and nonmanual economic status, by simple comparisons of lower nonmanual, and upper manual, individual incomes. This is so because the composition of these two categories by sex, and hence their members' position within households and basic economic functions, are different.

To compare "clericals" with skilled workers is to compare women with men; secondary earners with primary; persons whose job choices are limited, and whose work is likely to be interrupted by childbirth, motherhood, and a heavy load of housework with persons who are "heads of households," and whose careers benefit from the burdens their spouses shoulder. All this tells us much about the disadvantageous economic position of women, but much less about the measure of equality achieved.

We need to compare similarly situated "earning units," preferably ones whose earnings are central in determining the general welfare of others, those who have a large impact on the per capita figures: males, and preferably male household heads. This we have done, as the data allowed. We found, in average individual wage figures, moderate real overlaps between "clerical" and "skilled worker" males in Hungary, and a modest *advantage* of clerical males over their skilled worker counterparts in three Polish cities. Similar findings emerged from a comparison of lower white-collar males with *all* manual workers in Czech industry, offering at least the possibility that even in egalitarian Czechoslovakia the overlap might be no greater than in Hungary.

Shifting to average per capita income figures by household, we saw the overlap disappear in Hungary, and the nonmanuals' advantage increase in Poland. In both cases, per capita *household* income figures left the white-collar workers closer to the level of the intelligentsia than to that of the skilled manuals. If we consider the *per capita* income averages in households of different strata as equally important for inequality as are the individual wage averages in strata, then much of the socialist income revolution, insofar as it involves the wholesale overtaking of routine nonmanuals by the top of the working class in average incomes, disappears.

There *has* been a revolution, but it is to be sought in the diminished *distance* between average incomes of those in different strata, and not primarily in the inversion of the traditional statuses of nonmanual and manual work. The narrowing of differentials between nonmanuals and manuals may indeed be testimony of socialist sincerity, but the evidence of redifferentiation in the per capita figures shows that individual choices, and abilities to make them—of spouse, number of children, and other alternatives—raise average white-collar per capita incomes above those of skilled worker families. About these socialism has done, and probably can do, little.

The ready acceptance of the socialist claims of an altered hierarchy, as routine white-collar workers have fallen and blue-collar risen, seems to depend on failure to appreciate the significance of three things: the heavy feminization of lower white-collar work,[67] the relatively low status of women within this kind of work, and the generality, the non-unique quality, of that feminization.

About the first, we have already said enough. About the second, it should be observed that lower white-collar work is itself internally differentiated. There are very routine jobs—typist, clerk, secretary, and the like—and there are less routine, semi-supervisory functions, wherein one has a share in running an office, checking figures compiled by clerks, or other responsible activities less routine. Now, it *might* be that the female majority and the male minority in "lower nonmanual" work are evenly distributed across the positions, but what we know about other occupational categories and the incomes of men and women therein make it extremely improbable. All evidence strongly suggests that the upper part of the "lower" white collar ranks is heavily male, the routine remainder almost exclusively female.* It is misleading to compare these with skilled blue-collar workers, who are so predominantly male.

*The current author's (admittedly unsystematic) observations in various administrative offices in socialist countries also prompt this view. According to the organization of the office, one may find the supervisor at a corner desk, or in a cubicle clearly separated from the routine clerical personnel: but in either case, the routine personnel have been female, and the incumbent of main desk or occupant of cubicle has been male in the great majority of cases. Both are located in the "same" stratum, but the vertical distances are clear and important.

Finally, the feminization of lower white-collar work, and its contribution to the equalization of interstratum economic status, is scarcely unique to socialism. In the United States, and in other Western countries, up to the turn of the century and even until the first World War, many "clerical" occupations including typing (once felt to be too strenuous for women) were the preserve of men. These, too, were times when women's labor force participation was not so high as today. The same was often the case in the clerical world of Eastern Europe before the onset of socialism; perhaps especially so, given the traditional nature of these societies; and negative attitudes toward women's work outside the home in most of them. Changing attitudes and economies in the West have almost completely feminized such job categories, and left them in a worse economic position vis à vis manual production work than when *both* categories were predominantly male in composition. In the socialist states, wage policies necessitated a large inflow of women into employment outside the home, while production emphases economically favored manual workers. Men took and continue to hold the best of the clerical jobs, while the rapidly expanding routine clerical ranks took on, mainly, newly available women. Economic policy, and increased supply, dictated the lessening of nonmanual advantages in income, and these were more easily imposed on the newly working women, who were the supply source, than on men.

What remains of the claims about the inversion of the old order? Not very much more than the certainty that *some* portion of lower white-collar males do fall below *some* proportion of male skilled workers, as we move away from the average figures and examine ranges and standard deviations. This is not "nothing," but again it is not unique. Sensitive enough income classifications for Western Europe, Canada, and the United States would show similar overlaps "up and down" between portions of categories hierarchically situated according to their *average* incomes. And even an overlap of categorical income averages is not absent in the United States. Blau and Duncan, for example, report figures in their large stratification study (for employed males 14 and over in 1962) showing that the lowest nonmanual category—retail salesman, median income $3,044—was surpassed by *five* categories of manuals whose medians range from $5,482 to $3,223. These manuals made up 45.4

percent of the national total employed, as against 1.7 percent for the retail salesmen they exceed. Conversely, the highest manual category (craftsmen, with an income median of $5,482), making up 15.5 percent of the employed, exceeds the medians of both the retail salesmen and the next highest nonmanuals (clericals; median $5,173), who together make up 8.3 percent of the total employed.[68] This, too, is overlap, but it is hardly dependent on socialist revolution.

We dare not pursue this topic much further, having already gone, in what must be regarded by some readers as excruciating detail, into various minutiae. We can only add, concerning "fringe benefits" differentiating lower white- and upper blue-collar workers, that there *are* such, as Lane notes, in Poland at least[69] and only recently have they been moderated.[70] Evidence that the offspring of lower nonmanuals enjoy readier access to higher education than do those of skilled manuals has also been presented, following much of Lenski's discussion of the American "clerical" strata, the heightened mobility opportunities of both clericals themselves (in career terms) *and* the advantages of clerical sons over those of craftsmen in access to the "professional, entrepreneurial or managerial" classes.[71] Little else remains that can be said. In the next chapter we shall see that, not only do lower white-collar employees have slightly smaller households than skilled workers, but that their lesser housing density is also a function of larger (and better equipped) apartments; that lower nonmanual men marry more "advantageously" than their skilled manual peers, and that the households they head, far from being "proletarianized," manifest quite different life-style and consumption patterns than those of the upper manaul strata.

There is, then, some validity, but a great deal as well that is misleading, in the broadly conceived notion of a "revolutionary" change in the status of nonmanuals and manuals, especially in those socialist countries where the hierarchical tradition is so deeply rooted. The hierarchy is "shorter," but it persists. This needs to be clearly understood, if we are to separate the reality of socialism's impact from the myth, either in the sphere of material goods or the normative order.

Chapter Seven

The Structure of Socialist Households

Brzeska Street was not yet asleep. This was the fifteenth of the month, and as always on payday, men were standing around in front of their houses. Their shirts were unbuttoned, their chests, hair, and faces glistened with sweat. Before the day had gone, its leaden sky had harassed houses, bodies, pavements, and trees. There were those who stood and those who sat; those who walked from one end of their street to the other, from one little group to the next, from one street lamp to the next; those who lounged against the walls on patches of trampled grass; those whose disheveled heads leaned out from dirty ground floor windows—all were drinking: beer, vodka, and cheap wine straight from the bottle; they choked as they drank, and the liquor splashed over the sores on their hands, onto their sweaty shirts, and their soft relaxed bodies. The wind, like a tired animal, ran clumsily along the sidewalks, bearing the smell of their sweat, their tobacco, and their breath, hot and rancid with alcohol. Among them women glided to and fro, some in old dressing gowns or with overcoats hastily thrown over their slips, others wearing brightly colored dresses with dark half-circles of sweat under the arms; some were urging the men to come back home; others to go into town for further reveling. They quarreled with the men, drew them away from their comrades, snatched bottles out of their unwilling hands; and they reviled the men in the men's own coarse language.

—Marek Hlasko, *The Eighth Day of the Week* (1958)

THIS WARSAW street scene is by now a bit dated, but not overdrawn. It depicts the "grim" years, before any of the improvements of later times had touched the mass of Polish (or Hungarian, or

Czech, or Soviet) families. The scene is a working-class one, far removed from the life the elite lived.

Working-class families are better fixed today. Many have left the Brzeska streets for new housing developments, and the Brzeska streets, some of them at least, have themselves given place to new and more comfortable buildings. But the living standards of other strata have risen as well. And, as we have seen earlier, income levels, attitudes, aspirations, and assessments of the status of oneself and one's stratum all vary markedly. The households of Brzeska street lived in their own way in the 1950s, distinct both from the intelligentsia above and the peasantry below them; should we not expect differences to persist?

This chapter deals with *households,* as much as individuals, in addressing some questions of equality, differentiation, and homogeneity not confronted in earlier chapters. Households are important units for the allocation of status, influenced in their composition and style by the income, education, and occupations of their founding members, and in turn influencing the attitudes and aspirations of younger additions. We begin with the formation of the household, with patterns of stratum homogeneity of diversity (homogamy and heterogamy) generated by a multitude of individual decisions to marry, each of which determines that a particular sort of household comes into existence.

The physical environment of a household—the dwelling space available, the conveniences, the privacy or lack thereof afforded separate members of the household within the dwelling, and the durables and appliances acquired—has both display and utilitarian values. All these promote or inhibit comfort, convenience, and a feeling that one is living a decent and reasonable life. They index a household's place as against other households. We examine them in the second and third sections.

Finally, the section on life-styles deals with those partially constrained, partially free discretionary decisions that produce stratum-related patterns of friendship, association, and leisure pursuits. Here there is much evidence that households differ not only through choices they "freely" make, but also through attitudes, differing from one stratum to another, about "normal" and appropriate things to do.

MARRIAGE: HOMOGAMY, HETEROGAMY, AND THE PERSISTENCE OF STATUS

Socialist ideologues and propagandists have emphasized freedom and equality in the selection of marriage partners as a presumed benefit conferred by the socialist order which replaced capitalism. Economic security, the abolition of unemployment, the provision of work opportunities for women, have all been heralded as making way for love matches, free of economic calculation. Further, a general "democratization" of social life, allowing freedom to select mates across social strata, is contrasted to a presumably class-bound past when such marriages, especially across the manual-nonmanual line, were unheard of. Lacking data, we cannot readily judge the past. (One Polish study, conducted in a medium-sized town, concludes that "the criterion of social background or property has disappeared completely" as an element in marriage—but it also specifies education as a principal base of homogamy today. An exception—a woman doctor marrying a taxi driver— "gave rise to comment, although it was by no means a sensation among the townspeople."[1] But "exceptions" may specify where the current rules lie.)

Thus, we might view skeptically broad claims that marriage patterns are uniquely "democratic" under socialism, and thus distinct from those in the West. Too much is at stake in a marriage; there are too many psychological imponderables linked to social background influencing attraction and repulsion, for us to expect that the stratification variables explored in this book will not influence such choices. Both general impressions and popular journalistic evidence point in this direction. Girls with high-school education in Eastern Europe "overelect" nonmanual, clean office jobs, although factory work is sometimes better paid, and do not want to marry manual workers if they can help it. Urbanites frown on spouses from the countryside, even if they are skilled: a girl "does not want to go out with a young combine operator, because he is a collective farmer."[2] How much "circulation," then, takes place in the marriage market, and how much status insurance by way of homogamous marriage?

Our more systematic data do not cover all the socialist countries, but they do provide some insight into patterns of homogamy, hypergamy, and hypogamy, and in a way still rather atypical of data for

Western societies. Women are assigned status on the basis of *their* occupations, rather than their social origin—an approach that makes sense in societies where women's labor-force participation is quite high, and where the status of a potential wife is thus not simply a function of her family background before marriage and of her husband's status after marriage. (This does not mean that we "lose" all information about women's origin status in our data. Educational and hence occupational attainment of women in socialist countries are closely related to family background, even if their range of opportunities is smaller than that of men. Thus, the occupational status of working wives is to some degree an indicator of their premarital background. This will not satisfy but may somewhat allay the concerns of those who would prefer to see husbands and wives classified by social origins, in order to facilitate the comparability of these data with those from Western studies.) Women's work, in the main, does not signify that the male earner's status is not the dominant one in the household. We have seen the disadvantaged position of working women in the economic reward structure at every level, which limits the degree to which women's occupations determine their general status.

For these reasons, we have grouped our data below with an eye toward establishing what sorts of wives husbands of different occupational levels "select," and have categorized those levels, just as in the earlier discussion of mobility, as elite, routine nonmanual, worker, and peasant. Table 7.1 draws on data for four countries. The Czech data are national in coverage, the units being all marriages contracted in 1964 (*N* = 110,793). Thirteen original categories were collapsed to four, and three very small ones eliminated, producing a total of 110,150. The Hungarian sample is part of the 1963 Central Statistical Office study, also national in scope (*N* = 5,939). Polish data are drawn from the 1964–1965 studies in the three cities of Lodz, Szczecin, and Koszalin. In these urban data, peasants are missing, but the reporting of nonworking wives adds interest. An initial *N* of 2,361 has been reduced, eliminating the hard-to-classify artisans, foremen, and "physical-mental" workers, to 1,594 (including nonworking wives) and 1,060 (excluding such wives). The Soviet data derive from a 1966 study in Estonia; students graduating from academic secondary schools reported their parents' occupa-

Table 7.1.
Socio-occupational Categories of Wives, by Category of Husbands, Various Socialist Countries

Husband	*Wife*			
	1	*2*	*3*	*4*
1 Elite				
Czechoslovakia	38.2	28.6	30.5	2.7
Hungary	16.0	56.9	16.0	11.0
Poland I	48.2	48.2	3.6	—
USSR	38.2	30.9	26.6	4.3
Poland II	63.3	34.2	2.5	—
2 Routine nonmanual				
Czechoslovakia	21.7	37.6	37.6	3.1
Hungary	3.6	52.9	32.9	10.6
Poland I	11.1	71.2	17.7	—
USSR	7.7	53.3	27.7	11.3
Poland II	7.9	79.6	12.5	—
3 Worker				
Czechoslovakia	9.7	14.6	67.8	7.9
Hungary	0.8	10.5	50.3	38.5
Poland I	1.0	23.0	76.0	—
USSR	4.9	17.5	65.8	11.8
Poland II	0.6	14.4	85.0	—
4 Peasant				
Czechoslovakia	5.6	6.2	38.8	49.4
Hungary	0.0	0.0	3.0	97.0
USSR	1.4	4.3	7.3	87.0

SOURCE: adapted from : Vladimir Srb, "K dynamice socio-profesionalni heterogamie v CSSR," *Sociologicky casopis* 3 (1967), table 6; Central Statistical Office, *Social Stratification in Hungary* (Budapest: CSO, 1967), p. 126; Wielislawa Warzywoda-Kruszynska, "Zbieznosc cech spolecznych wspolmalzonkow," in K. M. Slomczynski and W. Wesolowski, eds., *Struktura i ruchliwosc spoleczna* (Wroclaw, Warsaw, Krakow, Gdansk: Wydawnictwo Polskiej Akademii Nauk, 1973), pp. 132–33; M. Kh. Titma, "The Influence of Social Origins on the Occupational Values of Graduating Secondary-School Students," in Murray Yanowitch and Wesley A. Fisher, eds., *Social Stratification and Mobility in the USSR* (White Plains, N.Y.: International Arts and Sciences Press, 1973), pp. 182–83.

tions. (These are not, then, necessarily typical of all Soviet marriages, or even all Estonian ones—but they are all the data we have.) Eleven categories in the original study have been collapsed to four, unknown and "other" occupations eliminated, reducing the base *N* of 2,250 to 1,515.

What sort of wives do men marry? Panel 1 suggests a strong tendency for elite men to marry, *contingent on their availability,* women of the same category. This is the modal pattern in the Estonian SSR and Czechoslovakia, and even more pronounced in Poland (variant "I" excludes nonworking wives, variant "II" includes such matches as homogamous, viewing wives' status here as derived from husband's). Hungary's elite males seem more "democratic" in their choices, but this is largely an artifact of somewhat different compositions of categories (Hungary's is "leading officials and intellectuals," a somewhat more restrictive term than Poland's "intelligentsia" and the parallel Soviet and Czech categories, and thus one in which women appear quite infrequently.) It *is* clear that elite men show an overwhelming tendency to marry women who do *not* work with their hands (or to ensure that their wives do not do so). Of the Hungarian elite 72.6 percent are married to nonmanual women, while the parallel percentage figures are 96.4 (!), 69.1, and 66.8 for Poland (I), the Estonian SSR, and Czechoslovakia.

Lower white-collar males (panel B) are also rather successful in finding nonmanual wives, although they marry women of elite occupations at an understandably lower rate than do men of that category. For Czechoslovakia, Hungary, Poland (I), and the Soviet sample, the proportions of lower white-collar males whose marriages are to women at or higher than their own level, are 59.3, 56.5, 82.3, and 61.0 percent.

Male workers, however, overwhelmingly marry working-class females, and these usually of the semi-skilled or unskilled variety, even when the male is himself a skilled worker.* That male manual

*The original data show that 18.6 percent of Polish skilled workers married semiskilled or unskilled women (versus 17.3 married to skilled) according to variant I, while in Hungary 14.0 percent of skilled workers had skilled wives, versus 47.0 who married semiskilled or unskilled. Of *all* Polish male workers, skilled, semiskilled, or unskilled, 48.2 percent married semiskilled or unskilled women, while the corresponding Hungarian figure was 41.6 percent. (In Hungary, an additional 38.5 percent of workers' wives, it will be noted, were in agriculture.)

Table 7.2.
"Supply" of Males and Females by Occupational Category among Married Populations

	Czecho-slovakia		*Hungary*		*Poland*		*USSR*	
	M	F	M	F	M	F	M	F
1 *Elite*	19.4	15.8	10.0	2.4	18.6	13.1	13.7	8.9
2 *Routine nonmanual*	6.4	18.4	10.7	16.4	33.1	43.7	18.1	22.0
3 *Worker*	70.2	57.5	48.6	30.5	48.3	43.2	39.2	36.6
4 *Peasant*	4.0	8.2	30.7	50.7	—	—	29.0	32.5

SOURCE: see source note to table 7.1.

workers have little access to elite women is not surprising: the miniscule figures for Poland and Hungary may be taken partially as a reflection of the weight of tradition in these historically most elitist of Eastern European states. But even the "mixing" that would come from marriage to a lower white-collar woman, a "routine clerical," is rare. Nowhere do more than one-quarter of worker husbands manage such marriages, and in three of the countries the total is under one-fifth.

Peasants generally content themselves with their female counterparts—a function of geography and human ecology as well as status. About the best a male peasant can expect to do is marry a wage-earning female worker, but even these matches are quite rare in Hungary and Estonia. More than one-third of Czech farmers contracted such marriages—an exception rooted in the larger supply of nonagricultural females and the relatively close mixing of agricultural and nonagricultural pursuits in the villages and small towns of this compact and well-developed country, which leaves the peasant population less isolated.

Thus far we have taken little account of the "differential supply" factor—that is, the fact that the occupational distribution of "available" women in our table differs from that of men, necessitating some heterogamy. We see from table 7.2 that the distributions of men and women are quite distinct in all four data sets. Given the supply of elite men, there is a shortage of women of the same category, while among the routine nonmanuals there is an excess of females over

Table 7.3.
Socio-occupational Marriage Patterns of Wives

	Homogamy	*Hypergamy*	*Hypogamy*
Czechoslovakia	59.4	20.1	20.5
Hungary	61.5	31.7	6.4
Poland	69.2	15.5	15.3
USSR	65.9	20.1	13.9

males. In the worker category, males outnumber females, but the reverse is true in the peasant stratum.

Elite men are, in a sense, sometimes forced to marry down. In seeking wives "outside," they have, apparently, first recourse to routine nonmanuals, thus entering into competition with the men of this stratum. This competition is moderated by the oversupply of women here, however, so that most routine nonmanual men still find wives in that stratum, except in Czechoslovakia. Larger numbers of routine nonmanual men, however, must take working-class wives than is the case with the intelligentsia. Male workers face a deficit of working-class women, and must marry up or down, while male peasants could, conceivably, all marry similar females.

These structural conditions set the stage for pronounced female hypergamy—a general pattern wherein females tend to marry males of higher status more frequently than males marry females of higher status. This pattern has been suggested as generally characteristic of societies,[3] in the context of origin status rather than current occupational status; but it should be noted that analysis of a large U.S. sample failed to find any such clear tendencies.[4] Calculations from the cell frequencies of the 4 × 4 (3 × 3 for Poland) matrices from which tables 7.1 and 7.2 were constructed, yield the patterns set out in table 7.3. The expectation of female hypergamy is met strongly in Hungary and the USSR. But in Czechoslovakia women marry down (hypogamy) slightly more than marrying up, and in the Polish cities the proportions are virtually identical. The *mean* for female hypergamy across the countries is 21.9 percent, exceeding the 14.0 mean for female hypogamy. The major tendency, however, is to marry within one's stratum—on the average, 64.0 percent of the marriages are homogamous. (A larger number of strata, sensitive to differences such as that between skilled and semi/unskilled workers, would, as indicated earlier, show more hypergamy.)

How would the picture look if not subject to the structural constraints of different male/female occupational distributions? We can answer this in two ways, both of which involve treating our original marriage matrices as "mobility" tables. Such, in a sense, they are. The cells contain husband-wife pairs, rather than father-son pairs, but otherwise the problems are similar in that we must control for the difference between the husband distribution (analogous to fathers in mobility tables) and the wife distribution (analogous to "sons"). We can, thus, make use of Boudon's I_B to index the amount of marital immobility that exists independent of structural constraints. Then, with the technique used earlier, we may generate *alternative* matrices to those that provided table 7.1, presenting the frequencies of homogamy-heterogamy as if the supplies of husbands and wives of similar status were equal.

Calculating I_B gives us the following values:

Czechoslovakia	.5655	
Hungary	.8279	
Poland	.7743	(3 × 3 matrix)
USSR	.7120	

Summarizing what the values tell us, it seems that Czechoslovakia ranks again as the most egalitarian case. With the "forced" heterogamy generated by unequal male and female distributions eliminated, only slightly more than half the Czechs who could have entered into heterogamous marriages avoid doing so in favor of homogamy. But over 80 percent of the Hungarians, and over 75 percent of the Poles, select mates from their own stratum, with the Estonians closer to these patterns than to the Czechs. This is evidence, all in all, of a rather high degree of homogamy, against assertions that socialist marriage is particularly "democratic."

Table 7.4 provides our "alternative" rates. Constructed in the same manner as table 7.1, it presents the picture as it would appear were the supply of males and females in each occupation category equal.

We see, first, that the tendency for elite homogamy is intensified (especially in Hungary), with majorities of intelligentsia males in

Table 7.4.
Socio-occupational Categories of Wives, by Category of Husbands, under Hypothetical Conditions of "Equal Supply"

Husband	*Wife*			
	1	*2*	*3*	*4*
1 Elite				
Czechoslovakia	48.2	10.4	40.1	1.3
Hungary	56.9	27.1	14.6	1.5
Poland I	64.3	32.1	3.6	—
USSR	52.9	20.9	23.8	2.4
Poland II	75.2	22.3	2.5	—
2 Routine nonmanual				
Czechoslovakia	29.8	14.8	53.8	1.7
Hungary	18.4	36.4	43.0	2.2
Poland I	18.2	58.7	23.1	—
USSR	13.5	46.2	31.6	8.7
Poland II	12.7	70.8	16.5	—
3 Worker				
Czechoslovakia	11.1	4.8	80.6	3.5
Hungary	4.8	8.5	77.3	9.4
Poland I	1.4	15.8	82.8	—
USSR	8.1	14.1	69.4	8.4
Poland II	0.7	10.1	89.1	—
4 Peasant				
Czechoslovakia	8.4	2.7	60.2	28.8
Hungary	0.0	0.0	16.3	83.7
USSR	3.0	4.6	10.3	82.2

SOURCE: see source note to table 7.1.

each country making such marriages. However, *across the board,* more men marry elite women, given the increase in their availability. "Equal supply" eliminates a large number of women from the routine nonmanual category, with differing effects on the marital fortunes of males depending on their stratum. The elite, except in Czechoslovakia, are not disadvantaged—in reality, averaging across the four countries (excluding Poland II), elite men's marriages with nonmanual women were 76.3 percent of their total; with equal supply, this increases to 78.2 percent. Though routine nonmanual males marry more elite women as their supply increases, their probabilities of strict homogamy fall off as the supply is equalized, and in general their rate of nonmanual marriages declines: from an average 20.5 to 17.2 percent. Male peasants, on the other hand, move a little from their low base: in reality 5.8 percent, and with equal supply 6.2 percent, marry nonmanual females. By and large, the changes of the gross, average sort are not large when equal supply is introduced (for the changes in individual categories/countries, the reader may himself examine table 7.4). The patterns of homogamy persist. Though traditional social structures may have changed, and though those traditional structures varied in their mixing of elitist and egalitarian components, there are still elements of status-matching quite evident in these data. One cannot see economic and social barriers, the kind that decree in general terms the sort of spouse to which one may "legitimately" aspire, in tables. But the data in the tables hint very strongly at their existence, and at the persistence of national differences we might expect. In conditions of equal supply, Polish and Hungarian nonmanual men marry manual women much less readily than do the males of traditionally more egalitarian Czechoslovakia, or of the USSR, where the processes of social change have been perhaps more pervasive, and certainly more convulsive.

HOUSING: TO EACH ACCORDING TO. . . . ?

In the socialist countries, the supply and quality of housing is a painful subject. While this is also the case in many other parts of the world, in the socialist states the problems are perennial, seemingly always far from solution, and more critically concerned with minimal space and amenities than they are in the West. Housing needs, of course, have been massive. The industrial migration generated tremendous demand. Aging and wartime devastation, both in the USSR and later in Eastern Europe, retired (or should have) a good deal of the older housing stock. The stage was set for governmental programs of a populist nature, to provide "adequate housing for all." The programs persist, but the outcome has been complex.

To casual outside observers, taking either an American or Western European perspective, the problems seem somewhat moderated by the fact that socialist rents are low—artificially so. Through most of socialist history, housing has been seen as a "welfare" item, a public expenditure. While this may seem good, there have been negative consequences. Industrial investment, seen as productive whereas housing was not, has enjoyed priority, and housing has finished far back in the race for investment. Additions to the housing stock in recent years have been impressive, but so have rises in demand. Socialist housing still suffers from the consequences of earlier policies—or the lack of viable policies. In the USSR, urban dwelling space was created in the 1920s and 1930s by the continued subdivision of existing housing into "communal apartments." One or two families to a room (in large cities especially) shared kitchens, bath, toilet facilities (where available), and corridors with other unrelated families, with all the attendant and predictable discomfort, rancor, spite, and conflict. Though the situation has eased, many still live this way, and it is almost a certainty that the majority of Soviet citizens over the age of forty who grew up in urban areas were raised in such circumstances.

Scarcity, small size, and low rents, combined with other factors, have made the distribution of socialist housing appear, to some Western observers, quite egalitarian. One's housing seemed to provide little hint as to one's occupation or income. In fact, this is scarcely the case, though it is not surprising that it should appear so.

First, although some significant exceptions exist,[5] clearly defined neighborhoods, the familiar cue to residential status, are generally still not part of socialist settlement patterns. The excess demand for space, state control over land use, the desirability of closeness to main lines of public transport where private cars are still rare, have all worked against the development of neighborhoods as the American knows them. Frequently households of quite distinct strata may be represented in the same building in Moscow, Warsaw, or Bucharest. There are, as we shall see, better and worse buildings or developments, but given the standardization of the outward aspects of apartment buildings, things generally look equal, if drab.

Another factor is that of selective exposure. When Westerners have the opportunity to visit socialist counterparts in their homes, they will find their colleagues' living circumstances generally modest compared to what they enjoy at home. Some discretionary purchases will be evident (art, books, stereo systems) and not unfamiliar: but the frame of this picture is, likely as not, a two- or three-room apartment, a tiny kitchen and small bath, with other rooms doing double or triple duty between at-home work, dining, sleeping, and entertaining. The rooms will be small, the whole apartment likely quite small by one's domestic standard (although here Americans will react more strongly than Western Europeans). The subliminal impression received is frequently one of marked egalitarianism in the distribution of housing. The socialist host, in prestige and income terms, may be of the elite—but surely his cramped apartment mainfests one area in which distribution takes little account of status? The visitor, I think, tends to assume that the "worker" can scarcely have much less space than this, that he can scarcely be doing without the minimal amenities. This is an error—for these, as we shall see, *are* absent from many workers' homes. Despite the appearance of egalitarian distribution and the persistence of official notions that housing is a welfare item where need is determinative, access to these scarce goods is also quite stratified. It has, in some measure, always been so. Earlier, we saw the Makarygin family, Solzhenitsyn's "new class" creations, enjoying *two* connected apartments in 1949 Moscow—when larger families occupied a single room or part thereof in a communal apartment. Fewer live this way today, but the Makarygins are still with us. How and why the inequalities persist, in a nonmarket housing system, deserves some comment.

The answers lie in the same tension that marks socialist wage and income policy—a tension between a promise of a progressive egalitarianism and the perceived necessity of differentiated, unequal reward in the here and now. No socialist commentator has pinpointed the conflict and outcome more succinctly than the (now exiled) Budapest sociologist Ivan Szelenyi. As he notes, construction lagged and shortages persisted in Hungary partly because "housing construction was not even considered economic investment, but an allowance made out of national income."[6] The existence of a large number of low-earnings households led to a building program, apparently dating from the late 1950s, aimed at providing new state-owned apartments at heavily subsidized low rents to the below-average earners. However, as Szelenyi and his collaborator, the novelist-sociologist Gyorgy Konrad found in the late 1960s,[7] it was not the working poor who got these accommodations (desirable because of the low fixed rents and the presence of amenities absent in older housing stock) but the higher earners, who needed housing subsidies the least! Those modest earners for whom the new state apartments were intended dwelt disproportionately in less-subsidized types of housing. In Szelenyi's words,

> the original aim of rent subsidies was to close those gaps to some extent which had opened in incomes in the interests of providing incentives for productivity. If, however, those flats systematically came into the possession of those enjoying higher incomes, the effect of the subsidy was the very opposite, differences in standards of living were widened and not narrowed. *Rent subsidies thus turned into wage supplements increasing the differences between low and high incomes.*[8]

Desirable apartments, then, were used as an incentive, and became an income supplement.[9] Employers, in a wage-controlled situation, could attract scarce talent by the promise of a new, comfortable, well-located apartment. The principle that dictated higher pay for scarce and valued services also dictated privileged access to desirable housing.[10] The "welfare" principle continued to determine the rents set on such apartments, guaranteeing that the absolute, as well as the relative, housing outlay of the affluent would often be less than that of the modestly paid worker. It was not a market system, yet there was little difference—as Szelenyi put it, the "*bureaucratic distribution of flats led to a result which resembled the likely one of distribution through the market*" (emphasis in the original).[11]

Thus it was in the Hungary of the late 1960s, and thus it has been elsewhere in the socialist world. In the USSR, the operating principles determining priorities in housing allocation show the same confused mix of welfare and incentive orientations, with little doubt about which will prevail in a conflict. Entitled to extra living space (an extra room, or up to 20 more square meters) are persons suffering from certain diseases, especially those with a risk of contagion, and very large families (7 children or more)—a need criterion. But "leading workers" and executives of state and party bodies, members of the various Academies of Sciences, holders of higher degrees or academic titles, persons who have received various honorific titles (Hero of Socialist Labor, Honored Artists, etc.), members of creative and artistic unions, military men ranking as colonel and above (and their opposite numbers in the KGB), certain doctors and dentists, etc., are all—by various laws and decrees dating from 1930 onwards—also entitled to extra space.[12] Certain apartment buildings in the large central cities, generally well above the average in their quality and amenities, are reserved for elite writers, scientists, etc.[13]

Some of the provisions make sense for functional reasons. Creative artists and academics need studios and studies, and many, since the crisis in work space affects cultural and educational institutions, do not have them available at their places of work. Such however is *not* the case with the bureaucrats and functionaries who do have offices to work in, and military and police personnel who are similarly provided for. All in all, the likelihood of extra square meters at one's disposal seems to increase with the weight of one's pay packet. Most of the categories described above are well paid by Soviet standards, and some receive the special salary components described in the previous chapter.

Nor are rents for extra space overly progressive.[14] Rents are theoretically pegged to income, but the rather low maximum rate is paid by virtually all people—even the average worker's wages cross this threshold. Extra space up to 4.5 square meters goes at the standard rate; above it the charge is trebled. The *base* is so low, however, that the best-housed will hardly pay much above the average 4 to 5 percent of family income going for rent in the nation as a whole.[15] Some special categories enjoy rent subsidies within this system. Military and KGB personnel above a certain rank pay a rate of 8 kopeks per square meter, while a rank-and-file worker whose income is much lower will pay the national maximum of 13.2 kopeks for the same space.[16]

Figures from Soviet research on the housing accommodations of different occupational groupings illuminate the results of this distribution system. An investigation of two factories in the Sverdlovsk area, one virtually *in* the city with a generally better housing stock, the latter 100 kilometers distant and less well-fixed, revealed differences even between the highly aggregated categories of engineering-technical employees and manual workers. In the first factory, about 80 percent of the former lived in private (i.e., noncommunal), well-equipped apartments, versus about 52 percent of the manuals. In the second, the engineering-technical category was so housed in about

65 percent of the cases, versus 36 percent for the manual workers.[17] Shkaratan's investigations among the personnel of the Leningrad machine-building industry and workers in other cities also showed differences. While the differences in square meters per capita between the households of "leaders of labor collectives" (7.8) and households of unskilled workers (5.6) in Kazan, (1967) did not seem overly large, the *quality* of accommodations was quite uneven; the industrial intelligentsia were 2 to 2.5 times more likely to be housed in private apartments or similar accommodations than were unskilled workers.[18]

The conflict between the need principle and housing as reward and incentive has generally been resolved in favor of the latter in the other states as well. As the Polish sociologist Stefan Nowakowski observed, in a shortage situation, the choice between allocating an apartment to a worker or to an engineer would be resolved in favor of the latter's higher skills and greater scarcity value.[19] As another Polish scholar notes, new apartments differ markedly in amenities: "in some industrial centers there are sharp differences in the furnishings of a flat provided for workers and one for technical intelligentsia."[20]

In the "marketized" Yugoslav economy, a private housing sector plays a larger role than elsewhere. Inequities are also pronounced. The "unskilled worker with an elementary education or less, and who lacks seniority, is most likely to pay the highest rent for the least desirable housing."[21] The sociologist Srdan Vrcan cites some revealing figures in an article in *Praxis*. Industrial plants, most of whose employees are manual workers, invest considerably less per employee (10 to 500 dinars per annum) in housing than do "government bodies, banks, business corporations, foreign trade firms, and socio-political organizations" (where staff is heavily weighted toward the white-collar categories). The latter range from 5,000 to 20,000 dinars per annum per employee.[22] Even within industrial enterprises, workers are disadvantaged—in one of the largest enterprises in Split, where rank-and-file workers made up 75 percent of the employed, they had received only 15 percent of the apartments placed at the enterprise's disposal since World War II.[23] Other research indicated that, among the modern apartments in new districts, modest size accommodations (60 to 70 square meters) were tenanted 84 percent by nonmanuals and only 8.6 percent by manuals, while in those larger than 80 square meters, no workers at all were found.[24]

Housing stratification assumes sharper outlines in some Polish and Hungarian data on apartment size (number of rooms), residential density, and presence or absence of that basic amenity, a private bath. Table 7.5 provides the data, drawn from the Polish industrial city of Lodz in 1965 and the Hungarian nationwide survey of 1963. The figures speak eloquently to differentials in access to housing. Generally, the higher the occupational group, the larger the apartment. Residential density declines as one moves up the occupational/income ladder, owing to larger apartment size but also partially to slightly smaller family size. The likelihood that a household has basic sanitary amenities increases with the status of the head. In Lodz, an intelligentsia household is *eight* times as likely as a skilled worker's household to have a private bath, while in Hungary the comparable ratio for bathrooms is 2.6 to 1. These average figures, of course, are rather insensitive to the extremes of inequality. As the Polish figures stand, they do not tell one, for example, that while only 5.5 percent of Lodz intelligentsia households were accommodated in one-room apartments, 46.7 percent of unskilled workers' households made do with such close quarters, nor that while 73.6 percent of intelligentsia households enjoyed the comparative comfort of three-room flats, only 22.2 percent of the unskilled households were so accommodated.[25]

Advantages of inheritance, contacts, and taste, as they affect the choices available to one in the disposal of income, also influence the type of dwelling occupied, judging from further data from the Hungarian national survey. On the average, 64 percent of the intelligentsia category enjoy apartments with private bath. Within this category, however, those whose head is of nonmanual *parentage* have a private bath in 77 percent of the cases, while those of peasant origin are so equipped only 44 percent of the time. The latter figure also reflects the presence in this category of the "rural intelligentsia," resident in the countryside, where the general quality of housing is a good deal lower. Skilled workers who are "skidders" are better housed than their hereditary counterparts: 59 percent of those with intelligentsia and 38 percent with routine nonmanual fathers have

Table 7.5.
Housing Size, Density, and Amenities; by Socio-occupational Category, Poland (1965), Hungary (1963)

	Poland (Lodz, 1965)				*Hungary (nation, 1963)*		
	persons per room	*no. rooms*	*% bath*	*% toilet*	*persons per room*	*no. rooms*[a]	*% bathroom*
Intelligentsia	1.31	2.90	71.4	79.1	1.77	1.92	64.0
Professional nonmanual	—	—	—	—	1.89	1.68	47.0
Technicians	1.58	2.28	22.4	44.8	—	—	—
Clericals	1.68	2.17	32.1	48.4	1.90	1.54	46.0
Physical-mental workers	1.91	1.95	18.8	38.6	—	—	—
Foremen, etc.	1.72	2.15	21.5	35.3	—	—	—
Skilled workers	2.09	1.85	18.3	28.7	2.31	1.46	25.0
Semiskilled workers	2.27	1.81	10.2	18.6	2.60	1.36	12.0
Unskilled workers	2.41	1.75	8.9	25.5	2.66	1.27	9.0

[a]Original data distribute each category across "1, 2, and 3 or more" rooms; 3.3 used as third category in compiling this table.

SOURCE: adapted from Anita Kobus-Wojciechowska, "Warunki mieszkaniowe i sytuacja materialna," in Wlodzimierz Wesolowski, ed., *Zroznicowanie spoleczne* (Wroclaw, Warsaw, Krakow: Wydawnictwo Polskiej Akademii Nauk, 1970), pp. 195, 197; and Hungarian Central Statistical Office, *Social Stratification in Hungary* (Budapest: CSO, 1967), pp. 27, 71, 75.

bathrooms versus 28 percent of those whose fathers were workers. In fact, moderate skidders—those of intelligentsia origin who are now lower white-collar—possess private bathrooms more often than current intelligentsia who rose from the working classes.[26] The generally older housing stock of 1963 reflected the role of direct housing inheritance (its effect would be less today), but there is no denying this evidence of "hereditary" housing advantage nearly twenty years after the socialist revolution.

Introducing income controls gives us some sense of what people of different socio-occupational categories value. Readiness to spend on or exert effort to acquire amenities (once again, our indicator is an apartment with private bathroom) seems to vary markedly with occupational stratum, independent of income. In the lowest reported income range (up to 600 forint per capita) 29 percent of intelligentsia households have bathrooms, 23 to 27 percent of lower nonmanuals, but only 18 percent of skilled and 5 percent of unskilled workers. Here, where money is tight, extra expenditure on housing amenities indicates some real differentials in relative evaluations, and readiness to do without some items in order to acquire others. Conversely, the highest income category (over 1,800 forint per capita) shows significant differences in what the affluent choose to do with sums permitting more free choice: 78 percent of the intelligentsia, and 48 to 58 percent of the routine nonmanuals obtain a bathroom—but only 44 percent of skilled and 18 percent of unskilled workers do.[27] This is evidence of different values and consumption styles under conditions where income is roughly similar, but it should not, however, be overstressed. First, the top range of incomes for intelligentsia in the over 1,800 *forint* category will be much larger than that for workers. Second, even at equal incomes, routine nonmanual household heads probably enjoy more access to upper management, to the bureaucrats who control the distribution of desirable housing, than do skilled manuals. Indeed, as Yanowitch observes on the basis of an investigation of a variety of Soviet data, whatever one makes of income statistics as they reflect the borderline between the routine nonmanuals and the skilled top of the working class, the inequalities in space of housing are "consistently in favor of nonmanual strata."[28] This greater closeness, promoted by similar work situations, dress, and even modes of speech, probably helps somewhat in getting access to scarce items one *is* willing to pay for.

One could argue that we make too much here of flush toilets. Certainly, we have seen evidence that the intelligentsia, and indeed nonmanuals in general, care more about these things than do manual workers. But it goes further: even with respect to central heating, running water in the apartment, and *sewer* connections, the Polish data show Lodz households in 1965 differentiated by head's occupation. On each indicator, the intelligentsia are well ahead, and the other nonmanuals (technicians and clericals) always do better than even the foremen and skilled workers. Of the intelligentsia, 54.9 percent are warmed by central heating, and only *10* percent of unskilled workers are. Running water comes in the apartments of 86.8 percent of the intelligentsia, 71.0 and 63.7 for clericals and technicians, and 53.3 percent for unskilled workers; 88 percent of the intelligentsia are hooked up to sewers, while the figures for the three strata of manual workers range from 53.3 to 47.1.[29]

We are, of course, dealing with a fairly poor country, Poland; an *old* city with an old housing stock, Lodz; and data over a decade old. To readers used to Western affluence, the Polish and Hungarian figures may seem simply to demonstrate how low general housing standards are. But to stop there is to miss much of the meaning of this brand of inequality to persons for whom American plumbing and comfort standards are, by and large, unattainable irrelevancies.

When we take these differences on their own terms, their importance appears in a different light. The general quality of one's housing is an index of where one stands, how one is regarded by those who control, presumably on the socialist principle of reward according to the *value* of work. The worker whose wife and two children are crowded into a single room, who shares corridors, sinks, toilets, and baths with other families, *knows* where he is. That his superior in the intelligentsia has only two or three rooms, a private bath/toilet, and kitchen is not a small distance. It bulks so large that he may hope to see his children cross it, but can doubt that he ever will.

What is a private bath/kitchen? It is freedom to set one's own schedule of cleansing and attendance to bodily needs, without taking account of others. It is less friction with those others. It is a modicum of *privacy*, of peace of mind. Such things affect children as well as adults, and help to determine the general quality of life and comfort.

What is an extra room? It is the advantage of Lodz intelligentsia over unskilled workers (actually "1.15 rooms"), just as 0.32 of a room is the advantage of a Lodz clerical household over that of a skilled worker. The differences in Hungary appear smaller, but were Budapest, or only cities, the focus, and rural residences excluded, the pattern would probably be closer to the Polish. Even here, an intelligentsia family averages 0.46 rooms more than a skilled worker. The extra room, or part thereof, is wall space to decorate with prints or paintings, to personalize and thus make the apartment more one's own. It is space that allows an extra measure of *intra*familial privacy, a relief from the friction that close quarters can evoke in the most loving families. It is, for younger members of the family, *a place to study* with some protection from distractions of noise and competing activities, in societies where the educational systems still rely on heavy doses of homework. For the intelligentsia or white-collar son in Budapest or Warsaw, working hard to attain his *erettsegi* or *matura* and thus move on the university, study space is not the least of the advantages he enjoys over the motivated sons of the working class. Such differences are not the insignificant things they appear to be in digits and decimals.

DURABLES: THE IMPEDIMENTA OF EVERYDAY LIFE

Eastern Europe and the USSR are less saturated with the appliances that fill the domestic landscape in the United States and Western Europe. From washing machines to TV sets, ownership of durables is simply less likely under socialism, whatever the stratum of the household investigated. But possession of many items is quite differentiated by socio-occupational status, and other variables as well—primarily education and income. (Our data are rather old here—averaging over a decade old. Today, items possessed by most of the intelligentsia in our data are now likely owned by all except for those who freely choose not to acquire them, while items almost unheard of in workers' households are present in many more. But our data do indicate the patterns, under the relative scarcity conditions of the mid-1960s, by which scarce items were distributed among social strata and income and educational groupings; despite changes in total supplies and average living standards, the patterns persist.)

Some aspects of the distribution of durables may seem rather odd to those more familiar with American patterns. The average socialist family is more likely to possess a radio or television set than a refrigerator, telephone, or vacuum cleaner. Much here has to do with supply. Electronic media provide another link between the citizen and the polity, and as such have received priority in state economic planning over such items as refrigerators. Possession of one item whose function is at least partly entertainment—a TV—and one utilitarian item—a washing machine—is determined mainly by income, but these are priority items even for families whose income runs toward the lower end of the scale. Thus, in a Polish urban study (1965), the intelligentsia were best equipped (TV, 78 percent; washer, 90.1 percent), but even unskilled workers' households had them in many cases (46.7 percent had TV, and 68.9 percent a washer). Nor is there any marked break between clerical and skilled workers as the nonmanual-manual line is crossed.[30] Similar conclusions may be drawn from a nationwide Hungarian survey,[31] and Czech data from 1967 offer further support. Correlation coefficients show income correlations higher for TV ownership (.386 with household head's income, with 75.2 percent of the total survey populations possessing a TV) and washing machines (.233, with 82.9 percent of the surveyed owning one) than were correlations with household head's education or occupational status.[32] About these items there is little differentiation according to taste. They are parts of a standard package of conveniences. While possession thus entails little in the way of conspicious consumption, their lack marks a household as poorly off by comparison to national norms.

Refrigerators play a moderate role in socialist household economy in general—something of an inconvenience, since without one, one must shop, frequently, every day for food. However, socialist *trade* in edibles is by and large still organized around the assumption of daily shopping. Few large supermarkets, and lagging development in the areas of frozen food, convenience foods, and packaging that retards perishability have reduced the advantages a refrigerator-

cum-freezer offers for long-term storage in other countries. This is all changing gradually, as consumption standards are upgraded, but today buying a refrigerator may still manifest as much a desire to seem well-equipped and modern as to maximize kitchen efficiency. Some data suggest that this is the case. Polish urban data show refrigerators present in 57.2 percent of intelligentsia homes, in 30.1 percent of clericals' and 20.7 percent of technicians' households, with a fairly substantial break between these and the 12.3 and 5.5 percent for skilled and unskilled workers' households.[33] In Czechoslovakia, the occupational status of the household head is more strongly correlated with refrigerator ownership (.406) than is income (.338) or education (.332).[34]

Strong differentials appear in the case of two seemingly quite utilitarian items—a vacuum cleaner and a telephone. Polish data (for Lodz) show a range of telephone hookups from 62.5 percent for intelligentsia families to 1.1 percent for unskilled worker households, with clericals and skilled workers sharply divided by figures of 21.5 and 2.0 percent, respectively.[35] Stated another way, if we guess from the single datum of "telephone" that the household possessing it is of the intelligentsia category, we will guess correctly with respect to 62.5 percent of the intelligentsia, and miss 37.5 percent. But our other erroneous guesses, wherein we misclassify other telephone owners as intelligentsia, will amount to only 5.7 percent of the guesses we have made about nonintelligentsia. We will not discriminate better with any other item on which we have data. Czech research also shows higher correlations of phone possession with occupational status (.379) and education (.329), than with income (.256).[36] The distribution of phones is much more inegalitarian than that of income.

This is not, then, simply a matter of the income component of stratification. Telephone service is not cheap, but neither is it prohibitively expensive. The supply, however, is small, and occupational position, connections, and organizational intelligence probably play a more direct role in acquiring phone service than cash in hand (short of direct bribery). Furthermore, however convenient a telephone is in general, its relative value is greater for those with less routine jobs, broader friendship and social networks, etc. Hence the probability, suggested by the Czech data, that in the socialist world (at least for so long as telephones remain scarce) their possession will indicate relatively elevated educational and occupational as well as income characteristics. It is probably as good a summary indicator of relatively high status as any we now have.

Possession of a vacuum cleaner is also strongly differentiated, with breaks between occupational strata and across the manual-nonmanual line larger than we would anticipate were income a deciding factor. The Polish data show vacuums in 73.6 percent of intelligentsia households, 51.8 of technicians', and 45.1 of clericals', versus only 23.9 and 12.2 for skilled and unskilled workers.[37] In Hungary, data from 1963 show lower total ownership rates, but still strong differentiations; intelligentsia and lower nonmanuals, 55 and 35 percent versus 17 and 5 percent for skilled/semiskilled workers and unskilled workers, respectively.[38] Czech data show vacuums correlated .463 with education and .519 with occupational status, but a lower .388 with income. Separate tabular data (not reproduced here) on the distribution of vacuums by income and education show comparatively large variations by education within income groups and rather less variation by income within groups similar in education. In the best-paid category (2,501 kcs. or more per month) university graduates had vacuums in 95 percent of cases versus only 26 percent for those of similar income who had not finished elementary school. On the other hand, 86 percent of university graduates in the lowest-paid group (under 1,250 kcs. monthly) had still managed to acquire a vacuum. The differences by income between the least educated are much larger: as above, 26 percent of the best-paid have them, but only 11 percent of the lowest-paid. The ownership ratios of income groups *within* educational categories are thus 1 to 1.1 for the university graduates and 1 to 2.4 for those who did not complete elementary school.[39] Soviet data, too, show a tendency for strong differentiation centered around vacuum cleaners.[40]

Why should the vacuum, as household durable, show this pattern with respect to stratification variables? No completely convincing answer is possible. Income, and the newer, more spacious housing that accompanies it, certainly does play a role—the income correlation is lower than those for education and status but higher than those for all 14 other income/durable pairings in the Czech data. But beyond this, much seems to depend on different notions, influenced by education and job status, as to what the proper household requires, what is defined as dirtiness and cleanliness, order and disorder in the home, and the priority of equipping women, upon whom the burden of housework still falls overwhelmingly, with labor-saving devices. That households with well-paid, well-educated, and high-status heads will also contain a relatively well-educated female spouse with an appropriate job is not improbable. Such households are likely to value both modernity and appliances that save time—a scarce resource in busy and active lives.

LIFE-STYLES

Statistics on marriage patterns, housing, and consumer goods tell us something of the framework of family life in different strata. But these still are mute on *how* people of different strata live. What do they do with free time? With whom do they associate, and in what sorts of activities? Is social life more intense and varied among those with higher-status jobs and lengthier educations, or is there a compensation for routine work and modest wages in a "mateyness" among the working classes, warmer and more sincere than the social relations of the intelligentsia? Who reads, attends the theater, watches TV? Do these activities differ among the strata, or is there the sort of homogenization one might expect after a generation of socialist attempts to make a common standard of culture available to all?

In their dealings with family life, American sociology textbooks have frequently been charged with a middle-class bias; with taking the middle-class family—presumably the kind in which most textbook authors grew up, and most of them live—as *the* family, the national standard. Critics, reasonably enough, worried that possibly quite distinct patterns of working-class family life were getting short shrift. In large measure, they seem to have been right. Two notable works, Komarovsky's *Blue-Collar Marriage*[41] and Young and Willmott's *Family and Kinship in East London*[42] explored the social patterns of working-class life, intra- and extrafamilial, in "Glenton," an American suburban community, and the London district of Bethnal Green. Their findings seemed in marked contrast with patterns of middle-class life.

Should we then expect class or stratum-related differences in the socialist states as well? The ideological emphasis has been on "democratization," on uplift of the lower classes, on economic leveling. Educational opportunities have expanded under socialism. And, as we have seen, mobility *has* been a common experience among today's socialist citizens. All these forces seem to press for a greater homogenization; yet everyday aspects of life may be the most resistant to large-scale social change. In fact, a considerable amount of evidence points to real differences in family life-styles, rather parallel to those uncovered in Western studies—enough to reject any hypothesis that there is no difference in the styles of families from different strata.

In London and in Glenton, for example, the role of (nonfamily) friends is an important, yet rather restricted one. Home, and hosting people there, is a matter of joint relations between relatives. Friends, even those seen frequently at work, on the street, in bars, are rarely invited home: a worker in Bethnal Green observes that doing so "doesn't seem right somehow. Your home's your own."[43] Komarovsky, too, notes that the "'pattern of entertaining' does not exist" among her blue-collar couples. Having nonrelatives home as guests was so strange a pattern that one of her informants "said that such a custom may have existed in the past but must have gone out of fashion because no one she knew followed it."[44] The social worlds of husband and wife are quite separate—wives have little contact with their husbands' male cliques,[45] husbands know little of their wives' female companions. The social life of the blue-collar strata seems less varied in content than that of the textbook middle classes.

Though the sort of research exemplified by Komarovsky and Young and Wilmott is rarely the enterprise of socialist researchers, it does find echo in the writings of Polish, Soviet, and Hungarian investigators. Irena Nowak's study of social contact patterns in Warsaw revealed marked differences between unskilled and skilled blue-collar workers on one hand, and the lower white-collar strata and intelligentsia on the other. The social life of the latter is wider and more active: asked whether they met with at least three friends once or more a month, 34 percent of the unskilled and 45 percent of the skilled manuals answered affirmatively, versus 57 percent of the white-collars and 62 percent of the intelligentsia. To the question whether one was visited *at home* by nonrelative(s) once or more a month, 47 percent of unskilled and 59 percent of skilled workers answered yes, versus 70 percent for the intelligentsia and 74 percent for white-collars with secondary education—those with only primary schooling fell below the skilled manuals, at 52 percent.[46] Gordon and Klopov's Soviet research revealed a slightly greater tendency for manuals to visit, and be visited by, relatives when compared to "specialists" (intelligentsia) and greater tendencies for specialists to visit and be visited at home by co-workers (26 percent, versus 18 percent for manuals) and by friends whose selection was not a matter of kinship, residence, or common work-place (73 percent, versus 46 percent for manuals).[47] (These figures are for males, but the parallel figures for females run generally in the same direction.)

Less direct evidence in the same direction emerges from the 1963 Hungarian household survey. Accounting for "noncultural" leisure activities (apparently "nonpurposive" social life), the intelligentsia and other nonmanuals state that about half their time is spent "in the family circle," while manual workers consume about two-thirds of this time thus, and peasants even more.[48] Later Polish research, by Warzywoda-Kruszynska in Lodz (1965), shows greater tendencies for manuals than nonmanuals to state that their acquaintances/companions are *also* their relatives, and a somewhat stronger tendency for working-class respondents to see their acquaintances as determined by residence and blood relationships rather than by "common interests."[49]

Nowak's Warsaw respondents were asked to name the two categories of persons with whom they spent most of their leisure time, from a list of "relatives, work-mates, neighbors, and other friends" with a "no acquaintances" category available as well. Skilled workers nominated relatives and work-mates (32 and 39 percent, with other friends named by 35 percent) while intelligentsia males gave each of the first two categories 29 percent and "other friends" 63 percent. Routine white-collar males with secondary education tended rather to resemble the intelligentsia, and those with primary education more the workers. The distance of the social worlds is emphasized in the responses of the unskilled as compared to the intelligentsia: only 18 percent of the former named "other friends," versus the intelligentsia's 63 percent, while fully 32 percent of the unskilled said they had *no* acquaintances versus only 10 percent of the intelligentsia. The reverse of a frequent choice of "other friends" was a frequent naming of *neighbors*—here, 16 percent of the unskilled did so versus only 6 percent for the intelligentsia (with a similar low figure for white-collar workers with secondary education).[50]

Nowak's data also partially support a phenomenon noted earlier by Komarovsky in Glenton: the separation of husband's and wife's social worlds. The "no common friends" pattern, reflecting the isolation of male and female cliques, was reported by 19 percent of unskilled workers versus only 4 percent for white-collars with secondary education and 7 percent of the intelligentsia. Skilled manuals and less-educated nonmanuals were even at 11 percent. The most common pattern (except for the better educated nonmanuals and intelligentsia) is one of totally common acquaintance, with 56, 42, and 60 percent of unskilled, skilled, and white collars with primary education reporting it, versus 37 and 28 percent for the white collar workers with secondary education and the intelligentsia. "Modal" for the latter two groups is maximum diversity: a set of common friends, and other friends specific to each spouse. Such is reported by 54 percent of the intelligentsia and 43 percent of the white collars, but by only *12* percent of unskilled and 27 percent of skilled workers.[51] The pattern that combines a shared social life with "freedom" of spouses to select other friends on their own is much better developed at the top than the bottom of the socio-occupational ladder (although it should also be noted that Nowak's respondents were males, raising the possibility of distortions that might well exaggerate the degree of "commonality" among the working-class respondents).

The forces that tend to make friendship a matter of social homogeneity—similarity of education, tastes, life-style, etc.—evidently work under socialism much the way they do elsewhere in the world. Friendship tends to increase as social distance decreases. Gordon and Klopov report from their Soviet data that 79 percent of specialist males name other specialists as their friends, while only 10 percent nominate workers. Conversely, workers name similar friends 73 percent of the time, and claim specialists in only 21 percent of the cases.[52] Assuming these figures to be accurate, this slight "upward" trend in workers' associations may reflect elements of patron-client linkages. As one Polish scholar observes,

> The engineer or technician may call in at the pub for a drink with a working man, but it is improbable that the engineer and workman would visit each other in each others' houses. If this does happen, there is an element of patronage, as for instance when the engineer acts as godfather to the workman's child, or attends his wedding.[53]

In any case, such friendships go against a general grain of homogeneity. Warzywoda-Kruszynska's study in Lodz included data on respondent's "closest friend."[54] A high degree of exclusivity prevails among the intelligentsia: 72.4 nominate other intelligentsia, 19.8 other nonmanuals (clericals and technicians), and only 3.9 percent workers (skilled) with the remaining 3.9 percent going to physical-mental workers and the "foremen, etc." category. Semiskilled workers nominate other manuals (including "physical-mental" and foremen) in 80.3 percent, lower nonmanuals in 9.1 percent and intelligentsia in only 1.5 percent of the cases. Especially interesting are the patterns at the borderline, between clericals and skilled manuals. Clericals (evidencing, perhaps, their aspirations) nominate intelligentsia as closest friends more (34.8 percent) than they do other clericals (20.3) and technicians (10.1) combined. Skilled manuals, on the other hand, locate only 7.3 percent of their "best friends" in the intelligentsia, and 18.4 in the two routine nonmanual strata. This nonmanual total of 25.7 percent is smaller than the total percentage citing other skilled workers alone (39.2 percent), and is *quite* far removed from the clericals' distribution pattern. Artisans, foremen, and physical-mental workers are "transitional" between clericals and skilled manuals, but are closer to workers than to any of the three nonmanual groupings. The break here is really between white and blue collar, as the two-by-two adaptation of the original data on nomination of closest friend show, below (all "transitional" groupings are classified as manual).

	1.	2.
1. nonmanual	78.3	21.7
2. manual	24.9	75.1

While some of this selectivity is no doubt a product of the ecology of workplace and dwelling, there is no reason to assume that this accounts for it entirely.

Warsaw is not Glenton, Budapest scarcely Bethnal Green, but the evidence suggests that they are very much on the same planet; that differences between the blue and white collar worlds are common properties of both. That the divisions seem in certain instances less radical than those inferred of Glenton and Bethnal Green may point to some moderate long-term impacts of revolution. But they may also simply reflect different residence patterns. In Glenton and Bethnal Green, most people find it possible, and desirable, to live close to family—and the course of the day shows frequent contact between the most tightly linked pair of wife and her mother. The settlement patterns of socialist cities involve two countertrends: the necessity of a young couple's living in a parental apartment while waiting for one of their own in their early years of marriage (with all the tensions inherent in such a situation) and the allocation system, which, likely enough, will provide an apartment, at last, farther from those parents than the young couple might like. The new apartment is too great an attraction to bypass (just as moving from the Bethnal Green tenements to a new housing estate was prompted not by weaker kin-ties among the leavers, but by the enhanced amenities of the new accommodations).[55] While the frequency of interaction with family decreases with distance, the values and attitudes that make for working-class familism may persist. In summary, surely there is much in the following words of a 43-year-old Budapest pipefitter familiar to those who have done fieldwork in working-class communities in the West.

> Those who work close to me are good friends of mine, but we don't go to each other's houses. I don't mind if they come to see us, but I refuse to sit about formally in someone else's house. We visit each other with my brother-in-law, he is a tanner at the Leather Factory, and his wife an office worker. They have two daughters about as old as ours. I call regularly on my mother who has been living alone at Ujpest for a year now. We try to go away somewhere for our summer holidays every year. If it falls through, there is always bathing near here.
>
> We are home-bodies. . . .[56]

That the same pattern persists in younger age groups, that they still depend heavily on the family circle, is manifest in the words of a 29-year-old worker living with wife and young daughter in a sublet basement room, and saving for the down payment on "his own place."

> We are trying to save money, so we don't go anywhere. . . . We take the evening meal home from the factory canteen. The fact is that at home it is impossible for us to cook, for three families are using the same sink. . . . When we have free Saturdays we spend Sundays at my mother's in Buda. We sleep there, and get breakfast, dinner and supper, and that means a saving of about 200 to 300 forints. My in-laws also occasionally send us sausages and ham, and apples and grapes.[57]

Home-bodies, indeed!

CULTURE AND THE HOUSEHOLD

Households of different socio-occupational strata structure their social lives in different ways, participating in narrower or broader social worlds. It may be expected that they will consume "culture" differentially, as well. In testing such expectations, our data force us to let a portion of the total stand for the whole, and generally concentrate on the printed word. This is an area in which contemporary figures should reflect a greater degree of egalitarianism than was achieved in the past. Increased education and the virtual elimination of illiteracy have made the capacity, and perhaps the subjective need to read (beyond the requirements of job), more widespread among social strata than previously. Thus, differences in reading and the propensity to acquire reading material that exist *today* should to some degree reflect persistent stratum characteristics. And, in fact, all the data indicate that the place of books and magazines in everyday life differs markedly with the occupational stratum of the household head and with two other important status components—education and income. Poland and Hungary, once again, provide the major sources of our data.

Who reads? The most general answer, one should state initially, is "everyone"; at least few admit reading nothing. Even unskilled workers report "some" reading in Eastern Europe—but scarcely as much as those whose jobs, education, and income place them in a higher position.

Research in Lodz (1965) found 30.7 percent of the intelligentsia surveyed responding positively to an inquiry as to whether they read more than three non-work-related magazines per month—only 1.1 percent of unskilled workers replied thus. The gap at the manual-nonmanual borderline was almost as striking as the confrontation of the extremes. Technicians and clericals gave positive answers to the totals of 27.6 and 21.5 percent, while only 6.1 percent of the skilled workers so responded. Only 3.3 percent of the intelligentisia admitted to avoiding magazines completely (12.1 and 19.3 percent of technicians and clericals), while 68.9 percent of the unskilled and 44.7 percent of skilled workers confessed the same.[58] Hungarian data for 1963 on subscribership to newspapers and periodicals, controlling for income, show generally high figures and less of manual-nonmanual break, but still indicate differences in the expected direction: 96 percent of the intelligentsia and 92 percent of clericals are subscribers, as opposed to a working-class range from 87 (for skilled) to 68 percent (for unskilled) workers.[59] Controls on the Polish data indicated a larger correlation of readership with educational level than with occupational stratum or income, although each had an independent effect.[60]

Book reading and acquisition are more differentiated than is consumption of an undifferentiated category of "newspapers and periodicals." Sixty-nine percent of Hungarian intelligentsia declared themselves "frequent" readers of books, as did 66 percent of the clericals, while only 40 percent of skilled and 21 percent of unskilled workers styled themselves thus.[61] Asked how many books they had read in the two months preceding, respondents' replies in Lodz averaged: intelligentsia, 2.0; clericals 1.73; skilled workers, 0.88 and unskilled 0.49.[62] Income had less to do with readership than did socio-occupational groups,[63] but education more. At the lowest level (less than complete elementary), respondents average 0.26 books. Complete secondary (academic) schooling lifted the average to 1.42 while a university degree generated a 1.98-book average.[64]

Possession of a personal library provides yet another indicator of differentiated patterns. Hungarian intelligentsia respondents possessed libraries of 200 books or more in 35 percent of the cases, clericals rather less (13 percent). But both were a far remove from the skilled manuals at 3 percent and the unskilled (2 percent). Education, again, was a powerful determinant (44 percent of university graduates had such libraries, versus 1 percent of those with less than 8 years' schooling), as was family background (36 percent of household heads who were *sons* of intelligentsia have libraries, regardless of current occupation, and 19 percent of other nonmanuals' sons, but only 7 percent of workers' and 1 percent of peasants' sons). Income accounts for 11 percent of the total variance, while stratum membership accounts for 29 percent. (Within strata, again, income accounts for only 3 percent, while stratum, within income groups, accounts for almost 20 percent of the variance). In more concrete terms, this means that in the lowest income category (under 600 forints monthly per capita) 12 percent of the intelligentsia nonetheless possessed libraries as against 1 percent of skilled workers and 6 percent of clericals. In the most affluent category (1,800+ forints) the intelligentsia rate climbed to 43 percent, the skilled workers to 4 percent, and the clericals to 15 percent. The line is sharply drawn between clericals and skilled manuals. Independent of income, clericals' 13 percent library ownership is well ahead of skilled workers' 3 percent.[65]

In Lodz, a respondent's "library" was defined as 50 or more books: 83.7 of the intelligentsia possessed such a collection, versus 50.6 percent of the clericals. Workers ranged from 15.3 percent (skilled) to 8.9 (unskilled).[66] Income differentiated the index less strongly (77.5 percent for those with over 4,000 zloty per month income versus 18.5 percent for those with under 2,000),[67] while education was stronger: complete and incomplete higher education (a combination that moderates the result) produced 77.0 percent rate of library ownership, while incomplete elementary schooling reduced the figure to an average 9.6 percent.[68] Within both education and income categories, clericals and skilled workers are still separated by a highly significant gap. Of those with complete secondary education, clericals possess a library in 65.2 percent of cases, but only 30.3 percent of skilled workers have one. Clericals may very well have a model of appropriate consumption they strive to follow. At a low income level (up to 600 *zloty* per month per capita) 37.5 percent of clerical households have libraries versus 11.4 percent of skilled workers, a difference that holds at medium and high income levels and thus manifests a greater readiness in general to spend for such cultural commodities.[69]

Similar, if more general, patterns of readership obtain in Soviet data,[70] and data for other socialist states. From such data, certain conclusions that are surely more than tentative may be drawn. First, behavior with respect to the printed media is markedly differentiated by the sort of socio-occupational categories employed here, with the differences running in the direction one would naturally anticipate. Not only persons in elite occupations, but also those in more routine nonmanual work, show greater proclivities to report a good deal of reading, and to acquire books and magazines, than do *any* of the manual strata. Second, the influence of income here is moderate compared to that of education and occupational category. The moderation of income differences under socialism has not wiped out the effect of other factors in this area of cultural consumption, and indeed even within similar education *and* income groups, nonmanuals acquire more books, and do more reading, than manuals. Third, insofar as "books in the home" and the example of reading as "normal" activity affect the household cultural atmosphere, we see here another factor contributing to the higher educational aspirations and better success rates of nonmanual offspring in their educational competition with manual children.

Other forms of cultural consumption as well are related to stratum. Intelligentsia in particular, and nonmanuals in general, are more frequent attenders of cinema and theater offerings than are manuals, with differences larger in the area of theater attendance than in filmgoing.[71]

Television, on the other hand, is on its way to becoming as "democratic" a medium in the East as it is in the West. The main determinant of TV ownership appears to be income, with most who can afford one acquiring a set, and differences in ownership by level of education or occupational category (with income controlled) rather smaller, although the data here are not very clear.[72] Data are, unfortunately, quite scarce on intensity and selectivity of utilization, although some Polish findings suggest that intelligentsia and other nonmanuals are more likely to watch (or to report that they watch!) more "serious" programs and somewhat less sports than the manual strata.[73]

The different intensities and qualities of cultural consumption for the different strata tell us something about the varying intensities at which they live, the diversity of stimuli they receive and to which they respond. Komarovsky, contrasting the blue-collar wives to Glenton to middle-class women, notes that the latter, despite being better equipped with the "good things" of life, feel a greater sense of pressure "generated by the sheer volume of the stimuli to which they respond and by their consequent awareness of the many uses to which they might put free time."[74] Attitudes toward time are revealing in the socialist states as well. Those lower on the occupational continuum feel the pressures of time and its scarcity less than those higher up, and generally have different ideas about what might be done with more time. Responses of Poles, as reported by Kobus-Wojciechowska, show the intelligentsia *least* likely (17.3 percent) and semiskilled workers *most* likely (61.0 percent) to report "enough" free time. Intelligentsia most frequently report "too little" time (77.9), followed by technicians and clericals at 67.1 and 58.9 percent—all well ahead of the workers, where skilled manuals lead in complaining of too little time (47.4 percent).[75] Manual-nonmanual differences hold whether the household includes children or not,[76] but vary interestingly with income within these two broad groupings. Among nonmanuals, as income rises, so does dissatisfaction with the supply of free time, while among manuals it declines. Some of this may be attributed to the nonmanuals' greater opportunities for extra work and tendency to reduce their time supply in quest of more income. But differences in the demands one makes of time, and their complexity, should play a role also. To the member of the intelligentsia, and to those nonmanuals who share partially the same life-style, time deficits mean books and magazines unread, concerts unattended, and other definable opportunities foregone, for which extra income is no more than partial compensation. For manuals who do not moonlight (and most lack the chance to do so on a regular basis) increases in income are more functions of wage raises and changes in job classification than time-consuming extra effort. Their relative satisfaction also derives from a less demanding attitude toward time. When books, the theater, etc. are for others, one does not miss them, and spending time passively comes more easily. If increasing one's free time to an "adequate" level involves the purchase of a few labor-saving devices, and a newer apartment with the conveniences that make stove-stoking and trips to a water tap in a building courtyard unnecessary, these *are* things that increased earnings can buy, and the worker can buy more time with them than can the member of the intelligentsia.

Research in the Soviet city of Taganrog provides more evidence of the relationship between attitudes toward the use of time, and educational level. A study of manual workers found diverse patterns in responses to a 13-item schedule of ways of utilizing more free time. Men with less than four years' schooling rated passive rest at home and TV viewing first, work around the house second (women in the same category chose the same pair, inverting their order). Men with some higher education chose study and "self-improvement" first, reading second, and visits to the movies, theater and other amusements outside the home third, placing rest at home and TV viewing eighth and work around the house ninth. (The men with under four years of school, conversely, rated study/self-improvement eleventh, and reading between fourth and fifth.)

Women in general reflected their burden of housework. Up to those with some higher education, housework rated no lower than third. Women with some higher education rated it only seventh, nominating reading, theater and movie visits, and at-home rest/TV as their first three choices. In this, they showed more resemblance to their marginally educated sisters than males did across similar educational boundaries.[77]

Differences in the way people employ their free time, and in the way they say they *would* employ additional free time were it available, seem to follow the other lines drawn between income, educational, and socio-occupational strata. Even data as few as those here push us further toward the view that socialist societies, no less than others, are mosaics composed of households whose composition and activity reflect their different places in the stratification hierarchy.

Chapter Eight

Socialism and Hierarchy in Perspective

> The conservative community demands habits of deference found only in individuals who can remain content in a status not of their own making. The radical community requires an altruism untainted by private property or individual ambition.
>
> —Andrew Hacker, *The End of the American Era* (1972)

READERS WHO have come this far will probably have impressions of two kinds. Some will indicate striking similarities in the meaning of success and advantage, in what striving for them entails, and in the way the pie is cut, linking their societies and those that are the subject matter here. Other impressions are of a different sort; the unfamiliar contexts of relative scarcity of many goods the Westerner takes for granted, the interaction between irrepressible human spontaneity and the planning that aims to foresee, divert, channel, and control it, the mix of elements of real (and bogus) egalitarianism and of what must seem, especially to an American, old-world snobbery.

Both sorts of impressions reflect realities. Socialist revolutions and their aftermath can be called an "experiment," but the socialist experiment proceeded not with inert but with *living* material—societies complex and heavy with historical experience. The USSR inherited not only the borders of the Eurasian land mass of the old Russian Empire but also the effects of a history that had diverged from the main currents of Western development for over 700 years. The complex of Eastern Europe included societies and cultures diverse in orientation, from Westernized to semi-Asiatic, all different in their own ways from Russia. Historical paths diverged, and socialism was introduced in different ways. Diversity was to be expected as well as unity, and impressions should reflect it.

This chapter attempts to focus some of these impressions, to tie up the various strands running through the book. First, it characterizes, in summary fashion, the broad common aspects of socialist stratification systems, without exhausting all their concrete characteristics. These we deal with in two succeeding sections that contrast and compare the United States with the USSR, and Eastern Europe with Western Europe—for reasons that should become clear as the reader proceeds. The final section is of a different sort, bringing us back to the normative issues dealt with in chapter 1. What, in the final analysis, is the "closing balance" of socialism? Does the degree of equality achieved, assuming equality to be desirable, so exceed that of Western capitalism as to outweigh the political repression socialism has visited on its citizens? Can such a question be posed in such terms? The reader will render his own judgment, on the basis of his own values and perceptions, at his own convenience. I offer mine in this chapter.

STRATIFICATION IN SOCIALIST SYSTEMS

Marx's vision of the postcapitalist future was a broad one, not heavy on detail. Is is thus fair game for the tempting, but not particularly illuminating, exercise of historical hindsight by those fated to live later than he. Here, it is sufficient to recognize that socialism, as achieved in the USSR and Eastern Europe, has not "transcended" capitalism and the modes of economic and political organization that have gone with it. The division of labor persists and grows ever more complex in East and West; the hierarchical organization of human effort survives as well. Mark's utopian vision of an individual spanning many occupations of different sorts in the course of a day is still unfulfilled.

What socialism has produced is another *form* of industrial society, an alternative mode of channeling the process of industrialism to the capitalist mode that marked nineteenth-century Europe. It has, obviously, dealt differently with problems of entrepreneurship, with the braking potential of preindustrial strata like the landed aristocracy, while borrowing heavily though selectively from the accrued technological experience of capitalist industrialism. In all, socialism has built societies different from capitalist ones, but hardly utopian. They are quite this-worldly in character and problems.

This is true as well of the stratification systems socialism has developed. Reviewing their elements, one finds not, certainly, a reproduction of capitalist patterns cloaked by a different rhetoric, as some critics might suggest, but one that, nonetheless, indicates the constraints the real world imposes on any set of revolutionary designs, and the impact of political decisions made for reasons other than the promotion of a new and more egalitarian social order.

The distribution of material rewards, as we have seen, *is* relatively egalitarian when we focus on individuals as receiving units—that is, more egalitarian by standard economist's measures than in the advanced capitalist states. Yet, in the concrete, as socialist citizens experience it, it is quite inegalitarian—nor, really, can socialist propaganda or exposition claim anything else. Early on, the socialist regimes acknowledged the relevance of scarcities of formal education, technical skills, and certain types of commitment to the reward process. Committed to development and growth, they could do no less, especially when, as new regimes of questionable legitimacy, they could not substitute adequate moral stimuli for material incentives.

Thus, the performance principle was enshrined—that work, not need, entitled people to rewards. Critical work meant significant rewards above the norm. Personnel valuable for *production* would reap them—so that the engineer, for example, was exalted. But the priority of control over the population dictated high rewards as well for those valuable for compulsion, and thus police and political officials have also come to benefit from the performance principle.

The state's virtual monopoly over employment and reward, and its effective blockage of the formation of independent organizations for the pursuit of class or stratum-related interests, has allowed it to play with the performance principle, emphasizing it or egalitarianism as circumstances dictate. Periods of increasing income inequality have alternated with periods of equalization. That same monopoly has made possible the exclusion from the normal market of many scarce goods and privileges, and their bureaucratic allocation to the favored. The importance of these must be emphasized, especially in economies where general affluence still lies far in the future.

In sum, socialism asserts that its object for the present and forseeable future is equity, rather than equality, a "fair" but not equal distribution of goods.[1] Those who abominate unearned income, the use of wealth to amass yet more, can be pleased that socialism has eliminated this, at least. Those who think of an equitable society as one that demands a new ordering of the rewards of occupational strata, and not simply a reduction of the distance between them (even including some of the sort of income overlap we have seen), are likely to be less pleased. One recalls here those socialist critics of inequality under socialism discussed in the first chapter, and perhaps best summarizes the problem by imagining their reactions to the words of a Hungarian, defending the differentiation of reward under the New Economic Mechanism in a discussion at a factory Communist Party meeting.

> There is a top, and meritorious, elite that has grown up under socialism which is doing far more for society in general than others. It deserves, therefore, to enjoy a special financial status, too. *This stratum is allowed to live in the style of and on a standard equal to, the former ruling class.*[2] [emphasis added]

His statement was condemned, but the fact that it was made indicates the readiness with which many accept what even they see as a return to the material gap that separated elite and mass in the years before socialism arrived. One need remember that the partisans of *more* differentiation—the Czech reformers, the "market socialists" sometimes denounced as "anarcho-liberals"—are also "socialists." Inequality, of whatever magnitude, seems likely to remain a problem; socialism surely shows no signs of outgrowing it.

The distribution of prestige fails to show many clear signs of a completely new order under socialism. Some old high-status groups have disappeared under socialist assaults, and some at the bottom as well. But for the groups that remain, ranking still seems to favor nonmanual over manual, urban over rural occupations, much as it did in presocialist times. Government policies have had some effect. The exaltation of the skilled manual worker, as well as his enhanced economic rewards, are real changes from the past. But the precise nature of the effect, versus that of the general trend toward prestige overlap across the manual-nonmanual line in some Western societies as well, cannot really be determined. Prestige, while it is in some measure a function of real and/or perceived income and power attached to a particular occupation or set of occupations, is distinct from them. Of the goods with which social stratification is concerned, it is *least* manipulable by the state, since its bestowal remains a free decision of individual minds reacting to a multiplicity of factors.

Of the distribution of power, we have already said enough, and need not linger on it now. Power is scarce to the point of nonexistence for most socialist citizens, and extremely abundant for the few. This concentration of power both reflects and facilitates state control over human and material resources. This, in turn, gives politics great control over economics, and produces a system of economic stratification shaped to political goals as well as economic realities. Here the East-West divergence is substantial indeed.

Of the dynamic aspects of stratification—of social mobility—the reader has seen a good deal in earlier chapters. Judgments based on bad data—the alternative to no data—must be provisional, but the broad coverage of those data for both capitalist and socialist societies does encourage some generalizations. The gross figures indicate a *range* of socialist mobility experiences not significantly smaller than those of capitalist societies. Socialist economic growth has produced mobile societies, but not extraordinarily mobile ones. Mobility has remained hostage to the heavy weight of an agrarian past, limiting manual to nonmanual movement, and giving greater place to mobility from peasant to worker. Socialist states initially better developed have had higher rates of manual to nonmanual transfer than those more backward. In these areas, the logic of numbers and their distribution across strata has been unbreakable.

The same logic, however, produces a major difference in socialist and capitalist mobility profiles—the inflow that shows large majorities of the socialist nonmanuals originating in the worker and peasant strata. As these strata expanded rapidly under the impact of revolution, their source of recruitment could only be external, and a proletarianization, demographically at least, of the nonmanual strata was the result. This outburst of long-range mobility may be just that—an artifact of revolution, not to be repeated. There is ample evidence that the first-generation incumbents of nonmanual and intelligentsia positions are quite as anxious as counterparts elsewhere to ensure their offsprings' succession to them, which would change greatly the inflow picture for the next generation. Our data do not cover enough points in time to permit us to state definitively that this is happening, but they do not provide any basis for concluding that it is not.

The other major difference affects few people directly and is submerged in our mobility data—the generally humble origins of the narrow political elite per se, compared to the generally middle or upper-class origins of political leaders in the capitalist states. This too is an echo of revolution, but not necessarily temporary for that. A career in socialist politics requires some of the education and training needed for other elite careers, but something else besides. The demands, insecurity, and uncertainty of such a career limit its attractiveness for many offspring of political and nonpolitical elite as well—and these are well-equipped to seek comfortable careers outside the political main line. Only time will tell, but currently politics seems a particular *kind* of mobility channel that few choose, but that *remains* open to persons of worker and peasant origin who have less initial disadvantage because of that origin in this than in other careers requiring deeper, but perhaps narrower, technical expertise. If time proves this characterization correct, the disparity in long-range mobility into the political elite between capitalist and socialist societies will be a durable, fundamental difference.

Socialism and the economic development it sponsored have made for more fluid societies that those of Tsarist Russia or interwar Eastern Europe. The mobility that marks socialism, as we saw earlier, has been attributable to the expansion of the total volume of opportunities, the space at upper and middle levels of the occupational hierarchy, rather than to an equalization of opportunities to rise (and to sink) across the board. People still have different mobility chances under socialism, depending on their stratum of origin. The particular nature of *this* inequality today is explicable by reference to the things socialism has done, and to the things it has not.

Socialism has, first of all, eliminated ownership of property in the means of production as a differentiating element in mobility chances, and thus in what Anthony Giddens terms "class structuration."[3] One cannot generally possess, bequeath, or inherit a productive enterprise, and thus transmit a certain capacity to maintain, expand, or sell and reinvest such resources. All, under socialism, must sell their labor, manual or nonmanual, to the state (private peasantry remaining a partial exception). Second, though one is generally free to pass on accumulated money, etc., to one's children, socialism legally prohibits, and in practice makes difficult, any attempt to *live* on such resources. Doing so, one is a "parasite," a violator of the dictate that "he who does not work, neither shall he eat," (to say nothing of the difficulty of surviving, even hypothetically, on the low interest generated by socialist savings accounts). Thus, the option of maintaining a certain living standard by inheritance is foreclosed. Third, socialism has broken in a rather decisive way with whatever automatic particularistic advantages sons might have in inheriting their father's profession of engineer, doctor, etc., through specific preferential access to the requisite training, etc. Meritocracy has taken hold, though as always with certain lapses and inconsistencies. Finally, university education per se is free, one does not pay tuition, and some receive living-expense stipends. This does not mean that it is without cost, that there are no expenses—there are, as we have seen. But ability to pay for direct education-related charges is no longer a differentiating element in chances to get into what we have seen to be the major channel of mobility—education.

These are all important breaks from the old presocialist systems, and should not be minimized. But the points where socialism has *not* broken with the past are equally critical. These, in a sense, resolve down to one point: socialism has left the family, the household, intact as a unit. Households are the units of which our four broad socio-occupational strata (elite/intelligentsia, routine nonmanual, worker, and peasant) are composed, and it is through them that young people acquire the characteristics that so heavily influence their mobility chances. For it is in the family that stratum-related advantages and disadvantages are transmitted from generation to generation. Cultural and intellectual resources, especially, are critical. We have written of mobility as contest, or competition. But not all households instill this view in their younger members.

Those youth who do view it this way are possessed of a rationale for striving that those from households (predominantly worker and peasant, though today probably a minority of these) where occupational outcomes are seen as chance or predetermined processes, lack. Among families committed to striving, to encouraging their children to compete, knowledge in general, knowledge of *all* sorts, is unevenly distributed. Intelligentsia families possess more of it than the others, and nonmanuals' families on the average more than those of manuals. The same seems true of attitudes. Ability to defer gratification, to focus on distant goals, to orient oneself toward adult concerns while still not adult, are present in all strata—but one finds them more commonly in the upper strata than in the lower.

The family's function in social placement goes beyond values and attitudes. Though money cannot buy education, it can pay for the tutoring that, increasingly, secondary school students receive in spare hours to increase their chances of passing university entrance examinations. As noted earlier, economically comfortable families can supplement government stipends for their children, often making the difference between a survival level and the security of reasonable accommodations and diet that conduce to academic success. A well-off family need not make the hard calculations about the costs of deferred earnings and additional years of dependence that a poorer family must. Finally, those families favored in both cultural and economic resources also are more likely than the rest to have contacts, at the point of university entrance and later initial job placement, that modify the strictures of bureaucratized meritocratic and universalistic procedures. One may or may not see this as corruption. But it is a real force, access to which is, itself, unequal for different social strata.

Socialism has given rise to a new type of hierarchy: not in the abstract, but in the here-and-now. It contains many elements, as we have seen, of the social orders it sought to replace, and still opposes. In the language of Andrew Hacker's lines at the beginning of this chapter, it has destroyed *most* of the conservative community that existed to some degree in the Russian and Eastern European past—but not all of it. It promised the "radical community" to its adherents, but has not, and cannot, deliver; for it depends for its survival on both individual ambition and on the attraction of the sort of private property even it has had to permit.

USA AND USSR

Unlike most of the Western or Eastern European states, unlike even the other European-rooted nations of Canada, Australia, New Zealand, the United States and the Soviet Union were *born* in revolutions that explicitly rejected not only monarchs but political structures and social arrangements that had earlier prevailed. There were significant differences between the two revolutions. America's was, apparently, socially less radical—a revolt of gentlemen landowners, merchants, and professionals that sought no diminution of the rights of property. Yet, it represented a radical break with the Europe of the day, with those principles and practices that had emphasized ascription over achievement, denied the equality of man in favor of the assumption that men were immutably unequal, and asserted the hereditary claims of some men to rule and the obligations of others to serve. Elective government, and equality before the law, even within the context of a quite inegalitarian distribution of economic resource and a linked restriction of the franchise, *were* radical principles in the context of the time, as was the developing ethos of a society open to achievement on the part of all.

Almost a century and a half later, Russia's revolution rejected and demolished a polity and society marked by anachronism and backwardness compared to the Europe of the time. The new regime recognized neither private property, hereditary privilege, nor divine justification, and set itself to the tasks of building a socialist state and an industrial economy. As in the United States, the break with the old order opened opportunities to the talented and enterprising. But unlike the United States, the emergent Soviet society was not to rely on individual choice or initiative, or on the market, to determine priorities. Nor was it quite ready to countenance, openly, extreme inequality, even that resulting from individual efforts—the promises of Marxism-Leninism included a much greater degree of equality of *result* than did the less-explicitly formulated ideology of the American revolution. But extreme economic inequality did emerge early on in the Soviet experience, requiring the formulation of a performance principle for its justification in the socialist phase of development.

Here are two revolutionary societies—each today a superpower, both partially European in orientation and heritage, yet both divorced in significant ways from Europe. Comparing the U.S.A. and the USSR is a frequent enterprise, fraught with difficulties yet also with promise. To compare the two systems of stratification is to compare advanced capitalism with mature socialism; it is also, in the words of one scholar, to compare "the *least typical* cases of each generic type of society."[4] Their relevance to our concerns lies in this fact, and also in the fact that each has had its impact on the "more typical" cases of each generic type—the industrialized states of Western Europe and the socialist countries of Eastern Europe.

Similarities between the stratification systems are perceptible in gross terms, however much the details differ. First, both societies have generated great economic inequalities while simultaneously stressing relatively open competition for highly rewarded positions in the labor force. American capitalism allows the fortunate and enterprising to enjoy large accumulations of wealth, transmissible to succeeding generations. The Soviet system has of course eliminated this, but both have developed economies wherein great disparities exist in labor-related incomes. The underlying rationale—incentive to performance, to greater effort—has been much the same in the USSR as in a capitalist state. Denouncing wage equalization in 1931, Stalin observed that under egalitarian policies an "unskilled worker lacks the incentive to become a skilled worker" and characterized as intolerable "a situation where a rolling mill hand in a steel mill earns no more than a sweeper."[5] Under Stalin, their rewards came to diverge quite markedly: despite moderation, they still do today. Add to the fairly large disparities in work-related incomes the material subsidies enjoyed by the small Soviet elite, and the real range of economic inequality is further magnified.

In recent years, the USSR has moved toward moderate leveling, toward greater income equality, by various measures already discussed. Given central control of the wage plan, the Soviet regime can more effectively do this than could an American government, even presuming that the latter wished to follow an explicitly egalitarian course. However, in its own way the United States too has in recent years attempted to move up the economic bottom of society. Various reformist programs aimed at eliminating poverty, or at least reducing its effects, among the elderly, racial and ethnic minorities, etc. have had some effect,[6] even if neither in rationale nor outcome do they satisfy those who view complete economic equality as social goal number one.

In both societies, restraints on the desirability and achievability of equality in material outcomes and social prestige have led to the enshrinement of equality of opportunity as a major value. As Paul Hollander puts it, it "emerged as an openly stated major American value while it was a more implicit admission of the deferment of the original Soviet aspirations of complete equality."[7] In neither nation are opportunities really equal in the sense of being independent of one's social origin, but in both real breaks have been made with the constricted opportunity structures of earlier societies.

For all of our previous strictures on the free nature of Soviet education and the skewed social composition of student populations, the USSR has developed a huge education system that serves as the ladder of opportunity for the talented and ambitious, doing better in this area than do most other nations (the United States, which enrolls a larger percentage of the age-eligible population in one or another form of higher education than *any* other nation, is also exceptional here). Competition for entrance into Soviet higher education *is* intense, but with some exceptions to be noted later, it is meritocratic, and is the channel through which many still rise to occupational status distant from that of their family of origin. Both American and Soviet societies, contrasting themselves to many others, can point to open social structures. Both stress equality of opportunity more than equality of result, with equally good reason.[8]

A second broad similarity brings us into an area mixing ambiguous terminology with realities hard to capture. In a number of senses, including generally accepted societal self-images, neither Soviet nor American societies are class societies, *however* far they diverge from egalitarianism. Groups or strata differ in their status, but do not take on the exclusivity of "classes." This phenomenon, "nonegalitarian classlessness," has been discussed at some length by Ossowski in his magisterial *Class Structure in the Social Conciousness*[9] but requires mention here as well.

Though Marxist analysis would deny *capitalist* America, by virtue of that very characteristic, any claim to classlessness, many other characteristics *do* tend to identify it as such. Such are (1) the lack of a feudal past, hence of a hereditary aristocracy/nobility, and the rejection, throughout American history, of European precedent in this area; (2) in the present, a belief, supported by the evidence of social mobility, that birth has not locked one into a particular status—that all, at least among the white population, can rise, though some will find it more difficult than others; (3) the lack of distinct legal or social barriers between economic or social groups in the hierarchy, as well as the lack of distinct privileges attached to any group wherever in the status hierarchy; and (4) relatively open, nondeferential contact between groups in the hierarchy, with no traditional, legally defined barriers to such contact.[10]

These characteristics, with a reality both external to and reflected in the minds of Americans (in the latter case in the tendency not to think of society in "class" terms), have supported a notion of "classlessness" in America, despite the fact that it *can* be divided into owners and nonowners of private property in the means of production. They operate independently of the core, orthodox Marxist definition of "class" in economic terms. If America then is "classless" in this sense, in what sense is the USSR so?

Here again we combine terminology with reality. *Sensu stricto*, the USSR is not "classless," but because of what Soviet writers regard as a historically unique class structure, it is free of the "antagonistic" conflicts of interest that divide classes in capitalist society. The bare-bones definition denominates two classes, workers and collective peasantry, distinguished by their linkage respectively to state and co-operative property (but linked by the fact that these are two forms of socialist property) and adds the intelligentsia (nonmanuals) as a "stratum." No impermeable barriers are seen to exist between the classes, no conflicts, nothing that imparts a "class character," in the negative sense, to Soviet society.

That truly private property in the means of production does not exist in the USSR *is* clear; to the degree that one is willing to take the sole existence of socialist property, state or cooperative, as signifying classlessness, one is welcome to do so. Beyond this, other elements also argue for a USSR less "class-based," in a general sense, than Western or Eastern European societies. Historically, as we saw in chapter 2, Russia was not a society of classes in the Western sense. Extremely inegalitarian, with yawning gulfs between the top and bottom of society, the Tsarist order still never saw the coalescence of groups with autonomy, self-conciousness, and clear positions in the social order that they maintained in opposition to or in balance with the central governmental power. Through economic changes, Russia remained to the end of Tsarism an "estate" society, where "official" status cross-cut economic boundaries, occupational groupings, etc. and delayed the coalescence of "classes" in any generally accepted sense. The particular nature of economic development in the twilight imperial years delayed the transformation of "peasants" into "workers" though they might toil in factory rather than field. The lack of adequate reflection of an increasingly complex occupational structure in the estate system delayed legal accommodations to emergent social realities. The autocracy survived in sufficient vigor to reduce possibilities of class formation. As World War I commenced, "Russian society contained, at most, only embryonic social classes."[11]

The Soviet regime was not hospitable to development beyond this embryonic state. Smashing the old society, it destroyed groups that had some chance of developing into classes, and substituted for the estate system another, even more tightly centralized, where rewards and status were largely under state control. "Classes" in the sense of autonomous groups in a hierarchy, with their own values, norms, and conciousness of interests, did not develop. Thus the Soviet regime, even more than the Tsarist, did not have to deal and negotiate with groups' representatives—the very stuff of politics in other systems. In assessing its support, the regime did not, as other might have, "calculate" that certain groups (classes) were its backers because their hierarchical position made them natural upholders of the system, while other classes given their position would naturally be less supportive. Instead, its monopoly of rewards allowed it to make hierarchical position a *consequence* of support and loyalty, to manipulate and reorder groupings as it chose.[12]

Thus, for different reasons, elements of classlessness are evident in both the USSR and the USA. America broke with Europe's old system, leaving room in the fluid operations of a capitalist economy for the growth of great inequality along material dimensions, but little ground for the formation of classes with the seeming permanence of their European counterparts. The Bolsheviks asserted control over society and economy, destroying the Tsarist system only to introduce one, equally unique, that prevented just as effectively the coalescence of hierarchical groupings into that degree of self-consciousness, self-identification, and exclusivity that would make them "classes." Again, taking Europe as the benchmark, Russia too lacked the structure, the "feel," of a class society.

This is important for the third area of similarity between the U.S. and USSR stratification systems—the relative lack of deference in relations between persons. That the United States is a nondeferential society needs little discussion—it is a quality of the national existence marked by European visitors and observers since the early nineteenth century. That the Soviet Union is also nondeferential many will find difficult to accept. What, they may ask, does the division of the population into those with access to "special" stores, resorts, hospitals and those barred from them signify but a society in which the many must defer to the few, in which "peasants" are still looked down upon by even the meanest city dwellers?

Let us allow, first of all, that interpersonal relations in the Soviet Union in many contexts show more elements of deference than in the United States. But here the comparison is a forced one. The United States lacks the deferential *tradition* of Imperial Russia and the relative poverty that accentuates social differences—with these, the Soviet regime has had to cope. The point is that, compared to some contemporary European nations, East and West, the USSR shows much less of traditional patterns of deferential behavior.

I find myself, I *think*, differing in emphasis here with Paul Hollander, who finds the deferential tradition and social structure of Tsarist Russia still partially persisting—noting the contempt of urbanite toward peasant and the premium many place on nonmanual work.[13] This is, perhaps, a matter of reference points, as the following section will show. Recent observers, such as Hedrick Smith in his well-known work, *The Russians,* also emphasize the palpable inequality of Soviet life, seeing a society "far more rank-

and-hierarchy conscious than Western societies."[14] Smith notes the profusion of hierarchical titles in Soviet organizations, and the penchant for personal titles ("Honored Artist," "Hero of Socialist Labor," "Poeple's Artist of the Soviet Union," etc.), observing that to an American "this comes across as strangely akin to the British with their system of peerages, knighthoods and orders."[15] But British titles do *not* guarantee access to special stores, to scarce items money cannot buy, to closed vacation retreats, etc. One may defer to a knight or a peer, but one is not compelled to do so, as Soviet citizens in a sense are; here *submission* is perhaps a better term than deference.

We are in a realm of subtlety here, where different observers will disagree; and observation is generally what we must go on. Linguistic usage has been democratized—polite terms of address of the "sir" and "madam" variety were effectively abolished from the common Russian language early on in the Soviet period; use of the familiar second person *ty* by superiors toward subordinates is seemingly less widespread than in the past, though its absolute incidence could readily be made a matter of dispute. The material privileges of the elite are indeed substantial, and create a gulf between them and the mass, but this is not the same thing as deference. More, it seems to me, than in the Eastern European socialist states, the Soviet elite enjoys its benefits privately, in closed settlements and the like. Some of the special stores are visible, but the very special ones are not. Those who enjoy these benefits shun publicity, command geographical isolation, and thus keep public perceptions of how elevated a life they lead vague. All this is aided by the fact that the USSR's is a *working* elite, with no leisure rich, "cafe society," etc.—the closed dacha settlements, the resort areas in the Black Sea and in the Baltic are not the equivalent, in reality or in public perception, of Palm Beach, Newport, or their Western European counterparts.

Titles such as "Doctor," "Professor," and the like will command respect in some social contexts, but neither these nor such obvious marks of status as expensive clothing seem to carry as much weight in the USSR as in some of the Eastern European states (see below). Salespersons, waiters, and other service personnel, in my experience, show little more tendency to grant diffuse status to such persons than to common folk. One may get results, in some situations, by asserting certain prerogatives—and if these can be credibly attached to one's office, to the hierarchical position one occupies, all the better—but to do this is to *force* deference, something different than to receive it naturally as one's due.[16]

Various travelers to and observers of the USSR touch on these points in different ways. What I characterize here as a nondeferential style of interpersonal relations will seem to some a simple crudity in behavior, perhaps attributable to a recent peasant past and an extended period of adjustment to an urban world. Matters, I think, are not that simple. There *is* some of this; evidence can be found in the standard Russian epithet for behavior that seems gross or obtrusive—"uncultured" (*nekul'turnyi*), so often applied to the behavior expected of peasants in the unaccustomed surroundings of the big city. But as the Soviet population's share of hereditary urbanites grows, it is difficult to trace any parallel development of a new set of "urbane" manners, as one might expect. The roots of the nondeferential Soviet style, the seeming disorder and lack of *politesse* that observers find annoying or charming, lie, it seems to me, in the violence and permanence of the revolutionary transformation that overtook the old Russia in the years 1917 to 1932. Whatever "old" rules of deference had decreed, new ones of a different kind, based squarely on power relations, developed. Power was too narrow a basis for the new society to elaborate a new, general structure of deferential relations, too tied to particular offices and positions of which an incumbent could be deprived tomorrow, and frequently was. Though from the mid-1930s on through the death of Stalin, some state promotion of visible bases of deference could be seen (among them the restoration of uniforms of various kinds for various levels in the civilian bureaucracies), these too were insufficient to structure relations of real deference.

Precise measurement, in the end, is impossible here. My own inclination is to emphasize the *lack* of deference in most contexts of Soviet interpersonal relations. (If the USSR appears deferential in comparison to the United States, a consideration of the Eastern European countries, where revolution has been neither home-grown nor so massive in its effects, may help to highlight the USSR's nondeferential characteristics more effectively.)

Differences in the two nations' stratification systems bulk large as well. These are rooted, primarily, in the vastly disparate political structures of the countries; the degree to which politics dominates, without completely subsuming, other sectors in the USSR; and the degree to which, in the U.S.A., it coexists with the other sectors, notably the economy, in a "negative reciprocity,"[17] leaving them relatively free to operate according to their own rules.

Despite the growing difficulties of striking out on one's own in an increasingly bureaucratized economy, the ambitious American *can* seek economic advancement and other sorts of mobility in two ways: through a career within an organization, private or public; and through a variety of independent entrepreneurial channels. Universities, corporations, the armed forces are three examples of the former. The range of the latter runs from traditional "small business" (which may grow big) to solo professional practice to entertainment. Though many qualities conducive to success are relevant in both societies, those uniquely qualified or desirous of going it alone will find few, if any, legally tolerated outlets in the USSR. Obviously, private business and solo professional practice are out—but even writers, artists, and entertainers find their opportunities and rewards controlled to a significant degree by their "trade-union" bureaucracies. If these do not promote their work, they do promote careers. Thus, in a general sense, the span of alternative channels for individual effort is more constricted in the USSR.

Despite the considerable rewards of success in the Soviet Union and the fairly impressive long-range mobility of many humbly born citizens (in the recent past, at least), these rewards remain conditional in a way that they are not in the United States. Allocation, in the final analysis, operates according to political-bureaucratic rather than market principles. Privilege, in the form of high salary, other material benefits, comfortable dachas, travel abroad, even power does not generally vest in oneself even for one's lifetime, much less in a form making it transmissible to one's offspring. The state, as the sole employer, controls privilege, and what it gives, it can take away. Paul Hollander notes the cases of "highly placed people who can be demoted, deprived of all privileges, and disgraced with astonishing speed, and who have no recourse to appeal, alternatives, or opportunities in a sphere other than that in which they failed."[18] With rewards so great, insecurity increases, since high rewards are associated with positions seen as extremely significant by those with ultimate political control. This contrasts greatly with the United States, where privileges and rewards *do* cumulate and form the basis for further accumulation. Hollander outlines the American situation, where

> while subjectively felt status-insecurity may increase with upward mobility, the objective conditions for loss of status and privilege do not. As the individual moves up, his security is enhanced and not diminished. The social position, once achieved, is unlikely to be lost or threatened, especially by administrative measures on behalf of political agencies and institutions.[19]

This is a difference in principle, and it is fundamental. Hollander's language may to some overstate the actual insecurity of Soviet elites and understate the slippery and ephemeral quality of some rewards of Americans, but the gulf it expresses is enormous. An American corporate executive, losing his high place in a power struggle, can leave his employer with substantial savings, spendable anywhere; retire to his large house, with all its comforts; continue to enjoy the company of friends; and if his capital is sufficient, live on the proceeds without working; or he can seek new employment. A high Soviet bureaucrat deprived of *his* job may have some savings, perhaps quite an amount. But with a demotion, he can also lose access to special outlets, a hard-currency component in income, his dacha, official car, chauffeur, and other things he *cannot* buy. His prospects for equivalent employment will be dim, his social circle contracted to those who do not fear to associate with a loser.

In day-to-day operation, however, the American-Soviet gap narrows somewhat. Soviet elite echelons have been, in recent years, rather stable. Stalin's purges and Khrushchev's various attempts to shake up the nationwide bureaucracy at all levels have given way to a stabilization under Brezhnev and Kosygin. One ignores at one's peril the fact that the USSR remains a "politicized" society with many semitotalitarian characteristics,[20] but it is well to recall that the USSR for the most part is composed of rather *apolitical* people—a situation the regime, for all its rhetoric, tolerates for the stability that it seems to provide.[21] Clearly, no espousals of alternative ideologies will be permitted, but ideological élan is no longer necessary for occupation of a high place, as long as standard formulas are repeated at appropriate times and there is no reason to suspect an individual of strongly held internal reservations. General conformity, energy, and a healthy degree of ambition and self-interest mark the kind of individual the system can use.

Thus, the Soviet regime has, for some years, consistently encouraged individuals to be ambitious—to develop needed skills, to acquire education. To them it has promised economic reward, interesting work, preference in access to scarce goods beyond wages and salaries. In this, it has applied the performance principle as its yardstick, much as has the capitalist United States. The difference, that which makes their resemblance here phenotypical rather than genotypical, in Goldthorpe's terms,[22] is that an authoritative political decision *could* significantly alter aspects of the whole current reward structure. This could only be done at certain costs, but the regime could make the decision to encounter them—while an American government, however great its power and everyday impact on individual lives has grown, could not. Finally, it is worth stating explicitly what has been implied—that as a general rule, power as an individual attribute can only be acquired by *direct* quest in the USSR, while it can, in some measure, be bought in the United States. The costs of pursuing a political career, of the quest for positional power, are high in the USSR, but not monetary. There, economic rewards of considerable size will flow *from* power; in the United States, the acquisition of behind-the-scenes power and the power that comes with public office both, generally, require substantial *prior* financial resource.

It is possible, of course, to gain great material benefits in the USSR without real power—as the rewards of favored artists, athletes, scientists, and the like show. But they cannot be retained or enjoyed *except* with the acquiescence and approval of those personalities who at that time dispose of power. It is also possible to accumulate wealth in the United States without attaining or even striving for power. But in principle, the systems remain distinct. It is, perhaps, testimony to the distrust of power, *openly* exercised at least, that *neither* American nor Soviet citizens, insofar as we can tell, accord the third of life's scarce goods—prestige—primarily to those who specialize in power.

EUROPE, EAST AND WEST

Profound political, economic, and social change came to Europe in the postwar period. On the war-ravaged continent, West and East, developed and backward portions, which *had* coexisted as parts of a European totality in the past, went their separate ways, each under the influence or domination of an emergent great power.

In the West, the United States, through economic aid, political pressure and sponsorship, and defense policy, helped in the construction of a political order of liberal-democratic character that consolidated trends dating back to the nineteenth century, and a capitalist economic order with admixtures of welfare-statism that provided material affluence beyond prewar dreams. In the East, the USSR pursued a different tack, imposing a centralized party-state, a socialist economic system, and a "mobilizational" style that emphasized economic growth through high investment rates and produced the opposite of affluence.

In some senses, the two Europes grew farther apart than they had ever been. Yet, it goes too far to state that they have been completely sundered, that the "Americanization" of Western Europe and the "Sovietization" of the East have destroyed all the old links. In assessing the structures of stratification of the socialist states, it makes sense to measure them against the structures of the Western European capitalist states, attending to differences born of more than thirty years of postwar experience as well as to persistent similarities.

The differences, the contrasting character of Europe's West and East are, of course, not to be denied or minimized. Though power is, in any society, a resource quite unequally distributed, its distribution in the East is clearly more unequal. In the developed parts of Western Europe, the postwar period brought what Dahrendorf called in the early 1960s the "social miracle" to completion. The rule of law and representative government, which had remained for all but small portions of the population promises of the French revolution never quite redeemed, assumed concrete reality.[23] Such limits on state power have not been established in the East, and this deficit seems a permanent property of those regimes. To the degree that power *has* been equalized in socialist regimes, it has been through a process of reducing strata that earlier enjoyed different amounts of power to a common low level, in favor of a tightly concentrated state monopoly.

The two Europes diverge as well in the social profiles of the holders of power. Though access to Western European elites is not so closed to those of humble birth as once it was, by and large those political elites are still self-recruiting, especially in the upper bureaucracy and civil service. In Eastern Europe, however, the echoes of what *may* have been a historically unique process are still in evidence: the positions of effective political power are occupied by persons whose origin lies in or close to the working class and peasantry. The subjunctive is warranted here: while the "functional" elites of science, art, technology, and the like seem increasingly headed for patterns of hereditary recruitment, the socialist "power elites," as in the USSR, have yet to exhibit the same tendencies. Sons of the major political figures find comfortable elite berths, but not generally in the direct line of power. Thus, given the stakes, it is possible that the political ladder will remain open to aspirants from the working class willing to do what they must to scale it.[24] The fact that Communist parties as a whole are statistically more dominated than ever by the well-educated does not militate against this, since even within the parties, the specialists in power and its exercise are few.

These differences are conditioned by the great East-West differences in the structure of *property*. Western Europe by and large retains a capitalist private-ownership system. Nationalization of certain basic industries has modified but not transformed the Europe of bourgeois capitalism. Socialism has, with few partial exceptions, deprived individuals and groups of ownership as a basis for accumulating and increasing wealth and power; the exceptions, in the agricultural and petty-artisan sectors, are not critical. It now confers power on those who, by virtue of political position, control *state* property for the duration of their terms in power. Few possess property that affords a hedge against governmental power, a basis from which to assert independence, in the sense of a real bourgeoisie. Of course, it is true that, East and West, fewer persons are self-employed or possessed of sufficient resources to *forego* employment in organizations. Yet the restrictions on financial independence are incomparably greater in the socialist states: *their* "new middle classes" are more dependent by far. There *is* an egalitarianism inherent in the general lack of private productive property in the East, not evident in the West. But much as with the distribution of power, it signals an equality where people share a comparable lack of resources.

The lack of accumulations of private resource and the reward-granting power of the state have, as we have seen, generated what seems a more equal distribution of *income*, earned and unearned, under socialism. This too differentiates the two Europes, but here the differences are not immense. The range between the highly qualified professional and the unskilled worker or peasant is compressed in the East, but scarcely inconsequential, especially given generally lower living standards. The hierarchy of groups is not so different in a Poland, Romania, or Yugoslavia from that prevailing in France, Germany, or Italy. Nor do our admittedly imperfect data on *prestige* reveal massive differences in East and West attributable to the transformations in the structure of power and property that have taken place.

However, the maintenance of a new hierarchy, and the removal of property and birth as qualifications for ascendancy, have given formal education a place in socialist systems somewhat more central than it occupies in the West. The political benefits to be gained from offering mobility chances to competitors of whatever origin, and from maintaining an equal-opportunity character in education (as well as the rationality of seeking scarce talent wherever it exists), have generated more egalitarian *access* to higher education in East than in West. In Great Britain, the approximately one-quarter share of university graduates produced from the working class has remained stable for a long time; in France and Germany, increases between the pre- and postwar periods in working-class university representation have been marginal, from bases of only 5 to 6 percent.[25] In the socialist states of the East, despite overrepresentation of elite and nonmanual offspring, the shares of the workers and peasants are larger. (In comparing West Germany with the German Democratic Republic, one analyst finds children of government officials occupying 5.5 times their share of university places in the former, while offspring of the comparable GDR category are overrepresented by a more moderate 2.6 times.)[26]

Such differences command attention, and point to an effective socialist assault on some patterns of an older European life. But these too are hardly sufficient to convey the total picture. From several standpoints, the character and structure of social hierarchy in Eastern Europe is better understood as *European* rather than *socialist.*

This is an elusive, no doubt imprecise notion. It is suggested in various reactions of a general sort. Travelers approaching a Warsaw or Budapest from London or Paris often have a strong impression of difference, of a distinct society encountered as one enters the East—but if their arrival is from Moscow, the feel is more one of entering the West, a more familiar Europe, and sometimes an older, more traditional society. There is a reality underlying such impressions, for the USSR's characteristics are not altogether typical of the socialist states as whole.

The system of stratification in Eastern Europe, to different degrees in different countries, retains traditional European elements, however much official ideology has commanded and announced their extermination. We suggested this in the close of chapter 2, and need examine it further now. First, social intercourse still contains a measure of deference, of the old *politesse* one connects with Europe—especially in the historically deferential societies of Poland and Hungary. It is unstructured observation rather than statistics that reveals this. The Soviet state successfully eliminated from general use the polite "sir" and "madam" forms of address (*gospodin, gospozha*), but in Eastern Europe they persist, and in Poland the equivalent forms (*pan, pani*) are in wider use than ever before, among strata of the population that would not have used them in the prewar period, as is the ritual of hand-kissing. Democratization of *ancien régime* forms may be egalitarian in a sense, but it is a peculiar outcome of proletarian revolution.

There is deference in behavior as well. In the academic contexts with which I am tolerably familiar, professor-student interactions are more formalized and mannered by far than those one encounters in the United States, and also more so than in the contemporary USSR. If informality or first names are to be utilized, it is the professor, not the student, who will initiate such a change in the normal pattern. Service personnel, in retail stores or restaurants, to cite two examples, seem less offhand with customers than in the Soviet Union or in the average American context—less surly, more generally accommodating.* In a more general context, titles (Doctor, Professor, etc.) seem to yield more return, are used more widely, and cherished more in Eastern Europe than in a less deferential society such as the United States. One notes that even in Yugoslavia, where traditions and rhetoric are more egalitarian, the tendency to advertise one's status is frequent—as one observer finds, Belgrade professionals are likely to list their titles on the brass nameplates they affix to their apartment doors.[27]

American academics and intellectuals who travel to Eastern no less than Western Europe have noted the deference with which professorial scholarly status and titles are treated, and have frequently concluded that the "social role of the man of knowledge" is elevated under socialism to a degree unknown in the money-oriented United States. They fall, I think, into the same confusion of part with whole that Lipset noted in the Western European context some time ago, missing the point that "open deference is given to *all* those with higher status, whether engineers, factory owners, or professors, while in [the USA] it is not given to *any* to the degree that it is abroad."[28]

We have seen data on the manual-nonmanual gap in previous chapters, and some of the differences even between borderline strata seem influenced by continuing convictions that work with one's hands, if no longer really demeaning, is still somehow less desirable than employment that offers white collar, tie, desk, and briefcase. More than ten years into Poland's social revolution, Ossowski noted that although "the new criteria of prestige" dictated otherwise, skilled Polish manuals saw moving to slightly lesser-paid nonmanual work as a promotion—in answer to the same priorities that led

*Many will surely dispute me on this, including satirical writers in Polish, Hungarian, and other Eastern European newspapers, who complain of poor service no less frequently or loudly than their Soviet counterparts. But experience as a customer and in observing others as such convinces me that the standards such writers apply are more demanding than any realistically applicable to the Soviet situation. Waiters, waitresses, and retail clerks are often slow-moving in Warsaw, Budapest, and elsewhere, and indeed poorly paid—there *is* reason to complain. But attitudes of contempt and unconcern for customers simply do not manifest themselves in the same fashion in Eastern Europe as they do with frustrating frequency in the USSR.

West Germans to view things similarly.[29] All this is changing, in both East and West, as the meaning and definition of "manual" and "nonmanual" grow blurred and as prestige ratings of high-level manual occupations creep up against some nonmanual specialties. And the *reality* of social transformation in Eastern Europe is undeniable. If Poland and Hungary, most of all, still seem elitist and deferential in the quality of their social life, they are less so today than in the past. Natives of those countries who are old enough to remember the presocialist order stress (with approval or disgruntlement) the magnitude of the transformation toward equality they have seen. To an American (with an understandably quite different frame of reference) the remarkable thing is how old-world these societies seem.

Social *mobility* is more stressed in the socialist East than in Western Europe—worker-to-minister (or to Party secretary) careers are cited as evidence of societies open to talent. Yet there is less, in everyday life, of the ready display of humble origins than one might expect. It has long been unfashionable, "uncultured" to go tieless—the open collar having once been a sign of a leader's solidarity with his class of origin. Not infrequently, veterans of revolutionary struggle, having achieved success, shed their old wives to marry daughters of the classes they had displaced, whose manners, diction, and general aura of "culture" fit them better for a new ruling elite. If there is not yet a pattern of concealing humble origins characteristic in some measure still of the British and Continental upper classes,[30] there is also no great urge to emphasize them, except for ceremonial-political purposes.

If there is a perceptible drift in Eastern Europe it seems to be toward a certain social elitism, toward assumption by the new ruling professional and managerial strata of some of the marks of the old presocialist elites. Manifestations are many, from the absurd to the mundane to the semi-tragic. The Budapest daily *Nepszabadsag* in 1976 noted tendencies toward "acquiring status symbols" to enhance "prestige."[31] Another source specified some of the symbols; old and expensive books (presumably unread) to add chic to one's shelves, old swords and weapons over the "stridently grotesque" hearths of new apartments "to suggest that the head of the house is of aristocratic descent."[32] Other examples abound.

Writers have stressed, from time to time, some of the tensions inherent in long-range mobility sundering the worlds of parents and children. Geoffrey Gorer has noted with sensitivity the costs of forming the British lower middle class in the nineteenth century. Power and money, as scarce resources, were replaced by a definition of nonmanual work as more "genteel," motivating many to stay in school and become "respectable," to qualify for the burgeoning administrative apparatus. The tensions were great, the hold on "gentility" precarious, the tendency to affirm it by despising and suppressing one's proletarian parentage and background strong.[33] Such extremes are not absent in the socialist context—the Warsaw paper *Polityka* recounted with appropriate egalitarian disapproval the shame a young researcher felt about his peasant mother, who had worked all the harder to see him rise and now found herself an unwanted visitor in her son's apartment, relegated to the kitchen during a party the night she arrived: "I heard someone ask who was the new guest, and Mikolaj [the son] answered that it was only a woman who helped with the cleaning. . . ."[34] It was not easy for his mother to *find* Mikolaj, either, since the brass plate on his door listed a new surname before the initials M. A., signifying his degree. As another woman in the building explains to his mother, "Well, he changed it. . . . Mikolaj didn't like his father's name. It was too peasant-like, too common. . . ."[35]

Nor is elitism limited to the conversion of old symbols and manners to the use of "new men." Descendants of old elites and bourgeoisie, as we have seen earlier, show discomfort and disdain for some of the new arrivals. Presumably, their attitudes still carry some weight, however reduced, with those who seek social, as well as occupational, acceptance. The acquisition of old status symbols by the newly successful hints at a desire to validate a new status, to conform to the presumptive expectations of reference groups that, if reduced in numbers and power, are still present.

Underlying much of this pattern of persistence is Eastern Europe's continuing legacy of underdevelopment, its more "traditional" labor-force composition. Hardly poor countries in global terms, the socialist states of Eastern Europe *do* lag significantly behind Western Europe in standards of living. Without the cloak of affluence, workers' dress stands out in greater distinction from that of the socialist middle strata, and many material differences are etched more sharply. Peasants still form a significant stratum of these societies, and the term "peasant"—never in general use in the United States, and increasingly rare in Western Europe—is still widely used. On the one hand, it is a demographic label, analytic and not evaluative. Everyone understands that today's peasant, generally literate, less isolated, with ambitions for his children, is not the faceless rustic of old. But on the other hand, he *still* occupies the bottom of the social hierarchy. Even in those countries where his income equals that of the average industrial worker, no one not *born* into the peasantry generally seeks to join it, and in this sense "peasant" still denotes an undesirable place in the general hierarchy.

The East presents an older Europe than the West in another way as well. While the socialist manual worker has come nearer his nonmanual counterparts in income and perhaps in prestige than his fellows in the West, actual work remains disparate. Over a decade ago, Dahrendorf cited technological changes in Western Europe that brought "the actual work tasks of salary and wage earners closer together," and asserted that "in modern light industries the working man is indistinguishable from the office clerk during as well as after working hours."[36] This may be a slight exaggeration for the West; it does not fit the East at all. There, a larger portion of the blue-collar work force remains in nonautomated, non-machine-assisted labor—dirty, noisy, arduous, and sweaty. While the socialist office worker is also disadvantaged by a lack of the automated solid-state gadgetry so common in the West, the gap between the setting of office and manual work still, on balance, is larger in the East.

The Soviet Union, then, has not duplicated itself in Eastern Europe. Neither in geography, population, nor history totally European, it remains atypical of socialist states, as the United States is atypical of those nations that fit the term "advanced capitalist society." The *authentic* revolution that overthrew Tsarism, the Civil War, and the rapid economic and organizational transformations that followed had, by the mid-1930s, created a new society, under a new polity no more democratic but more demanding and totalistic than the old. In Eastern Europe, only Yugoslavia and Albania forged their new social orders in partisan warfare and revolution—and after initial imitation of the "Soviet model," rejected it, each going its own way. (This has produced, in Yugoslavia, a society whose stratification system mixes elements of Balkan egalitarianism/traditionalism with market elements in the structure of economic reward in a unique combination—one hard to categorize, and different in significant ways from all the other socialist societies.) In the other countries, the Soviet model was imported and imposed *in lieu* of domestic revolution—and herein lies the key to some of the persistently "European" quality of those states. The Soviet superstructure was a product of experience as much as Marxist-Leninist design; it fit, in critical ways, the infrastructure of Russia. Its fit to the infrastructures of the Eastern European states was medium to poor, and remains so. In elitist and generally Russophobe Poland and Hungary, its Russian provenance compromised it badly. *No* large groups in either society agitated for Soviet-style socialism and its social order. Czechoslovakia's attitudes were, if anything, Russophile, but the Soviet model here was imposed on a society already at a level of economic development (in 1948) beyond that which the model had achieved in backward Russia. Romania, anti-Russian but economically backward, today manifests both attitudes in a maverick foreign policy line and an adherence to the Soviet centralist economic model. Only in Bulgaria, backward and linked to Russia by old historical ties, has the Soviet model really seemed to fit well—and Bulgaria remains the most docile satellite, with a social order closest in all respects to that of the USSR.

Their origin deprived the socialist governments of Poland and Hungary, especially, of legitimacy for a long time, and this legitimacy is still quite suspect in Poland, though less so by far in Hungary due to Kadar's capable political management. The alien superstructure remains somewhat alien to the domestic infrastructures. The tension between the two has left Poland and Hungary, not surprisingly, with distinct elements of their old elitist/deferential traditions.

It may indeed be that the persistence of old elitist attitudes and deference explains and underlies certain political differences between parts of Eastern Europe and the USSR. Today, of the states within the Soviet bloc, Poland and Hungary, the most traditionally elitist, also afford their citizens more freedom—in speech, in symbolic expression, in behavior—than the others, and a great deal more than the USSR. Power is centralized, and these freedoms could be revoked—but not without costs that the regimes seem unwilling to bear. The traditionally high status and critical attitudes of the intelligentsia, the deference they still command from the population as a whole, and their consequent greater assertiveness (compared to all but a small portion of the Soviet intelligentsia), the real though moderate play given to private enterprise in both societies, all are rooted in the past. Nisbet, in his concern with a "new despotism" in *all* advanced societies, decries the growth of power over human lives, which is "basically the result of the gradual disappearance of all the intermediate institutions which, coming from the pre-democratic past, served for a long time to check the kind of authority"[37] modern states developed. Though "intermediate institutions" may not be the most appropriate term, more elements of this sort have survived from the predemocratic past into a nondemocratic present in Poland and Hungary than elsewhere. They *are* "buffers to central power" albeit quite moderate ones, and they exist in some measure because equality of condition has *not* proceeded so far in these states as elsewhere in Eastern Europe.[38] The elements of the old order, however repugnant to some egalitarians and even sincere reformist socialists, are too deep rooted to be readily removed, and in their persistence have presented a barrier to even greater Sovietization of political life.

All these general observations come finally to touch upon questions of the costs and benefits of socialist revolutions—what they have bestowed on men, what they have taken away. Thus we come, finally, back to the questions raised in chapter 1—has the measure of greater *equality* socialist regimes have promoted in the material sphere been so linked to the "omnicompetent" and repressive qualities of those regimes, that its achievement has *required* the suppression of existing or potential freedom? And if so, has it been, from any point of view, worth it?

EQUALITY, SOCIALISM, AND LIBERTY

The questions are complex ones, with whose large-scale implications other writers have dealt more lucidly and grandly than I shall attempt here. For the socialist experience, an assessment must depend in large measure on the values one brings to the sorts of data and observations this book provides. "Ideological egalitarians" and "neoconservatives" (or libertarians) would presumably pose somewhat different questions in making their assessments (though this is not to say that the former are unconcerned with individual liberty, nor that the latter will countenance *any* sort of inequality that develops spontaneously). In assessing the socialist experience here, we will try to pose questions of both sorts.

At the outset, some avowal of personal perspective is in order. Simply put, I would rank myself more with those I have called "neoconservatives" than with the egalitarians. I am troubled by the implications of "equality of result" for individual liberty, were it to become the basis of government programs. Nor are egalitarians, in my view, really confronting the potential impact of the increased governmental intervention they see as necessary, though they are not evidently comfortable with it. To promote equality of result in the economic sphere alone would require an encroachment on individual choice and autonomy that would go well beyond economics. Here, the conflict between equality and liberty *is* real.

The moral rationales for "equality of result"—that justice demands no less, that inequalities are the products of "chance" and therefore indefensible, that individual differences in talent and capacity are characteristics over which their recipient has no control and are therefore "nonentitling"—fail to convince. "Chance" plays a role in determining one's social origin, and hence one's career prospects; and to the degree that these prospects are radically disparate because of old legal or traditional restrictions, attempts to generate greater equality of *opportunity* make sense to me, and to many who might be called "conservative." But "chance" and "luck" of the sort Jencks et al. discuss—sheer contingencies that generate different outcomes for those with similar backgrounds and education—seem part of the human condition, neither "just" nor "unjust" in the sense that social arrangements may be so judged. *Why* their operation must be challenged and beaten, as a matter of broad-scale policy, eludes me, however clear it may be to egalitarians.

Finally, individuals differ not only in talent and capacity—"givens," perhaps—but in the *effort* they invest in developing these.

Whether egalitarians see effort itself as unequally *distributed* as well as unequally exercised, I do not know. But I am unwilling to regard it as nonentitling, as they evidently do.[39]

All this is no defense of many varieties of inequality to whose eradication many libertarians are committed. Those legal, administrative, or political restrictions that have barred races, ethnic groups, or classes from occupations, locations, or necessary education to develop abilities and pursue goals; those extreme economic conditions that have left larger or smaller segments of societies at a brutalized, and precarious level of existence, are not defensible. The actions most liberal democracies, whether "capitalist" or "social-democrat," have taken to deal with them have restricted certain freedoms of the few to distribute a usable amount of freedom to the many, and have thus been crucial in sustaining the democratic character of those societies. These measures have been justified as promoting greater equality of opportunity, and they *have* promoted it. This is very different from the pursuit of equality of result.

This is my own position, which must dictate certain, by now probably predictable, evaluations of the socialist experience. As readers will, I think, understand quite well by this point, my use throughout this book of the word "socialist" to describe the USSR and Eastern European states has been the exercise of an option—since they are as readily characterized by many authors as "communist." My choice of terms simply reflects the fact that the regimes themselves claim to have established socialism, but not communism: it does not imply a failure to distinguish the "socialism" represented by European social-democratic parties from the political and economic reality of the countries of our concern. But in a larger sense, a major issue—perhaps the major issue of our age—is involved in the terminology here.

To contrast socialism with its supposed opposite, capitalism, is not, in an analytic sense, to contrast totalitarianism with freedom and liberty. But in the concrete as opposed to the analytic realm, the two contrasts *are* to a significant degree intertwined. A capitalist economic order, with its significant though generally far from total divorce of state from economy, of political from economic power, is surely not the "cause" of political democracy, of a free society—it is not a sufficient condition thereof. *But* the contemporary world strongly indicates that it is a likely *necessary* condition. There are, to be certain, capitalist economies that exist in authoritarian regimes—Chile, Brazil, South Africa come readily to mind—as well as societies that combine capitalism, political democracy, and a decent regard for human liberty, among them the Western European states with social-democratic governments. However, one will not find free and democratic polities where socialism has destroyed capitalism, where the state has through the exercise of its power absorbed the economy. Instead, one finds polities where the grip of the regime on the population is all the tighter, owing to its control of the economy, than it was under the often authoritarian regimes that preceded socialism.

Temptations toward an economic determinist view here should be resisted. It is in any case a rather "loose" determinism that sees a free-enterprise economy as a necessary but not sufficient condition of freedom, and socialism as an economic base, *but not the only base,* of a lack of political freedom. One need recall that, if the history of the socialist states teaches anything, it is that *politics* determines: political decisions, based on political power and coercion, brought socialism to their economies. They did not drift into a totalitarian political system because of a gradual socialization of the means of production.

Thus, the relationships among capitalism-socialism freedom-unfreedom are complex, though not *completely* indeterminate. Once political force destroys the private economic sectors, the strain toward an unfree polity seems, on the evidence, pronounced to say the least. And the problems, largely ones of politics, turn heavily, as do most political issues, on matters of values. Egalitarians and neoconservatives will disagree, as they must, on the *prospects* for the survival of their own values under "Eurocommunist" governments that may arise in the future, on what further government intervention in the economies of Western democracies may bring. Our task here is not to deal with these issues, but to review the evidence that the experience of the socialist states presents on issues by no means unrelated to them; and on the basis of that evidence, to make some judgments.

Let us commence from the egalitarian perspective. Here, taking both enhanced equality of opportunity and equality of result (the latter being, for some, perhaps the only convincing evidence that the former has been achieved) as desiderata, a major question would seem to be whether gains in this area balance losses in individual freedom. Another way of putting the question, slightly different, is: could whatever advances in equality socialist regimes have delivered also have been, conceivably, delivered by other regimes?

Answering these is a tall order. Despite the large amount of data in the pages preceding, we lack solid measures of presocialist inequality. Nonetheless, we can make some general, reasonably grounded observations.

First, we can stipulate that social mobility *has* increased under socialism, that the economic development it fostered has created opportunity to move up—more opportunity than existed under the old regime. Thus, although it still falls far short of the absolute, opportunity has been considerably equalized.

However socialism was not a *conditio sine qua non* for this change. Accelerated social mobility *could* have been produced by an intensive effort at economic restoration and development under capitalist auspices as well—the Marshall Plan, equally effective, worked in Western Europe, would have worked well in Czechoslovakia, and with some modifications for more backward economic bases, could have worked in the rest of Eastern Europe. Going further back into history, one can ask whether "capitalist" economic development in Russia would have produced mobility that would have been, *en gros*, similar to that achieved in the Soviet "plan era." This is a quite difficult, "what if" type of question. But one can argue, from the rapid rate of economic development in the later imperial years, that an extension of imperial economic policies into the 1920s and 1930s, had all of Europe escaped the war, might well have come quite close. Development would have been statist, but still its political auspices would probably have been less repressive than those under which Soviet development took place. The twilight years of Tsarism were ones of uncomfortable balance between old and new, but not ones of increasing repression; forces for reform were active, if still relatively weak. Certainly, the political regime installed in the 1920s in the USSR was more violent and repressive than that of Tsarism. Thus, history *could*, had certain things not been *quite* as they were, have seen an economic transformation, and high rates of gross social mobility, under a nonsocialist regime that for all its autocratic trappings would have left more room for personal autonomy than did Stalinism.

So much for such speculations—and for mobility across the manual-nonmanual line. Socialism and its "revolution" have produced a form of mobility capitalism would not have—a high degree of long-range mobility placing persons of humble origin in the dominant *political* positions in society. Continued Tsarist economic development, or Marshall Plan–type programs in Eastern Europe, would have relied more on elements of traditional elite and professional strata. Thus, these sorts of opportunities seem to be uniquely socialist products. But they have touched, and will touch, very few people, insofar as effective political power remains so tightly concentrated in socialist societies. Whether it can then be thought of as a significantly egalitarian innovation is doubtful, when balanced against the political subjection the humbly-born leaders of socialist regimes have imposed on the populations from which they arose.

With socialism has also come greater *equality of result* in the economic sphere; we need not question the judgments of economists here. The question we need pose, as temporary egalitarians, is whether the equality thus achieved is *remarkably* greater than that observable elsewhere. But income disparities under socialism are *still* quite significant in terms of gross figures, and greater by far when one takes into account the hidden material benefits enjoyed by the elite but not figured into income. No radical reversal or absolute equalization of the economic status of socio-occupational strata has taken place. The costs of being a loser, the rewards accruing to a winner are still significant—too much so, as we saw in chapter 1, for socialist intellectuals who stand on the egalitarian side. Judgments of the magnitude of egalitarian gains will vary according to perspective. In the light of the past, they are significant; in the light of *promised* transformations of society and its reward system under socialism, they are rather modest.

Were socialist regimes necessary to produce these results? Here, I think, the answer must be yes. Socialism as it grew in its Soviet version, and as it later came to Eastern Europe, involved broad, almost total expropriation of private property in productive resources; established a "command" economy, subservient to the polity, in place of whatever market existed; and developed a polity monist rather than pluralist in character.

Without this combination, it is difficult to see how the equalization that has occurred, could have. Frank Parkin notes that the pattern of advanced Western capitalism, wherein a market economy is combined with political pluralism, is a difficult one in which to bring about "redistribution of advantages between social classes."[40] However, under socialism, as he reasons,

> it is relatively easy for a government to alter the reward system in favour of previously disadvantaged groups. It is not simply the absence of a market which makes this possible, but the fact that privileged groups are not accorded the political rights and facilities for challenging or negating redistributive measures.[41]

This is the crux—political monism, the monopoly power of the socialist regime, restricts the ability of groups to defend themselves, to press their interests—and not only privileged groups. Parkin's words apply better to the transition period, perhaps, than to the total sweep of socialist history thus far. Quite *un*privileged groups as well lack rights to challenge or negate government economic policy (some privileged groups are *well* provided for in this area, since they themselves are part of the narrow bargaining process that socialism accommodates). Egalitarianism, such as it is, has been delivered on the basis of a lack of group and individual freedom. As Parkin puts it, shifting the focus to nonsocialist systems, perhaps

> socialist egalitarianism is not readily compatible with a pluralist political order of the classic western type. Egalitarianism seems to require a political system in which the state is able continually to hold in check those social and occupational groups which, by virtue of their skills or education or personal attributes, might otherwise attempt to stake claims to a disproportionate share of society's rewards. The most effective way of holding such groups in check is by denying them the right to organize politically, or in other ways, to undermine social equality.[42]

Thus, the socialist policy holds in check certain groups who might claim disproportionate rewards. An egalitarian may not have trouble with the term "disproportionate"—since any extra reward to any group will be bad, something to which nothing entitles it. But recall that the state alone judges *what* is proportionate and what disproportionate. The system Parkin describes restricts the rewards of *some* groups, bringing them to a level closer to that of the working class than elsewhere—but it also *elevates* the rewards of security police and other surveillance and compulsion specialists, since it deems *them* worthy of disproportionate compensation. The state machine that effectively denies groups the right of political organization to undermine "social equality" also denies them the right to organize for virtually any other unofficial purpose. These are not outcomes egalitarians wish for—but they seem to be a necessary part of the package.

Now, many may complain that the argument thus far suffers from lack of historical perspective—that "freedom" cannot be lost where it did not exist, that it does not exist where large portions of the population are denied the material basis for exercising choice. These are reasonable objections but, I would argue, lend themselves readily to overstatement.

First, granting that only Czechoslovakia really operated on liberal-democratic lines, and that Tsarist Russia and the rest of interwar Eastern Europe were not liberal democracies, we need remember that there are differences of no mean degree between *authoritarian* regimes, which these were, and *totalitarian* regimes, which the USSR and the Eastern European states all were for some portion of their postrevolutionary periods. The presocialist authoritarian regimes, repressive and unjust in many ways, left much of the economy and many spheres of life private, nonpoliticized, in direct contrast to what communist regimes have attempted. Thus, spheres of freedom (including, not unimportantly, the right to emigrate) were open to the populace. Nor did those regimes find it necessary to arrest and imprison so many as have socialist regimes—not a bad indicator of relative freedom and individual liberty in a world where these values are always imperfectly realized.

Second, it can be argued that socialist regimes, by their utilization of organizational weapons, have proven rather stable and enduring. While they have been so partly because they have tapped some real social energies, responded to some widely felt needs, their stability and endurance have also been effective brakes on the development of democratic, rule-of-law tendencies that *might* have emerged in a less totalitarian context.* This too must be accounted a cost by egalitarians, unless it can be demonstrated that *no* potential for political change in the direction of Western patterns existed or exists.

It may be, as some would argue, that the average socialist *citizen* has not missed freedom; that his presocialist poverty, his vulnerability to unemployment and other economic injury left him no mental room to think in such terms. In some measure, this is surely true—more true in the USSR and the historically less-developed states than elsewhere. But it is not at *all* clear that socialist strategies of development have been *more* effective at providing full stomachs than other strategies, not pursued, might have been. In fact, quite the reverse seems to be the case. The relatively low living standards in the contemporary socialist states are products not only of low developmental starting points but of state-imposed priorities favoring nonconsumption sectors as well. Socialist citizens could have gotten a better deal elsewhere.

More importantly, whether they miss freedom or not, they have suffered from the lack of restrictions on state control, of the rule of law, of immunities from interference that liberal democracies generally afford their citizens. These protect not only the politically active and articulate; they protect the apolitical as well from the *consequences* of their lack of interest in politics. Socialist citizens have been subjected to repression, arrest, and death more often because of these lacks than they otherwise would have been. And this is a cost in anyone's terms.

One would have to be committed indeed to equality-as-justice to

*One is tempted here to cite the examples of Spain and Portugal, two nations until recently seemingly mired in a legacy of underdevelopment of an almost Eastern European type, and authoritarian regimes ever more anachronistic. For all their regimes' repulsive qualities, they neither sought to, nor did they, penetrate society as Communist regimes have. At this time (1978) both seem well on their way out of the old molds, and toward some approximation of Western parliamentary politics—though their paths are still strewn with dangers. Could either a soldiers' revolt, or the death of a *caudillo*, produce the same prospects for political pluralism in a contemporary Communist state? One would be hard-pressed to argue so convincingly. Here, I think, we see evidence of the difference in *potential* for change left by an authoritarian as opposed to a Soviet-type regime, much of that difference being attributable to the "private" sectors the former leaves in the economy and elsewhere, which of their very nature limit the totalism and permanence of power.

countenance the repression visited upon the masses in socialist states, even were the equality achieved much greater. The measure of actual progress toward equality is too modest to give egalitarians any basis for accepting, however grudgingly, the lack of freedom under socialist regimes as a tolerable trade-off.

This is the judgment I think egalitarians should render—though I do not delude myself that they would necessarily do so in actual fact. From the conservative side, the issue is simpler. The suspicion and fear here are not of inequality but of the encroachment of the state on the individual, for good purpose of ill.[43] Taking some types of equality as "good purposes," even much *greater* equality of opportunity than has been reached could not justify the nature, scope, and seeming permanence of the subjection of socialist citizens to their regimes.

Indeed, from a libertarian viewpoint *nothing* could. The achievement of equality before the law, the legal equalization of basic human status that is the cornerstone of equality of opportunity, gave men in the West a measure of independence—imperfect, but immeasurably more than what had gone before. This involved state intervention, but moved the majority, hitherto outside or below the law, up. Intervention to produce equality of result levels *down,* and by the very nature of the mechanisms necessary to produce it makes men more dependent. Neither contemporary egalitarians nor the founders of Marxian socialism expressed a wish to trade equality for freedom: in the radically new and just society, material equality would be the base for an equality of liberty as well. But liberty of this sort is something different, or as Nisbet puts it, it amounts to "mere equal shares of somthing *called* liberty which bears little relation to the autonomies and immunities which are true hallmarks of liberty."[44]

Socialist citizens do not enjoy such autonomies and immunities. True, in some places, they are relatively free, in other states, hardly so at all. In either case, their "freedom" in its particular measure depends on the current persona of the leadership, the current policy, the current line-not on guarantees beyond which the state *cannot* go. One cannot, and should not, identify the Marxian promise of equality among men as the *sole* temptation that has led regimes backed by Marxian ideology to deny liberty to their subjects. Revolutionaries crave power, fame, wealth, and a host of other things, as well as the supposed welfare of those in whose name they act. But their pursuit (and as far as it has gone their realization), of egalitarian goals unattainable under the conditions of the market and a plural polity has been a major force in the design and construction of political systems inimical to individual and group liberty.

From this perspective then, there is little to cheer one in contemplating what the Soviet-East European brand of socialism has wrought; and, indeed, little reason to marvel that those in East and West who still denominate themselves as socialists and hold up socialism as an ideal refuse to identify their "true" socialism with any of socialism's concrete manifestations as they exist today. For those who hold it as their ideal, "socialism" remains today as much a matter of the future as it was over sixty years ago, before the world saw the establishment of the first socialist regime.

Epilogue

SOCIALISM ONCE represented, in many men's eyes, the future—the promise of a more just, decent, and egalitarian social order. Today socialism as a concrete mode of organizing government, economy, and society has a considerable history of its own—it has a past. That past, complex and widely divergent from the designs in the original blueprints, has been the subject of this book.

The presocialist societies all had problems—economic backwardness versus more developed European states; regimes whose inadequacies ran from the moderate to the near-criminal; internal social and political tensions that made pragmatic compromise at one and the same time essential and well-nigh impossible to achieve. All those societies fell in the chaotic destabilization of war, to give place to new socialist regimes—Russia earlier, the Eastern European states later. With the new regimes came the commitment to the construction of a new social order. The interaction of revolutionary design and social realities produced systems of stratification combining new and old elements—and these emergent hierarchies have, thus far, proven stable and durable. Tightly centralized polities support their basic outlines, and while adjustments continue to be made between "differentiation" (to stimulate effort) and "leveling" (to head off potential unrest), the hierarchies seem likely to retain their present forms.

Certain trends and latent possibilities, however, make it foolhardy to predict persistence of current patterns into the indefinite future. Socialism has endured and survived the problems of adversity of the early years. It seems due, soon, to confront the problems of success.

As noted earlier on, the mass mobility generated by socialist economic development in the early years provided a cushion against lowered general living standards. The upward movement of workers to administrative positions, of peasants to the urban environment and full and steady factory employment, defused a good deal of potential unrest that even the state's considerable coercive resources might not have contained. The upwardly mobile retained, in some measure (since they could scarcely avoid doing so) the frames of reference of their strata of origin. Thus, their destinations were *felt* as real advancement, and probably contributed to social stabilization, to depoliticization of attitudes. The system had delivered; the beneficiaries knew it—a political fact of which all, regardless of political persuasion, must take account.

Their stake in the system was one that they sought to preserve. Yesterday's underdog becomes today's success, and attitudes change with circumstance. As Andrzej Malewski found in a Warsaw survey as early as 1958, manual workers were more egalitarian in attitudes toward wage differentiation than engineers—not surprisingly. Engineers of working-class origin, showing the cross-pressures of origin and destination, were more egalitarian than engineers whose fathers had also been engineers (and thus, of the intelligentsia) but much *less* so than workers themselves. As Malewski cogently observed, "the influence of egalitarian tradition of the paternal home is extremely anaemic in comparison with the influence of the actual living situation."[1]

We are already twenty years on from the time of Malewski's inquiry. The "heroic" and convulsive years of social transformation are behind. The socialist elite no longer expands in size so rapidly, generating such demand for new personnel. The working class, now the dominant segment of society in statistical terms, no longer grows by annual leaps. The peasantry, smaller than ever before, no longer represents a massive pool of underemployed manpower to be drawn from, nor is there economic dynamism to draw them in the quantities of the past. Mobility data are not yet available to confirm this, but the logic of the maturation process and annual figures on laborforce distribution across sectors of the economy suggest that the mass mobility of the past cannot be duplicated. There is little evidence yet in socialist societies of the shift to a "service society," demanding accelerated manual to nonmanual mobility, wherein the nonmanual strata come to comprise most of the working population, as is occurring in some advanced Western states.

Whatever socialist regimes manage by way of greater material welfare for all their citizens, and by way of egalitarian distribution, the prospects for socio-occupational mobility in the future are still important, all the more so since the historical experience of an earlier expansion of mobility opportunities, *and* socialist rhetoric, have generated a greater and broader orientation toward mobility than has existed ever before in the socialist states. There is a risk here that frustrated aspirations will lead to unrest, to exactly that kind of *class* politics and orientation toward change that is moderated when opportunities for *individual* improvement of one's situation seem good. This would be a politics of the working class, particularly: the class that has been formed by socialism. Such a politics could be explosive.

Opposition to such politics is certain—from regimes reluctant to accommodate to *any* spontaneous politics (and such this would be) but also from incumbents of more favored socio-occupational strata, on the bread-and-butter issues of distributive justice. Increasingly, the intelligentsia's frame of reference will be that of the intelligentsia, not of recruits from lower strata; the workers', that of urban industrial workers, not that of ex-peasants, as the revolutionary wave of mobility and its effects recede. Expectations, if they do not undergo a revolutionary rise, may stabilize at a point that threatens to exacerbate the situation, rather than moderate it as in the past. The intimations are yet uncertain, but dismissing the restiveness of Polish workers[2] or the recurrent grumblings of some segments of the Hungarian working class[3] as portents of the future would not be justified.

Are the workers egalitarian, and are they a segment of society potentially responsive to appeals by egalitarian socialist intellectuals of the sort discussed in chapter 1? In response to specific inquiries, workers *seem* so, especially on economic issues[4]—as are in general the less educated and those of relatively low incomes (who make up, obviously, a substantial component of the working class). Yet worker-intellectual linkages remain generally weak in socialist countries. The "common cause" made by Polish dissident intellectuals and workers in 1976–1978 is remarkable for its break with previous patterns, and may not be indicative of future developments elsewhere. Nor, of course, is the working class without internal divisions. Though we have generally dealt with it as a single stratum in our four-stratum scheme, significant economic differences make it likely that different segments may think and act differently with reference to issues of reward differentiation. Furthermore, the *issues* most likely to mobilize workers, even the economic ones, are not necessarily limited to egalitarianism and/or poverty—it has not been the unskilled and worst-paid, those with the lowest hierarchical positions and greatest material need, who have created disorders in Poland.

The future, as always, is unclear. One should not expect that egalitarian grievances, if generalized into a movement capable of working change in socialist polities, will move them in the direction of *political* liberalism. If tolerance be a necessary element of the *social* base of a more liberal regime, workers do not exhibit it to any great degree. Nor, much as conservatives fear, do egalitarian attitudes, in general, seem to promote tolerance of diverse opinions.[5] Thus, worker militancy over bread-and-butter issues could certainly threaten stability to a point, but the threat it represents would not confront the current regimes with the necessity of accommodating to political reform in a democratic direction. Should "ideological egalitarian" intellectuals find responses among the workers, it will be the bread-and-butter aspects of their program that attract, not the vision of a "purer" socialism of egalitarian *political* participation.

It has been the pragmatic reformers, ready to countenance *greater* income differentiation and the "incentive" it should provide, whose programs have implied (and in the Czech case of 1967–1968 explicitly demanded) greater individual liberties, who have represented the greater, more profound challenge to systems whose ultimate power lies in the restriction of those liberties. The possibilities for various alterations in the stratification structure multiply to the degree that liberalization and loosening of the monist-centralist polity, which supports the current hierarchy of reward and opportunity, seems possible.[6]

Thus far, neither egalitarians nor liberal pragmatists have had major impacts in changing the direction of socialist systems. Such impacts, whether resulting in more liberty or less, more or less egalitarianism, would require a more effective linkage between intelligentsia and workers, cross-cutting their material interests (which continue to differ) in the pursuit of larger and longer-term goals, than any developed yet. The prospects for such changes depend on many factors beyond the immediate concerns of this book, and we cannot predict the way those factors will develop. But even in the face of the current relative stability, we cannot rule out a coalescence of factors that may produce radical changes. If such should come, the time for a new book on our topic will be at hand.

Notes

PROLOGUE

1. See Robert W. Jackman, *Politics and Social Equality: A Comparative Analysis* (New York: Wiley, 1975).

CHAPTER ONE EQUALITY AS AN ISSUE

The first quotation heading the chapter is from a Krakow area folk tale collected by the nineteenth-century Polish ethnographer Oskar Kolberg, as reported in Stanislaw Ossowski, *Class Structure in the Social Consciousness,* trans. by Sheila Patterson (New York: Free Press, 1963), p. 21. The second is reported by Irving Krauss, *Stratification, Class, and Conflict* (New York: Free Press, 1976), vii.

1. The original statement of the "functional" view, Kingsley Davis and Wilbert Moore, "Some Principles of Stratification," *American Sociological Review* 10, (April 1945), 242–49 is also available in a great number of readers on social stratification.
2. See Seymour Martin Lipset, *The First New Nation: The United States in Historical and Comparative Perspective* (Garden City, N.Y.: Doubleday, Anchor Books, 1967), p. 2, and passim.
3. Ibid.
4. Cambridge, Mass.: Harvard University Press, 1971.
5. New York: Pantheon, 1973.
6. New York: Basic Books, 1972.
7. Gans, *More Equality,* pp. 78, 63–64.
8. Ibid., pp. 64–65.
9. Jencks et al., *Inequality,* pp. 195–96.
10. Ibid., p. 8.
11. Ibid., p. 230.
12. Ibid. See also p. 15, *n* 2.
13. Robert A. Nisbet, "The New Despotism," *Commentary,* June 1975, p. 34.
14. Susan Ferge, "Some Relations Between Social Structure and the School System," in *Hungarian Sociological Studies (The Sociological Review Monograph,* no. 17, edited by Paul Halmos) (Keele, February 1972), p. 217.
15. Ibid.

16. Ibid., p. 219.

17. Svetozar Stojanovic, *Between Ideals and Reality: A Critique of Socialism and its Future,* trans. by Gerson S. Sher (New York: Oxford University Press, 1973), p. 212.

18. Ibid.

19. Ibid., p. 213.

20. Ibid., p. 214.

21. See ibid., pp. 215–16.

22. Ibid.

23. Ibid., p. 220.

24. Ota Sik, "Czechoslovakia's New System of Economic Planning and Management," *Eastern European Economics,* Fall 1965, p. 22.

25. Pavel Machonin, "Socialni rozvrstveni nasi spolecnosti," *Nova mysl,* April 1968, pp. 466–74. (JPRS Political Translations on Eastern Europe, no. 351, May 31, 1968, p. 50).

26. Augustin Kudrna, "Diferenciace v odmenovani," *Planovane hospodarstvi,* no. 9 (1968), translated as "Differentiation in Earnings," *Eastern Europe Economics,* Summer 1969, p. 37.

27. Frank Parkin, *Class Inequality and Political Order* (New York: Praeger, 1971), p. 177.

28. Ibid.

29. Wlodzimierz Wesolowski, "Social Stratification in Socialist Society (Some theoretical problems)," *Polish Sociological Bulletin,* no. 1 (1967), 33.

30. On the Soviet debate, see Murray Yanowitch, *Social and Economic Inequality in the Soviet Union: Six Studies* (White Plains, N.Y.: Myron E. Sharpe, Inc., 1977), pp. 91–96, and sources cited therein.

31. See Wlodzimierz Wesolowski, *Klasy, warstwy i wladza* (Warsaw, 1966), p. 22.

32. Nisbet, "New Despotism," p. 38.

33. See Gans, *More Equality,* pp. 66, 87, 204; Jencks et al., *Inequality,* pp. 197, 230.

34. Gans, *More Equality*, p. 66.

35. Robert Nisbet, "The Fatal Ambivalence of an Idea: Equal Freemen or Equal Serfs?," *Encounter,* December 1976, p. 10.

36. See, e.g., Irving Kristol, "About Equality," *Commentary,* November 1972, pp. 41–47.

CHAPTER TWO TRADITION, DEFERENCE, AND EGALITARIANISM

The passages that head this chapter are taken, respectively, from Karl Baedeker, *Russia, with Teheran, Port Arthur, and Peking: Handbook for Travelers* (Leipzig, 1914; facsimile edition, Random House, Arno Press, 1971). p. xliii; and from K. J. Jirecek, *Cesty po Bulharsku* (Prague, 1888), p. 35, as translated in Doreen Warriner, ed., *Contrasts in Emerging Societies:*

Readings in the Social and Economic History of South-Eastern Europe in the Nineteenth Century (Bloomington: Indiana University Press, 1965), pp. 255–56.

1. *Documentacni Prehled CTK*, no. 32 (July 30, 1974); see *Radio Free Europe, Czechoslovak Situation Report*, September 4, 1974, p. 1.

2. Hugh Seton-Watson, *Eastern Europe Between the Wars: 1918–1941* (3d rev. ed., New York: Harper and Row, 1967), p. 178–79. Seton-Watson's work was for many years the standard general history of the area and period, and we will have occasion to refer to it frequently.

3. The description that follows is drawn in great measure from Jan Szczepanski, *Polish Society* (New York: Random House, 1970) pp. 20–26. See also Michalina Vaughan, "Poland," in Margaret S. Archer and Salvador Giner, eds., *Contemporary Europe: Class, Status and Power* (New York: St. Martin's Press, 1971), pp. 318–21.

4. Seton-Watson, *Eastern Europe*, p. 123.

5. Ibid., pp. 86–87, 100.

6. Gyula Illyes, *People of the Puszta*, trans. by G. F. Cushing (Budapest: Corvina Press, 1967), p. 163.

7. See Charles Gati, "Modernization and Communist Power in Hungary," *East European Quarterly* 5, no. 3 (1971), 328.

8. See Frederick S. Pisky, "The People," in Ernst C. Helmreich, ed., *Hungary* (New York: Praeger, 1957), p. 71.

9. The Depression and its effects seen to have been a major spur here. On Hungary, see Gati, "Modernization," pp. 338–41.

10. For 1921 figures, Glowny Urzad Statystyczny, *Maly Rocznik Statystyczny 1930* (Warsaw, 1930), p. 10, table 19; for 1931 figures, Chief Bureau of Statistics, *Concise Statistical Year-Book of Poland 1938* (Warsaw, 1938), p. 30.

11. Pisky, "The People," p. 71.

12. See Gati, "Modernization," pp. 339–42.

13. For general historical background on the Balkans, see Robert Lee Wolff, *The Balkans in Our Time* (Cambridge: Harvard University Press, 1956); L. S. Stavrianos. *The Balkans since 1453* (New York: Holt, Rinehart and Winston, 1963); and the essays in Charles and Barbara Jelavich, eds., *The Balkans in Transition* (Berkeley and Los Angeles: University of California Press, 1963).

14. The phrases are those of Ivan T. Berend and Gyorgy Ranki; see their excellent *Economic Development in East-Central Europe in the 19th and 20th Centuries* (New York and London: Columbia University Press, 1974), pp. 188–89, 36–37. See also Norman J. G. Pounds, *Eastern Europe* (Chicago: Aldine, 1969), pp. 530–32, 576–77.

15. Serbia's dominant stamp on the new Yugoslav state had positive impacts in the area of landholding patterns, whatever problems it caused in other areas. The diversity of patterns in different areas (feudal in Bosnia,

large estates in Croatia and the Vojvodina) gave place, over the course of centrally directed land reform programs, to peasant smallholding similar to the Serbian model throughout much of the country—although, of course, the problems of technological backwardness, overpopulation, and agrarian underemployment remained. See Berend and Ranki, *Economic Development*, pp. 186–88; see also Bogdan D. Denitch, *The Legitimation of a Revolution: The Yugoslav Case* (New Haven and London: Yale University Press, 1976), pp. 60–62.

16. Jozo Tomasevich, *Peasants, Politics and Economic Change in Yugoslavia* (Stanford, California: Stanford University Press, 1955), p. 160.

17. Much more could be written here about the specifics of peasant living standards, but the chapter would grow unwieldy were these matters to be detailed. See Seton-Watson, *Eastern Europe*, pp. 75–110.

18. Tomasevich, *Peasants*, p. 173.

19. See Robert Redfield, *Peasant Society and Culture: An Anthropological Approach to Civilization* (Chicago: University of Chicago Press, 1956), pp. 68–70. While Redfield's formulation is not generally applied to "national" societies, its use in this manner here does not seem out of order. Poland and Hungary (the former despite the long period of partition from 1795 to 1918) preserved a high-cultural tradition, a "history," for a millenium. The peasant segments of these societies possessed, of course, their "little tradition," but it can be regarded as a "half-culture" incomplete without the broader culture, national symbolism, etc., represented by the "great tradition." In contrast, as we shall see, the Balkan states, due to the nature and length of the Ottoman domination, *lost* their "great tradition," preserved in a nonliterate culture only in songs and tales. None *but* peasants were left to "carry on," and peasants living a subsistence life under foreign domination for centuries could do little other than elaborate a "little tradition" and preserve it. No "great tradition," then, existed when, in the nineteenth and twentieth centuries, the Balkan states reclaimed their independence, and thus the new societies reflected their "peasant" nature with no real competition from a "higher," nonpeasant culture.

20. Julia Pardoe, *The City of the Magyar*, vol. II (London, 1840), in Warriner, *Contrasts*, p. 56.

21. Sandor Petofi, "A Magyar nemes" ("The Hungarian Nobleman") (1845), in *Collected Works* (Budapest: Akademiai Kiado, 1951), vol. I, p. 340; in Warriner, *Contrasts*, pp. 59–60.

22. W. S. Kuniczak, *The Thousand Hour Day*, (New York: Dial Press, 1966), pp. 162–63.

23. Boleslaw Prus (pseud. for Aleksander Glowacki), *The Doll*, trans. by David Welsh (New York: Twayne Publishers, 1972), p. 407.

24. Ibid., p. 44.

25. Alexander Gella, "The Life and Death of the Old Polish Intelligentsia," *Slavic Review* 30, no. 1 (1971), 15.

26. Gella's essay "Life and Death" is one of the most eloquent recent contributions in English to this literature. His citations (esp. pp. 3–4) provide a good guide to the main Polish-language sources.

27. Wlodzimierz Wesolowski, "Changes in the Class Structure in Poland," in *Empirical Sociology in Poland* (Warsaw: Polish Scientific Publishers, 1966), pp. 16–17.

28. Zygmunt Bauman, "Economic Growth and Social Structure: the Case of Poland," in Jerzy Wiatr, ed., *Studies in Polish Political System* (Warsaw: Ossolineum, 1966), pp. 17–18.

29. Though their number may have been *fewer* in interwar Poland than in the areas of pre-World War I Poland where the educational network was relatively well developed. See Gella, "Life and Death," p. 15.

30. Illyes, *People of the Puszta,* p. 222.

31. Thus, the conservative interwar Hungarian government of Count Bethlen, attempting to restrict the activities and appeal of trade unions and the Social Democratic Party, made a pact with the socialists that left them free to organize industrial workers on economic issues but barred them from organizing and agitating among the peasants, seen as a more critical mainstay of the traditional social order. See Gati, "Modernization," p. 338.

32. See note 19, above.

33. Two useful essays treating related topics are Stanford J. Shaw, "The Ottoman View of the Balkans," and Wayne S.Vucinich, "Some Aspects of the Ottoman Legacy," pp. 56–80 and 81–114, respectively, in Jelavich and Jelavich, eds., *Balkans in Transition.*

34. *Istorijska citanka, odobrani tekstovi za istoriju srpskog naroda* (Belgrade, 1948), as translated in Warriner, ed., *Contrasts,* p. 298.

35. Anon., *Betrachtungen über das Furstenthum Servien* (Vienna, 1851) as translated in Warriner, ed., *Contrasts,* p. 303.

36. Ivo Andric, *The Woman from Sarajevo,* trans. by Joseph Hitrec (New York: Knopf, 1965), p. 158.

37. Ibid., p. 120.

38. Ibid., pp. 171–72.

39. J. W. Ozanne, *Three Years in Roumania* (London, 1878), in Warriner, *Contrasts,* p. 159.

40. Miloslav Janicijevic, "Osvrt na Strukturalne Promene Jugoslovenskog Drustva," in Jugoslovensko Udruzenje za Sociologiju, *Promene klasne strukture savremenog jugoslovenskog drustva* (Belgrade, 1967). Direct quote is from English language summary, p. 304.

41. Serbia, once having gained its independence, *had* to be a relatively high-mobility society for the time, since, given its demographic profile, "there was no source of recruitment into its ruling establishment except the peasantry" (Denitch, *Legitimation,* p. 34). In the twentieth century, peasant offspring were certainly underrepresented in the universities, and the elites were generally *two* generations removed from the peasantry. Yet, some data

indicate that perhaps about 20 percent of the interwar Yugoslav elite were of peasant parentage, and such a figure might well have characterized the share of university places taken up by peasant sons, at least in some faculties. For the elite data, see Lenard Cohen, "The Social Background and Recruitment of Yugoslav Political Elites, 1918–1948," in Allen Barton, Bogdan Denitch, and Charles Kadushin eds., *Opinion-Making Elites in Yugoslavia* (New York: Praeger, 1973), pp. 51–52.

42. Seton-Watson, *Eastern Europe,* p. 142.

43. Ibid., p. 146–47.

44. Jaroslav Krejci, *Social Change and Stratification in Postwar Czechoslovakia* (New York: Columbia University Press, 1972), p. 1.

45. See Hugh Seton-Watson, *The Russian Empire, 1801–1917* (Oxford: The Clarendon Press, 1967) pp. 21–24.

46. On the estate system in general, see Cyril E. Black, "The Nature of Imperial Russian Society," in Donald W. Treadgold, ed., *The Development of the USSR: An Exchange of Views* (Seattle: University of Washington Press, 1964), pp. 177–78; Seton-Watson, *Russian Empire,* passim; Robert A. Feldmesser, "Social Classes and Political Structure," in Cyril E. Black, ed., *The Transformation of Russian Society* (Cambridge: Harvard University Press, 1960) pp. 238–40.

47. Feldmesser, "Social Classes," p. 240.

48. See Cyril E. Black, Marius B. Jansen, et al., *The Modernization of Japan and Russia: A Comparative Study* (New York: Free Press, 1975) pp. 46–47.

49. Data are from Seton-Watson, *Russian Empire,* pp. 534–35.

50. Ibid., p. 28.

51. Black, Jansen, et al., *Modernization,* p. 90.

52. See Seton-Watson, *Russian Empire,* p. 219.

53. See ibid., p. 27; for a valuable brief treatment of the development of the industrial working class, see Jerzy Gliksman, "The Russian Urban Worker: From Serf to Proletarian," in Black, ed., *Transformation,* pp. 311–23.

54. Gliksman, "Russian Urban Worker," p. 312.

55. See Seton-Watson, *Russian Empire,* p. 535.

56. See Gliksman, "Russian Urban Worker," p. 313.

57. Ibid.

58. Seton-Watson, *Russian Empire,* p. 405.

59. See the interesting and evocative portrait of the mercantile classes by a contemporary British observer in Sir Donald Mackenzie Wallace, *Russia: On the Eve of War and Revolution,* ed. by Cyril E. Black (New York: Vintage, 1961), pp. 186–93.

60. See Feldmesser, "Social Classes," p. 242.

61. See George Fischer, "The Intelligentsia and Russia," in Black, ed., *Transformation,* pp. 263 ff.

62. See Warren Eason, "Population Changes," in Black, ed., *Transformation*, pp. 82 ff.

63. See Seton-Watson, *Russian Empire*, p. 240.

64. Ibid., p. 239.

65. Ibid., p. 219.

66. Ibid., p. 221.

67. See Alf Edeen, "The Civil Service: Its Composition and Status," in Black, ed., *Transformation*, p. 281.

68. On the matter of Russian society as "classless" though inegalitarian, see Feldmesser, "Social Classes"; see also Stanislaw Ossowski, *Class Structure in the Social Consciousness* (New York: Free Press, 1963) pp. 100–18.

69. See Feldmesser, "Social Classes," pp. 248, 252.

70. Translated excerpts (at some length) of both the Szejnert article and the quick responses to it (*Zolnierz Wolnosci*, May 5–6, 1973; *Trybuna Ludu*, May 8, 1973; *Kultura*, May 13, 1973) are available in *RFE Polish Press Survey*, no. 2414 (June 28, 1973).

71. This phenomenon (which is also the subject of many jokes in contemporary Poland) is described briefly in Gella, "Life and Death," p. 25, and is also noted by J. Kopec, in the *Kultura* article aimed at Szejnert, and cited in note 70.

CHAPTER THREE OLD HIERARCHY AND NEW

Marx and Engels quotation is from Karl Marx and Friedrich Engels, "Manifesto of the Communist Party," in Lewis S. Feuer, ed., *Marx and Engels: Basic Writings on Politics and Philosophy* (Garden City, N.Y.: Doubleday, Anchor Books, 1959), p. 23. CPSU Program quote from Arthur P. Mendel, ed., *Essential Works of Marxism* (New York: Bantam Books, 1961), p. 380.

1. See Robert A. Feldmesser, *Aspects of Social Mobility in the Soviet Union* (Ph.D. diss., Harvard University, 1955).

2. Otto Ulc, *Politics in Czechoslovakia* (San Francisco: Freeman, 1974), p. 52.

3. Alexander Matejko, *Social Change and Stratification in Eastern Europe: An Interpretive Analysis of Poland and Her Neighbors* (New York: Praeger, 1974), p. 25.

4. Milovan Djilas, *The New Class: An Analysis of the Communist System* (New York: Praeger, 1960).

5. Jan Szczepanski, *Polish Society* (New York: Random House, 1970), pp. 105–46.

6. Ibid., pp. 141–44.

7. See Michal Pohoski, "Interrelation Between Social Mobility of Individuals and Groups in the Process of Economic Growth in Poland," *Polish Sociological Bulletin*, no. 2 (1964), 17–33.

8. See I. I. Kravchenko and E. T. Fadeev, "O sotsial'noi strukture sovet-

skogo obshchestva (sotsiologicheskaia konferentsiia v Minske)," *Voprosy filosofii,* no. 5 (1966), 143–54.

9. See, e.g., M. N. Rutkevich, "Problemy izmeneniia sotsial'noi struktury sovetskogo obshchestva," *Filosofskie nauki,* no. 4 (1968), 44–52; O. I. Shkaratan, "Rabochii klass sotsialisticheskogo obshchestva v epokhu nauchno-tekhnicheskoi revoliutsii," *Voprosy filosofii,* no. 11 (1968), 14–25; S. A. Kugel', "Izmenenie sotsial'noi struktury sotsialisticheskogo obshchestva pod vozdeistviem nauchno-tekhnicheskoi revoliutsii," *Voprosy filosofii,* no. 3 (1969), 13–22; V. S. Semenov, "Novye iavleniia v sotsial'noi strukture sovetskogo obshchestva," *Voprosy Filosofii,* no. 7 (1972), 20–30; and the report on another conference in 1972, in I. I. Kravchenko and O. N. Trubitsyn, "Problemy izmeneniia sotsial'noi struktury sovetskogo obshchestva," *Voprosy filosofii,* 6 (1972), 137–47.

10. Zev Katz, *Patterns of Social Stratification in the U.S.S.R.,* (Cambridge: MIT Center for International Studies, 1972), pp. 74, 76–100.

11. Ibid., pp. 37–67.

12. Ibid., p. 77.

13. Boris Meissner, "Totalitarian Rule and Social Change," *Problems of Communism* 15, no. 6 (1966) 58.

14. Szczepanski, *Polish Society,* p. 145 notes a similar pattern in Poland.

15. Katz, *Patterns,* p. 76.

16. See Pavel Machonin, "Socialni stratifikace v Ceskoslovensku 1967," in Pavel Machonin et al., *Ceskoslovenska Spolecnost: Sociologicka analyza socialni stratifikace* (Bratislava: Epocha, 1969), p. 134 ff. Essentially the same material is available in Machonin and Zdenek Safar, "Social Stratification in Contemporary Czechoslovakia," *Revue International de Sociologie* 6, nos. 1–3 (1970), 278–310; and in Machonin, "Social Stratification in Contemporary Czechoslovakia," *American Journal of Sociology,* 75 (March 1970), 725–41.

17. See Machonin and Safar, "Social Stratification," pp. 294–95.

18. The only readily available English-language report is on the early conclusions drawn from this set of studies, but will orient the reader to its general "shape," as we have recourse here and in later chapters to various aspects of it. See Wlodzimierz Wesolowski and Kazimierz Slomczynski, "Social Stratification in Polish Cities," in J. A. Jackson, ed., *Social Stratification* (Cambridge: Cambridge University Press, 1968), pp. 175–211.

19. See, e.g., Slomczynski and Wesolowski, "Proby reprezentaczyjne i kategorie spoleczno-zawodowe," in Wesolowski, ed., *Zroznicowanie spoleczne* (Wroclaw-Warsaw-Krakow: Wydawnictwo Polskiej Akademii Nauk, 1970), pp. 73–75.

20. See Alex Inkeles and Peter H. Rossi, "National Comparisons of Occupational Prestige," *American Journal of Sociology* 61 (January 1956), 329–39; and idem., "Multidimensional Ratings of Occupations," *Sociometry* 20 (September 1957), 234–51. See also Alex Inkeles and Raymond A. Bauer,

The Soviet Citizen: Daily Life in a Totalitarian Society (Cambridge: Harvard University Press, 1961).

21. See Adam Sarapata and Wlodzimierz Wesolowski, "The Evaluations of Occupations by Warsaw Inhabitants," *American Journal of Sociology* 66 (May 1961); a longer version is Sarapata, "Poglady mieszkancow Warszawy na strukture spoleczna," *Studia Socjologiczno-Polityczne*, no. 6 (1960).

22. See the essays in Adam Sarapata, *Studia nad uwarstwieniem i ruchliwoscia spoleczna w Polsce* (Warsaw: Ksiazka i Wiedza, 1965); also "Stratification and Social Mobility in Poland," in *Empirical Sociology in Poland* (Warsaw: Polish Scientific Publishers, 1966), pp. 37–52; and, for a recent statement, "Occupational Prestige Hierarchy Studies in Poland," in *Transformations of Social Structure in the USSR and Poland* (Moscow and Warsaw, 1974), pp. 363–96.

23. See Donald J. Treiman, *Occupational Prestige in Comparative Perspective* (New York: Academic Press, 1977). Treiman uses Vodzinskaia's 80-occupation data from occupational orientations of Leningrad secondary school students for the USSR. See V. V. Vodzinskaia, "O sotsial'noi obuslovlennosti vybora professii," in G. V. Osipov and J. Szczepanski, eds., *Sotsial'nye problemy truda i proizvodstva: sovetsko-pol'skoe sravnitel'noe issledovanie* (Moscow and Warsaw: "Mysl'," 1969), pp. 39–61. Most of this work is now available in English; see V. V. Vodzinskaia, "Orientations Toward Occupations," in Murray Yanowitch and Wesley A. Fisher, eds., *Social Stratification and Mobility in the USSR* (White Plains, N.Y.: International Arts and Sciences Press, 1973), pp. 153–86, esp. pp. 158–59. His Polish data derive from the well-known 1958 study by Adam Sarapata and Wlodzimierz Wesolowski, "The Evaluation of Occupations by Warsaw Inhabitants," *American Journal of Sociology* 66 (May 1961), 585, and another study of high school and advanced students (see Treiman, *Occupational Prestige*). Yugoslav data, rating 100 occupations, are from Eugene Hammel's unpublished manuscript, "The Ethnographer's Dilemma: Occupational Prestige in Belgrade." Finally, Treiman's Czech data derive from a 1966 study, V. Brenner and M. Hrouda, "Veda a vysokoskolske vzdelani v prestizi povolani," *Sociologicky casopis* 4, no. 5 (1967), 541–50 and 5, no. 1 (1968), 43–54 (German translation is available: "Wissenschaft and Hochschulbildung im Prestige der Berufe," *Soziale Welt* 20, no. 1 [1969], 11–27), and from the 1967 Machonin study. The former study, however, is not so tightly focused on prestige as it might be, and we use here only the 1967 data (see note 25, below).

24. In addition to the Hammel data, used by Treiman, a smaller-scale Yugoslav study is available. See Joze Goricar, "Vrednovanje nekih zanimanja," in Jugoslovensko Udruzenje za Sociologiju, *Promene klasne strukture suvremenog jugoslovenskog drustva* (Belgrade, 1967), pp. 253–68.

25. Jaroslav Kapr, "Obecna struktura prestize povolani v Ceskoslovensku," in Machonin et al., *Ceskoslovenska spolecnost*, pp. 377–99, esp. p.

386. The reader can find the rank-order list of 50 occupations in English—minus the NORC-type scores—in Jaroslav Krejci, *Social Change and Stratification in Postwar Czechoslovakia* (New York: Columbia University Press, 1972), pp. 99–100.

26. Sarapata, *Studia*, p. 117, table 8.

27. V. N. Shubkin, *Sotsiologicheskie opyty* (Moscow: "Mysl'," 1970), pp. 280 ff.

28. See Robert W. Hodge, Paul M. Siegel, and Peter H. Rossi, "Occupational Prestige in the United States, 1925–1963," in Reinhard Bendix and Seymour Martin Lipset, eds., *Class, Status and Power: Social Stratification in Comparative Perspective* (2d ed; New York: Free Press, 1966), pp. 327, 331.

29. Sarapata, *Studia*, p. 117, table 8.

30. See Kapr,"Obecna struktura," pp. 397–98.

31. Sarapata, *Studia*, pp. 179–80, tables 11 and 12.

32. See Hodge, et al., "Occupational Prestige," pp. 323–24.

33. O. I. Shkaratan, *Problemy sotsial'noi struktury rabochego klassa SSSR* (Moscow: "Mysl'," 1970), p. 48.

34. See Iu. V. Arutiunian, *Sotsial'naia struktura sel'skogo naseleniia SSSR* (Moscow: "Mysl'," 1971), pp. 108–11.

35. In the sample of Warsaw residents (see above).

36. This distinction is Ossowski's (*Class Structure*, pp. 185–86).

37. Lubomir Brokl, "Moc a socialni rosvrstveni," in Machonin et al., *Ceskoslovenska Spolecnost*, pp. 235–64. Fortunately (and alone among the chapters of this book) this piece has been fully translated, as "Power and Social Stratification," *International Journal of Sociology*, 1, no. 3 (1971), pp. 203–83. Succeeding page references are to the English-language version.

38. Ibid., pp. 219–20.

39. Ibid., p. 221.

40. Ibid., p. 218.

41. Ibid., p. 215.

42. Ibid., p. 221.

43. Ibid., p. 223, and graph 6.3, p. 224.

44. See ibid., p. 246.

45. See Paul Hollander, *Soviet and American Society: A Comparison* (New York: Oxford University Press, 1973), p. 230.

46. Geoffrey Gorer, *The Danger of Equality and Other Essays* (London: Cresset, 1966), pp. 63–71.

47. John H. Goldthorpe, "Social Stratification in Industrial Society," in Bendix and Lipset, eds., *Class, Status and Power*, pp. 648–59.

48. Ibid., p. 657.

49. Ralf Dahrendorf, "Recent Changes in the Class Structure of European Societies," in Stephen R. Graubard, ed., *A New Europe?* (Boston: Beacon Press, 1967), p. 319.

50. Zygmunt Bauman, "Officialdom and Class: Bases of Inequality in Socialist Society," in Frank Parkin, ed., *The Social Analysis of Class Structure* (London: Tavistock, 1974), pp. 141–46.

CHAPTER FOUR SOCIALISM, REVOLUTION, AND MOBILITY

The first quotation heading the chapter is from Stanislaw Ossowski, "Social Mobility Brought About by Social Revolution" (Working paper, Fourth Working Conference on Social Stratification and Social Mobility, International Sociological Association, Geneva, December, 1957) as quoted in Seymour Martin Lipset and Reinhard Bendix, *Social Mobility in Industrial Society* (Berkeley and Los Angeles: University of California Press, 1959), p. 282 (emphasis in the original). The second is drawn from Adam Wazyk's "A Poem for Adults," first published in *Nowa Kultura* (Warsaw), August 21, 1955; version here from Edmund Stillman, ed., *Bitter Harvest: The Intellectual Revolt Behind the Iron Curtain,* (New York: Praeger, 1959), pp. 121–32.

1. See, e.g., Joseph Lopreato and Lawrence E. Hazelrigg, *Class, Conflict, and Mobility: Theories and Studies of Class Structure* (San Francisco: Chandler, 1972).

2. See Stanislaw Ossowski, "Ruchliwosc spoleczna jako wynik rewolucji spolecznej," in *Z zagadnien struktury spolecznej* (*Dziela,* vol. 5) (Warsaw: Panstwowe Wydawnictwo Naukowe, 1968), p. 282.

3. For the Harvard Project findings, see Alex Inkeles and Raymond A. Bauer, *The Soviet Citizen: Daily Life in a Totalitarian Society* (Cambridge: Harvard University Press, 1961), esp. pp. 67–100. See also Robert A. Feldmesser, "Aspects of Social Mobility in the Soviet Union" (Ph.D. diss., Harvard University, 1955), for the most detailed treatment available of mobility in the early postrevolutionary period and the Stalin era, and also Zev Katz, *Patterns of Social Mobility in the USSR* (Cambridge: MIT Center for International Studies, 1973).

Some results of Soviet research dealing with inter- and intragenerational mobility on the basis of selected data from the 1960s are presented in M. N. Rutkevich and V. F. Filippov, *Sotsial'nye peremeshcheniia* (Moscow: "Mysl'," 1970).

4. Among such Soviet studies see, for example, N. A. Aitov, ed., *Nekotorye problemy sotsial'nykh peremeshchenii v SSSR* (Ufa, 1971); O. I. Shkaratan, *Problemy sotsial'noi struktury rabochego klassa SSSR* (Moscow: "Mysl'," 1970); Institut sotsiologicheskikh issledovanii Akademii Nauk SSSR, *Problemy effektivnogo ispol'zovaniia rabochikh kadrov na promyshlennom predpriatii* (Moscow, 1973). Descriptions and discussion of these studies, their utility and limitations, may be found by the reader in Murray Yanowitch, *Social and Economic Inequality in the Soviet Union: Six Studies* (White Plains, N.Y.: Myron E. Sharpe, 1977), pp. 114–24, and in Richard

B. Dobson, "Mobility and Stratification in the Soviet Union," in Alex Inkeles et al., eds., *Annual Review of Sociology*, no. 3 (Palo Alto: Annual Reviews, 1977), 306–11.

Polish studies at the sub-national level include a study of the occupational destinations of *peasant* sons: Michal Pohoski, *Migracje ze wsi do miast* (Warsaw: Panstwowe Wydawnictwo Ekonomiczne, 1963); see also by the same author "Interrelation Between Social Mobility of Individuals and Groups in the Process of Economic Growth in Poland," *Polish Sociological Bulletin*, no. 2 (1964), 17–33; an "early" (1959) urban study in Lodz, Jozef Kadzielski, "Miedzypokoleniowa ruchliwosc spoleczna mieszkancow Lodzi," *Przeglad socjologiczny* 17, no. 2 (1963), 114–28; a 1961 study of urban males, Stefan Nowak, "Psychologiczne aspekty przemian struktury spolecznej i ruchliwosci spolecznej," *Studia socjologiczne*, no. 2 (1966), 75–105. Finally, the 1964–1967 research in the three cities of Lodz, Szczecin, and Koszalin resulted in two reports on the mobility of the (male) respondents. See Antonina Pilinow-Ostrowska, "Ruchliwosc zawodowa i jej konsekwencje," in Wlodzimierz Wesolowski, ed., *Zroznicowanie spoleczne* (Wroclaw-Warsaw-Krakow: Wydawnictwo Polskiej Akademii Nauk, 1970), pp. 339–73; and Krystyna Janicka, "Ruchliwosc miedzypokoleniowa," in K. M. Slomczynski and W. Wesolowski, eds., *Struktura i ruchliwosc spoleczna* (Wroclaw-Warsaw-Krakow-Gdansk: Wydawnictwo Polskiej Akademii Nauk, 1973), pp. 61–101.

Yugoslav researchers have also taken to quite complex and sophisticated analysis of mobility, though they lean less toward *national* representative samples than toward those that try to capture the complexity of differential economic development by focusing on the *extremes*—often "Westernized" and modern Slovenia on the one hand and the quintessentially "Balkan" Macedonia on the other. For an example of such work, see Stane Saksida et al., "Social Stratification and Mobility in Yugoslav Society," in *Some Yugoslav Papers Presented to the 8th World Congress of Sociology, Toronto 1974* (Ljubljana, 1974), pp. 213–74.

5. Otis Dudley Duncan, "Methodological Issues in the Analysis of Social Mobility," in Seymour Martin Lipset and Neil J. Smelser, eds., *Social Structure and Mobility in Economic Development* (Chicago: Aldine, 1966) pp. 51–97.

6. Peter M. Blau and Otis Dudley Duncan, *The American Occupational Structure* (New York: Wiley, 1967), pp. 115–61.

7. Lopreato and Hazelrigg, *Class, Conflict, and Mobility*, pp. 368–78.

8. Raymond Boudon, *Mathematical Structures of Social Mobility* (San Francisco-Amsterdam: Jossey-Bass–Elsevier, 1963).

9. S. M. Miller, "Comparative Social Mobility: A Trend Report and Bibliography," *Current Sociology* 9, no. 1 (1960), 18.

10. Of all 1967 "workers," 13.9 percent were in the agricultural sector, according to data in *Statisticheski godishnik na NR Bulgariia, 1968*, p. 71.

11. The main report of this project (though it does not contain the table used here) is the work frequently cited in this book, Pavel Machonin et al., *Ceskoslovenska spolecnost: Sociologicka analyza socialni stratifikace* (Bratislava: Epocha, 1969).

12. As reported in *Anuarul Statistic al Republicii Socialiste Romania* (Bucharest: Directie Centrala de Statistica, 1973), p. 63.

13. See, e.g., Phillips Cutright, "Occupational Inheritance: A Cross-national Analysis," *American Journal of Sociology* 73, no. 4 (1968), 400–16.

14. Vojin Milic, "General Trends in Social Mobility in Yugoslavia," *Acta Sociologica* 9, nos. 1–2 (1965), 120.

15. Lawrence E. Hazelrigg, "Cross-National Comparisons of Father-to-Son Occupational Mobility," in J. Lopreato and L. L. Lewis, eds., *Readings in Social Stratification* (New York: Harper and Row, 1974), pp. 469–93.

16. Ibid., p. 474, *n* 9.

17. The original Hungarian-language report of this 1962–1964 study is *A tarsadalmi atretegzodes es demografiai hatasai. II. Magyarorszagon* (Budapest: Kozponti Statisztikai Hivatal, 1970). More accessible are Rudolf Andorka, "Social Mobility and Economic Development in Hungary," *Acta Oeconomica* (Budapest), no. 7 (1970), 25–45, and Rudolf Andorka, "Mobilite sociale, developpment économique et transformations socio-professionelles de la population active en Hongrie. Vue d'ensemble (1930–1970)," *Revue française de sociologie*, 13 (suppl.), (1972), 607–29.

18. See, e.g., Raymond Boudon, *Education, Opportunity, and Social Inequality: Changing Prospects in Western Society* (New York: Wiley, 1974); William H. Sewell, Robert M. Hauser, and David L. Featherman, eds., *Schooling and Achievement in American Society* (New York: Academic Press, 1976).

19. See Joseph R. Fiszman, *Revolution and Tradition in People's Poland: Education and Socialization* (Princeton, N.J.: Princeton University Press, 1972), p. 278.

20. Blau and Duncan, *American Occupational Structure*, pp. 156 ff.

21. See David V. Glass, ed., *Social Mobility in Britain* (London: Routledge and Kegan Paul, 1954), pp. 98–140 and 291 ff.; Gosta Carlsson, *Social Mobility and Class Structure* (Lund: Gleerup, 1958), pp. 124 ff.

22. See chapter 5.

23. See E. K. Vasil'eva, *Sotsial'no-professional'nyi uroven' gorodskoi molodezhi* (Leningrad, 1973), p. 49, as cited in Yanowitch, *Social and Economic Inequality*, p. 121.

24. Honorina Cazacu, *Mobilitate sociala* (Bucharest: Editura Academiei Republicii Socialiste Romania, 1974), pp. 82, 110, 196, 267–68.

25. See Josef Alan, "Uloha vzdelani v socialni diferenciaci nasi spolecnosti," in Pavel Machonin et al., *Ceskoslovenska spolecnost*, pp. 274–75.

26. The Czechoslovak coefficients are presented in Zdenek Safar, "Different Approaches to the Measurement of Social Differentiation of the Czecho-

slovak Socialist Society," *Quality and Quantity* 5, no. 1 (1971), 179–208; the Australian in F. Lancaster Jones, "Occupational Achievement in Australia and the United States: A Comparative Path Analysis," *American Journal of Sociology* 77, no. 3 (1971), 527–39, and those for the USA in Blau and Duncan, *American Occupational Structure,* p. 170.

27. Boudon, *Mathematical Structures*, pp. 29–34.

28. E. M. Beck, "A Canonical Approach to Assessing Occupational Mobility Matrices," *Social Science Research* 2, no. 3 (1973), 247–56.

29. Robert A. Feldmesser, "The Persistence of Status Advantages in Soviet Russia," *American Journal of Sociology* 59, no. 1 (1953), 26.

30. Ibid., p. 24.

31. See Miller, "Comparative Social Mobility," citing S. Baum and J. N. Ypsilantis, "Social Mobility in Hungary: A Society in Transition" (unpublished MS, 1960).

32. Rudolf Andorka, Istvan Harsca and Rozsa Kulcsar, *A tarsadalmi mobilitas torteneti tendenciai* (Budapest: Kozponti Statisztikai Hivatal, 1975).

33. See Seymour Martin Lipset and Reinhard Bendix, *Social Mobility in Industrial Society* (Berkeley and Los Angeles: University of Calfornia Press, 1959), p. 34, citing Gewerkschaftsbund der Angestellten, *Die wirtshcaftliche und soziale Lage der Angestellten* (Berlin, 1931), p. 43.

34. See especially R. Andorka, "Historical comparison of Hungarian social mobility, 1930–1963, by means of census data and retrospective life histories" (Budapest, 1974, mimeograph).

35. Calculated from original versions of 1938–1938 table, Andorka et al., *A tarsadalmi,* p. 66.

36. Ibid.

37. See Ferenc A. Vali, *Rift and Revolt in Hungary: Nationalism versus Communism* (Cambridge: Harvard University Press, 1961), p. 64.

38. On the "volatility" of occupational careers over time, see Sandor Szalai, "Restratification of a Society," *New Hungarian Quarterly,* no. 23 (Autumn 1966), 24–33.

39. See Rudolf Andorka, "Tendencies of Social Mobility in Hungary: Comparisons of Historical Periods and Cohorts" (paper for the Conference of the Research Committee on Social Stratification, International Sociological Association, Geneva, 1975; Budapest, 1975, mimeograph), p. 7.

40. On this change in the balance of advantages as they affect cooperative farm members, see my "De l'utopie à la societe 'pragmatique': les consequences sociales des reformes economiques en Europe de l'Est," *Revue d'Etudes Comparatives Est-Ouest* (Paris), 6, no. 1 (1975), 123–24, and sources cited therein.

41. Andorka calculates the mobility profile at the three time points for the 1962–1964 sample as follows:

	1938	1949	1962–64
stable	56%	53%	41%
mobile	44	47	59
(of which)			
structural	21	20	40
circular	23	27	19

Applying this method, as best we can reconstruct it, to the 1973 data yields:

stable	33%
mobile	67
(of which)	
structural	47
circular	20

Thus, we create a series of indicators that show, despite the slight rise in circulation in 1973 over 1962–1964, a decline in the ratio of circulation mobility to all observed mobility. Andorka's method, given his own objectives, has its own rationale and validity. The discrepancies between his results and ours suggest caution in basing hard interpretations on such methods.

In the original 10 × 10 tables (9 occupational categories plus "other") Andorka apparently defines "circular" mobility to include: all mobility from or into "other," whatever the origin category; all mobility *from* strata where marginal percentages increase over 1938–1962/64 *into* strata that decline, as well as movement from one declining stratum to another; all "downward" mobility not already included in the previous categories (from "skilled" to "unskilled" or "semiskilled" among workers, etc.) and "horizontal" mobility between equal or ambigously situated categories: artisan to skilled worker, etc. The same procedure was applied by the present author to the 1973 data in their 8 × 8 original matrix. See Andorka et al., *A tarsadalmi mobilitas*, p. 65.

42. See Blau and Dunca, *American Occupational Structure*, p. 94.

43. H. Najduchowska, "Dyrektorzy przedsiebiorstw przemyslowych," in Jan Szczepanski ed., *Przemysl i spoleczenstwo w Polsce Ludowej*, pp. 82–87, as cited in George Kolankiewicz, "The Technical Intelligentsia," in David Lane and George Kolankiewicz, eds., *Social Groups in Polish Society* (New York: Columbia University Press, 1973), p. 186 and appendix 3, tables 1–3. See also Janina Markiewicz-Lagneau, *Education, Egalité, et Socialisme* (Paris: Editions Anthropos, 1969), pp. 54–55.

44. Najduchowska, "Dyrektorzy," pp. 82–83 and 86–87.

45. Kolankiewicz, "Technical Intelligentsia," p. 186.

46. J. Janicki, *Urzednicy przemyslowi w strukturze spolecznej Polski Ludowej* (Warsaw, 1968), p. 166; cited in Kolankiewicz, "The Polish Indus-

trial Manual Working Class," in Lane and Kolankiewicz, eds., *Social Groups*, p. 123.

47. By 1958, 67.7 percent of enterprise directors were of "worker" social origin, but 52.5 percent of all directors had some sort of higher education. (Najduchowska, "Dyrektorzy"). This would seem to suggest that *these* directors are mobile sons of workers rather than ex-workers themselves.

48. Feldmesser, "Aspects of Social Mobility," p. 67, citing *Pravda*, March 7, 1929, p. 5.

49. Ibid., p. 241.

50. See ibid., pp. 103–20, esp. pp. 109–18.

51. Ibid., pp. 214–37.

52. Since it is, of course, these positions that are most critical to the new regime—but all in all, they represent a small proportion of all occupations. See David Lane, *The Socialist Industrial State: Towards a Political Sociology of State Socialism* (London: Allen and Unwin, 1976), pp. 198–99; also the comments by Anthony Giddens, *The Class Structure of the Advanced Societies* (New York: Harper and Row, 1973), p. 231.

53. This appears to have been a quite standard adaptation to "populist" policies, both in the USSR and the Eastern European states.

54. See Bogdan Denitch, "Mobility and Recruitment of Yugoslav Leadership: The Role of the League of Communists," in Allen Barton, Bogdan Denitch, and Charles Kadushin, eds., *Opinion-Making Elites in Yugoslavia* (New York: Praeger, 1973), pp. 115–16.

55. See Lane, *Socialist Industrial State*, p. 199.

56. Miller, "Comparative Social Mobility."

57. See Hazelrigg, "Cross-National Comparisons."

58. The basic techniques involved were explored some time ago in W. Edward Deming, *Statistical Adjustment of Data* (New York: Wiley, 1943), pp. 96–127, and adapted in a computer program by Thomas Wilkinson for this study.

CHAPTER FIVE CONTEMPORARY MOBILITY: ASPIRATIONS, BARRIERS, OUTCOMES

The first quotation heading this chapter is from Srdan Vrcan, "Some Comments on Social Inequality" *Praxis* 9, nos. 2–3, (1973), 237. The second is recollected from the author's conversation with the driver on a taxi ride in Moscow in spring 1969).

1. See Zdenek Salzmann and Vladimir Scheufler, *Komarov: A Czech Farming Village* (New York: Holt, Rinehart and Winston, 1974), p. 35.

2. See, e.g., Irene Winner, *A Slovenian Village: Zerovnica* (Providence: Brown University Press, 1971), pp. 90–91.

3. Edit Fel and Tamas Hofer, *Proper Peasants: Traditional Life in a Hungarian Village* (Chicago: Aldine, 1969), p. 274.

4. Ibid., pp. 275–78.

5. Anna Sianko, "Wybor zawodu a wzory awansu spolecznego mlodziezy wiejskiej," *Studia Socjologiczne*, no. 3 (1966), 55.

6. Irwin T. Sanders, *Balkan Village* (Lexington: University of Kentucky Press, 1949), p. 134.

7. See Jerzy Gliksman, "The Russian Urban Worker: From Serf to Proletarian," in Cyril E. Black, ed., *The Transformation of Russian Society* (Cambridge: Harvard University Press, 1960), pp. 313–15, on living conditions of factory laborers at the time.

8. Gyula Illyes, *People of the Puszta*, trans. by G. F. Cushing (Budapest: Corvina Press, 1967), p. 265.

9. Laszlo Nemeth, *Guilt*, trans. by Gyula Gulyas (London: Peter Owen, 1966).

10. Ibid., p. 28.

11. See Michal Pohoski, "Interelation Between Social Mobility of Individuals and Groups in the Process of Economic Growth in Poland," *Polish Sociological Bulletin*, no. 2 (1964) 22–24.

12. See Iu. V. Arutiunian, *Sotsial'naia struktura sel'skogo naseleniia SSSR* (Moscow: "Mysl'," 1971), pp. 236–39.

13. Salzmann and Scheufler, *Komarov*, p. 61.

14. Winner, *A Slovenian Village*, pp. 185–89.

15. Joel Halpern, *A Serbian Village: Social and Cultural Change in a Yugoslav Community* (rev. ed.; New York: Harper and Row, 1967), p. 319.

16. Figures recalculated from Robert Rosko, "K problemu identifikacie druzstvenych rolnikov s pracou," in *Dynamika socialnej struktury v CSSR* (Bratislava: Vydavatelstvo politickej literatury, 1966), p. 173.

17. See Vasile Morea, "Pregatirea fortei de munca si orientarea profesionala a tineretului, *Lupta de Clasa*, December 1970, pp. 48–49.

18. F. N. Rekunov, "Formirovanie zhiznennykh planov sel'skikh shkolnikov kak chast' problemy nauchnogo rukovodstva obshchestvom," in *Sotsiologicheskie problemy narodnogo obrazovaniia* (Sverdlovsk, 1967), pp. 65–66.

19. Zygmunt Bauman, "Social Dissent in the East European Political System," *Archives Europeenes de Sociologie* 12, no. 1 (1971), 38.

20. Stefan Nowak, "Psychologiczne aspekty przemian struktury spolecznej i ruchliwosci spolecznej," *Studia socjologiczne*, no. 2 (1966), 83, 96.

21. Alex Inkeles and Raymond A. Bauer, *The Soviet Citizen: Daily Life in a Totalitarian Society* (Cambridge: Harvard University Press, 1961), p. 301.

22. Ibid., p. 89.

23. Ibid., p. 104.

24. Ibid., p. 112.

25. L. A. Margolin, "Svoboda vybora professii kak uslovie i forma proiavleniia svobody lichnosti," *Filosofskie nauki*, no. 2 (1966), 39.

26. Julia Juhasz, "Secondary Education of Working Class Children," *New Hungarian Quarterly* 11, (Autumn 1970), 133.

27. See Istvan Kemeny, "Restratification of the Working Class," *New Hungarian Quarterly* 11 (Summer 1970), 34.

28. Morea, "Pregatirea," p. 49.

29. *Scanteia Tineretului,* March 16, 1974, in *RFE Romanian Situation Report,* March 22, 1974, p. 11.

30. Mihailo Popovic, "Social Conditions and the Possibilities of Education of the Young People in Yugoslavia," *Sociologija* (special issue in English, 1970), p. 251.

31. Hungarian Central Statistical Office, *Social Stratification in Hungary* (Budapest: HCSO, 1967), p. 89.

32. M. N. Rutkevich and F. R. Filippov, *Sotsial'nye peremeshcheniia* (Moscow: "Mysl'," 1970), pp. 140–41.

33. N. A. Aitov, "Sotsial'nye aspekty polucheniia obrazovaniia v SSSR," *Sotsial'nye issledovaniia* 2 (1968), 189, 190.

34. M. Kh. Titma, "The Influence of Social Origins on the Occupational Values of Graduating Secondary-School Students," in Murray Yanowitch and Wesley A. Fisher, eds., *Social Stratification and Mobility in the USSR* (White Plains, N.Y.: International Arts and Sciences Press, 1973), pp. 220–24.

35. Juhasz, "Secondary Education," p. 134.

36. HCSO, *Social Stratification* p. 89.

37. Morea, "Pregatirea," p. 48.

38. Data reported by C. Stanculescu, *Scanteia Tineretului,* December 4, 1973 (*RFE Romanian Situation Report,* December 18, 1973), pp. 15–16.

39. Nowak, "Psychologiczne aspekty," pp. 83–84.

40. Zsuzsa Ferge, "Social Mobility and the Open Character of Society," *New Hungarian Quarterly* 11 (Spring 1970), 93–94.

41. Kemeny, "Restratification," pp. 35, 37.

42. Nowak, "Psychologiczne aspekty," p. 96.

43. Wlodzimierz Wesolowski, "Changes in the Class Structure in Poland," *Empirical Sociology in Poland* (Warsaw: Polish Scientific Publishers, 1966), p. 28.

44. N. A. Aitov, "Obshchee i osobennoe v klassovoi strukture stran sotsialisticheskoi sistemy," *Filosofskie nauki,* no. 3 (1970), 87.

45. *Rude Pravo,* February 2, 3, 4, 1972 (*RFE Czechoslovak Press Survey,* 15 March 1972, pp. 8–9).

46. See Jaroslav Krejci, *Social Change and Stratification in Postwar Czechoslovakia* (New York: Columbia University Press, 1973), p. 191.

47. Ernest Gellner, "The Pluralist Anti-Levellers of Prague," *Government and Opposition,* 7, no. 1 (1972), 20–37, approaches such a conclusion in his discussion of the collective work of Pavel Machonin et al., while stressing their commitment to democratic norms and an eventual re-leveling of incomes when greater economic abundance would have been achieved.

48. *Klassy, sotsial'nye sloi i gruppy v SSSR* (Moscow: "Nauka," 1968), p. 160.

49. See sources cited in Murray Yanowitch, *Social and Economic Inequality in the Soviet Union: Six Studies* (White Plains, N.Y.: Myron E. Sharpe, 1977), pp. 109–114.

50. Nowak, "Psychologiczne aspekty," pp. 94–95.

51. HCSO, *Social Stratification*, p. 89.

52. Krystyna Lutynska, "Office Workers' Views on their Social Position," *Polish Sociological Bulletin*, no. 1 (1964), 79–83.

53. Unfortunately, in the original and longer Polish version of the report ("Opinia urzednikow o ich pozycji spolecznej," *Przeglad Socjologiczny* no. 2 [1963]), the data relevant to our concerns here are no more clearly presented.

54. Stefan Nowakowski, "Egalitarian Tendencies and the New Social Hierarchy in an Industrial-Urban Community in the Western Territories," *Polish Sociological Bulletin*, no. 2 (1964), 80. Also, as the Polish sociologist Widerszpil found, as against *engineers* of worker origin, office employees of the same origin, asked to identify the "class" to which they belonged, named the "working class" (45 percent versus 62 percent for engineers and technicians). See Stanislaw Widerszpil, "Changes in Polish Social Structure," special issue of *International Journal of Sociology* 4, no. 4 (Winter 1975–76), pp. 102–3. This issue is a partial translation of Widerszpil's *Preobrazenia struktury spolecznej w Polsce ludowej* (Warsaw: "Ksiazka i Wiedza," 1973).

55. Frank Parkin, *Class Inequality and Political Order* (New York: Praeger, 1971), pp. 147–48.

56. Yanowitch, *Social and Economic Inequality*, pp. 127, 129–30 and sources therein.

57. Shubkin reports data which demonstrate this movement toward the "homogenization" of aspirations. See V. N. Shubkin, *Sotsiologicheskie opyty* (Moscow, "Mysl'," 1970), p. 228.

58. See Janina Markiewicz-Lagneau, *Education, Egalite, et Socialisme*, (Paris: Editions Anthropos, 1969), p. 105 (table); Aitov, "Sotsial'nye aspekty," p. 193. See also Walter D. Connor, "Education and National Development in the European Socialist States: A Model for the Third World?" *Comparative Studies in Society and History* 17, no. 3 (1975), 330–34.

59. M. N. Rutkevich and L. I. Sennikova, "O sotsial'nom sostave studenchestva v SSSR i tendentsiiakh ego izmeneniia," in *Sotsial'nye razlichiia i ikh preodolenie* (Sverdlovsk, 1967), p. 52.

60. Are these data on social origins of students "typical" for the nations as a whole? As we lack for the most part reliable national data, only approximate answers can be offered. The Warsaw pattern, on the whole, is more "elitist," or seems to be, than for Poland in toto (see *Trybuna ludu*, August 18, 1972, p. 5; summarized in *ABSEES*, January 1973, p. 220). The

Soviet figures are probably nearer a national average—were the data based on the enrollment at Moscow State University, for example, the pattern would probably show an even more exaggerated overrepresentation of elite and other white-collar offspring.

61. *Nepszabadsag,* March 21, 1972 (*RFE Hungarian Situation Report,* November 7, 1972), p. 12.

62. Judit H. Sas, "Expectations and Demands Made upon Children in a Rural Community," in Paul Halmos, ed., *Hungarian Sociological Studies* (*The Sociological Review* Monograph, no. 17) (1972), p. 261.

63. Ibid., pp. 259–60.

64. Susan Ferge, "Some Relations Between Social Structure and the School System," in Paul Halmos, ed., *Hungarian Sociological Studies,* pp. 234–35.

65. On this, see Mervyn Matthews, *Class and Society in Soviet Russia* (New York: Walker, 1972), pp. 260 ff.

66. See, e.g., for Poland, *Trybuna Ludu,* November 6, 1971, p. 8 (summarized in *ABSEES,* April 1972, p. 202).

67. V. F. Neustroev, "Opyt sotsiologicheskogo issledovaniia problem narodnogo obrazovaniia na sele," in *Sotsiologicheskie problemy,* p. 25. See also Matthews, *Class and Society,* pp. 342–43.

68. *Nepszabadsag,* July 9, 1970, p. 9 (summarized in *ABSEES,* October 1970, p. 184).

69. See Jan Woskowski, "Primary School Teachers and their Social Position in People's Poland," *Polish Sociological Bulletin,* no. 1 (1964), 84–89.

70. See comments on this in the Polish weekly *Polityka,* November 21, 1970.

71. See, e.g., early (1962) data from Shubkin's work in Novosibirsk; V. N. Shubkin, "Social Mobility and Choice of Occupation," in G. V. Osipov, ed., *Industry and Labour in the USSR* (London: Tavistock, 1966) p. 93.

72. Adam Sarapata, "Privlekatel'nost' professii," in G. V. Osipov and Jan Szczepanski, eds., *Sotsial'nye problemy truda i proizvodstva* (Moscow: "Mysl'," 1969), pp. 67–69.

73. See, for Yugoslavia, Popovic, "Social Conditions," p. 255–56; for Poland, Wieslaw Wisniewski, "The Academic Progress of Students of Different Social Origin," *Polish Sociological Bulletin,* no. 1 (1970), passim.

74. The present author has examined these phenomena in two previous works. See *Deviance in Soviet Society: Crime, Deliquency, and Alcoholism* (New York and London: Columbia University Press, 1972), and "Deviance, Stress and Modernization in Eastern Europe," in Mark G. Field, ed., *Social Consequences of Modernization in Communist Societies* (Baltimore: Johns Hopkins University Press, 1976), pp. 181–203.

75. Dariusz Fikus and Jerzy Urban, *Spoleczenstwo w podrozy* (Lodz: Wydawnictwo Lodskie, 1968), p. 21.

76. Elzbieta Neyman and Andrzej Tyszka, "Cultural Differentiation and

Social Stratification of a Small Town," *Polish Sociological Bulletin*, no. 1 (1968), 90.

77. Julia Juhasz, "Secondary Education of Working Class Children," *New Hungarian Quarterly* 11 (Autumn 1970), 132–34.

78. Mikolaj Kozakiewicz, *Bariery awansu poprzez wykstalcenie* (Warsaw: Instytut Wydawniczy CRZZ, 1973), p. 190.

79. See, e.g., I. M. Musatov, "K voprosu o proizvodstva rabochei sily," *Izvestiia Sibirskogo otdeleniia Akademii Nauk SSSR* no. 9 (1965), 58; and Ferge, "Some Relations," pp. 227, 229–30.

80. Marko Veselica, *Vjesnik u srijedu*, January 10, 1968, p. 3 (*JPRS Sociological Translations on Eastern Europe*, no. 509, March 6, 1968).

CHAPTER SIX THE STRATIFICATION OF INCOMES

The first quotation is from M. Sakov, "Ot kazhdogo po sposobnostiam, kazhdomu po potrebnostiam," *Politicheskoe samoobrazovanie*, no. 8 (1960), p. 27, as cited in Murray Yanowitch, "The Soviet Income Revolution," *Slavic Review*, 22, no. 4 (1963), 697. The second is from Svetozar Stojanovic, *Between Myths and Reality* (New York: Oxford University Press, 1973), p. 190.

1. Peter Wiles is perhaps the most outstanding example of such a sleuth. See P. J. D. Wiles and Stefan Markowski, "Income Distribution under Communism and Capitalism: Some Facts about Poland, the UK, the USA and the USSR," *Soviet Studies* 22, no. 3 (1971), 344–369, and no. 4 (1971), 487–511; see also by Wiles, "Recent Data on Soviet Income Distribution," *Survey* 21, no. 3 (1975), 28–41.

2. Wiles and Markowski, "Income Distribution," p. 344.

3. Wiles, "Recent Data," p. 33.

4. Calculated from Glowny Urzad Statystyczny, *Rocznik Statystyczny 1974* (Warsaw, 1975) p. 167.

5. Leonard J. Kirsch, *Soviet Wages: Changes in Structure and Administration since 1956* (Cambridge, Mass.: MIT Press, 1972) is a recent monographic contribution to this literature. Its bibliography (pp. 187–227) provides a useful guide to the previous works, as does the discussion in Murray Yanowitch, *Social and Economic Inequality in the Soviet Union: Six Studies* (White Plains, N. Y.: Myron E. Sharpe, 1977), pp. 29–57.

6. In an illuminating article, Alastair McAuley estimates decile ratios for Soviet earnings distributions, differing somewhat from Wiles, which show the following progression: 1956—4.9; 1957—5.1; 1959—4.2; 1961—4.2; 1964—3.3; 1966—3.3; 1968—2.8. See "The Distribution of Earnings and Incomes in the Soviet Union," *Soviet Studies*, 29, no. 2 (1977), 225.

7. Murray Yanowitch, "The Soviet Income Revolution," *Slavic Review*, 22, no. 4 (1963), 696.

8. Wiles, "Recent Data," p. 31.

9. See Yanowitch, *Social and Economic Inequality,* pp. 24–26.

10. Peter Wiles, *Distribution of Income: East and West* (Amsterdam, Oxford, and New York: North-Holland–American Elsevier, 1974), p. 81.

11. Edward Taborsky, *Communism in Czechoslovakia, 1948–1960* (Princeton: Princeton University Press, 1961), p. 453.

12. See *Dubcek's Blueprint for Freedom,* with commentary by Paul Ello (London: William Kimber, 1969), pp. 141–42.

13. The words are Ernest Gellner's, from his review essay on the work of Machonin and his research team. See "The Pluralist Anti-Levellers of Prague," *Government and Opposition* 7, no. 1 (1972), 34.

14. As quoted in Alan Levy, *Rowboat to Prague* (New York: Grossman, 1972), p. 119.

15. Though we lack cross-nationally comparable time-series data on quantile distributions, such evidence as does exist suggests that *none* of our scattered USSR figures for different years touches the peak period of inequality there; the data for other socialist countries do not match the most "inegalitarian" data available *for* the USSR, nor do they challenge effectively the position of Czechoslovakia as "most" egalitarian.

16. This seems to be the conclusion of Lydall's meticulous multinational study, though he is careful to indicate the difficulties of dealing with socialist data and definitions. See Harold Lydall, *The Distribution of Earnings* (Oxford: Clarendon Press, 1968), pp. 156–57, 161–62, 210, 239.

17. See United Nations, Secretariat of the Economic Commission for Europe, *Incomes in Post-War Europe: A Study of Policies, Growth and Distribution (Economic Survey of Europe in 1965, Part 2)* (Geneva, 1967), ch. 6, p. 18; ch. 8, p. 41, for figures that yield such conclusions (quartile ratios).

18. For a painstaking analysis of the service sector in socialist societies, see Gur Ofer, *The Service Sector in Soviet Economic Growth: A Comparative Study* (Cambridge, Mass.: Harvard University Press, 1973).

19. See Yanowitch, *Social and Economic Inequality,* pp. 31–32, table 2.3.

20. See Kirsch, *Soviet Wages,* p. 174, and U.N., *Incomes in Post-War Europe,* ch. 8, p. 27.

21. Christopher Jencks, et al., *Inequality: A Reassessment of the Effect of Family and Schooling in America* (New York: Basic Books, 1972), p. 227.

22. See, e.g., Murray Feshbach, "Manpower Management," *Problems of Communism* 24, no. 6 (1974), 25–33; David E. Powell, "Labor Turnover in the Soviet Union," *Slavic Review* 36, no. 2 (1977), 268–85.

23. Yanowitch, "Soviet Income Revolution," p. 695.

24. See, e.g., Jeremy Azrael, *Managerial Power and Soviet Politics* (Cambridge: Harvard University Press, 1966), esp. pp. 28–64.

25. In Bulgaria, collective farmers' total incomes were below those of state-sector farmers in 1960, but rose moderately above them in 1965, 1970, and 1973—but were it not for their "auxiliary earnings" (private plots, etc.)

the collective farmers would fall well below the state-sector agriculturalists throughout the period (see *Statisticheski godishnik 1974,* p. 69). Receipts from *private* agriculture seem to vary greatly. In Poland, the average total received on private farms in general in the 1972–1973 growing year was 107,100 zl.; but this varied between averages of 65,000 for farms of less than three hectares to 202,500 for those of 15 and more hectares. It is difficult, then, to find the "average" independent peasant. (See *Rocznik Statystyczny 1974*, p. 338.)

26. Wiles and Markowski, "Income Distribution," pp. 347–48.

27. *Rocznik Statystyczny 1974,* p. 167.

28. Central Statistical Office, *Statistical Yearbook 1973* (Budapest, 1973), p. 112.

29. Augustin Kudrna, "Diferenciace v odmenovani," *Planovane hospodarstvi,* no. 9 (1968), 4. (This article is also available in an English translation, as "Differentiation in Earnings," *East European Economics* 7, no. 4 (1969), 25–37.

30. Jiri Vecernik, "Problemy prijmu a zivotni urovne v socialni diferenciaci," in Pavel Machonin et al., *Ceskoslovenska spolecnost: sociologicka analyza socialni stratifikace* (Bratislava: Epocha, 1969), pp. 300–1.

31. Kudrna, "Diferenciace v odmenovani," p. 2.

32. U.N., *Incomes in Post-War Europe,* ch. 8, p. 36, citing *As ipari munkasok munkakorulmenvei es berhelyzete,* vol. 82 (Budapest, 1966) p. 73.

33. These estimates are based on a grouping of what seem the most parallel categories in the 1970 census figures into aggregates comparable to Shkaratan's, from Tsentral'noe Statistichesko Upravlenie, *Itogi vsesoiuznoi perepisi naseleniia 1970 goda,* vol. 6 (Moscow: "Statistika," 1973), pp. 24–33 and 170–74.

34. Ibid., p. 174.

35. For more detail, see U.N., *Incomes in Post-War Europe,* ch. 9, pp. 4–5.

36. Ibid., ch. 9, pp. 5–6.

37. Ibid., ch. 9, pp. 6–7.

38. Ibid., ch. 9, p. 8.

39. Ibid., ch. 9, pp. 12–18.

40. Ibid., ch. 9, pp. 17–18.

41. Rimashevskaia's 1965 work shows this. See N. M. Rimashevskaia, *Ekonomicheskii analiz dokhodov rabochikh i sluzhashchikh* (Moscow, 1965) and the citations and references thereto in U.N., *Incomes in Post-War Europe,* ch. 9, pp. 30–31.

42. See Kazimierz M. Slomczynski and Krzysztof Szafnicki, "Zroznicowanie dochodow z pracy," in Wesolowski, ed., *Zroznicowanie spoleczne,* (Wroclaw-Warsaw-Krakow: Wydawnictwo Polskiej Akademii Nauk, 1970), pp. 153–64.

43. See, e.g., Gregory Grossman, "The 'Second Economy' of the USSR,"

Problems of Communism 26, no. 5 (1977), 25–40; Aron Katsenelenboigen, "Coloured Markets in the Soviet Union," *Soviet Studies* 29, no. 1 (1977).

44. Nora Murray, *I Spied for Stalin* (New York: Wilfred Funk, 1951), p. 84.

45. Nadezhda Mandelstam, *Hope Abandoned* (New York: Atheneum, 1974), pp. 529–30.

46. Roy A. Medvedev, *Let History Judge: The Origins and Consequences of Stalinism* (New York: Knopf, 1971), p. 540. The physicist Andrei Sakharov takes the same line in his well-known "manifesto," *Progress, Coexistence and Intellectual Freedom*, with introduction, afterword, and notes by Harrison E. Salisbury (New York: Norton, 1968), pp. 76–77.

47. See Mervyn Matthews, "Top Incomes in the USSR: Towards a Definition of the Soviet Elite," *Survey* 21, no. 3 (1975), 16.

48. Ibid., pp. 17–19, provides a summary of these outlets.

49. Ibid., p. 16; I have also received such information, for some cities other than those mentioned by Matthews.

50. The Soviet refugee respondents to the Harvard Project inquiry rated the socialized medical services a positive aspect of the system. See Alex Inkeles and Raymond A. Bauer, *The Soviet Citizen: Daily Life in a Totalitarian Society* (Cambridge, Mass.: Harvard University Press, 1961), pp. 236–42.

51. Ladislav Mnacko, *The Taste of Power*, trans. by Paul Stevenson (New York: Praeger, 1967), p. 144.

52. Tibor Dery, *The Portuguese Princess and Other Stories*, trans. by Kathleen Szasz (London: Calder and Boyars, 1966), p. 177.

53. Stanislaw Dygat, "Long Journey," in Edmund Stillman, ed., *Bitter Harvest: The Intellectual Revolt Behind the Iron Curtain* (New York: Praeger, 1959), pp. 43–44 (Originally published in *Przeglad Kulturalny* [Warsaw], September 9, 1956).

54. Aleksandr I. Solzhenitsyn, *The First Circle*, trans. by Thomas P. Whitney (New York: Harper and Row, 1968), p. 346. The short quotations that follow are from pp. 346–47, and 353.

55. Ibid., p. 353.

56. Leopold Tyrmand, *The Rosa Luxemburg Contraceptives Cooperative: A Primer on Communist Civilization* (New York: Macmillan, 1972), p. 236.

57. Otis Dudley Duncan, "Properties and Characteristics of the Socioeconomic Index," in Albert J. Reiss, Jr., et al., *Occupations and Social Status* (New York: Free Press, 1961), p. 158.

58. Robert W. Hodge, Paul M. Siegel, and Peter H. Rossi, "Occupational Prestige in the United States: 1935–1963," in Reinhard Bendix and Seymour Martin Lipset, eds., *Class, Status, and Power* (2nd ed.; New York: Free Press, 1966), p. 331.

59. Frank Parkin, *Class Inequality and Political Order* (New York: Praeger, 1971), p. 147. Parkin makes somewhat similar points in another essay, "Yugoslavia," in Margaret S. Archer and Salvador Giner, eds., *Contempory*

Europe: Class, Status and Power (New York: St. Martin's Press, 1971), pp. 300–6.

60. Mervyn Matthews, *Class and Society in Soviet Russia* (New York: Walker, 1972), p. 149.

61. Zev Katz, *Patterns of Social Stratification in the U.S.S.R.* (Cambridge: MIT Center for International Studies, 1972), p. 90.

62. David Lane, *The End of Inequality? Stratification under State Socialism* (Harmondsworth: Penguin, 1971), p. 78.

63. Parkin, "Yugoslavia," p. 304.

64. See David Lane, *The Socialist Industrial State: Toward a Political Sociology of State Socialism* (London: Allen and Unwin, 1976), pp. 179–80. Even more recently Yanowitch, while recognizing the heavy feminization of lower white-collar work, does not explicitly connect this with the issue of manual-nonmanual income overlap, nor with the marginal (if any) prestige advantage of lower nonmanual over manual work. See his *Social and Economic Inequality*, pp. 33–37, 105, 168–69.

65. L. G. Kamovich and O. V. Kozlovskaia, "Sotsial'nye razlichiia sredi rabotnikov umstvennogo truda na promyshlennom predpriatii," in *Sotsial'nye razlichiia i ikh preodolenie* (Sverdlovsk, 1969), pp. 102, 104.

66. For the Polish data, see Krzysztof Zagorski, "Changes of Social Structure and Social Mobility in Poland," in M. N. Rutkevich, W. Wesolowski, et al., eds., *Transformations of Social Structure in the USSR and Poland* (Moscow and Warsaw, 1974; mimeographed volume prepared for Eighth World Congress of Sociology), pp. 338–339.

67. Giddens, in an otherwise well-argued and stimulating book, argues that the overlap of skilled manual and lower white-collar pay "cannot to any great degree be explained away in terms of a concentration of female workers in the lower non-manual occupations." He notes the high work participation rate of women in socialist economies, and their more even distribution through the occupational system, including their high representation in the professions, compared to women in the West. This, however, does not take account of the fact that "professional" women tend to concentrate in the lower reaches of their professions, with men occupying the higher, or that some professions, such as medicine, do not enjoy the same prestige or material reward in the socialist states as in the West. Finally, that women are spread through the labor force in no way reduces the effects of their overwhelming dominance of lower white-collar work, a dominance that does seem to explain away a good deal of the overlap in incomes. See Anthony Giddens, *The Class Structure of the Advanced Societies* (New York: Harper and Row, 1975), p. 229, and p. 312 *n* 10.

68. Figures from Peter Blau and Otis Dudley Duncan, *The American Occupational Structure* (New York: Wiley, 1967), p. 27.

69. Lane, *Socialist Industrial State*, p. 78.

70. See *RFE Polish Background Report*, February 19, 1975, esp. pp. 6–7.

71. Gerhard E. Lenski, *Power and Privilege: A Theory of Social Stratification* (New York: McGraw-Hill, 1966), p. 372.

CHAPTER SEVEN THE STRUCTURE OF SOCIALIST HOUSEHOLDS

The quotation that heads this chapter is from Marek Hlasko, *The Eighth Day of the Week*, translated by Norbert Guterman (New York: Dutton, 1958), pp. 54–55.

1. Stefan Nowakowski, "Egalitarian Tendencies and the New Social Hierarchy in an Industrial-Urban Community in the Western Territories," *Polish Sociological Bulletin*, no. 2 (1964), 77.

2. S. Soskin, *O preodolenii sotsial'no-ekonomicheskikh i kul'turno-bytovykh razlichii mezhdu gorodom i derevnei v period stroitel'stva kommunizma* (Alma-Ata: "Kazakhstan," 1967), p. 98.

3. See, e.g., Lee G. Burchinal, "The Premarital Dyad and Love Involvement," in H. T. Christensen, ed., *Handbook of Marriage and the Family* (Chicago: Rand McNally, 1964), p. 654; Morris Zelditch, "Family, Marriage and Kinship," in R. E. L. Faris, ed., *Handbook of Modern Sociology* (Chicago: Rand McNally, 1964), p. 688.

4. Unfortunately, we cannot take account here of interesting problems raised some time ago regarding the probability of marriage for different sex/status groups; the most frequently cited being that of highly educated career-oriented women. Such, it has been suggested, are less likely to find marriage partners than less-educated women (and, for various reasons, would find it difficult to marry down). To test such a notion, we would need more complete data on a larger universe of marriage-eligible males and females, a universe that would include some elements of arbitrary definition. Neither our data, nor those of a recent American study, encompass such a universe. See Zick Rubin, "Do American Women Marry Up?" *American Sociological Review*, 33, no. 5 (1968), 750–60.

5. There are "special" cases, such as the closed or semiclosed settlements outside Moscow: Zhukovka, the "writers' colony" Peredelkino, etc., as well as the professionally specialized Akademgorodok outside Novosibirsk. Some areas of Belgrade retain desirability from presocialist times, and the hilly Buda section of Budapest has in recent years become the site of expensive cooperatives and villas for persons who have done well under the economic reform. Various small suburbs around Warsaw draw people with the wherewithal to arrange for the construction of small cooperative buildings with well-above-average apartments, or even detached houses. That these are not so conveniently situated for persons working in central Warsaw is true; but private cars tend to be part of the picture for dwellers in such areas. Such accommodations, while not remarkable by middle-class West-

ern European standards, are for that very reason quite remarkable, and visible, in their own national settings. As the writer David Tornquist observes, "the revolutionary leaders [have]chosen to reside in the villas of the former rich on the hill of Dedinye at the edge of Belgrade"; see *Look East, Look West: The Socialist Adventure in Yugoslavia* (New York: Macmillan, 1966), p. 9. See also, on the persistence of Belgrade neighborhoods, Sharon Zukin, *Beyond Marx and Tito: Theory and Practice in Yugoslav Socialism* (New York: Cambridge University Press, 1975), p. 38.

6. Ivan Szelenyi, "Housing System and Social Structure," in Paul Halmos, ed., *Hungarian Sociological Studies (The Sociological Review* Monograph no. 17) (University of Keele, 1972), p. 274.

7. Ibid., pp. 281–82.

8. Ibid., pp. 282–83.

9. The dimensions of the supplement to income received through housing allocations are, according to two other Hungarian researchers, remarkable. Hegedus and Markus calculated expenditures on housing across five income groups, from high to low, and found that the ratio of the highest income group (1) to the lowest (5) in housing expenditure was 0.7 to 1.0; a broader range separated group 2, "upper middle" incomes, from group 4, "lower middle," at a ratio of 0.57 to 1.00. See Andras Hegedus and Maria Markus, "Values in the Long Range Planning of Distribution and Consumption," in Halmos, ed., *Hungarian Sociological Studies*, p. 47.

10. Szelenyi, "Housing System," pp. 383–84.

11. Ibid., p. 292.

12. See Alfred J. DiMaio, Jr., *Soviet Urban Housing: Problems and Policies* (New York: Praeger, 1974), pp. 122–23.

13. Ibid., pp. 124–25.

14. On rents, see ibid., pp. 144–48.

15. Ibid., p. 144.

16. Ibid., p. 146.

17. These figures are estimated from N. V. Ivanchuk, "O preodolenii sotsial'nykh razlichii v bytovoi kul'ture razlichnykh grupp trudiashchikhsia promyshlennogo predpriatiia," in *Sotsial'nye razlichiia* (Sverdlovsk, 1969), p. 110 (graph 2).

18. O. I. Shkaratan, *Problemy sotsial'noi struktury rabochego klassa SSSR* (Moscow: "Mysl'," 1970) pp. 416–17.

19. Stefan Nowakowski, "Cohesion of Social Groups Within the Process of Socialist Industrialization in Poland," in M. N. Rutkevich, W. Wesolowski et al., eds., *Transformations of Social Structure in the USSR and Poland* (Moscow and Warsaw, 1974), p. 410.

20. Stanislaw Widerszpil, *Preobrazenia struktury spolecznej w Polsce ludowej* (Warsaw: Ksiazka i Wiedza, 1973); quotation is from the partial translation, published in *International Journal of Sociology*, 4, no. 4 (1974–75), p. 22.

21. Andrei Simic, *The Peasant Urbanites: A Study of Rural-Urban Mobility in Serbia* (New York and London: Seminar Press, 1973), p. 95.

22. Srdan Vrcan, "Some Comments on Social Inequality," *Praxis* 9, nos. 2–3 (1973), p. 235.

23. Ibid.

24. Ibid., citing V. Mlakar, "Stanovanja danes in jutri," *Teorija in praksa* 9, nos. 6–7 (1972).

25. Anita Kobus-Wojciechowska, "Zroznicowanie warunkow mieszkaniowych i sytuacji materialnej," in Wlodzimierz Wesolowski, ed., *Zroznicowanie spoleczne* (Wroclaw-Warsaw-Krakow: Wydawnictwo Polskiej Akademii Nauk, 1970), p. 193.

26. Hungarian Central Statistical Office, *Social Stratification in Hungary* (Budapest: HCSO, 1967), p. 74; see also p. 73.

27. Ibid., p. 75.

28. Murray Yanowitch, *Social and Economic Inequality in the Soviet Union: Six Studies* (White Plains, N. Y.: Myron E. Sharpe, 1977), pp. 40–41 and sources cited therein.

29. See Kobus-Wojciechowska, "Zroznicowanie warunkow," p. 197.

30. Ibid., p. 206.

31. HCSO, *Social Stratification in Hungary,* p. 79.

32. See Jiri Vecernik, "Sociologicke problemy vlastnickych struktur v ceskoslovenske spolecnosti," *Sociologicky casopis* 6, no. 1 (1970), p. 27.

33. Kobus-Wojciechowska, "Zroznicowanie warunkow," p. 206.

34. Vecernik, "Sociologicke problemy," p. 27.

35. Kobus-Wojciechowska, "Zroznicowanie warunkow," p. 206.

36. Vecernik, "Sociologicke problemy," p. 27.

37. Kobus-Wojciechowska, "Zroznicowanie warunkow," p. 206.

38. HCSO, *Social Stratification in Hungary,* p. 79.

39. Vecernik, "Sociologicke problemy," p. 27 and p. 24, table 1.

40. See, e.g., M. V. Timashevskaia, "O nekotorykh sotsial'nykh posledstviiakh gradostroitel'nogo eksperimenta," in O. N. Ianitskii, et al., eds., *Urbanizatsiia i rabochii klass v usloviiakh nauchno-tekhnicheskoi revoliutsii* (Moscow: IMRO, 1970), p. 287.

41. Mirra Komarovsky, *Blue-Collar Marriage* (New York: Random House-Vintage, 1967).

42. Michael Young and Peter Willmott, *Family and Kinship in East London* (Baltimore: Penguin Books, 1962).

43. Ibid., p. 108.

44. Komarovsky, *Blue-Collar Marriage,* pp. 28, 312.

45. Ibid., p. 28 ff.

46. Irena Nowak, "Some Differences of Social Contact Patterns among Various Social Strata," *Polish Sociological Bulletin,* no. 2 (1966), 136.

47. L. A. Gordon and E. V. Klopov, *Chelovek posle raboty: sotsial'nye problemy byta i vnerabochego vremeni* (Moscow: "Nauka," 1972), pp. 147–

48. (Other Soviet research also indicates greater likelihood of spending free time with relatives as job status declines: see Timashevskaia, "O nekotorykh sotsial'nykh," p. 291.

48. HCSO, *Social Stratification in Hungary,* p. 103.

49. Wielislawa Warzywoda-Kruszynska, "Zycie towarzyskie w roznych kategoriach spoleczno-zawodowych," in K. M. Slomczynski and W. Wesolowski, eds., *Struktura i ruchliwosc spoleczna* (Wroclaw-Warsaw-Krakow-Gdansk: Wydawnictwo Polskiej Akademii Nauk, 1973), p. 214 (table 1).

50. Data from Nowak, "Some Differences," p. 140.

51. Ibid.

52. Gordon and Klopov, "Chelovek posle raboty."

53. Nowakowski, "Egalitarian Tendencies," p. 80.

54. Warzywoda-Kruszynska, "Zycie towarzyskie," p. 230, table 8.

55. Young and Willmott, *Family and Kinship,* p. 126.

56. Agnes Simonyi, "How Do Workers Live? Interviews with Twelve Workers," *New Hungarian Quarterly,* 15, no. 53 (1974), 67.

57. Ibid., pp. 67–68.

58. Anita Kobus-Wojciechowska, "Zroznicowanie konsumpcji kulturalnej," in Wesolowski, ed., *Zroznicowanie spoleczne,* p. 218 (table 1).

59. HCSO, *Social Stratification in Hungary,* p. 91.

60. Kobus-Wojciechowska, "Zroznicowanie konsumpcji," pp. 221–23.

61. HCSO, *Social Stratification in Hungary,* p. 98.

62. Kobus-Wojciechowska, "Zroznicowanie konsumpcji," p. 242 (table 10).

63. Ibid., p. 246 (table 12).

64. Ibid., p. 244.

65. HCSO, *Social Stratification in Hungary,* pp. 99–100.

66. Kazimierz M. Slomczynski and Wlodzimierz Wesolowski, "Zroznicowanie spoleczne: podstawowe wyniki," in Wesolowski, ed., *Zroznicowanie spoleczne,* p. 123 (table 19).

67. Ibid., p. 125 (table 21).

68. Ibid., p. 124 (table 20).

69. Ibid., pp. 128–29 (tables 22, 23).

70. Gordon and Klopov, *Chelovek posle raboty,* statistical appendix, pp. 28–29 (tables 30, 31).

71. See HCSO, *Social Stratification in Hungary,* pp. 94,96; also Anita Kobus-Wojciechowska, "Ilosc czasu wolnego i formy jego spedzania," in Slomczynski and Wesolowski, eds., *Struktura,* p. 196 (table 13), and Jaroslav Krejci, *Social Change and Stratification in Postwar Czechoslovakia* (New York: Columbia University Press, 1972), p. 93 (table 43).

72. See HCSO, *Social Stratification in Hungary,* p. 95; Kobus-Wojciechowska, "Zroznicowanie konsumpcji," p. 260; Vecernik, "Sociologicke problemy," p. 25. See also Gordon and Klopov, *Chelovek posle raboty,* statistical appendix, p. 32 (table 35).

73. Kobus-Wojciechowska, "Zroznicowanie konsumpcji," p. 265.
74. Komarovsky, *Blue-Collar Marriage*, p. 59.
75. Kobus-Wojciechowska, "Ilosc czasu," p. 184.
76. Ibid., p. 188.
77. See Gordon and Klopov, *Chelovek posle raboty*, statistical appendix, pp. 60–61 (table 59).

CHAPTER EIGHT SOCIALISM AND HIERARCHY IN PERSPECTIVE

The beginning quotation is taken from Andrew Hacker, *The End of the America Era* (New York: Atheneum, 1972), p. 147.

1. See my essay, "Socialism, Work and Equality," in Irving Louis Horowitz, ed., *Equity, Income and Policy: Comparative Studies in Three Worlds of Development* (New York: Praeger, 1977), pp. 148–50.
2. *Partelet*, November 1973, as quoted in *RFE Hungarian Situation Report*, March 5, 1975, p. 13.
3. Anthony Giddens, *The Class Structure of the Advanced Societies* (New York: Harper and Row, 1975), p. 107 ff.
4. Ibid., p. 21.
5. See portions of Stalin's speech "New Conditions—New Tasks in Economic Construction," in Robert V. Daniels, ed., *A Documentary History of Communism* (New York: Vintage Books, 1960), vol. 2, p. 26.
6. The effect of more welfare measures sometimes, paradoxically, conduces to the appearance of persistent inequality. The lowest fifth of the United States (and some Western European) populations in income is increasingly composed of retired persons, whose pensions and other benefits allow them to remain separate from offspring's households (where in an earlier time they would have resided, with less effect on measurements of inequality). Their presence "lengthens the lower tail of the income distribution," but does not really manifest a decline in their relative or absolute welfare. See Simon Kuznets, "Income Distribution and Changes in Consumption," in H. S. Simpson, ed., *The Changing American Population* (New York: Institute of Life Insurance, 1962), as quoted in Seymour Martin Lipset, *The First New Nation* (Garden City, N.Y.: Doubleday, Anchor Books, 1967), p. 373.
7. Paul Hollander, *Soviet and American Society: A Comparison* (New York: Oxford University Press, 1973), p. 204.
8. See, for example, the comments of two Soviet sociologists rejecting "quota" programs for admission to higher education. M. N. Rutkevich and F. R. Filippov, *Sotsial'nye peremeshcheniia* (Moscow: "Mysl'," 1970), p. 144.
9. Stanislaw Ossowski, *Class Structure in the Social Consciousness* (New York: Free Press, 1963) pp. 100–118.

10. These, roughly, summarize Ossowski's view—see ibid., pp. 107, 109.

11. Robert A. Feldmesser, "Social Classes and Political Structure," in Cyril E. Black, ed., *The Transformation of Russian Society* (Cambridge, Mass: Harvard University Press, 1960), p. 245.

12. Ibid., pp. 248, 252. As Feldmesser puts it, "Loyalty to a political leader and his ideology is again the cause, not the consequence, of one's hierarchical position. . . . "(p. 248).

13. Hollander, *Soviet and American Society,* p. 208.

14. Hedrick Smith, *The Russians* (New York: Quadrangle Books/NYT, 1976), p. 200.

15. Ibid., p. 262.

16. Thus, George Feifer, a perceptive observer of Soviet life, refers to the sort of official privileges the Soviet elite enjoys and argues that these "would not be tolerated for a moment under the most unrestrained capitalist economy." Further, "the Russian masses, struggling in shops, shivering in queues, do not protest or even question this anomaly." Indeed, they for the most part do not; in my experience they tend to ignore it. And here, I think, the acceptance comes not so much from an attitude that the mighty are entitled in a moral sense to their privileges, but from the feeling that this is one of the immutable realities of power. Such acceptance does not, in my view, equal deference. "An Observer" (George Feifer), *Message from Moscow* (New York: Knopf, 1969), p. 109.

17. See Giddens, *Class Structure,* p. 34 ff. on "negative reciprocity."

18. Hollander, *Soviet and American Society,* p. 217.

19. Ibid.

20. See Allen Kassof, "The Administered Society: Totalitarianism Without Terror," *World Politics* 16 (July 1964).

21. On Soviet mass apoliticality, see the present author's "Generations and Politics in the USSR," *Problems of Communism,* September–October 1975, pp. 20–31.

22. See John H. Goldthorpe, "Social Stratification in Industrial Society," in Bendix and Lippet, eds., *Class, Status, and Power,* pp. 648–59.

23. Ralf Dahrendorf, "Recent Changes in the Class Structure of European Societies," in Stephen R. Graubard, ed., *A New Europe?* (Boston: Beacon Press, 1967), pp. 294–96.

24. Zbigniew Brzezinski and Samuel P. Huntington, *Political Power: USA/USSR* (New York: Viking, 1964), esp. pp. 139 ff.

25. See T. B. Bottomore, "The Class Structure in Western Europe," in Margaret Scotford Archer and Salvador Giner, eds., *Contemporary Europe: Class, Status and Power* (London: Weidenfeld and Nicholson, 1971), p. 401.

26. See Jaroslav Krejci, *Social Structure in Divided Germany* (New York: St. Martin's Press, 1976) pp. 95–97, 121.

27. See, e.g. David Tornquist, *Look East, Look West: The Socialist Adventure in Yugoslavia* (New York: Macmillan, 1966), p. 8.

28. Seymour Martin Lipset, *Political Man: The Social Bases of Politics* (Garden City, N.Y.: Doubleday, Anchor Books, 1963), p. 352.

29. See Lipset, *First New Nation,* pp. 208–9, citing Ossowski, "Social Mobility Brought About by Social Revolution," Fourth Working Conference on Social Stratification and Social Mobility (International Sociological Association, December, 1957), p. 3.

30. See C. A. R. Crosland, *The Future of Socialism* (New York: Schocken Books, 1964), p. 182; see also Seymour Martin Lipset and Reinhard Bendix, *Social Mobility in Industrial Society* (Berkeley and Los Angeles: University of California Press, 1959), pp. 82–83.

31. *Nepszabadsag,* August 25, 1976, quoted in *RFE Hungarian Situation Report,* September 14, 1976, p. 3.

32. *Nepszava,* September 5, 1976, quoted in ibid.

33. Geoffrey Gorer, "A Reconsideration of the Functions of Class Distinction," in *The Danger of Equality and Other Essays* (London: Cresset, 1966), p. 80.

34. *Polityka,* October 19, 1974, quoted in *RFE Polish Press Survey* (no. 2461), November 15, 1974, p. 4.

35. Ibid., p. 3.

36. Dahrendorf, "Recent Changes," p. 320.

37. Robert A. Nisbet, "The New Despotism," *Commentary* 59, no. 6 (June 1975), 31.

38. Ibid., p. 35.

39. As Charles Frankel puts it, "the man of twenty, in possession of a superior character that enables him to cultivate his abilities, can usually be shown to have done *something* to produce this character. Has there been no hard work, inner discipline, lacerating struggle with his soul? Is it all the throw of the dice?" See "The New Egalitarianism and the Old," *Commentary* 56, no. 3 (1973), 58.

40. Frank Parkin, *Class Inequality and Political Order* (New York: Praeger, 1971), p. 181.

41. Ibid., p. 182.

42. Ibid., p. 183.

43. As Robert Nisbet writes of bureaucrats, the "vast majority are honest, efficient, hard-working; a great many of them are dedicated. That is precisely the problem of bureaucracy: the better it is, the worse its impact upon culture and social order." "The Fatal Ambivalence of an Idea: Equal Freemen of Equal Serfs?" *Encounter* 47, no. 6 (1976), p. 19.

44. Nisbet, "New Despotism," p. 38.

EPILOGUE

1. Andrzej Malewski, "Attitudes of the Employees from Warsaw Enterprises toward the Differentiation of Wages and the Social System in May, 1958," *Polish Sociological Bulletin,* no. 2 (1971), 30.

2. See, e.g., Adam Bromke, "A New Juncture in Poland," *Problems of Communism*, September–October 1976, pp. 1–17.

3. See William F. Robinson, *The Pattern of Reform in Hungary* (New York: Praeger, 1973), esp. pp. 146–57, 314–545.

4. Malewski, "Attitudes"; see also Bogdan D. Denitch, *The Legitimation of a Revolution: The Yugoslav Case* (New Haven and London: Yale University Press, 1976), pp. 172–75.

5. See, e.g., Wieslaw Wisniewski, "Tolerancja a egalitaryzm," *Studia socjologiczne*, no. 2 (1963), 203–16; also Seymour Martin Lipset, *Political Man: The Social Bases of Politics* (Garden City, N.Y.: Doubleday, Anchor Books, 1963), pp. 87–126, on "working-class authoritarianism."

6. This observation is based on the arguments at the conclusion of last chapter on the "necessity" of a Soviet-type polity, with its restriction of group autonomy, etc., for the maintenance of a structure of inequality of the sort which exists now in the socialist states.

Index